THE PERSISTENCE
OF THE OLD REGIME

Also by Arno J. Mayer

POLITICAL ORIGINS OF THE NEW DIPLOMACY, 1917–1918

POLITICS AND DIPLOMACY OF PEACEMAKING:
CONTAINMENT AND COUNTERREVOLUTION AT VERSAILLES,
1918–1919

DYNAMICS OF COUNTERREVOLUTION IN EUROPE, 1870–1956

Arno J. Mayer

THE PERSISTENCE OF THE OLD REGIME

Europe to the Great War

Pantheon Books, New York

Library of Congress Cataloging in Publication Data
Mayer, Arno J
The persistence of the old regime

Bibliography: p.
Includes index.
1. Europe—Civilization—19th century.   2. Europe—
Civilization—20th century.   I. Title.
B204.M39   940.2'8   80–21645
ISBN 0–394–51141–7

First Edition

For Herbert Marcuse

Contents

Preface

I GAVE THE FIRST SKETCH for this book as the Carl L. Becker Lectures at Cornell University in the fall of 1977. I am grateful to my colleagues at Cornell for their many courtesies to me, and to Walter LaFeber in particular for emboldening me to change my topic at the very last minute. Originally I had promised to give a thematic exposition of my draft manuscript on the domestic causes and purposes of war since 1870. But then I had second thoughts. In the preceding year I had presented my thesis on the links between resurgent conservatism and war during the last century at the École des Hautes Études en Sciences Sociales in Paris; at the Institut Universitaire de Hautes Études Internationales in Geneva; at the universities of Bielefeld, Bochum, Düsseldorf, Jerusalem, and Leyden; and at the Lehrman Institute in New York. On all these occasions I was criticized not so much for overemphasizing the domestic rather than the diplomatic mainsprings of international conflict as for affirming rather than demonstrating the survival of the old order in Europe into the twentieth century. With time the force of this critique became so compelling that I finally decided to use the Becker Lectures to begin an examination of the perseverance of the *ancien régime* in the six major European powers that became embroiled in the Great War of 1914–1918. Caught up in this problem of historical inertia, I spent the following two years exploring it, at the expense of my study of war.

The result is this book, which is a work of interpretation based almost exclusively on secondary sources. The bibliography at the back of this volume lists the books and articles I found most useful and pillaged mercilessly. Because my quest became so maniacal I learned from everything that I read. This being the case, I decided not to burden and lengthen the text with footnotes, which became endless. I also decided not to attack by name historians with whom I disagree, since my differences with them bear on questions of interpretation rather than fact. My purpose is less to refute or debate other historians, from whom I cite occasional phrases, than to develop a new angle of vision and frame of analysis.

I conceive of this book as a Marxist history from the top down, not the bottom up, with the focus on the upper rather than the lower classes. The first chapter deals with the economic bedrock of the old order. Although some readers may wish to skim or skip over this ponderous discussion of the material base of society, without it my thesis would be altogether incredible. Indeed, this book is in the nature of an argument. Even though I qualify most generalizations, I make no pretense of presenting all sides of the question. In this instance I freely admit to being an ardent "lumper" and master builder rather than an avid "splitter" and wrecker. I agree with Jacob Burckhardt that no comprehensive historical vision is possible without recourse to organizing generalizations and principles. Needless to say, as Carl Becker reminded us, there is no finality to any such vision, and Burckhardt readily conceded that the same studies he used to construct *The Civilization of the Renaissance in Italy* "might easily, in other hands, not only [have] received a wholly different treatment and application, but also [have led] to essentially different conclusions." In the meantime he asked, as I do also, that he be granted "a patient hearing" and that his book be "taken and judged as a *whole*" and not only in its discrete parts.

In the course of my reading and writing I incurred numerous intellectual and scholarly debts. Above all I benefitted enormously from the detailed criticisms and suggestions of Perry Anderson, Hans-Ulrich Wehler, Charles Maier, and Alfred Rieber, who read early drafts of the first four chapters. Coming from different ideological horizons, they confronted me with hard and unsettling but not destructive questions. David Abraham, Jerome Blum, and Robert Tignor made valuable comments on chapter 1, while Richard Wortman cheerfully helped me find my way through the monographic literature on late imperial Russia.

Five steadfast friends genially tolerated my bringing our unbroken conversations around to my momentary obsessions. François Furet never tired of my cross-examining him about the *ancien régime* and aristocratic reaction in eighteenth- and nineteenth-century France;

Felix Gilbert patiently and subtly answered my irreverent questions about the old order and high society in Berlin between 1870 and 1933; Carl Schorske inspired, cheered, and tempered my foray into the study of high culture; Pierre Vidal-Naquet connived in my reassessment of the encounter of noble and bourgeois; and Sheldon Wolin encouraged me not to be daunted by canonical interpretations of liberalism, Nietzsche, and Weber. I fear that I cannot absolve my colleagues and friends of all responsibility for my blunders and distortions, for they lacked either the heart or the good judgment to dissuade me from rushing into hazardous historical waters.

I owe thanks to Shelley Baranowski, Vladimir Brovkin, and Dorothea Schneider for helping me with my research at crucial points. Helen Wright masterfully typed and retyped successive drafts, and the few mistakes she made invariably turned out to be mine after all. She knows the high esteem in which I hold her. I received financial support from Princeton's Center of International Studies and Committee on Research in the Humanities and Social Sciences.

Finally I wish to express my gratitude to Philip Pochoda of Pantheon. He brought his critical discernment to my manuscript and lightened the chore of preparing it for publication.

Princeton–Chérence
Summer 1980

ARNO J. MAYER

THE PERSISTENCE
OF THE OLD REGIME

Introduction

EVEN WITH THE PASSAGE of time the first half of the twentieth century stands out for having witnessed an unprecedented cataclysm and a major watershed in the history of Europe. Growing temporal and psychological distance is not likely to significantly lessen or normalize the enormity of the Great War and the Verdun Ossuary, the *outrance* of the Second World War and Auschwitz. But because of the fixed infamy and atrocity of this self-immolation and holocaust—including Hiroshima—historians will forever continue to probe their underlying causes. They will also keep trying to penetrate the agony and ferocity of the Bolshevik revolution and regime, which were the main ray of hope during one of Europe's darkest nights. Russia was fatally caught up in this colossal turbulence, sacrificing more blood and patrimony than any other nation. Paradoxically, though peripheral to Western civilization, Russia was nevertheless among its greatest destabilizers and ultimate saviors.

This book is intended as a contribution to the discussion of the *causa causans* and inner nature of Europe's recent "sea of troubles." It starts with the premise that the World War of 1939–1945 was umbilically tied to the Great War of 1914–1918, and that these two conflicts were nothing less than the Thirty Years' War of the general crisis of the twentieth century.

3

The second premise is that the Great War of 1914, or the first and protogenic phase of this general crisis, was an outgrowth of the latter-day remobilization of Europe's *anciens régimes*. Though losing ground to the forces of industrial capitalism, the forces of the old order were still sufficiently willful and powerful to resist and slow down the course of history, if necessary by recourse to violence. The Great War was an expression of the decline and fall of the old order fighting to prolong its life rather than of the explosive rise of industrial capitalism bent on imposing its primacy. Throughout Europe the strains of protracted warfare finally, as of 1917, shook and cracked the foundations of the embattled old order, which had been its incubator. Even so, except in Russia, where the most unreconstructed of the old regimes came crashing down, after 1918–1919 the forces of perseverance recovered sufficiently to aggravate Europe's general crisis, sponsor fascism, and contribute to the resumption of total war in 1939.

The third and major premise of this book is that Europe's old order was thoroughly preindustrial and prebourgeois. For too long historians have focused excessively on the advance of science and technology, of industrial and world capitalism, of the bourgeoisie and professional middle class, of liberal civil society, of democratic political society, and of cultural modernism. They have been far more preoccupied with these forces of innovation and the making of the new society than with the forces of inertia and resistance that slowed the waning of the old order. Although on one level Western historians and social scientists have repudiated the idea of progress, on another they continue to believe in it, albeit in qualified terms. This abiding and tacit faith in progress is coupled with an intense aversion to historical stasis and regression. There has been, then, a marked tendency to neglect or underplay, and to disvalue, the endurance of old forces and ideas and their cunning genius for assimilating, delaying, neutralizing, and subduing capitalist modernization, even including industrialization. The result is a partial and distorted view of the nineteenth and early twentieth centuries. To achieve a more balanced perspective, historians will have to view not only the

high drama of progressive change but also the relentless tragedy of historical perseverance, and to explore the dialectic
interaction between them.

But this book does not offer a balanced interpretation of
Europe between 1848 and 1914. To counteract the chronic
overstatement of the unfolding and ultimate triumph of
modernity—even the general crisis itself, including fascism, is
being credited with serving this universal design and outcome
—it will concentrate on the persistence of the old order. The
conventional wisdom is still that Europe broke out of its *ancien
régime* and approached or crossed the threshold of modernity
well before 1914. Scholars of all ideological persuasions have
downgraded the importance of preindustrial economic interests, prebourgeois elites, predemocratic authority systems,
premodernist artistic idioms, and "archaic" mentalities. They
have done so by treating them as expiring remnants, not to say
relics, in rapidly modernizing civil and political societies. They
have vastly overdrawn the decline of land, noble, and peasant;
the contraction of traditional manufacture and trade, provincial burghers, and artisanal workers; the derogation of kings,
public service nobilities, and upper chambers; the weakening
of organized religion; and the atrophy of classical high culture.
To the extent that economic, social, and political historians
accord any vitality to these vestiges of a dying past, they present them as using or misusing that vitality to delay, derange,
and complicate the ultimately inevitable growth of capitalist
industrialization, social leveling, and political liberalization. In
this same teleological spirit, cultural historians have pored
over the accomplishments of the artistic avant-gardes while
curtly dismissing academic cultures for being exhausted and
for obstructing the preordained march to modernism.

In order to reconstruct the historical matrix in which the
general crisis and Thirty Years' War of the twentieth century
originated, it may be necessary to reconceive and perhaps
even totally reverse this picture of a modern world commanding a recessive and crumbling old order. At any rate, it is the
thesis of this book that the "premodern" elements were not
the decaying and fragile remnants of an all but vanished past

but the very essence of Europe's incumbent civil and political societies. This is not to deny the growing importance of the modern forces that undermined and challenged the old order. But it is to argue that until 1914 the forces of inertia and resistance contained and curbed this dynamic and expansive new society within the *anciens régimes* that dominated Europe's historical landscape.

There are no value-free categories with which to address this reality. On the one hand, to speak of the Europe of the time as saliently premodern, preindustrial, and prebourgeois is to endorse the view, at least implicitly, that the forces of progress were on the verge of inheriting the earth. On the other hand, to refer to Europe as an *ancien régime* or a quasi-feudal society is to ratify the presumption that the forces and institutions of perseverance were on the point of collapse. Obviously, such labels and images have a retrospective inference, and the choice of one set over another is in itself a historical judgment. A book, however, which proposes to explore and reassess the dimensions of "oldness" in Europe between 1848 and 1914 cannot avoid applying and refining such notions as *ancien régime* and feudality.

Europe's old regimes were civil and political societies with distinct powers, traditions, customs, and conventions. Precisely because they were such integral and coherent social, economic, and cultural systems, they were exceptionally resilient. Even in France, where the *ancien régime* was pronounced legally dead between 1789 and 1793, it kept resurfacing violently and lived on in many ways for more than a century. Of course, Europe was not a single entity. There were vast national and regional variations of economy, social structure, legal tradition, and mental outlook, and these historical singularities cannot be ignored or minimized. Nonetheless, in its prime as well as in its perdurable extension into modern times, the *ancien régime* was a distinctly pan-European phenomenon.

The old order's civil society was first and foremost a peasant economy and rural society dominated by hereditary and privileged nobilities. Except for a few bankers, merchants, and shipowners, the large fortunes and incomes were based in land. Across Europe the landed nobilities occupied first place not only in economic, social, and cultural terms but also politically.

In fact, political society was the linchpin of this agrarian society of orders. Everywhere it took the form of absolutist authority systems of different degrees of enlightenment and headed by hereditary monarchs. The crowns reigned and governed with the support of extended royal families and court parties as well as compliant ministers, generals, and bureaucrats.

The Church was another vital constituent and pillar of the *ancien régime.* Closely tied to both the crown and the nobility, it was, like them, rooted in land, which was its principal source of revenue. The upper clergy was of distinguished social provenance, exercised far-reaching influence, and enjoyed important fiscal and legal exemptions. As a great corporate institution the Church exerted considerable sway through its quasi-monopoly of education and social services and its exclusive control of the sacred rites of birth, marriage, and death.

The entire regime was suffused with the legacy of feudalism that presumably expired with the Middle Ages and finally was declared "totally abolished" in France in August 1789. Since the term "feudality" remains controversial in discussions of medieval and early modern history, it is bound to be even more disputed in the study of modern and contemporary history. According to Marc Bloch no region in Europe ever had a "complete" feudal society, and different parts of Europe were feudalized to varying degrees and at differing speeds. But Bloch also stressed that notwithstanding great diversities in form, intensity, space, and time Europe's feudal societies shared important common features: the fractioning of the central state into fiefs; the ties of personal dependence, protection, and heredity implanted in the ownership and exploitation of land; the "honorable obligation to bear arms" reserved to the upper orders or vassals; and the extreme social and political inequality favorable to a small oligarchy of landed proprietors, warriors, and churchmen. Predecessor to the *ancien régime,* the feudal regime was characterized by a particular form of property, frequently by serfdom, and always by the payment of feudal and seignorial dues. This system of production that relied on the legal subjection and economic exploitation of a vast underclass was embedded in a complex structure of social and political institutions.

With the rebirth of the territorial state and the development of the idea of political sovereignty, monarchial authority put an end to political and military feudalism. Claiming the monopoly of coercion, the dynasties presided over expanded standing armies and centralized bureaucracies loyal to the crown. They also secured the fiscal independence needed to pay for this large and growing state apparatus without excessively bending to the nobility.

To the extent that political, legal, and military power was closely associated with landownership, the former declined much more rapidly and extensively than the latter. The enduring seignorial system left a deep imprint on the old regime by perpetuating the privileged noblemen who exalted and arrogated the ethos of personal loyalty, the exercise of martial virtues, and the duty of public service. To be sure this nobility was politically diminished by the loss of direct and exclusive legal and administrative authority over land and labor and by changes in military organization and technique. Even so, since they were not shorn of their stake in the landed property, agriculture, and processing of primary products that dominated economic life down to 1914, the nobles retained their wealth and status. Moreover, while working out a *modus vivendi* with the crown, the nobility of the sword infused the entire public service nobility, both civil and military, with its time-honored precepts. In fact, the kings themselves became imbued with this noble conceit. Seeing their own thrones tied to the hierarchical society of orders, they bolstered this civil society economically and socially. At the same time, though the absolute monarchs deprived noblemen and seigneurs of their sovereign political and military authority, they assimilated them into their state apparatus. The result was that by permeating the state apparatus, and in particular its officials of non-noble birth, with their own precepts, and by occupying key positions in the new armies and bureaucracies, the nobles compensated for their loss of private political power. The nobility also benefitted from close connections with the Church, whose top personnel was of high birth and whose wealth, like the nobles' own, continued to be overwhelmingly landed.

Clearly, then, feudalism endowed Europe's old order with much more than a mere integument of upper-class traditions, customs, and mentalities. It penetrated the *anciens régimes* through nobilities positioned to monopolize strategic economic, military, bureaucratic, and cultural stations. These postfeudal noblemen adjusted their ties of dependence, heredity, and ennoblement to reflect and enhance their privileged place in the ruling and governing classes of the new territorial states. Of course, the configuration and repressiveness of this prolongation of feudality differed by country and region. The dissimilarities between Europe east and west of the Elbe became most striking. In Russia and Prussia in particular, but also in Hungary and southern Italy, labor service and legal servitude actually intensified before they gradually disappeared. Throughout most of the rest of Europe, the landed nobles became postfeudal in economic terms as they adopted capitalist methods of agricultural production and land exploitation. But notwithstanding this growth of capitalism on the land, the nobility continued to suffuse high society, high culture, and high politics with its feudalistic spirit.

The European economies provided the material underpinning for this continuing pre-eminence of the landed and public service nobilities. Land remained the ruling and governing classes' principal form of wealth and revenue until 1914. No less significant, consumer manufacture continued to outweigh capital goods production in its share of national wealth, product, and employment. This was true even in England, where agriculture was radically reduced in economic importance, and in Germany, which experienced a spectacular spurt of industrial development between 1871 and 1914. Across Europe small and medium-sized firms that were family owned, financed, and managed dominated the manufacturing and

commercial sectors of the national economies. This entrepreneurial capitalism spawned a bourgeoisie that was at best
protonational. As a class this bourgeoisie shared economic
interests, but it had only limited social and political cohesion.
This manufactural and mercantile bourgeoisie could not measure itself with the landed nobility in terms of class, status, or
power. To be sure, in the last third of the nineteenth century
the growth of capital-intensive producer-goods industries
gave birth to an industrial bourgeoisie. But quite apart from
remaining of limited economic importance until 1914, these
magnates of industry and their associates in corporate banking
and the liberal professions were more disposed to collaborate
with the agrarians and the established governing classes than
with the older bourgeoisie of manufacturers, merchants, and
bankers.

Just as there was no complete or model feudal society, so
there was no archetypal postfeudal or preindustrial *ancien régime.* England was only one of its variants. Although England's
economy was dominated by manufactural and merchant capitalism, the aristocracy continued to be paramount. This was so
because land remained the chief source of wealth and income
despite the radical contraction of British agriculture in the
course of the nineteenth century. In other words, the monarchy and landed elite tamed the industrialization of England
without succumbing to it.

There is no denying that British agriculture was eliminated
"as a major social activity" and that the power of the land-
based nobility was transformed. But even after taking these
steps along the democratic route to modernity, England never
became a "bourgeois order" run by a "conquering" or "trium-
phant" bourgeoisie. Of course, the House of Commons,
elected by an expanding male franchise, controlled the executive, and regional and local bourgeois interests were represented in it. But there was no movement to remove the crown,
the royal court, the House of Lords, and the ascriptive public
service nobility. Despite the decline of agriculture and despite
insular security, which obviated the need for a strong military

caste, the landed classes managed to perpetuate this "archaic" political order and culture.

The major Continental powers, except for France, had none of Britain's advantages: the landed elites were intact, agriculture remained a major social activity, and insecure frontiers justified the military presumption of kings and nobles. This explains, in part, why Russia, Austria-Hungary, and Germany persisted as absolutist monarchies.

France alone among the major powers finally became a republic in 1875. But except for no longer having a king and for now being governed by a *petit bourgeois* political class, France stayed in tune with the rest of the Continent, its economy dominated by agriculture and traditional manufacture. Ironically, an excess of agrarian and political democracy impeded French industrialization, notably after the onset of the second industrial revolution in the late nineteenth century. If France became "a half-hearted republic in continual crisis," it was because its bourgeoisie was too weak and divided to steady it.

In any case, neither England nor France had become industrial-capitalist and bourgeois civil and political societies by 1914. Their polities were as "obviously outdated" and "stubbornly concerned with their longevity" as the polities of the other four big powers. All alike were *anciens régimes* grounded in the continued predominance of landed elites, agriculture, or both.

As Joseph Schumpeter saw so clearly, except in France the kings remained the divinely ordained "centerpieces" of Europe's authority systems. Their position was feudal in both "the historical and the sociological sense," not least because "the human material of feudal society" continued to "fill the offices of state, officer the army, and devise policies." Although capitalist processes, both national and international, generated ever larger shares of government revenue—for the "tax-collecting state"—the feudal element remained a *"classe dirigente"* that behaved "according to precapitalist patterns." While the entrenched upper classes took account of "bourgeois interests" and availed themselves of the "economic possibilities offered by capitalism," they were careful "to distance themselves from the bourgeoisie." This arrangement was not an "atavism . . . but an *active symbiosis* of two social strata" in which the old elites retained their political, social, and cultural primacy. In exchange they let the bourgeoisie make money and pay taxes. In Schumpeter's judgment, even in England "the aristocratic element continued to rule the roost *right to the end of the period of intact and vital capitalism.*"

By controlling what Schumpeter called the "steel frame" or "political engine" of the *ancien régime,* the feudal elements were in a position to set the terms for the implantation of manufactural and industrial capitalism, thereby making it serve their own purposes. They forced industry to fit itself into pre-existing social, class, and ideological structures. Admittedly, industrial capitalism distorted and strained these structures in the process, but not beyond recognition or to the breaking point. The old governing class was both resilient and flexible. It had the support of the landed nobilities and interests, which quite rightly considered the steel frame of the *ancien régime* to be the protective armor for their privileged but exposed positions. In addition, the managers of the state won the loyalty of the bourgeoisie by furthering or safeguarding their economic interests with government contracts, protective tariffs, and colonial preferments.

If the feudal elements in both political and civil society perpetuated their dominance so effectively, it was largely because they knew how to adapt and renew themselves. The public service nobilities, both civil and military, took in qualified and ambitious scions of business and the liberal professions, though they were careful to regulate closely this infusion of new blood and talent. Newcomers had to pass through elite schools, ingest the corporate ethos, and demonstrate fealty to the old order as a precondition for advancement. Besides, the highest ranks of the state bureaucracy and military services continued to be reserved for men of high birth and proven assimilation.

The landed magnates were no less effective in adjusting to changing times. Above all, they absorbed and practiced the principles of capitalism and interest politics without, however, derogating their aristocratic world-view, bearing, and connections. Some noble proprietors became improving landlords. Others combined the rationalized exploitation of the soil and agrarian labor with large-scale milling, distilling, brewing, and dairying. Still others turned to extracting timber, coal, and minerals from their lands and invested in industrial ventures. Moreover, all learned alike to resort to lobbying and logrolling as well as pressure and partisan politics to protect or promote their interests. Increasingly, the landed estate assumed the attributes of class and class consciousness, and acted accordingly.

This extensive and many-sided adaptation is usually considered evidence for the de-noblement and de-aristocratization of the old order, for the inevitable if gradual *embourgeoisement,* or bourgeoisification, of Europe's ruling and governing classes. But there is another way of viewing this accommodation. Just as industrialization was grafted onto pre-established societal and political structures, so the feudal elements reconciled their rationalized bureaucratic and economic behavior with their pre-existent social and cultural praxis and mind-set. In other words, the old elites excelled at selectively ingesting, adapting, and assimilating new ideas and practices without seriously endangering their traditional status, temperament, and outlook. Whatever the dilution and cheapening of nobility, it was gradual and benign.

This prudential and circumscribed adjustment was facilitated by the bourgeoisie's rage for co-optation and ennoblement. Whereas the nobility was skilled at adaptation, the bourgeoisie excelled at emulation. Throughout the nineteenth and early twentieth centuries the *grands bourgeois* kept denying themselves by imitating and appropriating the ways of the nobility in the hope of climbing into it. The grandees of business and finance bought landed estates, built country houses, sent their sons to elite higher schools, and assumed aristocratic poses and life-styles. They also strained to break into aristocratic and court circles and to marry into the titled nobility. Last but not least, they solicited decorations and, above all, patents of nobility. These aristocratizing barons of industry and commerce were not simply supercilious parvenus or arrivistes who bowed and scraped for fatuous honors from the parasitic leisure class of a decaying old order. On the contrary, their obsequiousness was highly practical and consequential. The bourgeois sought social advancement for reasons of material benefit, social status, and psychic income. In addition, and no less important, by disavowing themselves in order to court membership in the old establishment, the aristocratizing bourgeois impaired their own class formation and class consciousness and accepted and prolonged their subordinate place in the "active symbiosis of the two social strata."

But there was another result as well. As part of their effort to scale the social pyramid and to demonstrate their political loyalty, the bourgeois embraced the historicist high culture and patronized the hegemonic institutions that were dominated by the old elites. The result was that they strengthened classical and academic idioms, conventions, and symbols in the arts and letters instead of encouraging modernist impulses. The bourgeois allowed themselves to be ensnared in a cultural and educational system that bolstered and reproduced the *ancien régime.* In the process they sapped their own potential to inspire the conception of a new aesthetic and intellection.

Indeed, the self-abnegating bourgeois were among the most enthusiastic champions of traditional architecture, statuary, painting, and performing arts. This high classical culture had formidable state support. Academies, conservatories, and museums provided training, access to careers, and official prizes. The governments financed most of these institutions, awarded commissions, and sponsored individual and collective artistic activities. The churches and universities were part of this towering hegemonic edifice.

But to say that the conventions and idioms of high culture remained traditional and classical is not to say that they were archaic and lifeless. To the extent that Europe was an old order, its official high culture was congruent with it. It might even be said that some of Europe's finest cultural achievements were and continued to be "inseparable from the milieu of absolutism, of extreme social injustice, even of gross violence, in which they flourished." No doubt, judging by the tendency to formalist replication, overdecoration, and monumentalization, some of the arts were becoming sclerotic and trailed behind their times. But cultural productions were no less effective for being turgid and specious. Certainly the official cultures were not about to be subverted or toppled by the modernist avant-gardes, which kept being assimilated, defused, and turned back.

The mentalities of Europe's elites probably trailed even further behind economic developments than their social and cultural life. In any case, their mind-set changed very slowly and was perhaps most revealing of their continuing implantation in and allegiance to the old regime. The governing classes, in which the feudal element remained particularly conspicuous, were thoroughly imbued with nobilitarian values and attitudes. Their world-view was consonant with an imperious and hierarchical rather than a liberal and democratic society.

In the 1780s an aristocratic reaction in defense of fiscal, social, and bureaucratic privilege had become an important, possibly a decisive, underlying and immediate cause for the French Revolution, the first act of the breakup of Europe's *ancien régime.* At that time the lay and clerical nobilities resisted any further loss of control in political society, which had become an ever more essential shield for their privileged status. Similarly, between 1905 and 1914 the old elites proceeded to reaffirm and tighten their political hold in order to bolster their material, social, and cultural pre-eminence. In the process they intensified the domestic and international tensions which produced the Great War that started the final act of the dissolution of Europe's old regime.

Chapter 1

THE ECONOMIES

The Endurance of Land, Agriculture, Manufacture

DOWN TO 1914 Europe was pre-eminently preindustrial and prebourgeois, its civil societies being deeply grounded in economies of labor-intensive agriculture, consumer manufacture, and petty commerce. Admittedly, industrial capitalism and its class formations, notably the bourgeoisie and the factory proletariat, made vast strides, especially after 1890. But they were in no position to challenge or supplant the tenacious economic and class structures of the pre-existent capitalism.

Even in Western and Central Europe the economy was still dominated by merchant and manufactural capitalism, while monopoly, finance, or organized industrial capitalism was only in its first growing phase. This meant that cosmopolitan merchants and bankers, along with local manufacturers, continued to carry more weight than the owners and managers of big industry and corporate banking.

While progress in production techniques was prodigious and continuous, the process and rhythm of economic growth were spasmodic and uneven. The first industrial revolution reached its technological and economic climacteric in parts of Western and Central Europe in the late nineteenth century, when the second industrial revolution entered its infant stage. But this does not mean that by then merchant and manufactural capitalism was stagnating or disintegrating—nationally, regionally, or locally. Although some of its branches experienced a decline in production and in profit rates, other branches continued either to hold their own or to expand. On balance, the capitalism of the first industrial revolution not only remained robust during the transition to the new capitalism of the second, but also furthered this transition and gained from it.

The protracted but far from general economic crisis that lasted from the mid-1870s to the mid-1890s was not so much a watershed between the old and the new capitalisms as the costly catalysis of their early interpenetration. Nor did this crisis inaugurate an era of "sharpening conflicts between the growth of productive power and business profitability." While the new capitalism established itself as semi-autonomous growth centers within the existing economic structures and helped put an end to the persistent economic crisis, it was in no position to take command of Europe's political economy. During the quarter-century between 1890 and 1914 even the German economy did not fall under the control of its large and interwoven industrial and financial corporations. Indeed, it would appear that by 1914 monopoly and finance capitalism was in its first rather than its highest or last stage. To be sure, there was substantial and rapid industrial growth and concentration. Even so, the new capitalism did not "supersede" the old with the start of the twentieth century, nor was capitalism "transformed" into an imperialism driven by capital exports rather than the export of merchandise.

Not only the growth of industrial capitalism but also the

contraction of "premodern" economic sectors proceeded very gradually. The result was that agriculture and consumer manufacture continued to outweigh the capital goods sector, in large measure because key landed and manufacturing interests excelled at adapting new production techniques and at enlisting state support to cushion their relative economic decline. Despite dramatic advances by the new capitalism, agriculture, urban real estate, and consumer manufacture continued to provide the essential material foundations for Europe's *anciens régimes* between 1848 and 1914.

Except in the United Kingdom, the agricultural sector claimed a larger share of the labor force and also generated a larger proportion of the gross national product than any other single sector. Moreover, except in France—and particularly in England—vast property holdings occupied a paramount place either as estate agriculture or as land let out for cash rent or crop sharing. In addition, in all countries landed property was still without exception the principal form of personal wealth and the main source of private income, also because of rising real estate values in the cities. It is true that although agriculture and land remained first in absolute terms, they were losing relative ground to industry and movable capital. But this is not to say that the landed estate and the postfeudal seigneur were about to crumble. The large magnates in particular more than held their own. While in some areas they bought the lands of the faltering small gentry at advantageous prices, in others they benefitted disproportionately from rising land values. Furthermore, numerous big proprietors became improving landlords. They rationalized land management, went into food processing and lumbering, and diversified their capital by investing in urban real estate and business ventures. Last but not least, particularly during times of economic adversity, the big agrarians managed to secure favorable tariffs, interest rates, subsidies, and taxes because of their close ties with the feudal element in government. More often than not they obtained these government benefits by collaborating with spokesmen for traditional consumer manufactory and infant heavy industry that also clamored for state aid.

On every major score the manufacturing sector came right after agriculture, except in Great Britain, where it had stood first since midcentury. This sector consisted mainly of four branches of consumer goods production: textiles and apparel, food processing, leather (including shoes), and wood (especially furniture). The technology of consumer manufacture was that of the first industrial revolution, notably the application of coal and steam as well as the ready availability of iron and steel and of rail transport. This sprawling economic sector comprised, above all, single-unit enterprises of labor-intensive small workshops and medium-sized plants (below factory level) staffed by artisans and unskilled hands using simple, low-energy machinery. Because of their relatively small capitalization most manufacturing firms were family owned, financed, and managed. As for the class formations of this precorporate entrepreneurial capitalism, the owners of small workshops were the backbone of the independent lower middle class. In turn the proprietors of medium-sized as well as large plants, especially in textiles and food processing, constituted a bourgeoisie that was predominantly local and provincial rather than national and cosmopolitan. This bourgeoisie, including commercial and private bankers, acted less as a social class with a comprehensive political and cultural project than as an interest and pressure group in pursuit of economic goals.

For its part, the capital goods sector was like an archipelago surrounded by vast oceans of agriculture and traditional manufacture. Paradoxically this sector had its real beginnings during the protracted recession of 1873 to 1896, and it was still of only limited scope in 1914. These four decades saw the launching of the second industrial revolution with its organic chemistry and synthetics, electric power, turbines, internal combustion engines, nonferrous metals, special alloys, and streamlined iron-ore processing. These innovations in technique, energy sources, and materials went hand in hand with the growth of giant firms, some of which established their own research laboratories.

This dynamic lead sector of producer goods industry was

centered in the now stupendous iron and steel industry as well as in metallurgy and machine making, vehicle construction, and chemicals. These four branches saw the greatest concentration of multi-unit companies operating large factories with specialized and high-energy machinery manned by a work force of factory artisans and proletarians. The capital-intensive production that furthered labor's marginal efficiency called for a scale of investment that exceeded the financial capacities of family entrepreneurship. Even family-controlled enterprises became outposts of corporate and managerial capitalism that spawned a business bourgeoisie with a national perspective and with growing ties with both investment banks and government. Because of their high capitalization, the mining and railroad industries ought to count as part of the corporate capitalist complex that spurred the second industrial revolution.

Curiously enough, the ascending national bourgeoisie of industrial capitalism was even less a social class "for itself," with its own interests and objectives, than the local and parochial bourgeoisie of traditional manufacture. Throughout Europe the magnates and "robber barons" of industry, and their (subordinate) associates in the professional middle class, solicited indispensable state aid from governments that continued to be dominated by preindustrial and prebourgeois governing classes. According to Joseph Schumpeter there was a systematic trade-off: in exchange for economic benefits the bourgeoisie supported the "feudal elements . . . [that] filled the offices of state, officered the army, [and] devised policies." The new national bourgeoisie, for its part, secured advantageous tariffs, legal codes, and labor policies. In turn, the old governing class counted on industrialists and bankers to help modernize in particular the war-related branches of the *ancien régime*'s economy without claiming an independent say in politics and culture.

For Thorstein Veblen this amalgamation of "the latest mechanistic science and . . . machine industry" with the feudal elements in and out of government was the quintessential characteristic of the second German empire. Veblen quite rightly insisted that Germany's old regime succeeded in assimilating capitalist science and industry only because it was so "securely lodged in the interests and traditional ideals of the dynastic rulers and privileged classes." In fact, it was these ancestral elements that "extended the dominion and improved the efficiency" of the old order by facilitating the "technical advance" essential to large-scale industry and trade as well as to the "larger and more expensive equipment and strategy of war."

Admittedly, Meiji Japan was the only other country with a governing oligarchy as adept at harnessing the industrial arts for an *ancien régime* as imperial Germany's inveterate margraves. But the traditional governing classes of the other European nations, including England, also grafted industrial capitalism into inherited social and cultural structures. They did so with methods and consequences that were different in degree rather than kind.

The tertiary sector, for its part, was one of small finance, commerce, and trade. To be sure, there were a few large banks, trading firms, and shipping and insurance companies. Having long since become dependent on international trade, Great Britain was the uncontested leader in this sector, the City of London being a conspicuous outpost and symbol of this supremacy. Nonetheless, even England continued to be a nation of small shopkeepers, along with all the other European nations. The retail and service trades especially were dominated by petty operatives. In terms of turnover, floor space, and personnel the department and chain stores of the major cities were only of marginal importance. Smallness was also the rule rather than the exception in the wholesale, import, and export trades. Similarly, in finance the terrain was occupied by modest banking houses, though the capital needs of heavy industries stimulated the growth of a few large joint-stock investment banks.

In sum, even as late as 1914 the civil societies of Europe's old regimes were far from being industrial-capitalist and *grand bourgeois.* In what were mixed or dual economies, gradually contracting landlord agriculture, consumer manufacture, and

petty commerce remained substantially ahead of conspicuously but slowly expanding capital goods production, investment banking, and large-scale merchandising. To treat
Europe's dominant economic sectors as obsolete residues is to
distort reality, for these survivals were as massive as they were
vigorous. Although they gradually yielded and lost economic
ground to the new corporate capitalism, the landed and public
service nobilities maintained their social and cultural
hegemony in the capitals and countryside while the merchant
bourgeoisie claimed codetermination in the manufacturing
and port cities. In turn, this continuing social and cultural
dominance sustained the old elites' hold on the state that
helped them slow down their long-term economic decline and
soften the blows of the business cycle.

Despite its contraction as a contributor to national employment, income, and wealth, as late as 1914 agriculture still
remained the principal sector in most European economies.
Admittedly, by then agriculture accounted for only 12 percent
of the active labor force, 9 percent of national income, and 15
percent of national wealth in the United Kingdom. On the
Continent, however, it occupied an altogether more vital
place. In the tsarist empire easily 66 percent of all employment
was in agriculture and well over 80 percent of the population
lived in rural areas. Moreover, agriculture contributed 35 percent of Russia's national income, 45 percent of its national
wealth, and over 70 percent of its exports—Russia being the
world's leading grain exporter. In France, the land claimed
between 40 and 45 percent of the active population and generated between 30 and 35 percent of national income, or about
40 percent of the total national product. But even in the German Empire, which was in the forefront of industrialization
and urbanization, 40 percent of the population in 1907 still
lived in villages and towns of less than 10,000, and 40 percent
of the labor force worked the land to produce 20 percent of
the national income.

Looked at with wide-angled lenses, the Continent was a society of landlords and peasants clustered in and around rural settlements ranging from tiny hamlets of less than 100 people to agro-towns with populations of between 5,000 and 10,000. Needless to say, far from all peasants were small land-holders. In fact, legions of peasants either rented or share-cropped the land they worked, or else they were landless or near-landless agricultural laborers. Accordingly, they were in the grip of large landowners, who capitalized on the oversupply of rural labor stemming from the simultaneous population growth and "deindustrialization" of the countryside to enforce their exploitative control of the agricultural economy. Moreover, by enlarging their interest in brewing, milling, and distilling, the landed magnates strengthened their economic leverage over the market-oriented independent peasantry.

In spite of, indeed because of, their abject material and social condition the mass of peasants remained quiescent. To be sure, there were rural *jacqueries* in Russia before and during the upheaval of 1905, and there were intermittent strikes by agricultural laborers in Italy's Po valley after the turn of the century. But these insurgencies dramatized not only the resigned submission of Europe's overexploited peasantry but also the resolve and capability of the large agrarians and their political allies to repress popular rebellions.

Indeed, the large landowners, including the agro-business-men among them, were the chief economic and social supports of the *anciens régimes.* Large landed property was the principal source not only of the extravagant income and wealth of the agrarian elites but also of their inordinate social prestige, cultural pre-eminence, and political sway. In all respects, including numbers and wealth, the agrarians continued to surpass the magnates of business and the liberal professions.

Even in England the landed elite remained more consequential than the contracted agricultural sector would lead one to expect. In 1873, 2,500 individuals each with holdings of at least 2,000 acres owned 42 percent of the land in England and Wales while 3,500 individuals each with no less than 10,000 acres owned 66 percent of the land in Scotland. Some

7,000 persons monopolized 80 percent of all privately owned land in the United Kingdom. The duke of Sutherland held over 1 million acres, many of them of marginal quality; the earl of Breadalbane and the duke of Buccleuch, some 400,000 acres; the dukes of Devonshire, Northumberland, and Atholl, nearly 200,000 acres; and the earls of Balfour, Derby, and Moray, about 65,000 acres. By themselves the 525 peers of the British Isles owned about 15 million acres: 28 dukes owned 4 million acres; 33 marquesses, 1.6 million acres; 194 earls, 5.9 million acres; 270 viscounts and barons, 3.8 million acres. In addition some 1,000 greater gentry held between 3,000 and 10,000 acres, and about 2,000 squires between 1,000 and 3,000 acres. Taking account of land sales and reductions in the size of estates during the forty-five years to 1914, about 4,000 individuals still commanded 50 percent of all privately owned land in the United Kingdom. Most of these magnates belonged to the nobility and gentry, and their average holding was 4,000 acres. Fifteen hundred members of this landed elite held an average of 8,000 acres, or 40 percent of the total.

It should be added that the value of many of these landholdings was enhanced by virtue of their including substantial urban properties or mineral reserves. The dukes of Bedford, Norfolk, and Westminster, the marquess of Salisbury, and the lords Ebury, Kensington, and Southampton held considerable real estate in London, while the dukes of Newcastle and Northumberland, the marquess of Bute, the earls of Scarbrough and Radnor, and the lords St. Levan and Plymouth owned important properties in or near other cities. Three of these dukes and three of these lords also claimed mineral deposits, notably coal and iron ore, as did the duke of Leeds, the earls of Fitzwilliam, Abingdon, and Crawford, and the lords Bathurst, Dynevor, Leconfield, Loudoun, Mowbray, Rosslyn, Shrewsbury, and Stanhope.

These large properties enabled the nobility and gentry of the English countryside to eclipse and subordinate the business elite of the cities. Needless to say, this postfeudal aristocracy also had deep social, cultural, and political roots, but these would have atrophied long before had they not been so solidly implanted in landed property. Besides, quite apart from their contribution to national and rent income, many of the 2.2 million male agricultural workers provided England's landed elite with reliable and vital electoral support.

Germany's agrarian elite had no difficulty measuring itself with England's. Not that Germany had no small and medium-sized peasant holdings, for in 1907 there were 5.5 million individual holdings of between 2.5 and 50 acres that covered an arable surface of 39 million acres. But there were also 286,000 properties of over 50 acres encompassing a total of 57 million arable acres, and some 3,000 individuals owned close to 15 percent of Germany's cultivated surface.

Among the large proprietors, the nobility occupied first place. It claimed some 13.5 million acres divided almost evenly between arable and forest lands. In western, southern, and central Germany over 50 percent of this cultivated land was rented out, 25 percent of it to small peasants in the west, 18 percent in the south, and 5 percent in the center. By contrast, only 20 percent of the noble lands were rented out in the eastern provinces, and less than 10 percent of them to small operatives.

Above all, there were 23,566 estates of over 250 acres covering about 23 percent of Germany's cultivated surface, and 19,117 of these estates were concentrated in Prussia. Some 3,500 of these Prussian grain-growing estates had over 1,250 acres, the number of properties of over 12,500 acres being around 125. The nobility owned nearly all of the latifundia, and between 1895 and 1912 the surface covered by entailed estates actually expanded from 5.2 million to 6.2 million acres.

As Germany's largest landowner, William of Hohenzollern claimed close to 250,000 acres, three-quarters of them in forest lands. The five largest landowners after the emperor each owned between 70,000 and 120,000 acres, or an average of about 100,000 acres: Prince Hohenlohe-Oehringen, Prince Hohenzollern-Sigmaringen, Prince Solms-Baruth, Count von Stolberg-Wernigerode, and the duke of Ratibor. Meanwhile, the three-class franchise gave the postfeudal territorial aristocracy, in particular the Junkers of East Elbia, political control of Prussia, and through Prussia of the rest of Germany.

In the Dual Monarchy as a whole there were at least two dozen aristocratic families with over 250,000 acres apiece. In the Austrian half the most notable among these were the Schwarzenbergs and Liechtensteins. All told there were about 230 estates of over 12,500 acres in Cisleithania. In Bohemia alone some 500 proprietors owned 3.7 million acres. In southern Bohemia Prince Schwarzenberg lorded over a small kingdom of 360,000 acres, complete with scores of parishes and churches. His property included a dozen castles, the same number of breweries, close to a hundred dairies, two sugar refineries, twenty sawmills, and a few mining enterprises. In Silesia, in Moravia, and in Lower Austria about a dozen large proprietors owned 20 percent, 11 percent, and 9 percent of the arable land of their respective provinces. Throughout Austria the major landowners were nobles. To the extent that the bourgeoisie became landed, they acquired country houses rather than large producing estates. Around the turn of the century nearly 60 percent of the active labor force worked the land, and the landlord-dominated agrarian sector, including forest lands, generated over 30 percent of Austria's national product.

In Transleithania, where they accounted for less than 50 percent of the population, the Magyars were giant landowners, even by European standards. To be sure, the landed gentry with holdings of 250 to 1,000 acres declined from about 30,000 in 1848 to 10,000 in 1914. But during that same half-century the number of noble magnates increased significantly, having made massive gains at the expense of this failing gentry. By 1910 some 6,000 seignorial and ecclesiastic proprietors owning an average of 1,250 acres controlled 40 percent of the arable surface, and some 4,000 proprietors claimed about 33 percent of all the cultivated land. There were even 175 latifundia of over 12,500 acres comprising close to 20 percent of Hungary's privately owned and cultivated surface. The Esterházys alone held close to 1 million acres, followed by the Andrássys, Károlyis, and Schönborns. The profitability and prestige of estate ownership was such that Hungary's great businessmen and professionals, including the Jews among them, made massive land purchases. In the meantime, 2.5 million small holders were confined to 30 percent of the arable land. Moreover, 1.5 million agricultural laborers, or nearly 20 percent of the active work force, toiled for subsistence wages in an economy in which agriculture secured the livelihood of 65 percent of the population, and raw farm products accounted for 50 percent of Transleithania's total export value.

Tsarist Russia was a country not only of landless mujiks, small holders, and kulaks but also of large agrarians among whom the nobility were pre-eminent. Admittedly, between 1861 and 1914 the number of noble landowners declined by 25 percent and their acreage by close to 45 percent. Moreover, of the roughly 100,000 noble landowners, nearly 50,000 had estates of less than 270 acres. But the other half of the noble proprietors owned 97 percent of the 100 million acres of noble lands, and these still covered more than 50 percent of all privately held land in European Russia. More striking still, a bare 10 percent of the agrarian nobility with properties of over 2,700 acres owned 75 percent of all land in estates. There were even 155 supermagnates whose estate holdings averaged 270,000 acres and comprised 33 percent of all noble-owned land. Among these landed giants were Count A. D. Sheremetev with 29 estates totaling 600,000 acres, his brother Count S. D. Sheremetev with 26 estates embracing 400,000 acres, and Princess Z. N. Yusupova with 21 estates comprising 580,000 acres.

In sum, down to 1905 the nobility remained dominant among the large landowners, claiming nearly 70 percent of all holdings of over 270 acres and a considerably higher percentage of all estates of over 2,700. But in contrast to East Elbian Germany, in most of European Russia at least three-quarters of the arable land in great noble estates was not farmed by the owners themselves but was leased to peasants, most of it for cash rent.

In the immediate wake of the Revolution of 1905 there was an increase in the rate of yearly land sales by nobles. But this divestment tapered off as soon as civil and political society was restabilized and the price of land rose steeply, as it did down to 1914. In the face of pressure for land reform in the first two Dumas the internally divided nobility closed ranks around the autocracy as the essential bulwark of the *ancien régime*. Attuned to the landed element in the nobility, in mid-1907 Stolypin revised the electoral law to make sure that hereafter the Duma should be safe for the landed element. The result was that Russia's fledgling lower chamber became a brake on Stolypin's own land-reform project, moderate though it was. Himself a member of the landed provincial gentry, Stolypin proposed to expand the small and middle peasantry by making imperial and state lands available for purchase and settlement, and not by expropriating or squeezing gentry and church lands. Moreover, at the same time that he and his successors backed the "sober and strong" kulaks or individual proprietors over the "weak and drunken" peasants, they stepped up state aid for large estate owners in particular. In addition to maintaining high tariffs and low taxes, the government chartered a special land bank to bolster noble landholding with cheap credit and mortgages.

Although France was not a country of giant landowners and estates, neither was it a republic of small and comfortable independent peasants. Six million petty proprietors of less than 2.5 acres, many of them owning mere patches of land, bordered on poverty even with supplementary income earned by hiring out their labor. In 1906 small properties between 2.5 and 25 acres accounted for 75 percent of all production units. But these units covered only 23 percent of the total arable land, their average size was less than 12.5 acres, and more than half of them were family-operated without the help of hired labor. In sum, microfundia of less than 25 acres and covering 30 percent of the cultivated land area made up 84 percent of all production units, and 76 percent of them were family-operated with the help of at most one *journalier* or *domestique*. Moreover, since these peasants did not necessarily own all the land they farmed, the larger the production units in this category the greater the acreage leased from big landowners for cash rent or a share of the crop.

Clearly, then, in the Third Republic medium and large landowners, who were considerably less numerous than the small ones, owned and operated the bulk of the arable land. While petty and small holders with 2.5 to 25 acres worked 75 percent of all farming units and took up 23 percent of the cultivated surface, middle peasants with 25 to 100 acres operated barely 20 percent of the farming units but took up more than 30 percent of the surface. Moreover, even though properties of over 100 acres and averaging 400 acres covered between 40 and 50 percent of the cultivated land, they totaled only 4 percent of the production units. This category even included some 17,000 properties of over 500 acres that occupied 15 percent of the land.

No doubt a considerable portion of these large properties were in forest and relatively barren lands. Even so, they were the lead sector of commercial agriculture which included 45,000 farming units employing between 6 and 50 hired hands, among them 8,000 units with over 10 workers. This large-scale capitalist agriculture specialized in cereals and sugarbeet production north of the Loire (notably in the Ile de France, Picardy, and Artois), in viticulture in the south (Languedoc, Provence), and in cattle farming on the western grasslands. Because of its concentration in a few departments and its interlocking with large-scale food processing and distribution, this advanced agricultural sector weighed heavily not only in economic but in political terms, and the noble element cut an important figure in it.

In Italy about 60 percent of the active population was in agriculture, forestry, and fishing, which generated nearly 50 percent of the gross internal product. Eighty percent of the agrarian work force owned no land to speak of, and 54 percent were casual day laborers. Large proprietors owned most of the fertile lands, many of them renting out their lands rather than exploiting them themselves. The Mezzogiorno was dominated by large latifundia of hundreds of acres, notably in Calabria and Sicily. In Calabria two-fifths of the landlords were absentee owners, while of the less than 800 proprietors who owned one-third of Sicily at least two-thirds were nonresident. More often than not the southern magnates were noblemen, a good many having acquired their titles in the early nineteenth century. In and around Rome the Borgheses owned close to 85 square miles of land, and about six times that surface was claimed by a few other great families, the rest being owned by the Church.

In the province of Bologna, the center of agrarian capitalism outside the south, 200 to 300 landowners held 157,500 out of 232,500 acres, or 66 percent of the prime land. Half of these large proprietors were noblemen, many of them scions of old families. They dominated not just the economy but the social, cultural, and political life of the province, including the city of Bologna. In the other provinces of concentrated land ownership and agriculture the pre-eminence of the nobility was even greater.

As previously noted, many large landowners branched out into land- and agriculture-related business activities. They commercialized the lumber of their forest lands as well as the coal and iron from under the surface of their properties. But above all, they went into the refining, brewing, and distilling of agricultural commodities. In 1886 landed magnates owned 80 of the 120 beet-sugar refineries in Bohemia producing most of Austria's beet sugar. They were also proprietors of 500 of the 900 breweries and 300 of the 400 distilleries in Cisleithania. Similarly, in Russia in 1914 landed nobles owned 2,377 of the 2,978 distilleries that turned out the empire's spirits.

Throughout Europe, except in France, the vast majority of large landowners were noble or gentry. Quite apart from exercising a gravitational pull on non-noble landed proprietors, this time-honored elite had much to tie it together beyond a common mode of production and source of wealth. The titled proprietors of each country had a common upbringing, education, life-style, mentality, code of behavior, and political persuasion. In the countryside they lorded not only over estate workers, tenants, and peasants but also over blacksmiths, artisans, shopkeepers, professionals, and clergymen. Both locally and regionally they occupied the leading social, cultural, and philanthropic positions, and they monopolized, controlled, or carried great weight in political society, also or especially at the center.

Needless to say, the landed nobility was not homogeneous in terms of birth, wealth, status, and outlook. It may be said to have had three principal components: the affluent cosmopolitan nobility of dynastic and ancient lineage that lived in the capital cities; the lesser nobility or greater gentry with large and reputed estates and with regional visibility and influence; and the comfortable or poor squirearchy of merely local horizons and consequence. But whatever their differences in pedigree, wealth, residence, and range of influence, the agrarian elites were united by a shared material stake and world-view. Moreover, in spite of their intramural conflicts of interest and strategy, the major factions of the landed estate ultimately rallied to fight for the maintenance of their joint pre-eminence in civil and political society, particularly in times of common adversity.

The long-drawn deflation of 1873 to 1896 was such a time, in that it affected the key branches of agriculture, even if unevenly. Largely because of a flood of cheap grains and meats from overseas, prices slumped, driving down profit margins and rent rolls while driving up arrears in mortgage and rent payments as well as the number of bankruptcies. At the same time the price in land declined and many estates were sold or reduced, especially by smaller and less efficient proprietors. The result was that the grandees became even bigger, since they bought up much of the bargain-priced land that flooded the market. Although there never was any real panic, large landowners in particular became profoundly apprehensive about the future of agriculture and land values. There was the additional fear that the persistent downturn in agriculture would accelerate its decline in relation to industry.

As they looked for ways to stem the tide, the postfeudal agrarians, especially the nobles among them, discovered or rediscovered the cardinal importance of politics. Whereas the small peasantry was helpless, the agrarian elites were in a position to use their disproportionate hold on the state apparatus to enlist government aid in the form of tariff protection, subsidized transport, cheap credit, and tax rebates. Since the price recession also affected important branches of industry and manufacture, certain bourgeois elements similarly looked to government assistance. As agrarians and businessmen sought each other out, it became evident that in the logrolling between them the agrarians had the upper hand and secured the greater benefits. In fact, the lingering sectorial contraction brutally reminded the rising bourgeoisie that it was very much the weaker component in what Schumpeter called the "active symbiosis of the two social strata." Although the agrarians were no less capitalist than the industrialists in economic terms, because of their landed status they had privileged access to the feudalistic auxiliaries that "filled the offices of state, officered the army, [and] devised policies" favorable to themselves. In other words, the agrarians became more determined than ever to maintain a political society that, while "taking account of bourgeois interests," nevertheless gave priority to large-scale agriculture, which was the material base for their exalted social and cultural position.

In Germany, even though the tariff of 1879 consecrated the collaboration of the masters of rye and of steel, it also confirmed the political subordination of the claimant bourgeoisie. Moreover, after Bismarck's fall the removal of Chancellor General Count Leo von Caprivi in 1894 reaffirmed the resolve of the protectionist agrarians not to permit any dilution of the feudalistic element in political society, notably in the executive branch of the imperial government.

Beginning in the late seventies the governments of Italy, Austria-Hungary, and Russia also adopted protective duties, though essentially in response to agrarian pressure, there being no industrial interests comparable to those in Germany. In Italy and Austria, and more particularly in France, the agrarians collaborated with textile manufacturers. In fact it was these manufacturers, chafing under foreign competition and free trade, who pressed for a united front with landed interests once they realized that they needed the votes of deputies of rural France to pass tariff legislation in parliament. In return, however, French agriculture won the Méline tariff of 1892, which was exacted by a composite agrarian movement of large landowners with such postfeudal aristocrats as the marquis Élie de Dampierre, Le Trésor de La Rocque, the comte de Chambrun and the marquis Melchior de Vogüé as their chief spokesmen. Incidentally, in addition to exploiting large properties in Berry (south of the Loire), which he also valued for their ethical and deferential magic, Vogüé was a board member of the Suez Company and of Saint-Gobain.

Clearly, there is no denying the agrarian impulse behind the resumption or growth of government intervention in the economy. Traumatized by the great price fall, the large landowners and their auxiliaries were at least as determined as certain large manufacturers and industrialists to restrict free trade, the more so because they had much more at stake and were much more vulnerable. Accordingly, they organized lobbies, pressure groups, peasant leagues, and parties or factions within parties in order to strengthen their hand for punctual dealings with bourgeois elements and government ministries and to maintain their pre-eminence in political society generally, especially in anticipation of difficult times ahead. Even haughty landed aristocrats supported or at least condoned this change from deferential to interest, class, and plebeian politics.

To abstract agricultural developments from their historical context and present them with aggregate figures is to foster a serious misreading of Europe's *anciens régimes*. There is no gainsaying the relative economic decline of agriculture in face of the gradual growth of industry. But except in England, agriculture persisted as the single largest and weightiest economic sector until 1914, and even in England the concentration of landownership remained essentially undiminished. In turn, the amplitude, grandeur, and exploitation of the world of landlords and peasants perpetuated the primacy of pre-industrial forces whose political associates were at or near the switches for war in 1914.

*   *   *

Europe's economic profile is distorted not only by glossing over large landownership in agriculture but also by understating consumer manufacture in relation to capital goods production. In all major respects, until 1914 consumer manufacture outweighed capital goods industry in the nonagrarian sector of each national economy, and also in international trade. As previously noted, consumer manufacture had four major branches: textiles and apparel; food processing; leather and shoes; lumber and furniture. This sector was dominated by small single-unit firms. Family owned and operated, these old-style enterprises were highly labor-intensive and utilized simple and low-energy-consuming machines.

Centered in and around the older towns, the world of workshops and artisans overshadowed the factories and proletarian labor of the newer urban centers and industrial zones in terms of work force, capitalization, and production value. Paradoxically, the growth of factory production and cities benefitted artisanal workers and workshops by stimulating the demand for goods and services that only the latter could provide, especially the demand for housing, food, clothing, and precision machinery. In other words, while some branches of traditional manufacture no doubt stagnated or contracted, others flourished and expanded. Although it had a slower growth rate than the lead branches of capital industry, the world of workshops and artisans on balance more than held its own. Another reason for the resilience of consumer production was its considerable adaptive powers. Especially in textiles new machines displaced countless hand spinners and weavers, with cottages and shops giving way to plants and their large-scale and costly equipment. Even so, textiles continued to belong to the sector of traditional manufacture: the large mills remained family owned and managed, most of their machines were operated by nonproletarian female labor, and they looked to small jobbers, wholesalers, and apparel makers as their primary market. Much the same was true for food processing, except that there were few women in the unskilled labor force of sugar refining, flour milling, brewing, and distilling.

Large-scale and capital-intensive firms with long-term external financing and a proletarian work force remained very much the exception in the vast manufacturing sector. Petty operatives and family capitalists were the rule, and they ran small firms with high labor-fixed capital ratios. The bulk of the work force consisted of craftsmen and artisans toiling in cottages or workshops of between one and five workers, including the proprietor. Local families owned and operated the vast majority of these mini-firms. They produced staples for sale to the peasantry of the surrounding countryside and to the intermediate classes of cities that were provincial administrative and market towns rather than modern conurbations. As for the manufacture of luxuries, which held an important place in consumer production, it tended to be centered in major cities, including the capitals, and it too was concentrated in small and medium-sized workshops and not in large factories.

Certainly the giants of manufacture could not compare with the giants of agriculture and real estate in numbers and wealth, let alone in status. The disadvantages of these big family capitalists were compounded by their inability to establish the same social and political influence over the multitude of petty, small, and intermediate operatives that the big agrarians exercised over the vast and composite peasantry. In addition, the magnates of consumer manufacture tended to work at cross purposes with their counterparts in the capital goods sector, a cleavage that the agrarians exploited for their own benefit.

As for the artisans, although they continued to be the dominant element in the working class, they were being buffeted by the strains and stresses of capitalist modernization. Faced with major changes in production and distribution methods, artisans had to struggle hard to maintain their autonomy, skill, status, and living standard. To be sure, numerically they were not only strong but getting stronger. But unlike the workers in the capital goods, extractive, and railroad industries, who were organizing along industrial lines, they remained divided along craft lines. Jealous of their personal and professional independence, artisans found it difficult to develop instruments and strategies of self-defense to take the place of the guilds and legal safeguards which presumably had served them so well in other difficult times.

In 1911 Britain's consumer manufactures and capital industries combined claimed about 38 percent of an active population of 18 million, or a total of 7 million workers. The 2.1 million workers, or 30 percent of this combined labor force, that were in metals, machinery, vehicles, and chemicals contributed about 24 percent of total net output. By comparison, the manufacturing sector was of considerably greater importance. Admittedly, wood and furniture along with leather claimed only 450,000 workers and 3.3 percent of net output. But textiles, apparel, and food processing accounted for 3.9 million workers, or 47.5 percent of the labor force in manufacture and industry, and generated 41 percent of net output. By themselves the 1.5 million textile workers contributed close to 16.5 percent of net output, while the 1.26 million apparel makers contributed another 8 percent, to make a total of 24.5 percent.

This was still a time when textiles by themselves accounted for 38 percent of all British exports, the bulk of it in the form of cotton piece goods. As late as 1913 over 85 percent of all cotton yardage and over 50 percent of all woolen piece goods were sold abroad, and 43 percent of these exports went to India alone. Given this large market for mass-produced cloth it is not surprising that there should have been ten textile firms among England's fifty largest corporations (with a capitalization of over £2 million each). Although the percentage of the female labor force that worked in textiles dropped from 22 percent in 1851 to 16 percent in 1911 the work force in this branch—as also in domestic service—was nevertheless being feminized. While the number of women workers in textiles actually rose from roughly 635,000 to 870,000 after midcentury, that of male textile workers, who were more disposed to combine with the organized factory proletariat, fell from 661,000 to 639,000.

The thrust toward bigness and concentration, partly

through mergers, was equally evident in food processing, notably in brewing and distilling, which between them claimed seventeen of England's largest enterprises. On the whole, all but nine of the fifty biggest firms were in consumer manufacture. But even in the large textile mills and food-processing plants the workers remained as resistant to unionization as the laboring men and women in the smaller establishments of the consumer sector and the 900,000 white-collar employees in Britain's unsurpassed and internationally oriented commercial sector.

While England is said to have moved gradually but steadily toward industrial and finance capitalism, Germany is pictured as having raced down that same road to overtake Britain by 1914. In actual fact, only about 10 million workers out of an active labor force of 27 million, or about 30 percent, were employed in manufacture and industry combined. Moreover, the capital goods sector employed only 2.25 million workers, and this 25 percent of the combined manufacturing and industrial labor force accounted for no more than 25 percent of net national output. Even if the coal industry is counted as part of the capital goods sector, traditional manufacture stayed way out front.

To be sure, metal processing, including machine and vehicle construction, was by 1914 the leading branch outside agriculture in terms of employment, capitalization, and production value. With a work force of 1.7 million, or less than 7 percent of Germany's active population, it contributed around 10 percent of net output. But a considerable percentage of these metallurgical workers labored in workshops and plants of less than 50 workers. There were also many traditional artisans among them, even in the largest factories.

Besides, all the other branches employing over 1 million workers were in the consumer sector. Clothing and leather combined claimed 1.6 million workers, food processing 1.3 million, and textiles 1.1 million. Admittedly, 750,000 of these textile workers, half of them women, toiled in plants of over 51. But except for textiles, consumer manufacture was concentrated in petty, small, and medium-sized business units. In any case, apparel, leather, textiles, and food processing claimed a total of 4 million workers by themselves. To complete the picture of small firms and traditional artisanship, another two branches need to be taken into account: building construction with 1.5 million workers, and wood processing, including furniture, with a work force of close to 1 million. In sum, there were some 6.5 million laboring men and women in the five major consumer branches each of which claimed 1 million or more workers.

This bulging consumer sector accounted, in large part, for the continuing importance of small and medium-sized business in Germany. In 1907, 90 percent of all firms in the combined manufacturing and industrial sector still employed only 5 or fewer workers. Even though the work force in these small enterprises had declined by one-third since 1875, it still amounted to 31.2 percent of the entire manufacturing-industrial labor force. At the same time, the 8.9 percent of the firms that employed between 6 and 50 workers claimed 26.4 percent of this labor force. Accordingly, while firms of between 1 and 50 workers claimed 57.6 percent of the wage earners in manufacture and industry, the 1.3 percent of the firms with over 50 employees accounted for the remaining 42.4 percent (51–200: 20.8 percent; 201–1,000: 16.7 percent; over 1,000: 4.9 percent). No doubt producer goods industries claimed nearly all the 548 enterprises of over 1,000 workers with a total work force of 1.3 million. In turn, however, the consumer sector accounted for a large share of the 26,700 enterprises of between 51 and 1,000 workers with a total labor force of 4 million.

At any rate, not only did consumer manufacture in Germany continue to far outpace capital goods production, but within both sectors medium-sized and small firms decisively outweighed the corporate giants. If the swollen retail and service trades are taken into account as well, the noncorporate business of the family and *petite bourgeoisie* looms still larger.

Even more than in either England or Germany, consumer manufacture continued to be preponderant in France, as did traditional and small family enterprise. In an economy where agriculture and petty shopkeeping were ingrained, before 1914 manufacture and industry combined claimed at best 5.2 million, or 25 percent of an active population of 21 million.

Apparel and other cloth manufactures were the single largest branch, with 1.6 million wage earners, single-person operatives, and home workers. Although since 1870 the textile industry had slipped to second place—between apparel and metallurgy—it still employed over 900,000 workers. With the addition of the 325,000 workers in leather, especially footwear, the clothing-related sector alone accounted for almost 40 percent of the entire manufacturing-industrial work force, for 30 percent of net output, and for 20 percent of the national product. Since there were, furthermore, 500,000 workers in food processing and 700,000 in wood and furniture, consumer manufacture was in an impregnable position. If the 555,000 workmen in construction are counted as well, the prime component of the nonagrarian sector of France's economy occupied 4.5 million workers and created over 40 percent of net output. By comparison there were only about 850,000 wage earners in metallurgy, or 13 percent of the manufacturing-industrial work force, and they generated no more than 15 percent of net output. Even with the inclusion of 300,000 miners and 300,000 railroad and dock workers, this capital goods sector occupied a distinctly subordinate place.

Needless to say, the expanse and depth of consumer manufacture very largely accounted for the absolute primacy of small firms and production units. Indeed, the Third Republic was as much a nation of small workshops and artisans as it was of small farms and peasants, if not actually more so. Although in 1913 the number of *patrons* was one-third less than under the second Napoleonic empire, there were still two "bosses" for every five workers, and the number of individuals paying the license *(patente)* to operate a shop or business actually rose by over 500,000 to a total of 2.3 million.

Because of inconsistencies in the French censuses, these figures are at best approximations. But there is no gainsaying the preponderance of small and medium-sized firms in the manufacturing-industrial sector, and most notably in consumer goods production, including construction, except for a few large companies specializing in public projects. Again textiles, but not clothing, stood apart, in that some 60 spinning and weaving plants employed between 100 and 200 wage earners, though as in the rest of the textile and garment workshops, this work force was heavily female and hence heavily transient and juvenile.

But with this notable exception, consumer manufacture especially was heavily populated by small and medium-sized firms owned and operated by *patrons,* most of whom were also their own merchants. Taking consumer and industrial production together, and not counting self-employed workers with no helpers, there was a total of about 610,000 firms. Of these, 530,000 had between 1 and 5 workers, and 68,000 between 6 and 50. According to another calculation nine out of ten firms had less than 10 wage earners and employed close to 60 percent of the entire manufacturing-industrial work force, while 72 percent of this labor force worked in plants of less than 50 workers.

Of course, France had some bigger plants as well. In all, there were 9,000 firms with over 50 wage earners. Of these, over 5,000 had between 51 and 100 workers, and 3,000 between 101 and 500. There were also 515 establishments of between 501 and 5,000, and 13 giants with a payroll of over 5,000. But the majority of these large enterprises were in the atypical categories of capital goods and mining. At any rate, the sector of consumer production was crammed with firms ranging from petty to middling in size, and many of these firms were at best moderately efficient. Moreover, these firms sustained a numerous *petite bourgeoisie* of modest means and, to a lesser extent, a prosperous entrepreneurial bourgeoisie of parochial rather than cosmopolitan horizons. Obviously, the associated myriad of small retail and service outlets further tilted the balance toward the lower middle class.

In the Austrian half of the Habsburg Empire manufacture and industry claimed about 20 percent of the active population, the vast majority of them in consumer production. Textiles, including garments, and food processing alone accounted for 53 percent of the gross manufacturing-industrial product, metals and metal processing contributing a mere 18 percent. Again, with few exceptions, which in this instance included some breweries and textile mills, small firms remained dominant in the consumer goods sector. In 1912, 75 percent of the 966,600 firms in the combined manufacturing-industrial sector were *Kleinbetriebe*, or small firms. There were also some 5,300 registered artisanal guilds in Cisleithania, with 550,000 masters, 500,000 journeymen, and 174,000 apprentices.

With the turn of the century Vienna became a city of 2 million inhabitants. It was not only a sparkling political, social, and cultural capital but also the principal center of consumer, including luxury, manufacture, with a growing heavy industry in the newer outer districts. The city had some 56,000 firms and 375,000 workers in manufacture and industry combined. At least 116,000 of these workers were crowded into workshops that had only between 1 and 5 wage earners, 50,000 in 6,800 workshops of between 6 and 10, and 34,500 in 2,500 workshops of between 11 and 20. In other words, over 200,000 of the 375,000 workers were employed in the 53,800 out of 56,000 firms that had a work force of 20 or less. In addition, 70,000 workers were employed in medium-sized plants, half of them by 1,300 firms with 21 to 50 wage earners, the other half by the 450 firms with 51 to 100. As for *Grossbetriebe*, or large firms, there were only 410 factories of 100 to 1,000 workers with a labor force of 92,000, over half of them in units of 100 to 300. All eight factories of over 1,000, employing a total of 12,000 workers, were in the metallurgical branch. As in all big cities, small operatives dominated the retail and distributive sector. Only 15 percent or 22,000 of the 142,000 employees in this sector worked in the 153 out of 50,000 establishments that had over 50 employees, and this included the 4,000 workers of Vienna's tramway system. Clearly, the capital of the Dual Monarchy was principally a city of small to medium-sized workshops and retail outlets rather than of large factories, department stores, and offices.

The Hungarian half of the Dual Monarchy had about 1.2

million workers out of an active labor force of 9 million. While about 29.5 percent were independent craftsmen without hired labor and 33.4 percent were employed in workshops of between 1 and 20 workers, about 37 percent worked in plants of over 20. In both halves of the Dual Monarchy the proportions between consumer and capital industries were roughly the same, but within the consumer sector food processing, in particular milling, had almost twice the weight in "dependent" Hungary as in Austria, which exported textiles, apparel, and other light manufactures to Transleithania.

In tsarist Russia manufacture and industry, inclusive of mining, around 1910 employed about 5 percent of the economically active population and contributed some 20 percent of national income. Textiles, including apparel, and food processing accounted for 30 percent and 13 percent, or 43 percent, of this sector's work force, and for 28 percent and 22 percent, or 50 percent, of its output value.

Small-scale firms not only claimed the largest and still growing share of the labor force but also continued to generate a substantial though declining percentage of output value. In 1914 about 2 million artisans toiled in the small workshops, or *artyels,* of "urban" Russia, many of them in the Jewish Pale of Settlement. There were, in addition, between 2 and 8 million precapitalist and preindustrial cottage producers, or *kustars,* scattered throughout the countryside, nearly all of them working in their home dwellings and using hand tools. In terms of production value this dispersed sector of tiny and small manufacture contributed between one-quarter and one-third of the entire consumer and capital goods sector, and artisan manufacture met most of Russia's consumer needs.

Italy's combined manufacturing-industrial sector was not all that different from Russia's, except that it was somewhat larger. In 1911 consumer manufacture accounted for 3.4 million, or slightly over 77 percent, of the 4.4 million "industrial" workers. By comparison, the producer goods sector claimed only around 970,000 wage earners, or slightly over 22 percent. Textiles and clothing combined employed over 1.5 million workers, a large majority of them women. Consumer goods industries, including construction, not only provided by far the largest share of "industrial" employment but also perpetuated labor-intensive artisanlike production in small or at best medium-sized shops. Since labor was a relatively cheap factor of production, there was little incentive for employers to invest in labor-saving machinery and factory production. In any case, well over 90 percent of all firms employed 5 or fewer workers and provided jobs for 30 percent of the total labor force in consumer and producer goods production. To be sure, there were a few large steel-making and engineering plants and factories, but in the aggregate they employed relatively few workers, notwithstanding the rapid growth rate of capital goods production between 1896 and 1908.

No doubt there were also some big entrepreneurs and considerable fortunes in Italy's consumer goods sector. These grandees of manufacture were most heavily based in large textile mills and food-processing plants in or near large cities, notably in the industrial triangle of the north. But in this sector the self-employed owner-operators, the master artisans of small-scale workshops, and the *padroni* of medium-sized plants were infinitely more common. And they were of the *piccolo* rather than the *grande borghesia,* with limited contacts and little influence in the world of large banking and commerce.

As for the capital goods sector, it belonged far more to the future than to the present. Judging by the growth rate of steel, engineering products, and chemicals, along with coal and rail transport, industry was reducing the enormous gap with agriculture and manufacture. But though making giant strides, producer goods continued to lag far behind. Because of their massiveness, visibility, and novelty a relatively few steel mills and metallurgical factories gave the appearance of lording it over the thick undergrowth of farms and estates as well as of small workshops and medium-sized plants. In actual fact, depending on the country, in their overall economic importance the producer goods industries were still in either their adolescence or their infancy. Moreover, the new industrialization was circumscribed geographically: the Midlands and Lancashire; the Ruhr, Saar, Upper Silesia, and Berlin; northeastern France; Vienna and Bohemia; St. Petersburg and the Donets Basin; northern Italy; and major seaports.

All over Europe, industrial development had to be fitted into long-standing social, cultural, and political structures. Right down to 1914 industrial and finance capitalism, let alone managerial capitalism, continued to be of subsidiary importance not only in economic terms, including in the international economy, but also in terms of class, status, and power. Although liberal ideas flourished, industrial capitalism never generated sufficient material and social strength to challenge successfully and enduringly the *ancien régime* in favor of a liberal bourgeois order. It was not merely that the economic and social carriers of bourgeois liberalism remained relatively weak and supine. As noted above, paradoxically the second industrial revolution coincided with the prolonged recession of 1873 to 1896 and the new overseas imperialism. These far from unrelated developments not only incited and enabled the feudal and illiberal elements to reassert themselves, notably in political society, but also prompted significant factions of the new industrial bourgeoisie to draw closer to the old ruling and governing classes instead of contesting their primacy.

Obviously, not everything was mere portent. From 1870 to 1914 Europe's pig-iron output quadrupled. Between 1893 and 1913 England and Germany respectively increased their pig-iron production by 50 percent and 287 percent, their coal production by 75 percent and 159 percent, and their crude steel production by 136 percent and 522 percent (thanks largely to the Bessemer process). Of course, Germany's rate of growth was unmatched, except by the United States. Within less than twenty years the Second Empire quadrupled its iron and steel output, so that by 1914 its production practically equaled that of England, France, Italy, and the Low Countries combined. But even France tripled its coal production and doubled its pig-iron output between 1871 and 1913. Moreover, France scored a tenfold increase in crude steel production between 1880 and 1913, and it did so without direct access to most of Lorraine's iron-ore deposits. Similarly, between 1885 and 1914 Russia's output of iron ore rose tenfold, so that the tsarist empire overtook France to become the fourth largest steel producer in the world. Italy and Austria-Hungary also registered impressive advances in basic industries.

Simultaneously, and more particularly with the turn of the century, the second industrial revolution began to burst forth: electricity and dynamos; petroleum and internal combustion engines (motorcars); chemistry and synthetics (dyes, nitrogen, coal hydrogenation). The new technology of physics and chemistry spurred large-scale corporate, finance, and managerial capitalism, in that it called for firms capable of capital-intensive, energy-consuming, and assembly-line production.

To be sure, it was the capital goods sector that spawned the largest firms through autoexpansion or merger. But until 1914 giantism was essentially limited to steel and coal mining, with coal still providing close to 90 percent of the world's energy. Of course, rail transport was the other colossus, though except in England much of it was owned, subsidized, or operated by the state. The fast-expanding metal manufacturing and engineering sector (including machine construction) retained many small and medium-sized firms. As for the motor vehicle and chemical industries, they occupied a rather marginal place until 1914. While car making was heavily "artisanal" and intended for a narrow luxury market, chemical production, though highly capital- and energy-intensive, remained inconsiderable in both output value and employment.

Clearly, large-scale industrial enterprises were in full expansion. Even so, the outposts of corporate and finance capitalism were like so many enclaves surrounded not only by vast agrarian sectors but by thickets of small workshops and medium-sized enterprises of family capitalism in both consumer and capital goods production. Moreover, many of the largest industrial firms, notably in war-related industries, were heavily dependent on governments that were either dominated or significantly influenced by agrarian or feudalistic elements, or by both. The leading sector of industrial capitalism came nowhere near achieving either economic or social and political primacy or even parity.

The United Kingdom was slow to develop its enclave of heavy industry and corporate capitalism. It paid the penalty of obsolescence for having pioneered in the manufacture and trade of such consumer staples as textiles and hardware, and also was hampered by the relative neglect of science and technology by England's ruling and governing class and its elite higher schools. By 1914 iron and steel, machinery, vehicles, and chemicals combined employed only some 2 million workers, or 12 percent of a total labor force of 18 million, or 33 percent of the 6.2 million workers in both manufacture and industry. This producer goods sector accounted for 23 percent of net output and generated close to 10 percent of national income.

Until 1905 only 13 of Britain's 50 largest concerns were in capital goods production, the other 37 being in soft goods. Nine of the giants were iron, steel, and coal companies that were heavily engaged in government-financed shipbuilding and armaments production (notably Vickers-Maxim and Armstrong). In spite of their large size, these firms remained family-controlled, and few companies of other industrial branches were able to measure themselves with them. There were close to 3,500 engineering firms with a total work force of 600,000. Of the 3 chemical firms among the 50 top companies, only 1 specialized in the new chemistry (Brunner-Mond). As for the chemical industry as a whole, it had only 128,000 workers, but these generated 4.4 percent of net national output.

Actually coal mining and transport had grown more rapidly than the other industries, employment in these two branches having quadrupled since 1840. In 1913 coal accounted for about 1.2 million jobs, 6 percent of national income, 10 percent of total export value, and 80 percent of total shipping tonnage, nearly one-third of the entire coal output being sold abroad. Less concentrated and mechanized than in Germany, there were 1,750 coal companies, and only 8 percent of the yearly production of 270 million tons were mined by machinery. The labor force in transport was around 1.5 million, but of these some 600,000 were in road transport in which single and small operators were dominant, as over 375,000 in railroads and about 300,000 in water transport (seas, canals, docks). Mining and transport together claimed about 15 percent of the active working population and produced about 15.5 percent of national income. If mining and transport are counted as part of capital industry, the share of employment in this sector of advanced capitalism in 1914 reached 27 percent and its share of national income 25.5 percent. These figures overstate the "modernity" of this sector since they do not allow for its small and medium-sized concerns.

It is worth noting that neither the automobile nor the electrical engineering branches figured among Britain's largest firms. There were many manufacturers of components for motorcars that remained a luxury item and that were assembled by firms too small and unsteady to attempt continuous-flow production. In 1900 the largest company (British Daimler) made about 150 vehicles, and some 200 miniature firms sprang up within the next five years. By 1909, 11,000 cars were assembled, and by 1913 three times that number, or about 34,000. Of course, some 10,300 were produced by the five largest firms with an output of between 3,000 and 1,500 motorcars (Wolseley, 3,000; Humber, 2,500; Sunbeam, 1,700; Rover, 1,600; Austin, 1,500), the balance being assembled by small companies. For electrical machinery England was heavily dependent on America and Germany, there being only 62,300 workers making electrical machinery, apparatus, and appliances.

Coal mining, basic metals, including engineering products, and textiles were the backbone of the British economy, and they accounted for 70 percent of all exports. By themselves, these three branches employed 50 percent of the manufacturing-industrial labor force, or 20 to 25 percent of all gainfully employed individuals, and generated 50 percent of total value added or of net output. Paradoxically, even though the textile industry alone had many large firms that mass-produced cotton and woolen fabrics for export, their owners enjoyed relatively little prestige. By contrast the barons of coal and steel were men of exceptional influence and status, in part because the governing class increasingly considered energy and armaments vital for the preservation of the established order, though coal mining and metal production swarmed with small firms and contributed less of their output for export.

Of course, by 1914 Germany had the most extensive sector of large-scale and concentrated industrial and corporate capitalism. Just the same, capital goods industry together with mining and railroads—most of them state owned and operated —were far from achieving predominance. In fact, Germany's enclave of advanced capitalism was less impressive for its size than for the speed with which it expanded.

While the population rose by 33 percent between 1882 and 1902, the combined manufacturing-industrial work force increased by at least 180 percent to reach about 8.5 million, or 35 percent of an active labor force of some 27 million. Of these wage earners, 2.7 million, or 10 percent, were employed in iron and steel, metal processing (including machine making), vehicle construction, and chemicals, and they produced about 24 percent of net output. Counting the 1.2 million workers in the extractive industry and 1.1 million in transport, many of them state employees, the advanced industrial sector claimed a total of 5 million workers, of whom at least 10 percent, or 500,000, were clerks, managers, and administrators. Although the 4.5 million wage-earning workers in capital goods industry, mining, and transport constituted only 17 percent of Germany's total labor force, they did make up 55 percent of all workers in manufacture and industry combined.

These same years also witnessed a stunning increase in large firms. Between 1882 and 1907 the number of companies employing over 50 workers, including those in construction and mining, rose from 9,500 to 27,000 and their labor force from 1.6 million to slightly over 5 million. To be sure, firms of 1 to 5 and of 6 to 50 workers still accounted respectively for 90 percent and 8.7 percent of all production units, and they employed 29.1 percent and 23.2 percent, or 52.3 percent, of all manufacturing and industrial workers. But the large firms that made up only 1.3 percent of all business units employed the remaining 47.7 percent of these workers, and used 74 percent of the horsepower and 77 percent of the electric power consumed by industry. In addition, by 1907 close to 5,000 of the 27,000 large firms had a work force of between 200 and 1,000 and a total of close to 2 million wage earners. There were even 550 huge companies with over 1,000 or a total of almost 1.3 million workers. The number of these giants increased only slightly more rapidly than the number of concerns with a capital of over 10 million marks, of which there were about 230 by 1914. Undoubtedly the firms of over 1,000 workers, with an average work force of 2,400, and even many in the category of over 500 workers were concentrated in mining, iron and steel, and metal processing, especially by virtue of mergers and vertical combines.

In the extractive industry, notably in coal mining and processing, bigness was the rule rather than the exception as regards both work force and capitalization. Even in 1882, 75 percent of all miners worked for concerns of at least 200 operatives. By 1914 the proportion of miners working for firms of over 1,000 operatives had risen from 25 percent to 60 percent. Among these were such supergiants as the GBAG (Gelsenkirchener Bergwerks Aktiengesellschaft), which in 1914 employed 37,000 workers to mine over 10.3 million tons of bituminous coal and to produce 2.2 million tons of coke. Building upon its numerous collieries in the Ruhr, after 1900 the GBAG, under Emil Kirdorf, acquired iron, steel, and metal-processing plants in Luxembourg, Lorraine, Aachen, and Düsseldorf. Its capitalization grew threefold to reach 180 million within ten years. In the Ruhr there were another two huge coal-mining concerns that with time also expanded vertically. Before 1914 Harpener Bergbau owned over 20 collieries, employed 25,000 miners, and produced 6.6 million tons of hard coal and 1.5 million tons of coke, while Hibernia had a work force of about 20,000 mining 5.7 million tons of pit coal and producing 700,000 tons of coke. Bituminous coal alone provided employment for 650,000 mine workers, primarily in the

Ruhr, the Saar basin, and Upper Silesia, and thus used more unskilled workers than any other branch of industry. Although there were only about 445,000 workers in iron and steel making, huge firms were as notable in this branch as in mining because of the scale of capital required.

Germany's biggest corporations in heavy industry combined iron ore and coal mining with steel making and processing as well as machine construction. The best known—not to say the most notorious—were Krupp, Thyssen, and Gutehoffnungshütte in the Ruhr, Röchling and Stumm in the Saar, and Henckel-Donnersmarck in Upper Silesia and in the Rhineland. Having pioneered in cannon making, the Krupp dynasty and its managers pursued a course of vertical expansion as well as diversification. The work force of the Krupp conglomerate rose from 16,000 in 1870 to 68,500 in 1913, and its capitalization increased even more massively, though without ever relaxing family control. This growth was not atypical of the leviathans of heavy industry which occupied the commanding heights of the capital goods sector, not least because they were the purveyors, advocates, and profiteers of military and naval armament.

There is no denying the importance of this composite lead sector and of the preponderance of large firms in it. Even so, it was no match for either agriculture or consumer manufacture. After all, the entire capital goods sector, including mining, accounted for less than 15 percent of national employment. Moreover, metal processing and engineering, including both machine and vehicle construction, were permeated with small and medium-sized firms as well as artisanal labor. To be sure, there were large and even giant concerns in this branch as well. In particular, Rathenaus' Allgemeine Elektricitätsgesellschaft (AEG) and Siemens, heavily and conspicuously centered in Greater Berlin, occupied a towering position in the manufacture of electrical equipment. Leaving aside electrical equipment, which around 1910 was a relatively small though rapidly growing industry, the sprawling engineering and machine-construction industry had a labor force of about 1.5 million workers. In this branch small and middle-sized firms of less than 50 artisanal workers occupied a sizable position, and the majority of big firms of over 50 workers averaged a labor force of less than 100 workers, who had a large component of factory artisans among them.

The automobile and chemical industries were still in an embryonic state. In the last decade of the nineteenth century, including the year 1900, Karl Benz, the only major motorcar maker, produced a total of about 1,750 cars. In 1901 the automotive firms employing some 1,800 workers assembled just short of 900 cars and trucks, 400 of them produced by Benz. By 1909 yearly output rose to over 7,000 vehicles, and it reached 23,000 in 1913, the year in which a total of 70,600 cars were registered in Germany and vehicle construction generated at best 2 percent of net output. Of these 23,000 cars and trucks, 15,300 were produced by companies assembling 1,500 or more units (Benz, 4,500; Opel, 3,200; Brennabor, 2,400; Daimler, 2,200; Adler, 1,500; Stoewer, 1,500).

The chemical industry was certainly the most advanced outpost of the new capitalism not only in Germany but throughout the industrializing world in terms of its growth rate in capitalization, output, and profits. The rapid expansion of the industry owed most to the development of organic dyes, alkalies, and fertilizers, made possible by a corps of professional research chemists. Between 1870 and 1900 some 150 chemical firms with a capital of close to 400 million marks were founded. Among these Höchst, which was organized in 1863, came to be the largest by far, with a capital of 25 million marks and a labor force of 10,000 in 1913. By the turn of the century the industry began to consolidate its ranks, guided by Carl Duisberg of F. Bayer, and investment banks became important but junior partners in many of the big merger-bent firms. To avoid self-destructive competition, the leading chemical companies formed into two separate associations. In turn, the latter made cartel arrangements between themselves for select product lines. The one consisted of Bayer, Badische Anilin-und Soda-Fabrik (BASF), and the Aktiengesellschaft für Anilin-Fabrikation (AGFA); the other comprised Höchst, Leopold Cassella, and Kalle, in which Höchst virtually absorbed his associates. In 1913 the chemical industry had a turnover of 2.4 billion marks, produced 90 percent of the world's synthetic-dye output, and accounted for 10 percent of German exports.

Notwithstanding this hothouse expansion (growth rate in 1870–1913: 6.2 percent) and consolidation, until 1914 Germany's vaunted chemical industry employed under 170,000, or less than 2.5 percent of the combined manufacturing-industrial labor force (including mining), harnessed less than 3.5 percent of the machinery (horsepower) in the manufacturing-industrial sector, accounted for less than 5 percent of paid-in corporate capital in this same sector inclusive of transport, and generated less than 4 percent of net output.

Evidently, then, even in the German economy the capital goods sector occupied a distinctly subordinate place in terms of share of capital, net output, and labor force. Moreover, the score of towering giant firms did not obliterate the vast substratum of small and medium-sized companies with few links to investment banks and with an essentially artisanal work force. Even in Düsseldorf, which was one of the fastest-growing cities on the lower Rhine, big industry was not sovereign. To be sure, in what by 1905 was the fifth and tenth largest city in Prussia and Germany respectively, the proportion of large firms was high, notably in metallurgy and machine making. In 1914 Rheinmetall, the largest employer and producer of military hardware, had 8,000 manual workers. Moreover, around 40 percent of Düsseldorf's industrial workers labored in plants with over 50 operatives, five factories having over 500 workers. Yet not only were many of these workers factory artisans but 60 percent of them continued to work in plants of less than 50 hands. In addition, some 62,000 wage earners out of a total labor force of 132,000, nearly half of them female, worked in the city's consumer goods and tertiary sectors.

France was Europe's third and the world's fourth industrial power. Needless to say, Germany's rapid development of a redoubtable capital goods sector became the standard by which to measure France's allegedly gradual and limited advance into industrial and finance capitalism. But whatever the reasons for its unhurried pace—demographic stagnation, coal deficiency, narrow domestic and foreign markets, over-cautious and family-centered entrepreneurs, investment-shy bankers—it was not all that exceptional by European standards.

Although at its own tempo, the French Republic did enlarge its capital goods sector after 1875, and more particularly from the end of the long-lasting price slump in the mid-nineties down through 1914. This sector doubled its contribution to manufacturing-industrial production from 13 percent in 1870 to 25 percent in 1913. Between 1900 and 1913 the expansion in metal making and processing as well as in chemical production, along with a steady but unspectacular rise in coal output, accounted for a 3.7 percent yearly growth in production and 47 percent yearly growth of value added in manufacture and industry combined. While capital goods production increased, there was a relative decline in France's top-heavy consumer manufacture. Even so, this sector, inclusive of building construction, still claimed 72 percent of the manufacturing-industrial labor force and generated 25 percent of the entire economy's yearly value added. By comparison, only 18.5 percent of the combined manufacturing-industrial work force, or 5.5 percent of the country's economically active population, which amounted to 1.2 million wage earners, toiled in the capital goods sector, including the extractive industry, and contributed barely 10 percent of total value added, or at best 20 percent of value added by both manufacture and industry.

Metal making and metal processing were the driving force of this economic growth. Moreover, although small ateliers and medium-sized plants manufacturing consumer and luxury goods continued to dominate the nonagrarian sector, the growth of heavy industry brought with it large factories and firms. Of course, France had a few sizable textile plants (spinning, weaving, wool combing), but those with over 250 workers were rare. In 1901, alongside nearly 600,000 establishments of between 1 and 50 workers, there were some 8,000 firms with 51 to 500 wage earners and 530 with over 500 workers. By 1914 this latter category of over 500 workers may well have expanded to 700 concerns employing at best

850,000 workers, the vast majority of them in mining and metallurgy (metal extraction, production, and processing).

Actually, because of a poor natural endowment, coal production rose only marginally between 1870 and 1913 and the number of miners remained fixed at 300,000. To compensate and "fuel" its industrialization France increased its imports of coke by 70 percent during these same years (from 14.8 to 25.3 million tons). Moreover, as of 1906 France imported an average of 20 million tons of pit coal every year.

Thanks to these imports France's iron and steel production expanded considerably between 1870 and 1910. Though trailing Britain, Germany, and the United States, it achieved more than a threefold increase in cast iron (from 1.3 million to 4 million tons), nearly a fourfold increase of crude iron and steel (from 670,000 to 2.4 million tons, with steel overtaking iron), and a nearly fivefold increase in iron-ore production (from 2.75 million to 13.4 million tons, part of it for export). By 1913 the production of cast iron was up to 5.2 million tons and crude steel to 4.7 million, the rate of growth being fastest after 1900. With the intensified exploitation of the *minette* of Lorraine, the output of iron ore reached 21.9 million tons. The large firms were clustered in the north, the northeast, and the center. In Meurthe-et-Moselle alone there were four concerns (Société de Longwy, Senelle-Maubeuge, Micheville, Wendel), each with between five and ten blast furnaces and with as many Thomas converters or Siemens-Martin furnaces, and each producing about 300,000 tons of crude steel. There were three large companies (Aciéries de France, Denain, Anzin) specializing in cast iron in the north, while Schneider was the titan of the center at Le Creusot (along with Forges de Châtillon-Commentry and Aciéries de Saint-Étienne).

There were only about 110,000 men employed in metal extraction and production as such, which compared to metal processing also contributed considerably less value added. As in Germany, the truly giant firms were the ones that expanded vertically and by diversification. Accordingly, Henri Schneider started (1840–1898) and his son Eugène expanded (1898–1942) a conglomerate that in 1913 employed 20,000 workers in metallurgy at Le Creusot and at least another 100,000 at other locations and in nonmetallurgical activities. Similarly, operating on both sides of the Franco-German border, the Wendel dynasty employed a total of 30,000 wage earners, 4,000 at Joeuf in French Lorraine. In 1913 the twin Wendel firms mined 3.7 million tons of iron ore, which they used to produce 1.25 million tons of cast iron and 1 million tons of crude steel, of which 400,000 and 350,000 tons respectively were produced by the French company headed by Robert de Wendel.

Metal processing expanded much more rapidly than metal making in employment, output, and value added. By 1913 there were some 800,000 metal workers, the majority of them in petty, small, and medium-sized firms centered around Paris and France's other major cities. There was a particularly swift growth in metal finishing, arms production, machine and tool making, vehicle manufacture, and naval construction, there being a close to threefold increase in production and also in value added between 1900 and 1913. Naval construction occupied a disproportionately large place in that in the latter year it accounted for 1 billion of the total production value of 2.7 billion in metal processing.

Within metallurgy, writ large, the automobile industry had the single fastest growth rate, perhaps partly because France had a superior network of roads. By 1913 France was Europe's first car and truck maker, production having risen from 4,800 to 45,000 units since the turn of the century, 70 percent of it in the Paris region and 11 percent around Lyons. This thriving automobile manufacture was hailed as the French economy's principal emblem of "modernism" despite its being embedded in the artisanal tradition of the time-honored metal-working trades.

In 1913 all of 33,000 workers were employed by car-making shops that were either mere ateliers or larger plants in the nature of a cluster of ateliers under a single roof. Probably 70 percent of this work force was skilled and semiskilled, there being at most 10 to 15 percent unskilled hands. Most of the artisans came from machine- or bicycle-making shops, though some of these shops also began to manufacture bodies and components for cars on their own account. Because of heavy reliance on subcontractors it took little capital to start up a firm. The number of automobile makers increased from 30 in 1900 to 155 in 1913. But only 30 were major companies producing over 150 cars, and of these 12 produced over 1,500 cars, though not one of them had a mechanical assembly line. In fact, the automobile being a luxury product, successive models were manufactured in small numbers, each car hand-crafted and hand-assembled. In this artisanal context each worker built 1.6 cars per year, with the result that labor rather than capital remained the principal cost factor.

This was true even for the largest producers, notably Armand Peugeot (5,000 cars and 80,000 bicycles), Darragu (3,500 cars) and Marius Berliet (3,000 cars). Louis Renault, who was about to move into first place, started with a capital of 60,000 francs in 1898. But even though he was attentive to Fordism in America and raised his output to 4,704 cars within fifteen years, it took 4,000 Renault workers to produce these 4,704 cars. At least 2,800 of these operatives were skilled craftsmen. In sum, automobile manufacture was a dwarf, even in metallurgy. It used less than 100,000 tons of steel, its production methods were artisanal, and, except for trucks, it was compatible with France's bent for luxury and export production. Close to one-third of all cars were sold abroad.

As for the chemical industry, it was of course less innovative than the automobile industry, in part because of the shortcomings of professional chemistry in France. Growing by 5 percent yearly after 1900, it employed 35,000 workers by 1914. There were some 40 major companies, Saint-Gobain, Péchiney, and Kuhlmann heading the list in size. But even they were of only limited importance. Eighty-seven percent of all dyes used in France were imported from Germany, and of France's nine dyestuff plants, five were German.

Above all in Austria-Hungary, Russia, and Italy, large industries, notably in capital goods production, did not really develop until after 1890, if not later. Precisely because they started from close to zero, their absolute as well as relative growth appears enormous. In all three countries the state furthered the development of capital industry with tariffs, subsidies, and contracts, while investment banks and foreign lenders provided much of the needed capital. Bigness became this sector's trademark, less because of advanced capitalism's bent for concentration than on account of the unprecedented scale and cost of fixed plant and equipment. Meanwhile, as elsewhere in Europe, the growth of big firms stimulated rather than destroyed medium-sized enterprise, and even mini-industry managed to hold its own.

Although in 1910 Rudolf Hilferding pointed to the incipient fusion of industrial and banking capital in Austria as the model for organized capitalism on a world scale, the industrialization of Cisleithania had not really progressed very far. Nor had the banks established their mastery in the capital goods sector. Admittedly, the production of pig iron climbed by 8.3 percent yearly between 1891 and 1901 and by 11.4 percent between 1901 and 1911, while coal production and machine making respectively rose by 4 percent and 9 percent yearly during those two decades. But by 1914 barely 24 percent of the economically active population was engaged in the combined consumer and producer goods sector, and this sector generated at best 38 percent of Austria's gross national product. Moreover metals and metallurgy accounted for only 18 percent of the gross manufacturing-industrial product, in contrast to the 25 percent provided by textiles and 28 percent by food processing. Lastly, around 75 percent of all metal-processing, machine-making, and chemical firms were *Kleinbetriebe,* though there were also the giants of heavy industry, notably the Wittgenstein and Skoda combines.

By the turn of the century Karl Wittgenstein—father of the philosopher Ludwig Wittgenstein—was the dominant figure in the Dual Monarchy's steel industry. Starting with a rolling mill in Teplice, he bought up weak and failing mills, foundries, and finishing plants throughout Bohemia and eventually, in 1897, also acquired a majority position in the Oesterreichisch-Alpine Montangesellschaft, which in 1913 produced close to 2 million tons of pig iron. Albert von Rothschild and Max von Gutmann alone resisted absorption, in that they retained control of the Witkowitzer Bergbau, which made marketing arrangements with Wittgenstein. On the whole, though, Wittgenstein self-financed his acquisition and expansion drive, eschewing long-term bank loans in order not to compromise his full autonomy.

First Ernst von Skoda and then his son Emil and grandson Karl were equally jealous of their independence as they built a vast industrial complex making heavy equipment for steel-works, mines, and sugar mills. Above all, they specialized in the production of weapons and munitions, which shortly after the turn of the century accounted for well over half of Skoda's yearly turnover. A victim of his own success, by 1899 Emil von Skoda, having outrun his internal capital, was forced to seek financing from banks, thereby reducing but not surrendering family control.

No doubt Wittgenstein and Skoda, who also promoted the cartelization of key branches of the producer goods sector, measured themselves with Europe's largest captains of indus-try. Even so, they were hardly hegemonic in the economy, nor representative of their sector. More characteristic, perhaps, were the four-score firms that in the mid-nineties produced about 9 million scythes, sickles, and strawknives, 8 million of them for export, above all to Russia.

None of this is to deny the oft-noted trend toward bigness and the amalgamation of business and banking, which presum-ably was stronger in Austria than elsewhere. Quite apart from the largest family enterprises going public, investment banks not only placed funds in capital goods concerns—and large-scale consumer manufacture—but also were fierce advocates of monopolistic practices. Still, the control by banks of indus-trial firms that Hilferding noted was at best an incipient tend-ency. In 1914 there were relatively few joint-stock companies in Cisleithania, and their securities were inconsiderable in the capital market. Industrial shares and railroad bonds—the lat-ter being government-guaranteed—accounted for no more than about 3 percent of all outstanding issues, and 8 out of 10 of the industrial shares were issued by a few large capital goods firms.

In the Hungarian half of the Dual Monarchy, out of a total population of 18 million there were 1.6 million workers, or 20 percent of the active population, in manufacture and industry, including mining and transport. Of these, between 300,000 and 350,000 worked in firms with over 100 wage earners, one-third of them in and around Budapest. These large concerns of over 100 workers were dominant in mining and metal making, in that they claimed 51,000 of the 57,000 workers in these two branches. Of the 100,000 transport workers, two-thirds were employed by the railroads, most of which were state-owned. There were some 600,000 wage earners in consumer and capital goods production exclusive of mining, metal making, and transport, and of these only 144,000, or one-fourth, worked for 426 firms of over 100 workers. Again, it is worth noting that the textile and apparel industries by themselves accounted for close to 300,000 operatives, and building construction for close to 120,000. The work force in both of these branches was distinctly preproletarian.

By 1914 tsarist Russia had an impressive industrial sector in which large-scale and technologically efficient plants occupied a conspicuous place. Between 2.5 and 3 million wage earners were involved in mechanized factory production, alongside 750,000 miners and 1 million railroadmen, state-financed railroad construction serving as the principal spur to the development of the capital goods industries up to the turn of the century. Between 1900 and the outbreak of war the volume and value of mining, metallurgical, and engineering production rose significantly. These three branches were dominated by corporate rather than family firms. Joint-stock companies with substantial capitalization were also of importance in textiles, though less so in food processing. About 310 firms with a capital stock of over 2 million roubles each constituted not quite a quarter of all firms and owned two-thirds of the total corporate capital. Close to half of all industrial enterprises employed over 500 workers, and a relatively high proportion of firms employed over 1,000 workers.

But even though some of the foundations for a modern economy had been laid, Russia's capital goods sector remained a small, state-promoted enclave. The factory work force was only 5 percent of the empire's laboring population. Because key production processes in the largest plants continued to call for manual labor, Russia's factory proletariat had not only an important artisanal component but also a hard core of unskilled workers. Moreover, in 1914 mining, metallurgy, and engineering accounted at best for 20 percent of the output value and 25 percent of the work force of the combined manufacturing and industrial sector.

In addition, this advanced capitalist sector was peculiarly dependent on foreign capital, loans, technology, and expertise. Between 1895 and 1914 Russia imported an average of 200 million roubles annually. The servicing of the empire's accumulated foreign debt called for close to that same annual sum, which meant that the government had to push agricultural exports to meet these payments. Nearly 50 percent of the capitalization of the coal industry in the Donets Basin was foreign, and so was about 80 percent of the capital in iron, metallurgy, and oil. Even with this massive capital inflow, especially from France but also from England and Germany, certainly no more than 10 percent of Russia's population or barely 17 percent of its active labor force in 1914 earned its livelihood from industry and manufacture. This combined sector supplied less than 25 percent of the national income.

St. Petersburg was a striking microcosm and showplace of Russia's industrial parturition. The capital's population increased by 1.1 million between 1890 and 1913. One-third of this increase came in the years after 1907–1908, which also saw a rapid expansion of employment in industry. In fact, once the government restabilized the situation following the upheaval of 1905, St. Petersburg fully shared in Russia's newest industrial advance.

By 1914 the city's manufacturing-industrial work force was close to 220,000, a sizable number laboring in big factories. With the help of foreign capital, large-scale production was growing at a disproportionately rapid rate in branches that were able to combine the utilization of the latest and most expensive machinery, imported from abroad, with the continuing use of labor-intensive production methods, labor remaining the cheapest factor of production. Some 960 manufacturing and industrial concerns within the municipality of St. Petersburg accounted for 7 percent of Russia's total manufacturing-industrial employment and 10 percent of its total manufacturing-industrial output value. There were, in addition, 48 factories outside but within easy reach of the city. Among these were 8 state-owned firms making munitions and other military wares, including the armaments and shipbuilding complex at Kronstadt, and employing some 20,000 workers.

Within the city limits metal processing had the highest growth rate. During the six years before 1914 its output doubled to produce 35 percent of all production value and to employ 40 percent of all factory hands. The metallurgical branch also was at the forefront in bigness: of 284 factories 100 had over 90 wage earners and claimed over 90 percent of the 78,000 metal workers, while the 22 factories with over 750 accounted for 66 percent of these. Russia's only vertically integrated metal-producing and metal-processing giant concentrated its operations in St. Petersburg: the Putilov corporation, which had its own iron mines, employed some 13,000 workers in iron and steel making, steel processing, shipbuilding, and machine construction. It was, of course, as heavily dependent on government contracts, notably for the army and navy, as the Nevski shipyards, which had a labor force of 3,500 workers. Meanwhile, foreign capital (and tariff protection) were of crucial importance in the nascent manufacture of electrical equipment, including motors, which from the start was dominated by big concerns. With Siemens and AEG in the lead, Russia's capital city produced around 70 percent of the empire's total output of electrical equipment, which remained insignificant. Much the same was true of the chemical industry, in which the 2 out of 89 plants with over 750 workers employed 11,800 wage earners, or over 70 percent of the total work force of 16,500 in this incipient branch of capital goods production.

Although the factory proletariat of the large-scale producer goods industries claimed 40 percent of St. Petersburg's wage earners, the consumer sector accounted for the other 60 percent, with 44,000 workers in textiles, 20,500 in food processing, and 23,300 in paper and printing. To be sure, by 1913 no more than 3 percent of the spinning and weaving workers were employed in mills with a work force of less than 90, while close to 84 percent, or 37,000, labored in 23 plants of over 750 workers (compared with 53 percent, or 11,700, in 9 plants in 1890). Similarly, although the degree of bigness was lesser in food processing, 55 percent of that work force was concentrated in 10 plants of over 750 workers, and another 21 percent in 10 plants of between 270 and 750. Even so, these and other workers in the large plants of consumer manufacture, except for the printers, were heavily unskilled, female, and of peasant mentality. They were therefore disconnected from the restless industrial proletariat of St. Petersburg.

In Italy, where both railroad construction and military and naval procurement were important stimulants for heavy industry, the picture was not significantly different, even though the capital industry sector was larger and less dependent on foreign capital. Between 1896 and 1914 there was a tenfold increase in steel production, and overall industrial production rose by close to 90 percent. Some 3.5 million workers out of a total work force of 18 million were in industry and manufacture, and of these 87,500 were in iron and steel making and 475,000 in engineering. With 22 to 24 percent of the total work force, industry and manufacture combined generated about 25 percent of Italy's gross internal product, of which the producer goods sector alone, including the vital and fast-expanding hydroelectric industry, accounted for but a small fraction. Like Russia's, Italy's largest and technologically most advanced concerns were in the capital goods sector, which relied on four large private banks, rather than on foreign investors or government, to furnish investment funding.

By 1914 the Banca Commerciale and the Credito Italiano had become the two banking giants that dominated the supply of industrial capital. Because of their size they were in a position to provide much of the financing for the capital-intensive industries that increased their capital stock so significantly between the turn of the century and 1914: the hydroelectric industry from 37 to 559 million lire, metal processing from 62 to 415 million lire, and chemicals from 98 to 296 million lire. These were also the branches in which the banks fostered a strong bent to concentration under the aegis of the Edison conglomerate in electric power, the Società Ilva in iron and steel, the Cantieri Navali Riuniti in shipbuilding, and the Navigazione Generale Italiana in merchant shipping.

In 1909 in metal processing, including machine construction, there were 278 plants of between 100 and 500 workers, and 38 of over 500 workers, for a total of 95,000 out of 160,000 workers; in chemicals 83 of between 100 and 500, and 8 of over 500, for a total of 24,000 out of 45,000 workers; in electric power 19 of between 100 and 500, and 2 of over 500, for 6,000 out of 13,000 workers. Also, by 1914 Italy produced about 8,000 automobiles, Fiat being by far the largest car manufacturer and assembling more than half of them.

In manufacturing and industry combined, exclusive of family workshops without hired help, the number of concerns of over 100 wage earners was 3,266. They employed 900,000 out of a total of 1.5 million workers, there being 378 firms of over 500 wage earners that accounted for 340,000 workers. It is important to stress, though, that while in metal processing 145,000 out of 160,000 wage earners were employed by concerns with a work force of over 100 operatives, in textiles (exclusive of clothing) 462,000 out of 590,000 wage earners labored in mills with over 100 workers, and of these 455,000 were women, 89,000 of them girls of less than fifteen years of age.

Because in the aggregate consumer manufacture and agriculture remained inefficient and localist, they were unable to liberate domestic purchasing power to stimulate and justify the expansion of a modern sector. The result was that in their mutual dependence capital goods industries and investment banks increasingly relied on the state to provide protective tariffs and government contracts for Italy's expanding and economically unproductive army, navy, and merchant marine.

* * *

Of course, not only in Italy but throughout most of Europe financial institutions contributed significantly to the development of the capital goods sector. Investment banks in particular learned to finance the capital-intensive fixed plant of the second industrial revolution. These joint-stock financial houses extended short- and medium-term loans on current account, made advances against shares, and purchased stocks for their own portfolio. In addition, they underwrote company securities which they placed and promoted on domestic and foreign security markets.

The growth of investment banking went hand in hand with the expansion of the producer goods sector. Either singly or in syndicates the new promotional banks supplied the largest blocks of credit to established and sound firms in iron and steel, metallurgy, coal, rail transport, and shipbuilding. Rather than engage in high-risk ventures, these banks sought ties with firms that, having surmounted the pains and perils of their founding years, were primed for expansion. These would-be giants proposed either to enlarge their own plant or to acquire other companies through purchase and merger.

The new captains of banking and industry converged in branches of the economy in which the state assumed an increasingly important role. To foster the nation's war-making capability governments aided capital goods industries, railroads, and shipyards with tariffs, contracts, and financial warranties. Moreover, these same industries along with the finance banks were in the forefront of those foreign and colonial ventures that after 1870 depended on government collaboration, including diplomatic pressure and military intervention.

Although many industrial credit banks were of local or regional origin, by the turn of the century nearly all of them had their operating headquarters in the capital cities, which became the economic and political command centers of the symbiotic expansion of investment banking and heavy industry. Italy was the only exception, in that Milan continued to overshadow Rome as united Italy's financial—and cultural— capital.

To meet or create the demand for financial services and most notably for longer-term credit, the investment banks had to increase their working capital. In the first instance they did so by augmenting their own capital stock. But of much greater consequence was their systematic development of branch and deposit banking to build up time deposits. In fact, the Continent's joint-stock banks acquired their soaring capacity to finance big industry by mobilizing and aggregating the savings of thousands of small and medium savers and investors for lending operations. While private banks, many of them Jewish, continued to hold their own in mere capitalization, because they did not venture into branch and deposit banking their general financial power began to fall behind that of the new faceless and corporate financial institutions.

Without a doubt, by the turn of the century the great banks became the principal source of external financing for capital goods firms, and most notably so in Germany, Austria, Russia, and Italy. Even so, they were far from dominating banking, heavy industry, or the economy at large. Quite apart from their being limited in number, their reach remained circumscribed. Above all, although the interpenetration of industrial and banking capital proceeded apace, businessmen made sure that their financiers should be "on tap," not on top. The captains of heavy industry were no less committed to maintaining their independence than the consumer manufacturers and merchants of family capitalism. Believing in self-financing, they turned to outside capital only as a last resort. Moreover, they preferred short-term and intermediate loans to long-term financing, which raised the specter of external control. To hedge against the concentrated influence of any one lender, even the largest German industrialists preferred to meet their credit needs by dealing with two or more banks. Although they sought and even welcomed the expert counsel of their financiers, businessmen meant them to have little or no say in policy and decision making. French entrepreneurs may well have been particularly jealous of their autonomy. But on this score of limiting the voice of outsiders there were differences in degree rather than in kind between Schneider of Creusot, Krupp of Essen, Skoda of Pilsen, and Putilov of St. Petersburg. Admittedly, bankers sat on the corporate boards of client firms. In Germany around 1905 Bernhard Dernburg of the Darmstädter Bank and Carl Klönne of the Deutsche Bank served on 38 and 25 boards respectively. But how powerful were most boards, what was the influence of outside members, and how many bankers served on executive committees? Besides, without technical and managerial executives of their own, the banks were in no position to involve themselves in the daily operation of capital goods industries.

But above all, just as the capital goods sector was not yet able to measure itself with agriculture, consumer manufacture, and commerce, so joint-stock investment banking was far from dominating the banking world. In particular mortgage, savings, and commercial banks continued to gather, manage, and invest an enormous proportion of capital resources. Some of these banks were publicly owned, others privately or associationally, and still others corporately. The public and private mortgage banks granted long-term credit on land, especially in the agricultural sector but also in urban real estate. Not surprisingly, throughout Europe fixed-income mortgage bonds constituted a high percentage of the number and value of all outstanding securities, and they absorbed a larger percentage of capital than any other type of paper. Along with savings banks and mutual credit societies, the mortgage credit institutions mobilized local and regional savings to finance local economic activity. Legally they were all but barred from extending credit to commerce and manufacture. Accordingly they put the bulk of their resources into mortgage loans, municipal bonds, and state and state-guaranteed securities, including railroads, though they also made small-scale and short-term personal and business loans.

But it was left to the commercial banks to service most of the nonagrarian sector exclusive of capital goods industry. They were the principal source of credit for small and middle-sized consumer manufacture, domestic commerce, and foreign trade. Especially in countries where the national state bank carried out only limited discount operations, commercial banks provided operating (rather than fixed) capital by lending against commercial bills and promissory notes, back-stopped by personal signature.

Obviously, the large private banks combined the commercial and the investment function. Less local and regional than the average commercial bank, they catered to clients with proven reputations and credit ratings, who heretofore had included royal courts and governments. They not only made loans but also bought shares and went into business ventures of their own, many of them of an international character. Either by themselves or together with other banks, including joint-stock investment institutions, these private financiers underwrote new stock issues.

Because of their enormous personal wealth and prestige, Europe's private bankers were more influential than the bankers of mortgage, savings, and joint-stock investment institutions. Until 1914 they were the "aristocrats" of the financial world. At the center of the *haute finance* of capital cities and major commercial centers, private bankers were well connected in high society and government circles in which, notwithstanding their visceral conservatism, they tended to favor free trade over protectionism. By comparison mortgage, savings, and commercial bankers were less wealthy, esteemed, and visible, also because their fields of operation were rural and local rather than national or international. Besides, since many of the mortgage and savings institutions were publicly or cooperatively owned, their executives were middle-level bureaucrats of modest status. As for the directors of the large joint-stock investment banks, they were not nearly as rich, opulent, and socially prominent as the patrician owner-directors of private banks. Whatever sway they had they owed to their association with big industrialists of the capital goods and transport sectors, many of whom relied on government contracts and preferments, notably protective tariffs.

*   *   *

The capital goods sectors and investment banks continued to be surrounded not only by agriculture and consumer manufacture but also by a tertiary sector of commerce, public service, the professions, and household help. Instead of withering away, retail and service outlets continued to multiply roughly in proportion to the urban population growth. Moreover, down to 1914 small shops held their own in relation to department stores. At the same time, the ever expanding government bureaucracies and the large-scale manufacturing and industrial firms swelled the fourth estate of clerks, technicians, managers, and professionals who were only indirectly or partially "productive."

Clearly, while the independent *petite bourgeoisie* of shopkeepers and service operatives proved its resilience and adaptability, the dependent intermediate class of white-collar workers and lower professionals—including entertainers, writers, and artists—claimed ever greater economic, social, and political space. As for domestics, their numbers were declining slowly and relatively rather than in absolute terms, so that in 1914 they were still a large component of the work force. Incidentally, household service, both live-in and day-laboring, was being rapidly feminized. By virtue of their work situation, domestic servants, in spite of being overworked, were closer to the world-view of the aspiring *petite bourgeoisie* than to that of the overexploited urban or rural underclass. In any case, even without counting the white-collar workers and lower professionals of manufacture and industry, the sprawling tertiary sectors claimed large work forces throughout Europe, ranging from 35 percent of the active population in Great Britain down to 11 percent in Austria-Hungary.

Most of the "unproductive" labor in the tertiary and manufacturing-industrial sectors was centered in Europe's capitals and largest cities. To be sure, department stores with their vast show windows, floor surfaces, and sales personnel became salient urban landmarks of conspicuous consumption for the monied upper classes. But like large-scale factories, these retail emporiums inspired a mixture of awe and curiosity, primarily by virtue of their uncommonness. Especially small shopkeepers—not unlike historians after them—overestimated the weight of department and chain stores in retail sectors where petty commerce and service continued to predominate and even expand. In addition to being the natural habitat of the independent lower middle class of small tradesmen and service operatives, the city was the primary workplace and residence of the fast-expanding dependent lower middle class of white-collar workers of both the public and the private sector, as well as of the subordinate professionals. Because of its burgeoning numbers and geographic concentration, as well as its relatively high educational, social, and material status, this composite *petite bourgeoisie* was a match for the working class, the more so because many artisans, craftsmen, and other labor aristocrats saw themselves as belonging to the lower middle class rather than the proletariat.

In other words, in numbers the lower and professional *petite bourgeoisie* challenged the working class for first place in the capitals and large cities (over 100,000) as well as in medium-sized towns (50,000 to 100,000). Needless to say, the growth of cities predated the second industrial revolution: at midcentury London and Paris had populations of over 2 million and 1 million respectively, and Berlin and Vienna had approximately 400,000 inhabitants. By the 1870s both the Habsburg and the Hohenzollern capitals crossed the 1 million mark; St. Petersburg and Moscow, as well as Glasgow, Liverpool, and Manchester, were either within reach of or over 500,000; and Europe as a whole had around 40 cities of over 100,000. Of these large cities 9 were in Great Britain and 8 in Germany, accounting for 11.5 percent and 4.8 percent of their respective populations.

Between 1870 and 1914 the population of London rose from 3.3 to 4.6 million. Since the British capital underwent a certain deindustrialization during that half-century, its continuing growth reflected, above all, the vitality of London's finishing industries and commercial sector, both of which were heavily oriented toward overseas trade and the local luxury market. By 1914 the population of Liverpool was over 700,000, while Manchester and Birmingham advanced to 600,000. In the United Kingdom some 20 percent of the population now lived in cities of over 100,000.

From the foundation of the Second Empire down to 1910 Germany's population rose from 41 to 65 million, or by 58 percent. During those forty years, while the rural population in settlements of less than 2,000 decreased by about 1 percent to 26 million, the urban population in settlements of over 2,000 increased from 15 to 39 million. Moreover, the number of cities of over 100,000 went up from 8 to 48, and their aggregate residents from 2 to 14 million, to account for about 21 percent of Germany's total population. Of these 48 large cities, 16 had over 250,000 inhabitants and 7 in excess of 500,000. Between 1880 and 1914 this latter category registered the most dramatic gains: Leipzig expanded from 150,000 to 590,000; Cologne, from 145,000 to 516,000; Dresden, from 220,000 to 550,000; Breslau, from 273,000 to 512,000; Munich, from 230,000 to 533,000; and Hamburg— the Second Empire's principal port—from 290,000 to 932,000. As for Berlin, it nearly doubled its population to 2 million. Actually, it came close to quadrupling its population, since Greater Berlin, with its industrial periphery, counted 3.75 million people. Unlike London and Paris, the German capital continued to be an important industrial and manufacturing center. Borsig, Siemens, AEG, and Schering located large-scale plants in the outer city, while small-scale clothing makers compensated for the decline of the capital's textile industry, providing employment for women of working-class families. But since Berlin was also the imperial capital, it had a thriving tertiary sector which occupied around 40 percent of its work force.

In part because of demographic stagnation, urban growth was much less significant in France than in either England or Germany. By 1914, 23 million, or close to 55 percent of the Third Republic's population, still lived in rural settlements of less than 2,000, and 6 out of 10 Frenchmen were resident in rural communes of less than 4,000. But now there were also 44 cities of over 50,000, which claimed 7.5 million inhabitants, as compared with 2.5 million in 1870. Among the 15 cities of over 100,000 people, Paris, Lyons, and Marseilles remained way out front.

In 1910 Austria's 7 cities of over 100,000 claimed 3.1 out of a total population of 28.6 million, of whom 18 million were in rural settlements of less than 5,000. With slightly over 2 million people, Vienna was in a class by itself, its population having more than tripled since 1870. Like Berlin and St. Petersburg, the Habsburg capital developed an important concentration of large-scale production in its outlying districts, which became an additional stimulant for the inner city's consumer manufactures and tertiary sector. The other cities of over 100,000 were Prague (225,000), Lemberg (206,000), Trieste (161,000), Cracow (152,000), Graz (152,000), and Brünn (126,000). Budapest had the same growth rate as Vienna, its population increasing from 280,000 in 1870 to 800,000 in 1914. But except for this growth of the capital, there was relatively little urban expansion in Transleithania.

Between 1870 and 1914 the population of St. Petersburg rose from 750,000 to 2.2 million, and that of Moscow from 400,000 to 1.65 million. Even so, though Russia's two leading cities were important industrial centers, the working class was far from dominating the labor force: while there were 220,000 wage earners in the capital, a good percentage of them in large plants, there were 240,000 of them in Moscow, 160,000 of them artisans in small consumer goods firms. Both cities had large tertiary sectors, St. Petersburg being the seat of the highly centralized tsarist bureaucracy, and Moscow the empire's principal commercial hub.

The place and growth of each nation's tertiary sector were embedded in its urban matrix. In Great Britain, the country of shopkeepers and merchants, the number of stores increased by 50 percent and employment in distributive trades doubled, between 1871 and 1911, to a work force of 2.5 million. Incidentally, there were only two large department stores, both of them in London: William Whiteley and Harrod's, respectively with 5,500 and 4,000 employees. Between them the public service and the liberal professions now claimed 1.5 million individuals. Around 1914 Britain's white-collar work force, which was close to 19 percent of the economically active population, was composed of 989,000 salespersons (many of them female), 822,000 clerks, 631,000 managers and administrators, 560,000 lower professionals and technicians, 237,000 foremen and inspectors, and 184,000 high professionals. England also led Europe in the employment of household help, there being about 2 million domestics, which included 40 percent of all working women outside agriculture. Indeed, Europe's most industrialized nation had as many domestic servants as workers in producer goods industries, each category claiming 10 percent of the total labor force!

Similarly, in Germany commerce and trade were the fastest-growing branches of the economy. Between 1895 and 1907 the number of retail establishments increased by 42 percent and the number of employees within them by 55 percent. Although one-man retail outlets declined in favor of retail shops with between 2 and 5 employees, in 1914 there were some 318,000 of the former as over 475,000 of the latter. In terms of per capita employment, retail stores, hotels, restaurants, insurance agencies, and banks expanded more rapidly than the population. Taking commerce and trade together, there were 1.1 million small firms of up to 5 actives with a total work force of 2 million. This represented about 93 percent of all the firms and 59 percent of all the employees in this sector. There were also some 49,000 firms with a staff of between 6 and 10 helpers, and 28,000 with between 11 and 50, or a total of 77,000 medium-sized establishments with 906,000 employees. Although Germany had some large commercial firms of over 51 employees whose work force totaled 466,000, there were only 380 with between 201 and 1,000 employees and 36 with over 1,000, so that no more than 7 percent of all actives in this sector, or about 250,000, were on the payroll of large establishments of over 200.

Among these large-scale establishments the department

stores had the greatest visibility, there being some 400 of them in 1911. With few exceptions, department and chain stores with a sales force of over 10 and a yearly turnover of over 400,000 marks were located in the largest cities. Of the 73 department stores paying the special turnover tax in Prussia in 1903, 27 were located in Greater Berlin. In the capital, retail firms with over 100 employees claimed a heterogeneous work force of around 14,000 salespersons, supervisors, buyers, clerks, packers, artisans, coachmen, chauffeurs, and charwomen. The single largest house was A. Wertheim on the Leipzigerstrasse, whose book value (inclusive of real estate) was estimated at 33 million marks. By 1900 it had a storefront of 313 meters, a sales surface of 16,560 square meters, a turnover of about 60 million marks, and 4,670 employees, the majority of them women, except for supervisors and buyers. Next in importance was the house of Hermann Tietz, which also had the biggest of its three Berlin stores on the Leipzigerstrasse and claimed close to 2,000 employees in 1910. But while Wertheim was essentially limited to one city and one major parent store, Hermann Tietz was part of the Tietz family chain, with sales of about 30 million marks in seventeen stores in fourteen cities, the largest branches after Berlin being in Cologne, Krefeld, and Düsseldorf.

The symbolic significance of these and lesser retailing giants, most of which were Jewish, cannot be denied, the more so since populist conservatives made them a key target of their denunciation of capitalist modernization, which was saturated with anti-Semitism. Even so, it should be noted again that retailing continued to be thoroughly dominated by petty and small family shopkeeping. To be sure, between 1882 and 1907 there was a fourfold increase in the number of stores with 50 or more employees, for a total of 1,000 such establishments. But according to the best estimates, with their total yearly turnover of at best 550 million marks Germany's 400-odd department and chain stores accounted for no more than 2.2 percent of total national retail sales of about 25 billion marks.

At this time Germany counted some 506,000 *Angestellte,* or salaried employees, in commerce and trade. Moreover, there were 686,000 white-collar workers in industry, now that there was 1 salaried employee for every 16 wage workers in coal, iron, and steel, 1 for every 6 in machine making, 1 for every 5 in chemicals, and 1 for every 11 in textiles and food processing. The public service and the professions combined claimed 1.1 million persons, while domestic service claimed 1.3 million.

The pattern was somewhat different in France. The number of small shopkeepers remained relatively unchanged between 1870 and 1914, in that the number of *petits commerçants*—grocers, bakers, butchers, haberdashers, clothiers, publicans, restaurateurs—only rose from 700,000 to 800,000. The vast majority of these establishments were family owned and operated by husband and wife, in some branches assisted by 1 to 5 helpers. Especially shops with over 5 employees became more numerous, though department stores remained of limited importance and confined to Paris.

Actually, the French capital had pioneered in large-scale merchandising of consumer goods exclusive of food: the Magasin Ville de Paris had been founded in the 1840s, the Bon Marché and the Louvre in the 1850s, the Printemps, the Belle Jardinière, and the Galeries LaFayette in the 1860s, and the Samaritaine in the 1870s. By 1910 the twelve major department stores had estimated sales of over 500 million francs, or about 16 percent of the capital's total retail turnover. The two largest stores were the Bon Marché with a capital of 40 to 50 million francs, 6,000 employees (4,000 salespersons), and 200 million turnover (1902), and the Louvre with a capital of 22 million, 4,000 employees (2,500 salespersons), and sales of 145 million (1900). In contrast to Germany, in France the greater part of the department-store personnel, including the sales force, was male.

All told, in France commerce, trade, banking, and transport claimed a work force of 2.3 million proprietors and employees. There were, in addition, some 550,000 white-collar *fonctionnaires* in government service. Among the 250,000 in the liberal professions there were 20,000 physicians, 56,000 lawyers, and 46,000 writers and artists. And it was a sign of the feminization of domestic service in France that in 1914 at least 40 percent of all working women in Paris were household workers.

The tertiary sectors easily overshadowed manufacturing and industry in both halves of the Dual Monarchy as well as in tsarist Russia. Both empires had large bureaucracies, not counting their military establishments. Around 1914, 13.6 percent of Vienna's work force were salaried employees, and the Austrian capital had some 63,000 retail and service outlets. In Russia commerce and transportation claimed 2.2 million or 7.1 percent of the active population; public service, 1.2 million or 3.8 percent; and domestic help, 1.6 million or 5.2 percent. In 1910 retail activities in St. Petersburg occupied 150,000 persons. Of course, compared with the other European capitals, Russia's still swarmed with between 14,000 and 18,000 street vendors, some of them operating out of makeshift stalls and most of them peasants. There were, in addition, some 20,000 regular retail shops, two-thirds of them selling food products. Even the "department stores" on the Nevski Prospekt were merchandise marts that clustered small shops under one roof. Accordingly the capital's four-storied *passazh* (arcade) housed approximately 60 retail shops specializing in high-quality apparel, jewelry, and other luxury items primarily for women. The city's eighteen open-air markets similarly accommodated over 3,000 shops and booths, two-thirds of them in the four largest marketplaces.

Clearly, the growth of petty, small, and medium-sized shopkeeping accompanied the urban, industrial, commercial, and governmental development that enlarged the ranks of clerks, technicians, cadres, and professionals in the work force. Admittedly, in terms of employment and value added, this composite tertiary sector, even counting domestics, could not measure itself with agriculture, manufacture, and industry. But even if only in the growth of its labor force, this sector may be said to have kept pace with the expansion of the proletarian labor force in capital goods, mining, and transport. Even Germany counted as many shopkeepers, office workers, civil servants, and professionals in the soft branches of its economy as it counted wage earners in its fast-growing heavy and mechanized industries.

In conclusion, in the early twentieth century Europe, except for England, was still predominantly rural and agrarian rather than urban and industrial. Moreover, all over the Continent as well as in England consumer manufacture and shopkeeping significantly outclassed capital goods production, mining, and rail transport in every major respect. Even Europe's predatory economic relations with the colonial and semicolonial world were anchored in manufactural and mercantile rather than industrial and finance capitalism. As we have seen, agriculture, consumer goods manufacture, traditional commerce, and local banking were not mere remnants in Europe's political economies. In fact, these supposedly declining modes of capitalist production, distribution, and credit continued to be dominant and to define class relations and status structures.

That most economic sectors recurrently needed and received state support to lessen the damage of cyclical downswings and foreign competition is not to say that without such assistance they would have been ruined overnight. In particular agriculture, the understructure of these essentially preindustrial but not precapitalist economies, periodically managed to secure government aid, not least because the landed nobilities—in France, commercialized agriculture—continued to command vast political power. But postfeudal nobilities and landed elites generally survived into the twentieth century not simply or primarily because of their privileged political, social, and cultural positions but also because of their still massive, if slowly decreasing, economic weight. Even in England and Germany the wealthiest men and families still came from the landed estate, bolstered by the rising value of urban properties and mineral-rich domains. The great landowners were not only numerically important but their fortunes far exceeded those of businessmen, though the latter's wealth was now growing more rapidly.

Moreover traditional manufacture, banking, and commerce remained economically vigorous, both individually and collectively. Banking and trading dynasties still claimed the largest fortunes in the nonagrarian sectors, ahead of the magnates of manufacture and industry, while small shopkeeping provided large segments of the independent *petite bourgeoisie* with an adequate income. Accordingly, the interest and class formations dating from before the second industrial revolution were not just relics of archaic production relations that incongruously lingered on within the capitalist societies of nineteenth-century Europe. Of course, each national economy was a mixture of different forms and relations of capitalist production and finance. But in Europe's mixed economies large-scale capital goods production and corporate finance remained a subordinate element in civil society. They were more a portent of the future than an accomplished reality of the early twentieth century. Much the same was true of mechanized assembly production and mass consumption. The motorcar was still being handcrafted for the very rich, many of whom had personal chauffeurs, while department stores catered to a clientele that was only slightly less prosperous.

Chapter 2

THE RULING CLASSES

The Bourgeoisie Defers

THE RISING BUSINESS and professional classes were in no position to challenge the landed and public service elites for parity or first place in Europe's ruling classes, let alone in its governing classes. Quite apart from their numerical and economic disadvantage, the rising bourgeoisies were weakened by internal cleavages between heavy industry and large-scale consumer manufacture and their respective banking associates. They were also estranged from petty manufacture and commerce, which left them without much of a popular base. But most important, the new-fledged industrial and financial bourgeoisies as well as the subaltern free professions lacked a coherent and firm social and cultural footing of their own. Unsure of themselves, they remained obsequious in their relations with the venerable notables of land and office.

The nobilities were not only larger than the rising bourgeoisies but also more cohesive and self-confident. Of course, there is no denying the defeudalization of Europe's nobilities, in that they were being divested of their legal and prescriptive military, administrative, and judicial prerogatives and responsibilities. But this is not to say that during the course of the nineteenth century they were reduced to archaic and impotent leisure classes trapped in virtually bourgeois societies. In fact, it was the rising national bourgeoisies that were obliged to adapt themselves to the nobilities, just as advancing industrial and financial capitalism was forced to insert itself into preindustrial civil and political societies. The nobilities comprised not only the largest landed proprietors, including many driving agrarian capitalists, but also the high and highest civil and military servants of the state. Whereas the former were rooted in slowly shrinking agrarian sectors, the latter, except in France, were thoroughly anchored in fast-expanding government structures.

These landed and public service nobilities were not identical with the aristocracies, though they were closely interwoven with them. The aristocracies were altogether more exclusive and restricted. Composed of only a few large families bound by kinship and wealth, they claimed superior birth, breeding, and status. In addition to commanding precedence at grand public rituals and social functions, also on the pan-European stage, the blue-bloods considered the top posts in the public service theirs by entitlement. Although aristocrats earned their living in these nonhereditary positions, they did not man them for the sake of money. Indeed, they relied on their lands to provide the (unearned) income and wealth that underwrote their presumptive, not to say presumptuous, ethos, comportment, and world-view.

The royal families outranked both the nobilities and the aristocracies. But in postfeudal times the nobilities were peculiarly dependent on crowned heads, who could make nobles but not aristocrats. Kings, emperors, and tsars were the fountainheads of new titles and honors that, along with provident marriages, revitalized the nobilities by infusing them with fresh wealth and talent. By absorbing outstanding members of the fledgling counterelites of the third estate—notably of the *grande bourgeoisie,* bureaucracy, and professions—the nobilities preserved not only themselves but also the aristocracies. The titled society owed its longevity as much to its remarkable absorbency as to its inherited landholdings and ascriptive positions and privileges. Nothing ever really interfered with this reproductive process which assimilated notables of movable wealth and public office into the nobility.

Like the rising bourgeoisie, the nobility was far from homogeneous. It was marked by fine but telling gradations of status and influence due to differences in birth, wealth, residence, office, and talent. The nobility cemented its unity, however, with ancient but living collective representations and traditions, shared social and cultural presumptions, and common political predilections. In addition, while the business magnates remained essentially solitary, the landed notables were able to use their prestige and mastery to tie much of the poor gentry and deferential peasantry to themselves.

Evidently, the old nobility of the land and the new magnates of capital never really embarked on a collision course. At most they jostled each other as they maneuvered for position in ruling classes in which the bourgeoisie remained liegelike suitors and claimants. Inveterate nobles firmly occupied and controlled access to the high social, cultural, and political terrain to which the bourgeoisie aspired. With characteristic flexibility and adaptability, and capitalizing on the bourgeois element's craving for social status and advancement, the grand notables admitted individual postulants from business and the professions into their midst. Rather than yield institutional ground, they opted for this selective co-optation, confident of their ability to contain and defuse its attendant ideological and cultural contamination. This strategy or gamble paid off, for the fusion of the two strata remained manifestly asymmetrical: the aristocratization or nobilization of the obeisant bourgeoisie was far more pervasive than the bourgeoisification of the imperious nobility.

Except in France, anointed dynasts and royal courts were the apex and fulcrum of Europe's stratified nobilities. Kings, emperors, and tsars alone could legally confer new and higher titles, and throughout Europe landed estates provided the required nimbus. In descending order the noble estate comprised, on the Continent this side of Russia, dukes, princes, marquises, counts, viscounts, barons, and knights; across the Channel in England, dukes, marquesses, earls, viscounts, and barons. Although the various ranks no longer reflected distinctions in wealth and status as accurately as in the past, they nevertheless remained an approximate index of grandeur and influence. The high aristocracy combined blue blood with enormous wealth in land, including urban real estate, and with considerable political influence or power. These peerless peers, many of them courtiers, had privileged relations with the royal families, who shared their concern for not diluting the status of their rarefied caste with needless ennoblements. Moreover, the extended royal and aristocratic families shared a pan-European predilection for the French language, the English hunt, and the Prussian monocle, which they displayed at the Continent's fashionable resorts. Yet while Europe may be said to have had a single aristocracy, it had as many nobilities as there were nations.

The intermediate nobilities were of more modest and recent descent, landed wealth, and overall position. They also served as receptacles for the newest recruits from big business, the grand professions, and the high public service. There were, in addition, those distended layers of mere nobility. They kept being replenished by automatic or quasi-automatic ennoblement for civil and military service, by the purchase of ennobling patents, and by the aristocratization of family names. Superambitious Englishmen fancied the use of *sir* or *lord* before their names, Frenchmen the particle *de,* and Germans and Austrians the prefix *von.* The Italians, for their part, had a penchant for tripling or quadrupling their surnames by adding the names of their mothers and grandmothers, thereby making them longer and more noble-sounding. Precisely because Russian nobles, high and low, had surnames without title and prefix, they were uniquely punctilious about the uniform and the form of address that were prescribed for each of the numerous grades reaching back to Peter the Great.

Even with all the genuine and counterfeit newcomers to its ranks, the venerable elite continued to be small in both relative and absolute numbers. Ennoblement was used sparingly and inconstantly. In order to feed the aristocratizing ambition honors were kept rare and valuable, and the criteria for awarding them remained shrouded in mystery tempered by presumed merit. The entire system was at one and the same time open and closed, the barriers being adjustable to enable desirable postulants to clear them. The press for admission fostered the elemental solidarity of the multitiered nobility at the same time that it pitted rigid exclusionists against flexible absorptionists. Whereas hidebound purists spurned bourgeois upstarts for polluting the aristocracy's blood, social code, and life-style, pliant integrationists had no such fears. Confident of their superior wealth and gravitational pull, they deemed the individual and subordinate assimilation of fresh blood, wealth, and talent, as well as the appropriation of new ideas, to be a measure of the nobility's continuing vitality. But even this intramural dissension was functional in that the disdain of the purists quickened the parvenus' rage for social acceptance at the same time that it gave the integrationists a deceptively open image.

Although ennoblement, above all elevation into a hereditary rank, was the most coveted recognition, commoners were also encouraged to value such lesser badges of distinction as decorations, titles, and honorific orders of different grades. Some of these were in the nature of prerequisites and tryouts for ennoblement. In Russia the higher degrees of the orders of Saint Anna and Saint Stanislav actually conferred personal nobility. In addition, the crowned heads invited aspiring wealthy and famed commoners to court while eminent families received them in their city mansions and country houses. Simultaneously, their sons were admitted to exclusive schools as well as to honorable bureaucratic and military careers. And then, of course, members of the old society accepted or pursued the progeny of suitable commoners as marriage partners, substantial dowries or fortunes being *de rigueur.*

By encouraging and implementing so many contacts and

associations the nobility diluted its own stock and invited permeation from below. To be sure, the bourgeois aspirants steadfastly courted and invested in this assimilation, as they sedulously emulated and cultivated those they considered their superiors. But in the process they also left their imprint on the amaranthine world that indulged their ambitions. While the nobility encouraged aspirants to social promotion to imitate its ways, it did not remain immune to new influences itself. Imitation was reciprocal between noble and bourgeois, though the balance remained weighted in favor of the stately elite. The result was not so much a profound debasement of the old society as a surface change that left its vitals intact. Even the ingrown aristocracy never became particularly degenerate, dissolute, or worn.

While the traditional and heavily landed elite was inordinately absorbent and resilient, the bourgeoisie was singularly impressionable and flaccid. The magnates of capital and the professions never coalesced sufficiently to seriously contest the social, cultural, and ideological pre-eminence of the old ruling class, only in part because the nobility kept co-opting some of the wealthiest and most talented among them. Above all, because of his sycophancy the bourgeois, bent on social climbing and yearning for ennoblement, eagerly denied himself. His supreme ambition was not to besiege or overturn the seignorial establishment but to break into it. For the socially and psychologically insecure business, financial, and professional grandees the upper bourgeoisie "was but an antechamber to the nobility," and their "highest aspiration was first to gain admission to the nobility and then to rise within it." At the same time that these magnates sought acceptance by high society, or in exchange for it, they reconciled themselves to their continuing political subordination, not to say vassalage. Except in England, the bourgeoisie cannot be said ever to have abandoned or departed from economic and above all political liberalism, never having embraced it to begin with.

There is no disputing the sempiternal *rise* of the bourgeoisie. Instead, what remains problematical is the congenital inability of the grandees of business and the professions to fuse into a cohesive estate or class of more than local dimension. As Schumpeter noted, although "the bourgeoisie produced individuals who made a success at political leadership upon entering a political class of nonbourgeois origin, it did not produce a successful political stratum of its own." Through the centuries rich and wealth-accumulating commoners of the cities and of the nonagrarian economic sectors were bent upon rising out of their "bourgeois" stations into the nobility that was their archetypal model.

In *The Waning of the Middle Ages* Johan Huizinga cautioned against overemphasizing the genesis and growth of absolutism, merchant capitalism, and the city patriciate during the transition to the Renaissance while dismissing feudalism and chivalry as "remnants of a superannuated order already crumbling into insignificance." Admittedly, he himself overstated the growth of "new forms of political and economic life and new modes of expression." But Huizinga also insisted that the upper classes never ceased to look to the chivalric nobility "as the foremost social force and . . . the crown of the whole social system." He stressed that no matter how exaggerated, this elite perception should be treated as an "important [historical] fact," the more so because it remained deeply embedded in the "illusions, fancies, and errors of the time."

Huizinga's caution should be remembered when contemplating the development of the new forms and modes of life during the transition from the *ancien régime* to the modern world. For one thing, liberal democracy, industrial and finance capitalism, the *grande bourgeoisie,* and cultural modernism were not nearly so far advanced as many historians would have it. For another, in the opinions of the elites of the time the postfeudal nobilities of land and public service remained "essential factors in state and society." In particular, just as the affluent burghers of the late Middle Ages and early Renaissance continued to be "dazzled and seduced" by the splendrous life of the chivalric nobility, so the *grands bourgeois* of the second half of the nineteenth and the early twentieth centuries imitated and adopted rather than scorned the forms, habits, and tones of the noble life that still dominated their societies.

Indeed, ever since the Middle Ages the notables of the would-be bourgeoisie had been driven by a propensity, not to say a compulsion, to emulate the nobility in preparation for their own elevation into it. Gabriel Tarde considered this "propensity to ape one's superior" to be a "fact" of all stratified societies and to have a logic and dynamic of its own. Though socially envious and feeling slighted, not to say affronted, lowborn individuals imitate those they idealize as their betters by internalizing their values and attitudes, which they then seek to act upon and externalize. To follow Tarde, having assimilated the reigning cultural ideas and societal objectives, both immediate and long-term, upstart financiers, entrepreneurs, and professionals imitated the tone-setting nobility's accent, carriage, demeanor, etiquette, dress, and life-style. While some were vague, confused, and spontaneous in their emulation, others were precise, rigorous, and studied. But whether flexible or slavish the bourgeois remained self-doubting and self-abasing. Perhaps their behavior was so timorous because deep down they never stopped doubting their own social legitimacy.

As Bernard Groethuysen suggests, the Catholic Church—but other religious sects as well—sanctified those who were born noble, powerful, and wealthy, affluence being taken as an external sign of high social position. This was perhaps a natural stance for an ecclesiastic establishment that historically had such close family, social, and economic ties with the landed elite, though the churches also hallowed the poor and the meek. But neither doctrine nor clergy considered those of "intermediate" status to be in the grace of God. The Church was distrustful of robber barons and preached humility to the economic, intellectual, and social upstarts of the cities. Indeed, the bourgeoisie lacked the legitimating force of time, which was on the side of the old ruling class whose superior wealth, breeding, bearing, and authority were sanctioned by their venerable origins.

As well as suffering from a lack of religious and temporal consecration from above, the insecure bourgeoisie was without a mass following that acknowledged its superiority and provided a warrant of popular support or furor. And last though by no means least, no matter how solid its economic foundations, except locally the formless bourgeoisie continued to be politically impotent. As a consequence it had to do without the agglutinating force of the ritual, mystique, and patronage attendant on the exercise of state power.

Although offended and incensed at being held in disesteem, the self-made men and their progeny never became consumed or paralyzed by resentment. Instead, they sought to overcome the stigma of their humble social origins and dishonorable economic callings by imitating the ways of the old ruling class. The entrepreneur almost brazenly set out to become a *bourgeois gentilhomme,* and so did the members of the free professions. They would, in the first instance, adopt noble ways and places of living and socializing. Even in the seventeenth century La Fontaine noted that "tout bourgeois veut bâtir comme les grands seigneurs." Both then and later their city villas and, except in Russia, their country houses were designed to flaunt wealth, claim status, and command influence. Would-be nobles also sent their sons to elite schools, pressed them to enter honorable professions, and pushed them into suitable marriage unions. Along the way the shoguns of industry, commerce, and finance purchased land that not only conferred social prestige but also provided a hedge against bad times and a vehicle for capital diversification. Some set themselves up as landed gentlemen with operating estates and country houses, though a greater number acquired land for rent while building an urban or a rural villa, or both. In whatever form, *real* estate, like state and ecclesiastic offices, brought a blend of social-psychological and economic dividends.

On this score England was typical of much of Europe. Until the early twentieth century the new magnate of money who did not invest in a landed estate with a country house was the exception. Because of the limited supply of old and sought-after country houses in prestigious locations, would-be nobles had architects build new ones, invariably in traditional styles. To be sure, country houses with time expressed social status stripped of political pretension, and therefore came to be less stately. Even so, by purchasing or building country houses girded by extensive lands, England's merchants, bankers, and industrialists struck an aristocratic rather than a bourgeois pose as they steered their sons away from the world of business.

On both sides of the Channel new wealthholders climbed the irregularly spaced steps of the social ladder to ever higher noble stations. Once there, many of the novices became snobbish purists, leaving it to more poised and accomplished—and perhaps also wealthier—social transvestites and their patrons to admit new men and ideas into the time-honored establishment. Down to 1914 even the most zealous and brazen social climbers were rarely satirized as vainglorious fools, there being few Figaros to taunt and trick counterfeit nobles without falling prey to their wiles.

Of course not all nonlanded magnates aspired to pass, there being men of great new fortunes who proudly spurned the aristocratic embrace. Immune to the lures of high society, they declined official honors and ennoblement. But quite apart from being rare exceptions, even these self-conscious and self-willed recusants were more nobiliar than bourgeois in mentality and demeanor. Besides, since their children were educated and socialized in elite schools and cultural institutions, many of these resistant families could not help but drift into the orbit of the old establishment, a movement that more often than not was intergenerational. Perhaps it should be added that the mounting need for economic preferment from the state made the bourgeois element that much more disposed to pay homage to the noble element which dominated civil and political society.

Although half-admired and half-feared for being the prototype of modernization, England continued to be very much a traditional society past the reign of Edward VII into that of George V. In 1914 nine-tenths of the membership of the far from lifeless House of Lords still consisted of landed aristocrats, most of them with country houses. On the whole, the aristocracy remained landed and accounted for England's most substantial fortunes. Intensely loyal to Crown, Church, and Empire, it occupied important political and bureaucratic posts and constituted the backbone of diehard conservatism. Headed by its oldest families, the titled aristocracy occupied the summit of the social edifice. With undiminished self-confidence it presided over a full calendar of gala affairs, country-house parties, weekend hunts, horse races, and cricket matches.

Admittedly, the landed establishment became increasingly intertwined with the business world. By 1914 nearly one-third of the peers were company directors, notably of large railroad, insurance, and international trading firms. But probably most of these board members served in nominal capacities, and there was little danger of their defecting to bourgeois society.

Ennoblement was designed to perpetuate the primacy of this landed aristocracy. Significantly, a large proportion of the businessmen who received new titles or were raised into the peerage during the nineteenth century bought estates before being dignified, or enlarged them soon thereafter. In any case, of the 463 individuals elevated into the peerage between 1835 and 1914 the overwhelming majority were of noble or gentle provenance. To be sure, many of these new peers of high lineage were connected with commerce and industry. Still, of 89 officials honored for their service to Great and Greater Britain, only 16 were of professional and business background, the other 73 being nobles and gentry. Similarly, after 1885 about 31 percent of all new peers were tied to the business world, but of these 80 percent were of landed origin.

Not surprisingly, during the thirty years before 1914 about half of the 200 new peers were of this same descent. To be sure, of the 100 of nonlanded origin, 70 were bankers, merchants, and industrialists. But 35, or half of these, had previously acquired landed estates and country houses. Fourteen were sons of landed families, and many of them were simultaneously officeholders and company directors. Especially as of the last quarter of the nineteenth century, entrepreneurs and bankers who had also turned landowner could aspire to a hereditary patent of nobility in their own lifetime. Between 1886 and 1914 about 62, or slightly over a quarter, of 246 new titles went to representatives of business and finance. In particular Lord Salisbury, who reclaimed the premiership from Gladstone in 1886, understood the importance of attaching the new wealth to the Conservatives if it was not to become a prop for the Liberals in this era of universal male suffrage. He set the pace by recommending the ennoblement of successful businessmen such as Edward Guinness, the brewer who had acquired an estate in Suffolk; Henry William Eaton, the cloth-maker who purchased 34,000 acres in Yorkshire; and William Armstrong, the iron and arms master for whom Norman Shaw built an ostentatious mansion on his vast estate in Northumberland. The Prince of Wales continued along these same lines when he sponsored Julius Wernher, the mogul of precious metals, Ernest Cassel, the Jewish banker, and Thomas Lipton, the pioneer of chain retailing. In the meantime the Liberals had become equally adept at the honors game, ennobling manufacturers of linoleum, tobacco, and cotton. Presently, however, among businessmen the captains of heavy industry secured the greatest percentage of peerages. They also excelled at finding marriage partners of landed and professional status, matrimony being a safer and faster avenue of social promotion than education. But in spite of this somewhat accelerated rise of self-made magnates of business and banking, the landed class continued to provide an inordinate share of newcomers to the peerage. No wonder the 35 nonlanded business peers went largely unnoticed among the 570 members of the House of Lords, which even after the Parliament Act of 1911 remained a citadel of prebourgeois influence and power. One reason they were so invisible was that most of them were mere barons in a chamber in which dukes and marquesses stood out for their prestige and wealth. The last dukedom was conferred upon a nonroyal worthy in 1899.

A greater number entered the peerage through politics and the public service than through commerce, industry, and finance. Not only were prominent ex-ministers and members of Commons raised into the House of Lords but so were the outstanding proconsuls of empire: Earl Roberts of South Africa, Viscount Milner of Egypt and South Africa, Viscount Kitchener of Egypt, and Lord Elgin of Canada. The far-flung empire and the expanding imperial services became particularly useful channels for the advancement and ennoblement of commoners, also because the romance and struggle of overseas Greater Britain opportunely regenerated the archaic ethos of heroism, glory, and honor. With the aristocracy unable to staff the imperial bureaucracy, both civil and military, the governing class recruited properly educated and homogenized sons of the middle classes for potentially honorable overseas careers. With increasing frequency, sterling service in the colonies, like meritorious government service in the British Isles, was rewarded with a personal knighthood or baronetcy. A special Order of the British Empire was created to accommodate the new influx.

By 1914 the fast-circulating lesser life orders, which expanded rapidly from the late nineteenth century, claimed some 1,700 members, among whom were precious few entrepreneurs. While nearly 70 percent were knighted for outstanding public service and about 17 percent for distinction in the professions, including the arts and sciences, only 3.6 percent were honored for achievement in the business world—among them Sir Henry Bessemer, Sir Hiram Maxim, Sir Henry Oakley, and Sir James Inglis. Clearly, even if one were to count exclusively as businessmen the 150 knighted local officials who were leading local merchants and manufacturers, this second order, like the peerage, would not allow itself to be overrun by the new plutocrats.

England's landed elite co-opted prominent new men of business, the professions, and government service not only by inducting them into the peerage or knighthood but also by taking them in socially. Provided they denied their origins by assimilating the patriciate's social code, they were invited, not to say summoned, to participate in high society. While titled ladies of the uppermost aristocracy stood out as sparkling hostesses, notably in London, their primary function was to smooth the social intercourse between men of old and new families as a prelude to their forming economic and political ties. Dinner parties in city mansions and weekends in country houses smoothed the way for landed peers to become corporate directors and to invest in business, including overseas ventures, and for entrepreneurs to become candidates for ennoblement. In sum, the receptions and invitations of bluebloods—which the new-bloods imitated—served as catalysts for the ongoing fusion of the old nobility of land and office with the new magnates of capital and the liberal professions on terms favorable to the aristocratic element.

The educational institutions also fostered this fusion. From the mid-nineteenth century and into the twentieth, the fast-expanding public schools, isolated in rural and estate England, imparted the manners, customs, and values of the old society to the sons of the middle classes, who with the help of the classics were prepared for a gentlemanly rather than a "productive" life. Since the prestige universities—notably Oxford and Cambridge—all but ignored science, mathematics, and modern languages, headmasters were not motivated to modernize the public school curriculum, the less so now that the empire needed administrators whose sense of duty and service could be nurtured with the Greek and Roman classics. Profoundly tied into the inveterate landed society, the great public schools and elite universities deflected the sons of the ever apostatizing bourgeoisie from disesteemed industry, trade, and engineering, which were considered unworthy, into honorable careers in the civil and colonial service, the Church, the military, and the law.

It bears repeating that the landed elite remained paramount because its social, cultural, and political primacy had such firm material foundations. Until the turn of the century half of Britain's wealthiest men were landowners, and until 1914 landowners continued to be the single largest group among the richest men and families, their fortunes being larger than those of the wealthiest merchants and manufacturers. The London estates of the duke of Westminster alone were estimated at £14 million, and at least another seven peers were almost equally wealthy. Backed by a sizable stratum of landed nobles of less extravagant fortunes, these super-rich aristocrats were based in London, where they were at the center of both civil and political society.

The second largest and wealthiest group came out of banking, trade, commerce, and shipping. To be sure, not until after 1918 did businessmen begin to leave estates on the scale of the giant landed proprietors. Still, England's banking, mercantile, and shipping fortunes were large and many, the most illustrious being those of the Barings, Harrisons, Liptons, Montefiores, Rothschilds, Sassoons, Selfridges, and Whiteleys. Like the landed grandees, these financial and business tycoons, many of them ennobled, were based in the capital, most of them in "the City" itself.

Both of these groups outranked the large manufacturers and industrialists in numbers and wealth. Although the manufacturers of Manchester, Birmingham, and Bradford were celebrated for pioneering and realizing the first industrial revolution, their fortunes remained relatively modest. Between 1800 and 1914 only one Manchester cotton manufacturer left an estate of over a million and only two others left estates of around half a million. When John Bright died in 1889 he left a patrimony of £86,000, while on his death in 1914 Joseph Chamberlain's estate was valued at £125,000. Although the patrimonies of the giants of the capital goods sector were of greater magnitude, they were as yet few in number.

Indeed, into the Edwardian twilight there were fewer and smaller fortunes in manufacture and industry than in landowning, commerce, and private banking, and the bulk of them were in provincial cities and towns. Not only in terms of wealth but also of income England's "producing" bourgeoisie occupied third place. Moreover, with notable exceptions, it was disconnected from the neighboring landed elite at the same time that it had difficulties raising its own project and ideology from the local and provincial to the national level.

In the meantime the carriers of large landed and commercial fortunes and incomes drew closer together in the capital. The fact that most of London's businessmen were Anglicans, or

had converted to Anglicanism, facilitated their social intercourse with the old aristocracy and predisposed them to enroll
their sons in the elite schools. At the same time that the new
banking and mercantile families pressed their assimilation into
high society, the great landed dynasties relented in their dis-
paragement of "the City." Gradually the younger generation
sought or accepted positions in board rooms which assumed
a gentlemanly air, thereby furthering the amalgamation of the
notables of land and capital not only in the ruling but also the
governing class.

Both major parties reflected this commingling on terms set
by the traditional nobility of land and service. Before leading
the Tories Benjamin Disraeli had totally styled himself in their
image. Lord Rosebery, the future Liberal Imperialist prime
minister, took Hannah de Rothschild as his wife in 1878, when
she was the sole heir not only of £2 million but also of Ment-
more Towers, the imposing Buckinghamshire manor that tes-
tified to her and her family's boundless aristocratizing zeal.
The third marquess of Salisbury and Lord Balfour of Burleigh,
who between them led the Conservative party for twenty-six
years and served as premiers for seventeen years, were of
absolutely impeccable lineage, education, wealth, and bearing.
Only in 1911, after three lost elections, did the Conservative
party choose a leader of a radically different mold to repair its
fortunes by practicing politics in a less genteel key. Andrew
Bonar Law, who eventually—in 1922—also became prime
minister, was an iron and steel merchant who eschewed aristocratizing, although he remained apprehensive that the Conservative establishment might desert him for lacking blue
blood, school tie, and landed estate.

Not that the deans of the Liberal party so easily or rapidly
broke free from the spell and lure of title, country house,
public school, Oxbridge, and empire. Herbert Henry Asquith
was the first prime minister to come from a nonlanded family,
and that was in 1908. A stalwart Liberal, Asquith was nevertheless infected by the aristocratizing ambition which consumed
his second wife, Margot Tennant. She was the daughter of
Charles Tennant, the Glasgow industrialist, merchant, and

land speculator who in 1885, after purchasing an estate of 4,000 acres, had been awarded a baronetcy. In any event, down to 1914 landed aristocrats and assimilated businessmen and professionals, notably lawyers, claimed at least half the cabinet posts even under Liberal administrations. Moreover, the old elite not only kept almost exclusive possession of the Foreign Office and diplomatic corps but also occupied most of the highest permanent posts in the state and imperial bureaucracy.

The kings of Prussia and emperors of Germany, like their English cousins, made full use of the ennobling mechanism, except that as quasi-autocrats they were less bound by the advice and consent of their ministers. Between 1871 and 1918 they raised 1,129 men into the nobility and advanced 186 Prussian nobles to higher ranks. While 1,094 novices, or over 98 percent of the total, were honored with the rank of mere *von,* the Hohenzollerns also created 151 barons, 54 counts, 15 princes (some with the right to be called "Serene Highness"), and one duke, most of them of enormous landed wealth. William I ennobled the bankers Schickler, Friedrich Wilhelm Krause, Adolf Hansemann and—with less enthusiasm—Gerson Bleichroeder, and during his short reign his successor, Frederick III, dignified the Berlin banker Ernst Mendelssohn and the industrialist Karl Ferdinand Stumm.

William II awarded 836 titles, or an average of about 30 per year between 1890 and 1918. He was predisposed to ennoble landowners, generals, and senior civil servants, almost all of whom were of Protestant faith and many of whom came from Prussia. Of the new patents 65 percent went to agrarians and army officers, who during these years suffered a marginal decline in their overall position in favor of bankers, entrepreneurs, and professionals, only a few of whom were non-baptized Jews, notably two members of the Goldschmidt-Rothschild clan. For certain, in 1914 traditional landed noblemen, soldiers, and bureaucrats heavily dominated the German peerage. These stayed far ahead not only in numbers but also in rank, the higher titles being, as always, reserved for descendants of venerable families of land and office. In fact, of the 221 conferments of baron and above, 205 went to sons of patrician families and a mere 16 to sons of bourgeois fathers. While men of landed background monopolized the apex of the aristocratic pyramid, those of bourgeois and upper-middle-class extraction tended to cluster in the broad supporting base of that pyramid. Clearly, Germany's ennobling strainer was still rather fine. Nearly all the 350 lowborn neophytes who constituted 30 percent of the bottom rank had an aristocratic mother or wife.

Until 1914, like that in England, the mighty landowning nobility in Germany claimed the most numerous and largest fortunes and incomes. These great agrarian fortunes were bolstered by venerable aristocrats who exploited the coal, minerals, and lumber of their extended landholdings. In 1910, 4 such magnates figured among the 10 wealthiest individuals of Prussia: Prince Henckel von Donnersmarck; Prince Christian Kraft of Hohenlohe-Oehringen (duke of Ujest); Prince Hans-Heinrich XV of Pless; and Count Hans-Ulrich von Schaffgotsch. Although Bertha Krupp von Bohlen und Halbach headed this list, it also included the bankers Baron Max von Goldschmidt-Rothschild and Kommerzienrat Eduard Beit von Speyer. Judging by the roster of the 100 wealthiest families in Prussia—the Prussia that was the demographic, economic, and political pivot of the Second Empire—the fortunes of the blue-blooded nobles and of the financial and mercantile magnates outpaced those of the captains of industry. While Thyssen, Tiele-Winkler, Daniel, Stumm, Stinnes, Siemens, Borsig, and Waldthausen figured prominently on this list, they were far from dominating it. Besides, 90 out of these 100 super-rich, regardless of the *source* of their wealth and income, belonged to the old society: 25 were old aristocrats, 40 were newer nobles, and 25 held officious titles. Even though August Thyssen and Hugo Stinnes, having spurned ennoblement, were among the 10 "commoners," neither their mentality nor their politics was bourgeois, and their progeny eagerly climbed into the preindustrial establishment.

Indeed, not only in Prussia but throughout Germany the nonagrarian economic elites and their retainers in the free professions never sought or found an autonomous social, cultural, and political ground from which to challenge the old society. The new men of exceptional wealth and talent fervently solicited or accepted the imperial and noble seal. In particular during the half-century preceding 1914, the "enriched bourgeois" systematically pressed their procurement of titles that legitimized "their connection with the dominant class and . . . adapted the new social forces to the old aristocratic environment," thereby also "reinvigorating" the formerly hostile nobility with "new blood and new economic energy." With equal effectiveness and greater frequency the new capitalists, after appropriating the aristocratic life-style, propelled their sons to become reserve officers, to join dueling fraternities, and to marry into the old society. This social climbing, including the ennobling marriages of daughters, never really waned. Nor was it dismissed as either ludicrous or eccentric. In fact, it may be said to have intensified with the atrophy of liberalism before 1914.

With few notable exceptions the Jewish banking, mercantile, and industrial dynasties, including those at the top of the wealth pyramid in Berlin, were consumed by this same ardor for upward assimilation, which many of them expressed through their rush to baptism, presumably a precondition for admission to imperial Germany's ruling class. Accordingly, the Mendelssohn-Bartholdys, Friedländer-Fulds, Schwabachs, Oppenheims, and Weinbergs sued for their titles and kept them, even though conversion did not remove the Jewish stigma that debarred them from high Christian society.

This massive, obeisant, and venal social and cultural adaptation helped to open channels of access to political society, which the feudalistic element continued to dominate. In other words, the magnates of capital bartered their political rights and claims for economic advantage, social status, and civic privilege. Especially once they perceived the Social Democrats as a clear and present danger, they practically abandoned what

remained of their bid for a share of political power commensurate with their newly acquired material positions. Rather than
press for political democratization, the German bourgeoisie
rallied around parties that were shaped in its own subservient
image and that essentially confined themselves to the defense
and promotion of its economic interests. Social feudalization
and class abdication were both cause and effect of political
emasculation.

For ambitious, deferential, and well-to-do *Grossbürger* who
were not ennobled—and they were the vast majority—there
were other badges of recognition and acceptance. Of all the
decorations the graduated orders of the Red Eagle, the Black
Eagle, and the Knight's Cross of the House of Hohenzollern
were the most coveted. Should fathers go unrecognized in the
private or public sector they could always push their sons to
join archaic fraternities at major universities in order to contract purposely conspicuous dueling scars that flashed a liegelike signal. Thereafter they could become officers in the army's
reserve system whose honor code and values helped assimilate
ambitious bourgeois and middle-class elements into the Prus-
sianized and aristocratic civil and political society. These were
so many steps toward preferment in the public service nobility.
The rage for nobility was less pronounced in the southern
states, but they hardly typified the spirit of the Second Empire.

In comparison with England, there was less socializing between the old aristocracy and prominent commoners in city
salons and country mansions, and the imperial court was almost totally closed to them. But instead of fostering the formation of a counterelite, this haughty exclusion motivated
prosperous entrepreneurs and distinguished professionals to
redouble their efforts to win acceptance by their superiors
through making large public benefactions and through simu-
lating a society of ranks among themselves. Under the auspices
of local, state, and national officials they created their own
nonhereditary "peerage," which was designed to provide the
social nimbus for which they yearned. While waiting in "the
antechamber to the nobility," they could secure and display
such officious titles as Kommerzienrat, Justizrat, Baurat,

Medizinalrat, and Regierungsrat—first and second grade. And not surprisingly, the emperor quite readily bestowed the additional distinction of privy councilor *(wirklicher geheimer Rat)* on many of these pseudonobles, thereby entitling them to be addressed as "Excellency." William II did so in large part to compensate for the virtual absence of parliamentarians from his ennoblement lists, an absence calculated to dispraise the Reichstag.

The Hohenzollerns and other princely houses showered with decorations even those few industrial giants who either declined or missed out on ennoblement—most notably Kirdorf, Klöckner, Stinnes, Thyssen, Werhahn, Wolff, and Krupp. August Thyssen alone resolutely resisted social cooptation, even at the cost of alienating his own sons. Although the first two Krupps, Alfred and Friedrich Alfred (Fritz), chose to remain commoners, they did nothing to disavow or distance themselves from the *ancien régime* which made their fortune. By 1854 Alfred proudly accepted his first decorations. After 1871, once he built the pompous and pretentious Villa Hügel (Hillside Villa) with between two and three hundred rooms, he made sure that there would be special quarters worthy of William I of Hohenzollern, who graced him with a yearly visit.

During Alfred's lifetime, in 1882, his son Fritz married Baroness Margarete von Ende from a family of Prussian service nobles. Living as a *grand seigneur* and with his principal residence at the Hügel, Fritz Krupp acquired two additional mansions in the Rheintal and in Baden-Baden. While he went to the Baltic Sea for the Kieler Woche, the grand yachting event, he spent the social season in Berlin. Fritz Krupp also cultivated his ties with William II, who saw to his becoming a member of both the Prussian Staatsrat and Herrenhaus and who appointed him privy councilor first class. He was now "His Excellency" Krupp and as such entitled to high precedence at court.

Having helped to find a suitable marriage partner for Bertha, Fritz Krupp's eldest daughter and heir, the kaiser attended the nuptials on October 15, 1906, at Villa Hügel, accompanied by Prince Heinrich, Chancellor Prince Bernhard von Bülow, and a score of ministers, generals, admirals, and aides-de-camp. Moreover, in his wedding address, William II entitled Gustav von Bohlen und Halbach, the carefully selected but undistinguished bridegroom, to assume his bride's maiden name, so that he became Krupp von Bohlen und Halbach. Thereafter the emperor witnessed the christening of their son Alfried. He saw to it, furthermore, that Gustav became a reserve captain in the Leib-Garde Husaren cavalry regiment, vice-president of the Kaiser Wilhelm Gesellschaft, extraordinary ambassador and plenipotentiary minister of Prussia, a right honorable knight of the Protestant Order of Johanniter and of the Order of the Red Eagle (second class with oak leaves and royal crown), a commander first class of the Prussian Order of the House of Hohenzollern, etc. To celebrate the centennial of Alfred Krupp, on April 26, 1912, the emperor of all Germans came to the Hügel with all the Hohenzollern princes, with Chancellor Theobald von Bethmann Hollweg and his entire cabinet, and with the general staff and all naval admirals. For the occasion, Gustav Krupp proposed to stage a medieval tournament of mounted knights with lances on the grounds of Europe's most modern manufacture of war matériel, but it was canceled at the last minute out of respect for the victims of a great mine disaster.

None of the other industrial titans who remained in the third estate received quite so many honorable and stately accolades. Just the same they too stayed well within the orbit of the old order and society. They prided themselves on being as much the masters in their own industrial domains as the Junker proprietors were on their estates. Needless to say, none of the great industrialists ever joined any of the floundering bourgeois-progressive parties. In fact, many of them became exceptionally fierce supporters of the semi-autocratic and conservative rule of the landed and public service nobilities. In any case, the recusants of integration into high society and state service remained a microscopic minority.

While the banker Gerson von Bleichroeder was ennobled, the shipping magnate Albert Ballin remained a commoner. But because both chose to remain Jewish, the old aristocracy treated them and their kind with even greater disdain than they did their Christian counterparts and then baptized or ennobled such Jewish businessmen and bankers as Ernst von Mendelssohn-Bartholdy, Fritz von Friedländer-Fuld, and Paul von Schwabach. Even so, with emperors and chancellors enlisting their economic services, Bleichroeder and Ballin sought to make themselves socially acceptable. In spite of being humiliated by the ostracizing anti-Semitism of Junker aristocrats, they took these aristocrats as their model: Bleichroeder acquired the landed estate of Field Marshal Albrecht von Roon, and Ballin a sumptuous mansion in Hamburg's Feldbrunnenstrasse, to stage a conspicuous display appropriate to the rank to which they aspired and to entertain old notables, including the Kaiser, in the style to which they were accustomed.

The external style and domestic decor of these bourgeois palaces replicated rather than defied the academic cultural conventions and tastes of their day. It should also be noted that university professors were not beyond being dazzled by the old society. They, too, exchanged political emancipation for *Bildung und Besitz* (classical education and property). Characteristically Otto Gierke, Gustav Schmoller, and Adolf Harnack eagerly accepted the ennobling *von* between their first and last names.

Even more than in England, where party politics and the House of Commons were effective fulcrums for the gradual bridling of the feudal element, the traditional elites in Germany remained supreme. The Bentincks, Stolbergs, and Castell-Rüdenhausens still had a princely presence—and great estates—in what once had been "their" principalities. There were, in addition, the princes created by successive Prussian monarchs, among them the Blüchers. Bülows, Eulenburgs, Hatzfels, Radolins, Plesses—and Bismarcks. Whatever their internal cleavages and rivalries, which were more than offset by the three-class franchise, the nobles, old and new, retained enormous wealth as well as social and cultural sway with which to bolster their primacy in political society. Backstopped and abetted by the emperor, they used the Prussian "parliament," the army, and the bureaucracy to curb the hapless Reichstag, which was in no position to effectively loosen their strangle hold.

Following the Revolution the titled nobility in France ceased to have a political and statutory existence. Although many nobles resurfaced and returned from exile after 1815, their political disestablishment all but continued, in large part because of the debilitating infighting between Louis XVIII, Charles X, Louis-Philippe, and their respective descendants and followers down through 1875. Throughout the nineteenth century the French aristocracy lacked the legitimating warrant of a hereditary and church-anointed crown, the mystifying theater of a royal court, the invigorating stimulus of periodic ennoblements, and the binding force of political patronage. Louis Napoleon's empire with its sham imperial nobility and make-believe court at Saint-Cloud merely kept alive hope that with time an authentic royal and aristocratic establishment would be reinstated.

But although it never recovered its political moorings, the nobility managed to perpetuate and reproduce itself. Even under the Third Republic dukes, marquises, counts, and barons occupied such prominent economic, social, and cultural positions that the *grands bourgeois* never ceased to revere and emulate them. The aristocratic world remained so seductive that many bankers, entrepreneurs, and professionals who failed to marry into it sought to pass themselves off as nobles by simply attaching the particle *de* to their names. The republic which still entrusted high diplomatic and military posts to noblemen had no intention of disallowing this spurious enlargement of the old elite, even though the political loyalty of so many aristocrats lapsed in times of crisis. In fact, the republic officially recognized the honorific quality of noble titles, and their holders retained the legal right to use them.

The survival of the leading noble families with large estates and castles was crucial to the perseverance of the nobility. The wealth and income of these notables who reclaimed their patrimony was and continued to be primarily in land. Some of them resumed operating and renting out their farmlands, though not too many of them became improving landlords in their own right. Others sold some or all of their holdings with a view to investing the proceeds in urban real estate. In particular wealthy Legitimists moved to provincial cities and especially to Paris, but retained their country seats or castles as a political base and for vacation and hunting seasons. It was from their elegant mansions and apartments in the Faubourg Saint-Germain in Paris that the grand Legitimists managed their rural properties and their growing stake in the nonagrarian sectors of the economy. Conversely, many of the Orleanists who had made their fortunes in banking, manufacture, and trade acquired large-scale estates to diversify their investments and enhance their social standing. Of course, in some provinces numerous *hobereaux* (squires) with modest landholdings perpetuated their disproportionate social and political sway, usually with the help of the Catholic Church. On balance real property never ceased to be the principal though shrinking material foundation of this heterogeneous nobility.

Above all, some of the larger and most prestigious grandees branched out into banking, industry, and commerce. In 1870 they figured prominently among the two dozen *conseillers généraux* who had an annual income of over 300,000 francs and were the vertex of France's plutocracy. Needless to say, such commoners as the bankers Emile Péreire and Adolphe Fould, and the iron and steel master Eugène Schneider belonged to this core of the super-rich, and so did the ennobled banker Baron Alphonse de Rothschild. But this select group also included the duc de La Rochefoucauld-Doudeauville, the comte de La Rochefoucauld, Baron de Graffenried, the marquis d'Albon, Vicomte Aguado, the prince de Beauvau, Baron Gourgaud, the marquis de Talhouet, the marquis de Vogüé, the duc d'Audiffret-Pasquier, and the marquis de Chasseloup-Laubat. The last four of these eleven nobles had made much if not most of their fortunes in banking, industry, and trade and probably also in urban real estate. Though not on this list, there were also a few pioneers of industry and manufacture among the aristocratic families: the Wendels in iron, the Moettes in champagne, the comte de Chardonnet in artificial silk, and the marquis de Dion in motors. As for plebeian entrepreneurs who ennobled themselves, they made their mark through the Decazes and the Talabots in iron and steel, and the Davilliers and Neuflizes in banking.

Their enduring prestige and social connections as much as their wealth won old aristocrats memberships on the boards of large corporations. Around the turn of the century they provided close to one-third of all the directors of railroad companies and nearly a quarter of the big steel and banking firms. They were also well represented on the board of the Compagnie Marocaine, one of the overseas investment and trading firms of Eugène Schneider, whose quest for social grandeur was boundless: among his directors he had Comte Albert Armand, the marquis de Chasseloup-Laubat, Comte Robert de Vogüé, Comte Robert d'Agoult, the duc Decazes, and the comte de Cherisey, while the marquis de Froudeville and Baron Henri de Freycinet sat on the executive committee with Schneider and Gaston de Caqueray. Similarly, in 1914 five of the eleven directors of the Comité des Forges were nobles.

While the aristocrats, even with all their investments and directorships, were no economic match for the untitled manufacturers, merchants, bankers, and industrialists, the new giants of business nevertheless continued to encourage their sons and daughters to marry into the nobility. Through matrimonial alliances the *grands bourgeois* of champagne, sugar, steel, and banking became united with such renowned dynasties as d'Uzès, de Mun, Poniatowsky, Polignac, Broglie, Brissac, Nervo, and Breteuil. Meanwhile Eugène Schneider steered his four daughters into marriages with noblemen, and one of his grandsons married into the house of Orleans. Moreover, like Krupp at Essen, Schneider adopted a regal life-style at Le Creusot, where he made his home in the château of the ancient royal manufacture of crystalware, which became a fortress of wealth and luxury that not only was secluded from but also lorded over the industrial serfs of France's largest iron and steel complex.

By the turn of the century the top layers of the aristocracy and bourgeoisie formed an amalgam whose influence was far-reaching with the Third Republic's governing class, which was drawn from the *classes moyennes*. While a few notables went into politics, far more commonly successful politicians of modest social provenance were raised into the social establishment by serving its economic interests as lawyers, directors, and lobbyists. Particularly after the Dreyfus affair the blue-bloods of the ruling class shelved or renounced their royalist convictions and reconciled themselves to the republican regime. But this reluctant *ralliement*, which the Catholic hierarchy blessed, also meant that they joined their bourgeois associates in a campaign to make the republic conservative, which in 1913 culminated in Poincaré's election to the presidency. By then Maurras's royalist *Action Française* had rekindled the antirepublicanism of a noble *fronde*.

Although relegated to the margin of the republican polity, the French aristocracy maintained its social and cultural preeminence. As if to compensate for its absolute political fall and relative economic decline, it became more self-consciously mannered and proud-minded than any other European nobility. Old highborn families learned to valorize their renowned names and ancestries. Some thirty grand aristocrats married American heiresses during the Belle Époque, while many others forged family alliances with indigenous fortunes, including Jewish ones. But this marriage strategy worked only because the aristocracy as a whole continued to seduce the bourgeoisie with what were so many inflated illusions and appearances. Rather than standing out as decadent, corrupt, idle, and vain, the French nobility dazzled Paris and foreign notables with its charm, elegance, and finesse. In addition, worried about social leveling and unrest, the bourgeoisie appreciated the aristocracy's unfailing hierarchy, continuity, and stability through a century of adversity. At any rate, no longer inclined to vaunt themselves, wealthy bourgeois were enraptured rather than repelled by swaggering aristocrats. In turn, the exclusive aristocracy, even if condescendingly, opened its gates sufficiently to admit bourgeois apostates into its salons and clubs.

In the hope of passing these barriers business magnates not only married upward and sought company directors among the titled nobility but also built or bought elaborate country houses. Indeed, the French countryside abounded in châteaux. Many of these were authentic and ancient, cast in medieval, Renaissance, and Louis XIII through Louis XV style. But thousands of imitation castles or stately manors were built in the course of the nineteenth century. In 1910 some 4,500 Parisian notables owned châteaux set in parks and surrounded by considerable lands. These secondary residences were prime badges of seignorial status or pretension and provided rarefied space for socializing during the summer and shooting seasons. The Rothschild clan had six palatial estates in the Paris region alone. While few other recent moneyed dynasties had quite that many rural seats, new notables nevertheless must have accounted for much of the mushroom growth of country mansions after 1848.

Just as France's château society was far from a lifeless fossil, so the kindred salon culture of Paris also retained a certain vitality. With few exceptions the salons were aristocratic rather than bourgeois, especially once the bourgeoisie looked to *tout Paris* to certify and enhance its social position. In wealth and education the aristocrat and the bourgeois were on the same level, but the former set the terms for their encounter. The aristocrat made the bodily, facial, and verbal gestures which the bourgeois not only strained to imitate but, above all, scrutinized for clues to his own uncertain standing.

Not that all drawing rooms were alike or equally snobbish. While none were without an aristocratic impress, the salons of the modest or counterfeit nobility were distinctly more literary and artistic than those of the *ancienne noblesse,* which were not dependent on intellectual leaven for their renown. In any case, even though Edmond Goncourt had long since declared the death of the salons and of high society, and Léon Daudet saw the cafés displace them in importance, they remained very much alive into the twentieth century. The salon culture of Paris was in the nature of a substitute court for a swarm of aristocrats without a king and without an aristocracy. The comtesse de Greffulhe and the comte Boni de Castellane gave majestic receptions for visiting royalty. Moreover, they and other luminaries of the highest society—the prince de Sagan, the comte de Montesquiou, the princesse de Polignac—applauded such advanced but also socially unthreatening cultural innovations as the Bayreuth festival and the Ballets Russes.

The most exclusive salons, usually animated by the distaff, were in the fashionable *hôtels* of Comte Aimery de La Rochefoucauld, Comte Jean de Castellane, Comte Robert de Montesquiou, the marquis de Portes, the marquis de Dion, the marquis d'Albufera, and the comte d'Haussonville. On balance, this pseudocourtly world was royalist, Catholic, and nationalist, and fervently anti-Dreyfusard. To be sure, there were also some authentically republican salons, notably those of the comtesse de Greffulhe, Madame Arman de Caillavet, Madame Émile Straus (*née* Geneviève Halévy, widow of Georges Bizet), Madame de Saint-Victor, Madame de Pierrebourg, the marquise Arconati-Visconti, and, to a lesser degree, Madame Ménard-Dorian. But they were anomalies in an otherwise politically disloyal social establishment. The Dreyfus affair merely exposed the reactionary predilections of most of *tout Paris,* and its outcome hastened the decline of the salon culture and the transmutation of its devotees into forced republicans. But both before and after this great divide the literary, musical, and artistic salons had an aura of unpolitical refinement that was anything but bourgeois. As Marcel Proust recounts in *Le Côté de Guermantes,* the aristocracy lorded over the famed drawing rooms and clubs which forged the moguls of business, the professions, the arts, and the civil service into a ruling class whose temper was traditional rather than modern.

Another index of the prebourgeois cachet of the French ruling class was the survival of dueling as an empty but not inconsequential convention. In Germany the duel was confined to student fraternities—and the army—and was intended to produce a conspicuous facial scar flaunting loyalty to the old order. In Paris, by contrast, it flourished in the interstices of high society where swords or pistols revalidated and challenged the ancient code of honor. Between 1888 and 1895 there are said to have been at least 150 duels over political, journalistic, or literary "affairs of honor." The agitation around Captain Dreyfus brought an upswing of dueling during the next ten years, and bloodless encounters for literary *lèse-majesté* remained quite frequent down to 1914, the government making no effort to outlaw them. Between them Jean Joseph-Renaud and Ronzier Dorcières arranged and refereed some 400 ritualized and frequently publicized contests.

Around 1910 there was also a revival of dandyism in Paris. According to Baudelaire dandyism tends to surface "in periods of transition when democracy has not yet become all-powerful and aristocracy is only partially weakened or discredited." In its essence it was, if not a remnant of the mannered past, a hankering after it. The dandies, many of whom were swordsmen and sported monocles, were nonproductive men of leisure. They constituted a self-chosen elite of artificial but simple, individual vestiary elegance as well as of intellectual originality, daring, and unpredictability. In revolt against both self-esteeming aristocrats and bourgeois philistines, but with a greater affinity for the former, the spirited fops of Paris put intellectual, aesthetic, and sexual eccentricity ahead of ostentatious material refinement.

Of course, even in Paris not all nonlanded magnates sought to deny their humble and obscure social origins. But especially in the provincial cities successful local businessmen lived in inconspicuous comfort in exclusive neighborhoods. Although they kept to themselves and were immune to the aristocratic temptation, these wealthy capitalists were not bourgeois in either world-view or life-style. But unlike the cosmopolitan, thoroughbred, and prodigal traditionalism of *tout Paris,* theirs was Arcadian, unaffected, and severe.

Following the *fin du siècle* the old and the new notabilities, fearful of the labor and socialist challenge, increasingly pulled together. They looked to the Catholic Church, which ceased to be anathema to the bourgeoisie, to sanctify their union. Indeed, the bourgeoisie, which had once been a force for "democratic progress, secularization, and resistance to aristocratic pretensions based on birth," became so uncompromising in its resistance to social change that it even considered scuttling the republic it had helped to fashion.

The highest aristocracy of the Austrian half of the Dual Monarchy may well have been exceptionally closed to new ideas and blood right down to the fall of the Habsburgs. But notwithstanding its haughty disdain for the principles and makers of the achieving society, Austria's archaic "first society" was not a moribund vestige marked for instant death. This aristocracy of birth of 300 to 400 families gravitated around the court of Emperor Francis Joseph I and after 1906 also around the shadow court of Francis Ferdinand, the heir apparent, who was Europe's archetypal ultraconservative. Predominantly Austro-German and large-landowning, this caste-bound *Hofadel* wielded enormous influence throughout political society, except in the impotent Reichsrat, and occupied commanding positions in the social, cultural, and religious life of the entire ruling and governing class.

To be sure, following the upheaval of 1848 many of the top aristocrats retreated from Vienna to their provincial estates. But although they turned their castles and manors into their principal residences, they also maintained resplendent villas or apartments in the most exclusive quarters of the capital, partly because Vienna was an irresistible magnet for their offspring. For the self-perpetuating older generation hunting weekends became reassuring and reinvigorating reprieves from the rigidly and ornately choreographed social life in Vienna through which the aristocracy continued to mediate its own reproduction. This social life, which was at one and the same time cosmopolitan and Austrocentric, revolved around the salons of the princely Schönburgs, Schwarzenbergs, Metternichs, Hohenlohes, and Dietrichsteins, and as of the later nineteenth century, around those of countesses Larisch, Lanc-koronska, Sternberg, Andrássy, and Schlick. Unlike the upper-most salon culture of the other European capitals, that of Vienna tended to exclude not only the intellectual and artistic elite but also the aristocracy of new wealth.

But this is not to say that the whole establishment, which was considerably larger than this innermost circle, was self-enclosed and resistant to the co-optation of new elites and the patronage of innovative artists. For there was also a second aristocratic society, and this one was much more numerous, open, and heterogeneous. Although the old feudals snubbed this lesser and more recent nobility, which was estimated at over 250,000 males, they also looked to it to man and defend the *ancien régime* which guaranteed their common interest and destiny.

More than in any other country, in Austria the privilege of dueling became almost as important a criterion of member-ship in the ruling class as birth, wealth, and education. Al-though outlawed, the duel was tolerated since the old elites considered it both a right and a duty, to be denied to the lower classes, national minorities, and Jews. With the dawn of the twentieth century dueling actually became more frequent, ca-reer and reserve officers being the leading but far from the only zealots of this exclusionary social code and ritual.

In any case, the sluicegates of ennoblement were in safe hands, in that they were operated by the emperor with the counsel of his trusted courtiers, ministers, and bureaucrats. The result was that all aspirants absorbed and internalized the social code of the first society, which set the tone for the entire establishment. Admittedly, important bankers, large manufac-turers and traders, big industrialists, and prominent profes-sionals rarely if ever were raised into the peerage. But it was not impossible for them to be decorated with the orders of Maria Theresa, the Iron Crown, Saint Stephen, Franz Joseph, Leopold, or Elizabeth; to be appointed to the squirearchy, which entitled them to insert the *von* into their names; or even to be advanced to nonhereditary baron *(Freiherr)* in a society in which "no one less than a baron was considered a man." To signal their candidacy these *grands bourgeois,* concentrated in Vienna, assimilated the norms and values of the nobility, and conspicuously adopted an aristocratized life-style which facilitated their dealings with the imperial bureaucracy on which they depended for economic preferments and general advancement. Above all, the wealthier social climbers, including the Jews among them, acquired city mansions and country houses. In style and decor these residences were modeled after those of the prosperous aristocracy in the hope of breaking and blending into the dominant culture. The salons of the new patricians, such as those of Josephine von Wertheimstein (formerly Wertheim) and Theodor von Hornbostel, were faithful replicas of aristocratic originals, although some of them were religiously and ethnically less exclusionist, politically more liberal, and culturally more venturesome.

Between 1800 and 1914 there were a total of about 9,000 ennoblements in Austria. Of these, slightly over 1,000 titles went to prominent bankers, merchants, manufacturers, and industrialists; while 460 were rewarded with a simple *von* and 385 were taken into the knighthood, only around 170 were elevated into the hereditary baronage. Between 1867 and 1914 an average of 13.67 of an average yearly ennoblement list of 95 went to businessmen, but this average was reduced to 8.64 between 1885 and 1913. There was also a marked decrease in the number of barons and knights in favor of the lowest rank of mere *von.* None of these recruits from the business estate (a total of 630 between 1867 and 1914) were raised or promoted to either count or prince, the hereditary peerage remaining reserved for the landed and public service nobility.

Clearly, the civil and military service bureaucracy never ceased to claim the vast majority of the list of honors, in part because of the automatic awards to officers for extended service and for active participation in military campaigns. Taking the period 1700 through 1914, civil servants received 33 percent and officers 50 percent of all patents, as over 12 percent for businessmen and 5 percent for artists and scholars, including scientists. Between 1885 and 1914, 14 bureaucrats and

44.14 officers were ennobled every year, or 58.14 civil and military state servants, as compared with 8.65 businessmen and 2.25 artists and scholars. Moreover, every year 5.32 state servants became barons as over 1.72 businessmen, and the 26 counts and 2 princes that were invested during this same quarter-century were promotions from within the bureaucratic, military, and landed caste.

On the whole the late Habsburg regime was sparing with patents of nobility, in particular with the higher titles, except in 1908, when Francis Joseph marked the sixtieth anniversary of his reign with 100 nonhereditary and 105 hereditary creations. No doubt some commoners—sons of middle-class and bourgeois families—made their way into the "second" aristocratic society through state service. But in order to do so they had to internalize the habitual ethos of imperial rule, much as businessmen and professionals with status ambitions had to assimilate the social and cultural code of Vienna's high society (and Jews, of course, had to convert to Catholicism). Evidently, in spite of a significant influx of new blood, wealth, and talent the "second" society, let alone the "first" one, remained solidly nobilitarian. Even though only a small fraction of entrepreneurs and professionals ever managed to secure ennoblement, they did not temper their aristocratizing drive. The archaic splendor, selectiveness, and mystery of imperial society kept mesmerizing them, the more so because they were without a world-view and social code of their own. Moreover, their endless but respectful wait in the establishment's antechamber was made tolerable by economic favors and by participation, even if only peripherally or vicariously, in the sparkling social life of the capital's elite. Vienna's Ringstrasse district was in the nature of a vast public salon in which the different layers of high society met without mixing. To be sure, the Schwarzenbergplatz and the Opernviertel were the residential preserve of the highest aristocracy and time-tested gentry. But wealthy businessmen, successful professionals, and important government officials, both ennobled and would-be-noble, moved in ever greater numbers into the Börsen-, Textil-, and Rathhausviertel where many of them bought or rented their expensive houses and apartments from noble proprietors who had invested in urban real estate. The unanointed among them eagerly mingled with their social betters while strolling in the streets, parks, and squares of the Ringstrasse, or while attending its Opernhaus or Burgtheater, visiting its museum, and patronizing its shops and coffeehouses.

But the conventions of this cohabitation were fixed, not by the ambitious yet insecure bourgeois, but by the self-assured aristocrat. Moreover, the urban space wherein the elites fused into a fragile amalgam favored the continuing pre-eminence of the aristocracy. Quite apart from the Haussmann-like layout of broad avenues and emplacement of military and police headquarters, the Ring quarters were bordered and interspersed with monumental public buildings and statues whose style was relentlessly historical. The hesitant modernist stirrings of the *fin du siècle* were squashed by a revival of traditionalism during the immediate prewar years, under the retrogressive sway of Francis Ferdinand.

As previously noted, even the economy of the Cisleithanian half of the Dual Monarchy continued to be distinctly preindustrial. Accordingly, the moguls of the nonagrarian sector were bankers, merchants, and manufacturers of consumer goods rather than captains of heavy industry.

But it is worthwhile to note some characteristics that marked Austria's trailing industrial sector, for these account for a peculiarity in the configuration of the ruling and governing class of Vienna. Because of a limited domestic market and the pressure of foreign competition the producers of iron and steel, metal products, electrical equipment, and, to a lesser extent, chemicals formed trade associations (cartels) to regulate prices and sales and to lobby for tariffs. They also established close connections with banks that became ever more deeply involved in the financing of firms and the promotion of cartels that were dependent on the growing protective and subsidy system. By 1910 this close intertwining of banking, business, and government served Rudolf Hilferding as a model for his theoretical and prognostic conception of *Finanz-*

kapital in a system of nascent organized capitalism. But Schumpeter saw a different pattern in this same reality. For him the bankers of Austria-Hungary were an ideal-typical incarnation of the bourgeoisie and the capitalism of which the preindustrial *classe dirigente* availed itself in order to perpetuate its own power.

Schumpeter quite correctly portrayed the bankers and industrialists, who held the key to military preparedness, as being in "an active symbiosis" with the old elites that monopolized the state. The fact that over 80 percent of Austria's banking entrepreneurs were Jewish, even if largely converted, made it that much easier for the inveterate elites to continue subordinating their indispensable helpmates.

These Jewish financiers never acquired social status commensurate with their economic importance. They were neither *hoffähig* nor *salonfähig,* nor were they considered worthy of dueling. With one or two notable exceptions, they were not received at Schönbrunn, nor did the nobility of birth, land, and public service invite them to their city mansions or country estates. To compensate for this social ostracism and in the hope of raising their status, the Jewish nobility of money became conspicuous patrons of the arts (opera, symphony, theater, painting) and of charities.

Similarly, these bankers and their associates were politically impotent. They had no hold on either political parties or parliament, and they remained suitors and suppliants in their dealings with the finance, industry, and foreign ministries. As a consequence, they were unable to effect changes in trade, fiscal, and diplomatic policies, which were designed and implemented by the time-honored governing class in close collaboration with the Austro-German and Magyar agrarians. Jewish financiers and businessmen reproved these agrarians for tariffs that, by inflating food prices, stimulated social unrest. Furthermore, they believed that by inciting other nations to take retaliatory measures these tariffs undercut Austria-Hungary's export of manufactures and balance of payments. For their part, Jewish businessmen and bankers wanted commercial treaties that would let in cheap foods, especially from the Balkan countries, including Serbia, in exchange for preferential markets for Cisleithanian manufactured goods.

Admittedly, this heavily Jewish *grande bourgeoisie* of finance and business lacked the political leverage to dictate a more "liberal" course. Giving priority to economic gain and interest, it never really considered renouncing its privileged but debased position. Even though the establishment, especially in Vienna, silently condoned or encouraged anti-Semitism, Jewish entrepreneurs not merely accepted but actively craved and solicited official favors, honors, and titles. While they sought to enhance their low social status by patronizing the arts, they meant to prove their civic virtue and gratitude for economic preferments by being fervently *kaisertreu,* especially in moments of international crisis. They did not intend to break with the imperial system and to renounce their place in the hegemonic bloc even though they were treated as social pariahs and were locked into compliance with domestic and foreign policies that injured their dignity and long-term welfare.

Since the Jews were disproportionately important not only in banking but in commerce, manufacture, and industry, as well as in the professions and the arts, their counterparts in the dominant Austro-German society and their sympathizers in the ruling and governing class would have had to accept them fully for a bourgeois and liberal project to become a real historial possibility. As it was, the latent but also increasingly active anti-Semitism that permeated even the new economic, professional, and cultural elites seriously impeded the consolidation of a critical mass to mount and sustain a credible bourgeois alternative in and to the *ancien régime.* In part because of this fatal flaw the capitalist bourgeoisie, the professional middle class, and the cosmopolitan intelligentsia remained too weak and craven to effectively challenge the hegemony of the *classe dirigente.* Indeed, the feudal element remained sufficiently strong to continue harnessing the economic and financial energy of entrepreneurial capitalists and the expertise of technical and intellectual cadres without granting them access to political society, not least because it was in a position to use material rewards and the lure of social promotion to defuse their political aspirations.

In Hungary the entrepreneurial and professional bourgeoisie was even smaller than in Austria and thus less capable of measuring itself with the landed magnates and the public service nobility. Partly because the haughty Magyar ruling and governing class disvalued business pursuits the field was wide open for non-Magyar enterprise. Especially Austrian and German entrepreneurs made a substantial place for themselves in the advanced nonagrarian sectors of the Transleithanian economy. But because of their external economic ties and political loyalties their influence was circumscribed, notably after the onset of the Magyar "independence" movement. At any rate, whatever the importance of this foreign capital, it remained socially and politically subordinate.

The same was true of Jewish business and banking, which had no external connections. By 1914 there were 1 million Jews in Transleithania, or about 5 percent of a population of 18.3 million. The majority of them had come from the east to take advantage of the emancipation laws of 1848–1849. Close to 75 percent of working Jews were active in industry, commerce, and banking and another 9 percent in the liberal professions. Nearly 25 percent of the Jewish population was concentrated in Budapest. In the capital Jews accounted for 200,000 out of 800,000 inhabitants and constituted 65 percent of the population active in commerce, 90 percent in finance, and 25 percent in petty manufacture. Ten Jewish families—among them the Ullmans, Fellners, Kornfelds, and Lánczys—owned the largest Hungarian banks and through them, as in Austria, also controlled much of large-scale commerce, manufacture, and industry.

Grateful for being provided with so much civic and economic space, the Jews became the most loyal of all the subject nationalities in Transleithania. While conversion and intermarriage were uncommon, the Jews eagerly learned the Magyar language and even became fervent Magyarizers among the other national minorities. Under the restricted franchise their relatively privileged economic and educational condition gave them, along with the gentry, a disproportionately large voice at the polls. Especially in Budapest, where every other qualified voter was Jewish, they furnished a broad electoral base for political conservatism.

There seems little doubt but that in the course of the nineteenth century the Jews provided the bulk of Hungary's business and professional elite. The Magyar ruling and governing class quite recognized, even appreciated, the vital contribution of this community that valued its religious, cultural, and social separateness. Between 1800 and 1918 it ennobled thousands of male Jews of about 350 different families, of whom 28 were raised into the peerage with baronial rank. In addition, 17 Jews were appointed to the upper house of parliament and 10 became privy councilors. These ordinations tended to be paired with titles of nobility and with religious conversion.

All but a few of these nobles were created after the Compromise of 1867, and easily half of them between 1900 and 1914, when 25 Jews were elevated into the hereditary baronage and 300 were rewarded with titles of personal nobility. Close to two-thirds of these nobles lived in Budapest, where the vast majority were in finance, commerce, and industry. By 1913 Jews dominated the boards of the largest banks, the stock market, the chamber of commerce, and the association of industrialists, and easily over half of these Jewish directors were ennobled.

Many of Hungary's Jewish millionaires accumulated their "first" capital in agriculture-related trade, commerce, and manufacture, notably as grain merchants and millers, distillers, sugar refiners, and lumbermen. Following this primary accumulation Brüll, Lipót Popper, Hatvany-Deutsch, Manfréd Weisz, Károly Kohner, and Mayer Krausz branched out into banking, stockbroking, and industry. Not surprisingly the vast majority of Jewish nobles living in cities other than Budapest plied these same trades. This is not to say that Jews owned no land. In 1893, 46 members of the Jewish nobility were among Hungary's 1,000 largest landowners, 3 of them ranking among the top 100 landed magnates. More generally, by 1910, 20 percent of the owners of over 1,250 acres were Jewish, and so were 19 percent of those of between 100 and 500 acres. No doubt the pursuit of social standing and ascent largely accounted for this stake in landed property, in a period when most Jewish notables acquired country houses. But even Jewish capitalists who had converted, owned country estates, and had close business and professional connections with the grand aristocracy, the government ministries, and the officious political parties were never really accepted in high society.

In the meantime, the radical gentry and lower middle class in particular were becoming stridently anti-Semitic, not least because Jews had become formidable competitors in the liberal professions and for government jobs. Well over 50 percent of all doctors and lawyers in Budapest were Jewish. Self-styled spokesmen for the declining gentry and *petite bourgeoisie* denounced the Jews for being the vanguard of the capitalist modernization that was undermining the old regime and accused the ruling and governing circles of tolerating this insidious corrosion. But Budapest never saw the equivalent of Vienna's Christian Social movement and Karl Lueger. Being smaller and less industrial, the Hungarian capital had a narrower reservoir of *petit-bourgeois* frustration and discontent. Besides, the Jews themselves occupied a large place in the intermediate class of independent artisans and petty shopkeepers that typically provided the reserve army of far-rightist and anti-Semitic politics, and they remained beholden to the conservative politicians and bureaucrats who had been their sponsors. As for the rebels within the Jewish community, notably the young professionals and intellectuals, they became partisans of radical as well as social democracy, thereby providing another convenient target for ultraconservatives who charged the Jews with polymorphic subversion.

The Jewish weight and stigma merely compounded the natural weakness of the bourgeoisie and middle class vis-à-vis the discordant yet ultimately conjoined large landowners and civil service nobility. Hungary's preindustrial *classe dirigente* had no difficulty using the so-called mercantilists without admitting them into the inner circle of power. In particular those ruling and governing circles that pressed or accepted gradual capitalist and bureaucratic modernization as a strategy of social and political defense were prepared to give the bourgeoisie subsidies, tax exemptions, and tariffs in exchange for political support against the aristocratic *fronde* and the radical gentry. Until the late nineteenth century this arrangement worked quite well: agrarian magnates, gentry bureaucrats, and bourgeois mercantilists collaborated to maintain the Compromise and the established order essentially unchanged.

But with the *fin du siècle* this conservative synthesis, which was neither liberal nor liberalizing, came under attack. A far right of besieged aristocrats, gentry, and *petit bourgeois* set out to reduce or eliminate the influence and power of the bourgeoisie, which they systematically distorted and exaggerated. Notwithstanding the allegations of this composite *fronde,* the mercantilists were neither a liberal nor a commanding force, though they were the promoters of the creeping industrialization, urbanization, and bureaucratization that was disfiguring the old order ever so slowly.

In Russia neither the reforms of 1861 nor those of 1905 significantly changed the lordly and autocratic relations of class, status, and power. Much as in Germany and Austria-Hungary, capitalist modernization was being forced into the *ancien régime.* The civil and military service nobility played an important role in determining the form, extent, and speed of industrialization whose imperatives were both national and international. The causes, purposes, and outcomes of the Crimean and Russo-Japanese wars demonstrated this close interpenetration of domestic and foreign affairs. In any case, without the government-fostered and government-directed economic development, of which railroad construction became the principal motor and symbol, the mutations in Russia's class and status structure would have taken place at an even more glacial pace. At the same time, there was never any doubt that the last three tsars and their ministers, and in particular Nicholas II, attached greater importance to maintaining the old order than to reforming it to accommodate those new forces and ideas which their own reluctant modernization quickened.

The landed nobility was Russia's ruling but not governing class. The latter consisted of a vast bureaucratic estate that despite close ties to the land was quite independent of it. In fact, in their own ways the landed and the service nobilities were more beholden to the autocracy than they were to each other.

With a few outstanding exceptions the status of Russia's peerage derived not from territorial rights or ancestral claims but from loyal and extended service to the autocracy. Through the centuries the tsars had awarded titles for civil and military service to the crown. While many of the patents of nobility had included grants of landed estates, with time such ceased to be the case. An ever greater number of nobles was nearly or completely landless. Unlike the surnames of the other European nobilities, those of the Russian aristocracy had no particles, prefixes, or titles to associate them with the locality of their birth, estate, or residence. Moreover, by 1914 a majority of the ennobled career servants lived on their government salaries, without supplementary income from land. Still, the remaining and probably also the more influential half of the service estate continued to have links to the land; the extended imperial family, headed by the reigning tsar, had vast landholdings; and Russia's landed nobility, in spite of internal divisions, continued to be the single most powerful and effective political pressure group.

Compared with the Hohenzollerns and Habsburgs, the Romanovs awarded titles rather freely. There was a table of ranks of fourteen parallel grades for military and civil career servants, with emphasis on time served rather than merit. Until 1896 military officers of non-noble provenance acquired hereditary status upon entering the fourteenth or lowest rank, while civil bureaucrats of low origin had to rise to the eighth grade to attain this distinction. Thereafter, to avoid inflating the "peerage," only the first seven and five ranks respectively conferred hereditary rights and privileges. In addition to these automatic promotions into the nobility, the tsar had the discretionary power to award patents of both hereditary and nonhereditary nobility through his personal list of honors. After 1882 the tsars conferred the majority of these nonautomatic ennoblements on commoners through the orders of Saint George, Saint Vladimir, Saint Anna, and Saint Stanislav. The first or hereditary degree of these orders remained relatively rare.

In 1858 there were around 610,000 hereditary nobles in the fifty provinces of European Russia (a figure that would be cut in half by not counting the nine Baltic, White Russian, and Lithuanian provinces, which had a disproportionately high number of Polish and German nobles). At that time there were also around 277,000 tsar-appointed personal nobles. By 1897 these figures had risen to 886,000 and 487,000 respectively, or a total of 1,373,000 nobles of both sexes, of whom about 55 percent owned land. Although at first sight this increase seems striking, it is well to remember that proportionately the population as a whole increased even faster and that these were years of considerable bureaucratic and military expansion. Throughout the nineteenth century the relative weight of newcomers remained fixed between 7 and 8 percent. Accordingly, although a growing number of commoners entered the first estate through the table of ranks and honorific orders, they did not challenge or dilute the dominance of the older noble families.

An imposing array of blue-blooded and titled nobles traced their ancestry back to before 1685. In 1900 there were about 800 such distinguished families of princes, counts, and barons, mostly in Georgia and Poland, and among them 40 princely families claiming descent from the ruling house of Kievan Russia. Moreover, at the turn of the century over 45 percent of the hereditary nobility was concentrated in nine western guberniya (Grodno, Kiev, Kovno, Minsk, Mogilev, Podolia, Vilna, Vitebsk, Volhynia) and about 15 percent in the guberniya around St. Petersburg and Moscow, or a total of at least 60 percent. In 1910 St. Petersburg had 75,000 hereditary and

63,000 personal nobles. These 138,000 individuals, inclusive of dependents, accounted for 7.2 percent of the capital's population. Only about one-fourth of these nobles lived off their lands and few of them were in the world of business and finance, the majority being civil servants. Even so, the old and landed nobility continued to have disproportionate sway not only in St. Petersburg society but also at court and with the bureaucracy.

The fact that until 1914 the nobility accounted for about 1.5 percent and over 7 percent of the population of the country and capital respectively is likely to have perpetuated the ennobling passion of the social climbers in the literate and achieving sectors of society, the more so since these were relatively small. (Incidentally, in 1789 there were about 300,000 nobles of all varieties in France, or 1.5 percent of the population.)

Obviously, this nobility was immensely heterogeneous: old-new; cosmopolitan-provincial; wealthy-poor; landed-bureaucratic; business-professional. There were sharp gradations in social standing, influence, and power. The higher the official grade the fancier not only the prescribed dress uniform but also the form of address (which ranged from "Wellborn" to "High Excellency"). And it goes without saying that when it came to service assignments and promotions as well as appointments to high office, hereditary nobles had a distinct advantage. In 1903 most generals of all grades had been born into the nobility (10 out of 140 full generals were members of the imperial family) though the great majority of lieutenant and major generals owned little or no land. In other words, the highest-ranking military officers and civil servants continued to be of noble origin and to rise within service castes that, in spite of being heavily diluted by commoners, nevertheless maintained and reproduced their lordly mentality, bearing, and web of connections. Since the tsar picked his closest collaborators almost exclusively from this same civil and military bureaucracy, they were certain to perpetuate the imperious ethos throughout the state machinery. Admittedly some of the key ministers and advisers of the last of the Romanovs—Giers, Kornilov, Kuropatkin, Plehve, Pobedonostsev—were of middle-class provenance. But as a condition for being asked into Nicholas II's inner circle of power, such officials of common birth had not only acquired noble status through the mechanical table of ranks but had also demonstrated their assimilation of the sanctified world-view. In fact, they probably compensated for their lowly origins by becoming exceptionally zealous champions of the *ancien régime*. At any rate, they did not dilute the public service estate with bourgeois or liberal attitudes.

Certainly until the Risorgimento the large landed nobility, nearly inseparable from the aristocratic church hierarchy, all but dominated Italy's ruling class. Thereafter mercantile and professional elements moved to the fore, but far more in the governing than the ruling class. It is not true that after unification the Italian nobility, both north and south, went into headlong decomposition and was left with little except its rapidly decaying social status. Most important, the leaders of the Risorgimento, themselves fearful of the underclasses, had been careful not to alienate the landed nobility, which they and their successors considered an essential force for order in Italy's heavily rural and agrarian society.

Count Camillo Benso di Cavour himself personified a salient characteristic of the Italian ruling class since the fourteenth century. As the younger son of a noble family he made his fortune by engaging in both agriculture and finance without in any way betraying or defiling his caste. Through the centuries the Italian nobility had been an amalgam of agrarian and mercantile families. While the grandees of merchant capitalism acquired landed estates and titles, the old feudal families branched out into commerce and trade. But the gradual fusion between them took a nobiliar form. Wealthy merchants and bankers denied their own social origins by acquiring large landed properties and searching for titles. The result was that even cities that drew their lifeblood from commercial capitalism spawned a patriciate that was heavily nobiliar.

To be sure, the Italian nobility never had the military prerogatives of the Junkers or the benefit of the national arena in which the English nobility forged its political conventions and ascendancy. Even so, the elite was feudalistic rather than bourgeois. Notwithstanding the abrogation of feudalism, peasants continued to be infeudated to their landlords in an agrarian society in which large landholding still prevailed. The masters of the soil maintained their extravagant control largely because the steep population growth compelled both small tenants and day laborers to accept their own overexploitation. Moreover, in the event of rural uprisings, the large proprietors could always use their local or regional political authority or influence to get the state to restore order.

In any case, proportionately the Italian nobility, including its aristocratic component, may well have been the largest in Europe. In part it was hidden to view because except for the princely names that figured in the *Almanach de Gotha,* there was little to distinguish the names of nobles from those of commoners. Even allowing for those who artificially elongated their names, the majority of the nobility were not readily recognizable by name alone. Still, there were great families known locally, regionally, and even nationally.

Although divided between "black" papalists and "white" nationalists, the aristocracy of the capital constituted a formidable social establishment. The descendant relatives of popes and cardinals were the oldest and wealthiest nobles. Not surprisingly, after 1870 the Barberinis, Borgheses, and Chigis, as well as most of the Colonnas and Orsinis, refused to shift their loyalty from Vatican City to the Quirinal Palace. Even among the lesser members of the old Roman nobility there were few avowed nationalists, though eventually this lesser nobility joined the newer nobility of merchants and bankers who were among the first to gravitate toward the court of the House of Savoy. In sum, Rome's primal aristocracy with few exceptions supported the Holy Father in his defiance of the secular Italian nation, while the rest of the nobility bolstered the conservative forces of postunification civil and political society by rallying around the crown.

Farther south the nobility was less clerical and more feudalistic. The old kingdoms of Naples and Sicily may be said to have been teeming with nobles. There were scores of princes and dukes, as well as countless *marchesi* and barons. While the richest among them were absentee landlords who exhibited their burdensome eminence during periodic visitations, the rank and file remained on or near their lands, where they also exercised political power and carried enormous social and cultural weight.

While many landed grandees of the south were sluggish agrarians and scorned all other professional pursuits, their counterparts north of the Apennines were considerably more efficient and entrepreneurial, not least because they were increasingly challenged by aggressive agrarian capitalists who were untitled. Emilia and especially the Po valley contained outposts of intensive commercial farming. As previously noted, Bologna was the northern capital of capitalist agriculture. Although relatively declining landed notables, Counts Cavazza, Isolani, Malvezzi, Mazzacorati, and Salina remained socially pre-eminent, overshadowing such untitled estate owners as Enrico Pini. Not only in Bologna but in the cities of the Piedmont and Tuscany, the titled landed nobility retained its primacy in the local patriciates.

There are virtually no studies of nobility and ennoblement in nineteenth-century Italy, and there are no profiles of the crown's honors lists after 1870. But this does not mean that after 1848 or 1870 the bourgeoisie completely outclassed the nobility. Contemporary Italy inherited an authentic nobility, some families tracing their lineage to Roman, medieval, and early modern times, others, such as Rome's Torlonia family, to the relatively brief Napoleonic interlude, and still others to the recent past. Through the ages titles had been conferred or validated by kings, popes, republics, cities, chivalric orders, and venerable ruling families. In addition, perhaps more than any other European society, Italian society was consumed by the rage for nobility, judging by the massive usurpation and misuse of titles. Personal and nonhereditary titles were irregularly transmitted to descendants, and frequently titles to be transmitted only by male primogeniture were extended to younger sons and to daughters. But in addition to these and other improper manipulations of genuine titles, innumerable commoners simply invented titles for themselves. This abuse reached sufficient proportions for the regime to take official notice of it. In June 1889 the crown established the register of the College of Arms (Consulta Araldica del Regno), and in July 1896 it ordered the Ministry of the Interior to codify legal norms for the use of titles and for the prosecution of usurpers. In February 1903 Giolitti, as interior minister, notified all prefects that the College of Arms kept receiving complaints about "the abuse and usurpation of titles." Determined to put a stop "to this intolerable state of affairs," Giolitti instructed the prefects to enforce the regulations of 1896 and to arraign "transgressors" before appropriate judicial bodies.

Beginning in 1906 regional registers were published, and in 1922, not counting the page listing the twenty princes and princesses of the House of Savoy, the updated *Elenco ufficiale nobiliare italiano* ran to 1,015 pages with an average of at least twelve entries per page. Only a close study of official regional and national registers, of self-ennoblement, of the conferring of lesser orders, and of decorations can reveal the degree to which the new economic and professional men of united Italy sought to climb into the old social establishment. But *prima facie* it seems that like their predecessors in early modern times many of them rushed to join the traditional nobility, thereby buttressing its social and cultural reign. Admittedly, this time-honored elite no longer enjoyed the same pre-eminence in politics and government. Even so, its political sway cannot be dismissed by emphasizing that between 1870 and 1914 the monocled Marquis Antonio di Rudinì and Baron Sidney Sonnino were the only titled nobles to serve as prime minister, or that the nobility, like so much else in Italy, was too disjoined to constitute a coherent hereditary upper chamber. By converging around the monarchy, providing high military officers, and patronizing the Church, the nobility bolstered the *ancien régime.* Significantly both Rudinì and Sonnino were spokesmen for the conservative *destra* with which even the irreconcilable "black" nobility collaborated to guard the status quo on both the local and the national level.

It would appear, then, that down to 1914 the interwoven landed and service nobilities throughout Europe continued to be dominant in the ruling classes. Except in England and France, they also maintained their primacy in political society. Their position was solid and awesome, not precarious and quaint, precisely because their immense capital was not only cultural and symbolic but also economic. To be sure, their time-tested and resilient material base was being impaired because of the relative decline of the agrarian sector. But the nobilities, especially the magnates among them, bolstered their failing economic fortunes by securing government supports, by investing in the nonagrarian sector, and by adopting clever marriage strategies.

The ascendant and claimant *grands bourgeois* had little beyond their economic capital with which to challenge this comprehensive, coherent, and formidable upper establishment. They were at a disadvantage in every major respect: social, cultural, and political. The future was acknowledged to be theirs, but the nobilities, for the present, blocked their path. Doubting their own legitimacy and in no position to subvert or conquer the old ruling classes, the new big businessmen and professionals decided to imitate, cajole, and join them.

Chapter 3

POLITICAL SOCIETY AND THE GOVERNING CLASSES

Linchpin of the Old Regime

IN 1914 EUROPE WAS not only heavily agrarian and nobilitarian but also monarchic. Republicanism was as uncommon as finance capitalism. There were, of course, the inveterate Helvetic Confederation and the fledgling Portuguese republic. But among the major powers, France alone had a republican regime. Although contested by royalist and Catholic irreconcilables, both old and new, the Third Republic endured as a country without a king but with an aristocracy. The other nations had both, the crowned heads and the nobilities needing and using each other. The nobilities combined their social predominance with inordinate political influence and power. They relied on their enormous political leverage to brake their chronic economic decline, which, had it continued unimpeded, threatened to undermine their lofty status. Particularly in the view of the landed nobilities, the authority systems that were disproportionately responsive to them were essential bulwarks of their privileged economic, social, and cultural standing. No doubt the *anciens régimes* would have contracted faster and sooner without this protective political armor.

Leading social thinkers have wrestled with the intricate relationship of political power, economic strength, and social status. Far from viewing class domination in purely economic terms, Marx and Engels probed the reciprocal dependence of economic, social, and political factors in different historical eras to gain political insight into the power configurations of their own times. Although they overestimated the speed and extent of the growth of manufacturing and industrial capitalism, they never really ignored the persistence of earlier forms of landed property and capital. They stressed, furthermore, that the governments which mediated the conflicts between owners of different types of property and capital commanded varying degrees of autonomy. In fact, Marx explicitly insisted that the state was "a separate entity beside and outside civil society" and that "the independence of the state was only found nowadays in those countries where the estates have not yet completely developed into classes, where the estates, done away with in more advanced countries, still have a part to play, and where there exists a mixture, countries . . . in which no one section of the population can achieve dominance over the others."

Of course, Marx expected that in each country the capitalist bourgeoisie would challenge the landed estate—whose members increasingly behaved like a political class—until such time as the national bourgeoisies dominated all the governments in a world system of competing states. But judging by his non-philosophical and nontheoretical writings, Marx fully realized that political society was not about to become a pure instrument of bourgeois rule, for prebourgeois and nonbourgeois class fractions continued to wield enormous political influence and power. Similarly Engels recognized that industrial capitalist developments were "not followed by any immediate corresponding change in political structure." In his judgment "society became more and more bourgeois, while the political order remained feudal." There is no denying that in their ideological conception Marx and Engels foresaw capitalist societies in which the bourgeoisie would monopolize and use the state to subjugate the wage-earning proletariat. But in their historicized political analysis and praxis they never ceased wrestling with the role of autonomous political societies that were far from neutral whenever they acted to counterbalance and conciliate the interests of the declining landed nobility and the rising capitalist bourgeoisie, to the advantage of the former.

In the wake of 1848 Marx concentrated on the economics of capitalism in his theoretical writings, while dealing with political developments in his conceptually inspired newspaper articles, letters, and pamphlets, notably in *The Eighteenth Brumaire of Louis Napoleon.* Although he and Engels sought to grasp and expose the dynamics of the interconnections of civil and political society that issued in repression and war, they did so with historical concretion rather than in search or application of a coherent political theory, which they in any case abjured.

Max Weber went in an almost opposite direction, especially after his Freiburg inaugural lecture of 1895, in which like Engels, he stressed the lack of congruence between society and polity in the second German empire. Stressing social and economic developments in his articles on contemporary affairs, Weber dealt with political society in his theoretical work. Specifically, as part of his discursive construction of concepts and ideal types he elaborated a typology of three forms of public authority or domination: charismatic, traditional, bureaucratic. But he only barely examined the structures and processes of specific political systems, probably for fear of discovering that none of them fitted his construct. Weber never faced up to the structural complexities of governmental systems that were mixed in the extreme and therefore dangerously strained. Above all, he dreaded rather than probed the repressive impulses of modern and contemporary authority systems. Instead, Weber focused on the pressure for symbolic and ideational legitimation by incumbent political actors.

Thorstein Veblen brought yet another perspective to the study of social and political statics. In his scheme, leisure classes that were overtaken by economic developments became obstacles to progress and champions of obsolescence. Although material interests also fueled the resistance of this wealthy elite, these were secondary to its "instinctive" drive to oppose change in the established "cultural scheme." Veblen saw this hegemonic fabric as essential to established regimes. For him it consisted of closely interwoven and time-honored habits of thought and action, refined manners, and public rituals that by force of "prescriptive example . . . stiffen the resistance of all other classes against innovation, and fix men's affections upon the good institutions handed down from earlier generations." Rather than defining this moving "instinct" and "class interest" of the leisure class, Veblen delineated the workings and effects of its conduct. The institutional system of any such culture being "an organic whole," the leisure class rejects "any change in men's habits of thought" for fear of "shaking the social structure at its base, . . . reducing society to chaos, . . . and subverting the foundations of morality." Accordingly, the hereditary fraction of Europe's ruling class perpetuated the "archaic traits, habits, and ideals . . . of the early barbarian age" in its cultural scheme. It also impressed these on the "lower orders" by virtue of its exalted social position. Although in normal times both the working and the middle classes were peaceable, in times of crisis they embraced the warlike and predatory spirit that the ancestral caste perpetually vaunted as the most honorable and essential component of its barbarous heritage.

Both the elite's archaic cultural display (spectacle) and the disposition of so many publics to be swayed by it remained most solidly implanted in those sectors of European societies which were "the most remote from the mechanical processes of industry and which were the most conservative also in other respects." But it was Veblen's central thesis that the hereditary elements of the leisure-class establishment had such an extravagant prescriptive reach beyond these premodern sectors precisely because they were able to "conserve, and even to rehabilitate, that archaic type of human nature and those elements of the archaic culture which the industrial evolution of society" would ultimately eliminate. To the extent that he treated the hereditary leisure class as a lofty status group whose sources and instruments of persuasion were essentially psychological and ideational, Veblen was closer to the Weberian concern with the nature and operation of legitimating creeds than to the Marxian preoccupation with the interconnections of material interest, ideology, and political control.

As previously noted, for the analysis of Europe's political societies Schumpeter provides an exceptionally useful framework. He went beyond Marx in clarifying the interpenetration of the landed and bourgeois interests and elites; beyond Weber in specifying the authority structures in modern systems of domination; and beyond Veblen in circumscribing the state apparatus as a vital rallying and operative center for the refractory leisure class. Schumpeter characterized the *ruling* class as an "active symbiosis" of the landed nobility and the bourgeoisie but stressed that the *governing* class was heavily or completely feudal. In most of Europe the entire state apparatus continued to be saturated with "the human material of feudal society, and this material still behaved according to precapitalist patterns." In all major respects the dynasties, the royal courts, most representative councils, the bureaucracies, and the armies had a feudal consistency. To be sure, political society went through considerable mutations by accommodating bourgeois economic interests and assimilating bourgeois and middle-class talents, but without its essence being affected. Although the uneasy alliance between the two social strata in civil society was not without consequence for government, the socially archaic landed and service nobilities maintained their political primacy, in part because they successfully enlisted bureaucratic and military modernization to promote their own conservative objectives.

In his own way each of these social theorists is helpful to historians interested in examining Europe's tradition-bound governing classes and institutions. Marx and Engels provide critical class perspectives on the autonomy but also the partiality with which states mediate between declining nobilities and rising bourgeoisies. Once desacralized and historicized, Weber's construct serves to explore the reciprocal dependence of charismatic, traditional, and bureaucratic authority in the syncretic polities of the *anciens régimes*. As for Veblen and Schumpeter, they direct attention to the continuing vitality of the old order's allegedly atavistic social classes and feudalistic political components.

In trying to explain why the dead continued to rule the living, Marx noted that "old, surviving systems of production [were] handed down with all their anachronistic social and political relations." Above all, as we have seen, there was no denying the enduring importance of agriculture and the landed elites. England went furthest in taming the agrarian sector and breaking and transforming the old nobility. Even so, the landed upper class did not vacate the political scene. Nor, judging by the battle over the House of Lords and home rule for Ireland after 1905, did it subordinate or adjust itself to the new plutocracy.

If successful democracy was contingent on the elimination of agriculture and land rent as major social activities, then it is hardly surprising that most of Europe should still have been governed by nondemocratic authority systems. To be sure, feudalism had passed into history. Personal servitude, seignorial justice and prerogatives, manorial taxes, local tolls, venal state offices, and church titles were a thing of the past. But to abolish feudal political, administrative, and legal rights was not to abolish the entire civil and political society of the old regime. Even in France, after the Revolution, there remained powerful material interests, social forces, customs, traditions, cultural settings, and mental structures that continued from before. In economic, social, and psychological terms feudalism outlived its juridical disappearance, most notably among Europe's elites. This was so in large measure because the landed and public service nobilities, supported by the Church, aggregated and translated these feudal residues into political influence and power.

Despite internecine conflicts of interest and outlook, the feudal elements retained a formidable place in Europe's authority systems. Their high and secure social origin and location gave them inordinate political potency as well as privileged access to institutional positions of power. By virtue of historical practice and presumption the nobilities of land and office kept reproducing a governing class that not only staffed the state bureaucracy but also kept replenishing the higher echelons of political leadership. This unbrokenness in political personnel and direction, which had profound societal moorings, accounts for the feudal element surviving as more than a mere integument of the state.

In 1914 the kings were still "the centerpiece" of civil and political society "by the grace of God, and the root of [their] position was feudal, not only in the historical but also in the sociological sense." Certainly there is no denying that following the preventive "regicide" at Sarajevo the sovereigns of the Hohenzollern, Habsburg, and Romanov empires—William II, Francis Joseph I, Nicholas II—played a crucial role in pushing Europe over the brink of war. As autocratic rulers all three commanded ministers and advisers who were nobles of one sort or another and who were creatures not of party, parliament, or movable capital but of the inveterate public service estate. As for George V of England and Victor Emmanuel III of Italy, they were more than reigning figureheads, although their prerogatives and powers were rigorously and constitutionally limited. Neither of them exerted himself to dampen the fires of war. Of course, being a republic, France had no king, though the incumbent president, Raymond Poincaré, increasingly acted like one. Abetted by aristocratized *notables,* he adopted a military and bellicose posture considerably ahead of the Chamber of Deputies and the cabinet.

But between 1848 and 1914, whatever the differences in their powers and prerogatives, all the kings exercised grave and impressive ceremonial and representational functions which heavily benefitted the hereditary leisure class, including the dynasties themselves. King, emperor, and tsar remained the focus of dazzling and minutely choreographed public rituals that rekindled deep-seated royalist sentiments while simultaneously exalting and relegitimating the old order as a whole. The coronation was the most solemn and resplendent of these studied spectacles of power, and it was saturated with historical and religious symbolism. Although the relationship of throne and altar was left studiedly ambiguous in this supreme ceremony, a high priest—appointed or approved by the sovereign—solemnly administered the oath of office and consecrated the initiate's crown, scepter, and sword. At the same time, this elaborate inaugural pageant, though centered on the king, displayed and ratified the latest ranking of status and influence in civil and political society at large. There were, of course, other rites of passage and rededication of comparable pomp, display, and mystery: the christenings, weddings, funerals, and jubilees of the ruling houses. At all these punctiliously staged sociodramas the grand, costumed, and rank-ordered nobles of blood, land, office, and church totally eclipsed even the most prominent un-uniformed commoners. Foreign royalty and nobility which invested these occasions with a cosmic aura and sanction also overshadowed them.

Nor did the kings hesitate to appropriate the highest religious and national holidays for the benefit of the feudalistic elements in the *anciens régimes.* In addition, as the incarnation of the warrior tradition, they flaunted their martial powers at infantry and naval maneuvers, military parades, and the changing of elite guards. Last but not least, the crowned heads dominated the social scene with their grand receptions, soirées, and hunts.

All these civil and social rituals invigorated the monarchy, cemented the discordant nobilities, and heralded the latest changes in the order of precedence. This ceremonial rearticulation of calibrated cohesion in the upper class was as significant as the institutional enaction of laws and forewarnings to control counterelites and underclasses. The populace, high and low, was to be awed rather than cowed by the effulgent uniforms, vestments, and decorations that intensified the magic and mystery of rites in which the kings lorded over the fusion of the scepter, the altar, the sword, and the national flag. Furthermore, the kings embodied and sustained this conflated potence during the state visits they paid one another.

These king-centered ceremonial rounds may appear stilted and contrived because of the ebbing of public ritual in recent decades. At the time, however, they were still very much alive and genuine. If anything, the use of old-world attire, transport, and splendor intensified the spell of meticulously staged pageants in tradition-soaked societies. Except in France, the royal family and the nobiliar notables dominated the nation's ceremonial calendar, which remained linked to high rather than low culture. The succession of spectacular civic rites reinforced hegemonic ideas, values, and feelings that braced the prebourgeois elites. This political ritual also integrated the lower orders by catering to their craving for dazzling spectacles, which was the counterpart of the passion for strict hierarchy among the upper orders.

The funeral of King Edward VII in May 1910 confirmed the continuing authenticity and sway of European royalty. Even before the foreign dignitaries and their suites arrived at Victoria Station on May 18, a queue of bereaved citizens, six to eight abreast, stretched seven miles to the entrance of Westminster, where the body was lying in state in William Rufus Hall. Just as this was the largest popular crowd to congregate in the British capital before 1914, so the assemblage of crowned heads, grand dukes, and crown princes was without equal in recent European history, except perhaps for the Diamond Jubilee of Queen Victoria in June 1897. On May 20, with an estimated two million people solemnly lining the streets, a truly extraordinary funeral cortege accompanied King Edward's remains to Paddington Station, from where a train took the coffin to Windsor Castle for burial in the crypt beneath Saint George's Chapel.

To be sure, there was nothing unusual about the glittering bodyguard escorting the gun carriage that bore the dead king's body, nor about the king-emperor's favorite charger following the royal bier with upturned boots attached on either side of the saddle. Perhaps it was even unexceptional that, led by a Highland gillie, another privileged escort should have been Caesar, the dead king's beloved white fox terrier. But what followed then was stunning and spectacular by any standard: King George V, riding on horseback, led a brilliant array of ruling kings, royal dukes, and hereditary princes, all of them on horseback as well. There were nine monarchs, without exception descendants of William the Silent, their order of precedence governed by kinship. In the first file, along with the new but yet to be inaugurated king, rode the duke of Connaught and Emperor William II of Germany, respectively Edward's brother and nephew. As Europe's most swaggering warlord, Kaiser Wilhelm stood out for "sitting his horse like a centaur, his face stern and set as a Roman effigy." In the next three files rode Haakon of Norway, George of Greece, Alfonso of Spain, Ferdinand of Bulgaria, Frederick of Denmark, Manuel of Portugal, and Albert of Belgium. In this august procession Nicholas II of Russia was represented by his brother, Grand Duke Michael; Francis Joseph I of Austria-Hungary by his heir apparent, Archduke Francis Ferdinand; and Victor Emmanuel III of Italy by his cousin, the duke of Aosta. Among the mounted notables there were, in addition, princely and ducal representatives of Holland, Sweden, Rumania, Montenegro, Serbia, Turkey, Egypt, Japan, Siam, the German states, and the English royal family. Prince Tsai Tao of China and his suite rode in the seventh of twelve state carriages, while Theodore Roosevelt, representing President William Howard Taft, shared the eighth coach with Stephen Pichon, the French foreign minister, representing President Fallières. The American ex-president who had once been a Rough Rider stood out as the only high personage not to wear either a uniform or a display of decorations. The Third Republic's plenipotentiary was considerably less jarring with his ribboned diplomatic frock coat. The distaff side of the royal and princely houses, led by Queen Mother Alexandra, the Russian Dowager Empress Maria, and Queen Mary of England, along with their ladies-in-waiting, occupied the other carriages.

There was not a single false or discordant note. Though 1910 marked not only the highest point of the fiery battle over the House of Lords but also an upsurge of labor, Irish, and suffragette unrest, the police anticipated no disruptions.

While the coronation of George V in London on June 22, 1910, followed an ancient and majestic ritual, his proclamation as king-emperor in Delhi was a ceremony of entirely new vintage for which Sir Edward Elgar composed "The Crown of India." On December 12, 1911, at a spectacular durbar in Delhi some 100,000 people gathered around a specially built amphitheater holding 10,000 invited guests, who were treated to a picturesque array of Hussars, Royal Horse Artillery, Imperial Cadets, Tiwana Lancers, trumpeters on white horses, and massed bands. With nearly all officials in uniform, this assemblage was convened to witness and legitimate George's exaltation. Dressed in coronation robes, their trains held by richly vested pages of princely Indian blood, Their Imperial Majesties mounted the steps to an extravagantly elevated dais isolated in the center of the amphitheater. Seated in two resplendent throne chairs surrounded by maces and emblems, they accepted the homage of their servants and subjects. Lord Hardinge, the governor general, in his political uniform and the flowing robes of the Order of the Star of India, ascended the raised platform in a bowing posture to kneel and kiss the king-emperor's hand. Once the members of the viceroy's council had made their reverence from the foot of the throne dais, it was the turn of the proud and striking but compliant ruling maharajas of India and the tribal chiefs of the frontier areas to make obeisance to their overlord.

The twenty-fifth jubilee of the reign of Emperor William II was celebrated in June 1913. It, too, was designed to reaffirm the unflagging primacy of the old ruling and governing class.

On June 15 the head of the House of Hohenzollern arrived by car for a solemn service in Potsdam's Garnisonkirche dressed in the uniform of the first Guard Regiment, displaying the Order of the Black Eagle, and accompanied by his self-effacing empress. There followed the crown princess; the crown prince and heir apparent, William of Prussia, with his wife and sons; the Hohenzollern princes of Braunschweig, Sachsen-Meiningen, Hessen, Schaumburg-Lippe, and Prussia. The emperor's suite included War Minister von Heering, Chief of Staff Count von Moltke, Lord Marshal Count zu Eulenburg, Adjutant General Baron von Lyncker, and General von Plessen. Before the arrival of this imperial party nearly all the generals and regimental commanders had taken their assigned seats in the church.

The following day, June 16, there was not a single *Grossbürger,* Progressive, or Social Democrat among the delegates of some eighty associations who were privileged to congratulate the kaiser in person. That evening the kings, grand dukes, princes, and ranking counts of the member states of the German Confederation arrived in the capital. Only Bremen and Hamburg, the Free and Hanseatic cities, were represented by non-nobles.

The special honors list offered additional proof that the emperor meant to use his jubilee to vaunt the *ancien régime.* Capitalizing on Bethmann Hollweg's penchant for military rank, William II chose this occasion to promote the chancellor of the German Empire and the first minister of Prussia from major to lieutenant general. The three nobles who were raised to be dukes held honorary military ranks and were proprietors of large entailed estates in East Elbia, two of them also serving as *Kammerherren,* or chamberlains: Baron von Bodschwingh-Plettenberg (hereafter Count von Plettenberg-Heeren), Baron von Richthofen, and Kleist-Retzow. Of the thirty-five promotions to hereditary nobility two were *geheime Kommerzienräte* and three court physicians, all the others being large agrarians and military and naval officers. The fourteen appointments to the Herrenhaus went to nobles, high public servants, and privy councilors, but included Edward Arnhold, Franz von Mendelssohn, and Bernhard Dernburg, three converted Jews, Dernburg being the controversial former minister of colonies. As for the decorations, they too were to reward or encourage loyalty and conformity. Wilhelm von Siemens and Georg von Simson (a Krupp board member) received the Order of the Crown, second and third class respectively, James Simon and Arnold Guilleaume the Red Eagle second class, while Arthur von Weinberg was designated *geheimer Regierungsrat*. Members of the liberal professions, including academics and artists— "the knights of the spirit" *(die Ritter vom Geist)*—were similarly honored. But again, the highest ranks in all the orders were reserved for Fleet Admiral von Tirpitz, Chief Court Chaplain Dryander, Lord Marshal Count zu Eulenburg, Prince Fürstenberg, Prince Solms-Baruth, and a complement of commanding generals. As Theodore Wolf noted in the *Berliner Tageblatt,* liberalism was kept away from the "banquet tables" and the emperor and his ministers gleefully exploited the *Bürgertum's* impotence.

Moreover, the emperor decorated Dr. Bovenschen, president of the Reichsverband gegen die Sozialdemokratie (Imperial Society *Against* Social Democracy), and Count Ernst von Reventlow, the editor of the archreactionary *Deutsche Tageszeitung,* thereby underscoring the ostracism of the Social Democrats, who absented themselves from the special jubilee sitting and dinner of the Reichstag. In addition, rather than take notice of the socialist-inspired free trade unions, the main body of organized labor, William II received delegations from the rival but compliant Protestant, Catholic, and National labor associations. He also reviewed what may well have been the most colorful event of the jubilee in Berlin: a procession of masters and journeymen of artisanal guilds ranging from bakers, blacksmiths, chimney sweeps, glassblowers, and coachmen to paper hangers, shoemakers, silversmiths, waiters, and wigmakers.

Equally striking was the sixtieth or diamond jubilee of Emperor Francis Joseph's apparently interminable reign, inaugurated in 1848. Even more than the ruling Hohenzollern, the senior Habsburg conspicuously put forward the members of his dynasty and all but secluded himself among them and his courtiers. Especially on this occasion the emperor surrounded himself with innumerable Habsburg arch and grand dukes and duchesses, as well as with military attendants. The gala evening at the Hofoper on December 2, 1908, was a particularly revealing occasion. Vienna's highest society was invited for a performance of *The Emperor's Dream* by Countess Christiane Thun-Solm, a specially commissioned one-act opera set in the time of Rudolf of Habsburg and celebrating the founding and accomplishments of the dynasty. Following an intermission the stellar audience reveled in *Aus der Heimat,* a musical by Joseph Hassreiter and Josef Bayer invoking the dances and songs of the major nationalities and culminating in an allegorical tableau in which all the peoples united to glorify the emperor. The foremost artists of both the Staatsoper and the Burgtheater actively participated in this apotheosis.

The first to arrive for this festive occasion were the higher officers of the army and general staff, who were assigned to standing room around the parquet circle. They were followed by an imposing cast of dignitaries, all of them in full-dress uniform, who occupied the choice orchestra seats: active and former ministers, top-ranking generals, upper civil servants, privy councilors, Hungarian magnates, and, in colorful vestments, Catholic prelates. There was only an occasional notable in civilian dress in a sea of uniforms: Dr. Weiskirchen and Dr. Starzynski, the president and vice-president of the lower house of parliament; Ambassador Baron Gali; former Finance Minister Dr. von Korytowski; and Baron Albert von Rothschild.

The loges, of course, were reserved for the top layers. Among those in the box seats of the third floor were the chancellor, Baron von Bienerth; the mayor of Vienna, Dr. Karl Lueger; and the police chief of the capital, Brzesowsky. The highest aristocracy occupied the loges of the second floor, along with the leading ambassadors. While the court retainers filled the parterre boxes, the archdukes Friedrich, Eugen, Rainer, Leopold Salvator, Karl Stephan, Josef Ferdinand, and Peter Ferdinand claimed the boxes of the first floor. Once they had made their great entrance, the emperor entered the great imperial loge on the same floor, dressed in his marshal's uniform and flanked by Duchess Maria Theresa von Württemberg and his oldest daughter, Princess Gisela von Bayern. The rest of the immediate family occupied the seats behind them. The 4,020 ennoblements, promotions, and decorations marking the jubilee fully confirmed this old-worldly status hierarchy of German Austria and hence of the Habsburg Empire.

Following a year's prescribed mourning for Alexander III, whose reign had been marked by an aristocratic reaction, Moscow in May 1896 became the scene for a coronation steeped in history, tradition, and religion. Having spent twenty-four hours in the outlying Petrovsky Palace, Nicholas II and Alexandra Feodorovna majestically moved first to the Alexandria and then to the Kremlin. The procession to the Kremlin was headed by mounted imperial guards, elite Cossacks, and Muscovite nobles. There followed on foot the court lackeys, the imperial hunt, and high government officials. Then came Nicholas, on his white horse, completely set apart, followed at a distance by the grand dukes of Russia and foreign princes, all of them on horseback.

Though colorful and imposing, this long procession paled in comparison with the short passage from the Red Staircase of the Kremlin to the Dormition Cathedral. On May 14, once the court choir had performed Tschaikovsky's "Fanfare," the Dowager Empress Maria Feodorovna headed the cortege to the coronation ceremony in Russia's holiest shrine. She walked under a canopy carried by sixteen high-ranking notables, her purple train brought up by four chamberlains and two masters of the hunt. No sooner was the dowager seated in the cathedral than thirty-two field officers brought a magnificent canopy held up by sixteen posts to the foot of the Red Stairs, where they were relayed by thirty-two generals. But it was only after Protopresbyter Yanyshev had sprinkled the procession path with holy water and two metropolitans had censed the Imperial Regalia at the entrance to the cathedral that Nicholas and Alexandra emerged to take their place under the canopy for the march to the high service. The emperor was attired in the uniform of the Preobrazhensky Guards and decorated with the orders of Alexander and Saint Andrew; his consort wore a dress of silver brocade embroidered by the sisters of the Ivanovsky Convent and topped with the Order of Saint Catherine. Once they arrived at the church they were escorted to two hallowed and precious thrones dating from the seventeenth and fifteenth centuries for the service to begin. Having kissed the cross held by the Metropolitan Pallady of St. Petersburg, Their Majesties were sprinkled with holy water and the tsar recited out loud the confession of the Orthodox faith. After Nicholas had risen and crossed himself three times, Count Miliutin brought the nine-pound imperial crown to the Petersburg metropolitan, who in turn handed it to the tsar of Russia to crown himself. Now wearing the crown and holding the scepter and the orb in his hands, the emperor reoccupied his throne. Immediately thereafter he freed his hands in order to place a small crown on the head of the empress, who knelt on a cushion before him. The coronation completed, Russia exploded into a paroxysm of joyful official receptions and popular festivals marred only by a stampede for free beer on Khodynskoe Field in which scores of people were either trampled to death or wounded.

Thirteen years later, in February 1913, Russia marked the tricentenary of Romanov rule. First in St. Petersburg and then in Moscow, Nicholas and Alexandra again acted the central role in the empire's theater of power. Notwithstanding major industrial and urban growth since the last great pageant in 1896, ancient rituals, symbols, and sacraments still freighted the principal ceremonial spectacles. The grandiose and brilliant procession from the Winter Palace to the Kazan Cathedral for the solemn *Te Deum* capped a full calendar of festivities. At the thanksgiving service the congregation of dignitaries consisted, as before, of high nobles, bureaucrats, officers, and diplomats, most of them with glittering swords and attired in resplendent uniforms covered with decorations and medals. Characteristically the Russian autocrat chose this notable occasion to create Baron V. B. Fredericks, minister of the imperial court, a count; to present a portrait of himself to his premier, Count V. N. Kokovtsev; to confer special orders on his ministers of war, navy, and foreign affairs; to offer a ceremonial cross to the metropolitan of St. Petersburg; and to confirm N. A. Maklakov, the prominent and ruthless diehard, as minister of internal affairs. Even more than his counterparts in Berlin and Vienna, the tsar intentionally all but ignored the nation's elected representatives. Michael Rodzianko, the ultraloyal president of the lower house, secured a few seats for Duma members in the cathedral with great difficulty, though neither they nor any of Russia's new men were asked to the gala dinners at the Winter Palace and the Imperial Opera's performance of Glinka's *A Life for the Tsar*. The imperial family's pilgrimage to Kostroma, seat of the first Romanov, and the observances in Moscow, Russia's real capital, were equally fixed. So were the tricentennial's officially sponsored exhibitions of restored icons and commissions for public buildings and statues.

On June 4, 1911, Rome celebrated the fiftieth anniversary of the unification of Italy. The principal ceremony was built around the inauguration of the teratogenic monument to Victor Emmanuel II, the first king of the new nation. The idea and public funds for this memorial were approved as far back as 1878, and Count Giuseppe Sacconi, whose design won the competition, was appointed chief architect in 1885. Significantly it was decided to place the monument on the Capitoline Hill, the capital's prestigious high point. The foundations were finally completed in 1892, when work aboveground began.

The day of the jubilee Victor Emmanuel III and Queen Helena proceeded in full state from the Quirinal to the ceremonial site. The veils having fallen away from the gilded statue, the royal party occupied the central platform immediately below the ponderous equestrian statue of Victor Emmanuel II and the altar of the Patria high above the level of the Piazza Venezia. The king and queen were surrounded by Queen Margherita, the duke and duchess of Genoa, the dukes of Aosta and the Abruzzi, Princess Letitia, and the prince of Udine. As a group they overshadowed the presiding officers of the two houses of parliament and Giolitti, the premier, who stood with them. They also dwarfed the senators and deputies assembled on a less protrusive platform of the multitiered royal shrine, which was crammed and overdecorated with bronze statuary, columns, vestibules, and fountains.

But the crowned heads did not reign by symbols and ceremonies alone. In fact, their sway owed much to their real resources and powers, of which they never hesitated to avail themselves. It bears repeating that the dynasts were Europe's largest landowners and as such felt themselves to be *primus inter pares* in the landed estate. The English crown lands stretched over 300,000 acres and included valuable properties in London. It was only fitting that a royal family with such vast estates should have four stately country residences besides Buckingham Palace. While British sovereigns were discreet about their landed and other possessions, William II by contrast personally reassured an assembly of landed Junkers in Königsberg in 1894 that as Germany's "greatest landowner" he shared their worries in what he knew to be difficult times for agriculture. As for Nicholas II, since his holdings were by far the greatest in Russia, he took no objection to being registered as "landowner" in the census of 1897.

The immense crown lands provided not only the income but above all the appropriate aura for sovereigns who in addition to being premier aristocrats were the sole founts of honors. Beyond this tacit prerogative to create and advance nobles, the emperor-kings of Germany, Austria-Hungary, and Russia were invested with power to appoint and dismiss ministers; issue ordinances; convoke, adjourn, and dissolve elective bodies; promulgate and enact laws; grant pardons; command the armed forces; make treaties; and decree martial law. In theory a limited parliamentary system was in force in all three empires —in Russia since 1905. In actual practice, the ministers remained exclusively responsible to the crown and not to the popular house. Admittedly, the lower chambers punctually tempered the will and willfulness of the monarchs, but they lacked not only the legal power but also the political discretion to curb them effectively and consistently. As a last resort, the imperial sovereigns could always ignore defiant legislatures; armed with emergency powers, they could either suspend or dissolve them, or call new elections, if need be after tampering with the franchise. The emperors of Germany, Austria-Hungary, and Russia excelled in the use of this tactic, and the heir to the Austrian throne even promised to outdo their imperiousness.

Of course, there were variations between the three empires in the constitution, custom, and practice of royal absolutism. The head of the House of Hohenzollern derived his panoply of powers less from being German emperor (he was not even "emperor of Germany") than from being king of Prussia, which was Europe's most concentrated and notorious seignorial and feudalistic outpost. There was no constitutional text to say where his authority as king ended and as kaiser began. At any rate, by virtue of exercising nearly unlimited power in Prussia, the largest state of the German Confederation and the one with a potent veto, William I and William II ruled the Continent's mightiest nation.

Francis Joseph I, who occupied his throne into his eighty-sixth year—longer than any other monarch—claimed some twenty titles, but he was first and foremost "Emperor of Austria and Apostolic King of Hungary." As of the turn of the century important landed elements of the Magyar ruling and governing class sought to bolster their own power by clamoring for greater autonomy for Transleithania under the dualist Compromise of 1867. When Francis Joseph failed to bridle them in his imperial capacity, he intervened in Budapest as the rightful holder of the Crown of Saint Stephen, confident that the *joint* armies were sworn and ready to do his will.

There were no such ambiguities about the constitutional and territorial locus of the Romanov crown. To be sure, Alexander III and Nicholas II vaunted their lordship over some fifty kingdoms, principalities, and provinces which had gradually been forged into a centralized state. But the clause of their interminable title that conveyed the full force of their iron grip was "Emperor and Autocrat of all Russians."

As for the powers of the king of England, over time they had, of course, been drastically trimmed in both law and customary practice. Even so, they were not inexistent. Benjamin Disraeli —the single most accomplished and effectual convert to the feudal element of the nineteenth century—actually recharged the dynastic office by proclaiming Queen Victoria empress of India. Hereafter in the oath administered by the archbishop of Canterbury, king-emperors—rather than emperor-kings— vowed to lawfully govern the peoples not only of the United Kingdom of Great Britain and Ireland but also of the domin- ions, the colonies, and the "Empire of India." The king was sworn to uphold the Protestant Reformed Church and to be the nominal fount of justice. Edward VII and George V prom- ised all of this and more, in what, even by the extravagant standards of their time, were the most glorious, bombastic, and stylized of Europe's coronations. The landed and aristo- cratic elements never doubted that the shimmering and mysti- cal splendor of the monarchy, heightened by the newfound imperial—not to say imperialist—luster, helped compensate for their contraction in the House of Commons, to which the king's ministers were responsible.

But even the British sovereigns retained executive respon- sibilities and advisory prerogatives beyond their ceremonial, representational, and authenticating functions. Because of the hallowed esteem in which they were held, they could and did abet, criticize, sometimes even obstruct certain policies of their cabinets. While Queen Victoria sustained her Conserva- tive ministries, she inhibited her Liberal governments, and George V asked for a second general election in 1910 during the House of Lords crisis as a precondition for agreeing—or agreeing to threaten—to pack the high chamber with pliable peers. In July 1914, when he was in close contact with Prime Minister Asquith, King George presumably favored interven- tion rather than neutrality in the Continental war, though he urged inordinate leniency toward the excesses of the Ulster rebels and their Tory sponsors.

The crown also had its word in the selection of prime ministers and cabinet members. Victoria chose Rosebery over Harcourt, while Edward VII influenced Arthur Balfour and Henry Campbell-Bannerman in the choice of some of their ministers. Both of them as well as George V allegedly stood over the appointment of the foreign secretary, the war minister, and some ambassadors and proconsuls. Predictably the foreign, military, imperial, and colonial services were special fiefs of the nobility as well as of aspirants to gentlemanly position and power. The English monarchy had no fist, and certainly no mailed fist. From Buckingham Palace, where the corridors of power were relatively well lit and straight, the crown reigned within the letter and spirit of the law, with subtlety and directness, but also without hastening the contraction of political society's feudal element, of which it was a benign but vital component.

Judging by the letter of the *Statuto,* the Italian throne was originally modeled after England's. But after 1870 sectionalism and government instability, which the wrangling of patronage parties and politics both expressed and aggravated, left the king of Italy much greater room to maneuver than his English counterpart enjoyed. With coalition cabinets falling apart and frequently re-forming, the crown was able to use to good advantage its prerogative of designating new prime ministers and sanctioning new elections. Although the Vatican and the Church kept their political reserve and the "black" aristocracy gathered around the papal court, much of the Catholic establishment silently but firmly joined the "white" aristocrats, the grandees of illustrious cities, and the service notables in rallying around the Quirinal. They did so because they considered the monarchy indispensable to the survival of a stable social order in a political regime haunted by the specter of Mazzinian republicanism. Accordingly Humbert I (1878–1900) and especially Victor Emmanuel III (1900–1946) of the House of Savoy—Europe's oldest reigning family—could always count on considerable support as they maneuvered in the interstices of a fragile constitutional system to consolidate and enlarge the royal prerogative. By the turn of the century, even leading conservative "Liberals" such as Baron Sidney Sonnino advocated restrengthening the power of the crown and Senate over the Camera to promote cabinet stability and to check social reform.

Historically the kings both subdued and upheld the nobilities. The nobilities of land and service needed the kings just as the kings needed the nobilities, but their mutual dependence was not symmetrical. Certainly by the second half of the nineteenth century the kings had become indispensable allies rather than dangerous rivals to the nobility. Of necessity they continued to champion policies of economic, military, and bureaucratic modernization that hastened the erosion of aristocratic privilege. But the crown had also become an essential rallying point for the feudal element in government that resisted sacrificing the landed nobilities to either bureaucratic or capitalist interests, or to a combination of both. The state was now the pivotal agency of aristocratic defense: in addition to protecting the nobility's and the gentry's property, it guaranteed respectable government places to their sons and to their own washouts. Even in France the kingless state continued to perform this function. Accordingly, political society served to perpetuate Europe's nobilitarian high society whose ostentatious life-style and presumption, which spanned national borders, demanded country castles and hunts, city villas and salons.

Not surprisingly, the nobilities eagerly participated in the court life which not only glorified the sovereign but also tightened his hold on his acolytes, both actual and potential. Besides being the principal locus of monarchial authority and pageantry, the court was the venerated and secluded social and cultural space in which members of the highest landed, service, and monied nobility vied to establish, maintain, and improve their standing in relation to the king and to each other. They did so for the usual mixture of reasons: power, wealth, prestige. Status and connections at court were the key to coveted sinecures in the royal household as well as to commanding positions in the government, the bureaucracy, the armed services, the Church, and the cultural establishment. For some posts competition was limited to descendants of the oldest, purest, and wealthiest aristocratic families; for others it was open to lesser and newer nobles, provided they had broken into court society themselves or through connections, usually after making large benefactions.

Although some courts were more exclusive than others—Vienna was much more select and snobbish than Berlin—intrigue and rivalry marked all of them. But none of this infighting among courtiers and different court factions in any way diminished the aura and lure of this exemplary leisure-class institution. This probity was maintained, in part, by assigning the highest and most conspicuous royal or imperial offices to illustrious and affluent peers who were as imperious as they were incorruptible. Accordingly, men of the finest pedigree of blood and land were appointed first chamberlain, grand marshal, great cupbearer, as well as master of ceremonies, of the hounds, of the stables, and commander of guard regiments. Of course, eminent noblewomen considered it a singular privilege to serve as mistress of the robes, lady-in-waiting, or lady of the bedchamber.

This innermost core of court society at once staged and performed in the royal repertoire of societal and diplomatic receptions, gala dinners, charity balls, and devotional services. While the courtiers did not prostrate themselves before Their Majesties on any of these occasions, they nevertheless followed a rigid protocol of ceremonial obeisance, vestment, and language. In turn, they initiated and drilled lesser nobles and mortals in this elaborate code of etiquette and precedence.

In all the monarchies every old, new, and would-be noble wanted to be *hoffähig,* to be invited and reinvited to court, and —*mirabile dictu*—to be graced with a royal visit at his city mansion or country estate. No matter how mannered, this ritualized and exclusive aristocratic game was far from empty. Whoever played it had to have both wealth and leisure. Although the conventions were similar all over, there were also distinct national or dynastic variations. The Austrian court was exceptionally rigid. Besides the extended Habsburg family only nobles with a direct lineage of fourteen generations were admitted to the highest functions, which included the extraordinary maundy ceremony at which Their Majesties knelt to wash the feet of twelve old men and twelve old women. In St. Petersburg the barriers were lowered to permit state officials of the top five ranks—after 1908 the highest four ranks—to witness the most exalted occasions. Incidentally, between the middle and the end of the nineteenth century the number of officials in the highest four grades rose by 1,000, from 850 to 1,850, while the incumbent masters of the Romanov court, hunt, and stable increased from 24 to 213. Crown and nobility continued to bestow both symbolic and real power upon each other.

In the capitals the royal and imperial courts were also the control centers of official culture. They hosted and sponsored operas, concerts, and plays; bought, commissioned, and exhibited paintings, sculptures, and furniture; and commissioned public buildings, monuments, and gardens. Kings and nobles played a key role in the promotion and reproduction of the visual, plastic, and performing arts that—as we will see in Chapter 4—perpetuated a persuasive ideology supportive of the *ancien régime.*

Obviously court society and culture strengthened the position of the throne as the centerpiece not only of the leisure class but also of the authority and hegemonic system. Even the diehard nobility and gentry that decried the state's promotion of capitalist and bureaucratic modernization for conservative purposes had no alternative but to remain loyal to the crown. While the royal sovereign personified and shielded the feudal element in political society, his court embodied and validated the archaic mentality and life-style that were their common patrimony.

In addition to the monarchs and their courts the "upper" chambers were redoubtable outposts of the feudal element or, as in the case of France, of the *grands notables,* among whom nobles and agrarians loomed large. Their founders having designed them as bulwarks of vested interests and privileges against ascending claimants, these select houses, councils, and senates never lost the marks of their origin.

Except for the French Senate, which by the turn of the century was entirely chosen by indirect election, these second chambers were nonelective. Membership was based on birth, wealth, and rank in public service, with a decided bias toward men of advanced age. With the usual exceptions, the members of these assemblies of notables were royal appointees or liege-men, in contradistinction to the popularly chosen lower houses which predated and constantly encroached on them. Nearly everywhere there was a mix of heredity and royal ap-pointment.

Britain alone had an upper chamber with a membership that except for a few bishops and judges was entirely hereditary, though the crown affected the composition through the yearly honors list. In 1911 only between 60 and 65 of the 570 heredi-tary peers in the House of Lords were business notables. Even though close to 100 were first-generation peers of nonlanded background—mainly recruited from among government serv-ants—the Lords remained a citadel of the landed aristocracy. Only 104 peers declared themselves to be Liberals, and 59 of these had been invested during the preceding twenty years.

No wonder that after the Second Reform Act of 1867 the predominantly Conservative House of Lords increasingly acted to amend and reject the progressive bills of Liberal governments. With periods of remission during Conservative administrations, this confrontation between Lords and Com-mons continued until 1914, and with particular intensity after 1890.

Between 1892 and 1895 the upper chamber defeated mea-sures concerning Irish home rule, Scottish local government, succession to real property, and employers' liability. Even at that time leading Liberals called for constraining the Lords, whose rights and responsibilities were enshrined in customary practice and not in statutes. In 1906 the Liberals were swept back into power to form the first cabinet in the history of England in which the majority of ministers, including the pre-mier, were nonaristocrats. Beginning with amendments to an education bill, the Lords resumed their petulant obstruction until finally, in 1909, they overwhelmingly vetoed the finance bill. They thereby intentionally challenged the House of Commons, whose fiscal prerogatives had become established in practice over three centuries but were not without ambiguity. In turn, the Liberals moved a parliament bill to reduce formally the hereditary and ordained peers in relation to the elected representatives.

The trigger for the Lords' audacious move was a benign land tax that Lloyd George, the "Radical-Liberal" chancellor of the exchequer, had put into the budget, presumably to taunt the Lords into overreacting. He charged that England's government continued to be monopolized by "the leisured classes who had nothing else to do except govern others" and who derived their power from "ten thousand people [being the] owners of the soil and the rest of us trespassers in the land of our birth." Not surprisingly, the proposed levy along with the irreverent rhetoric infuriated the normally poised peerage. In the House of Lords 112 temporal peers and 2 bishops pressed for a showdown with Commons, which with their siege mentality they feared forever lost to England's long-regnant elite. Who were these diehards who in addition to mobilizing the upper house hoped to galvanize the king, the army, and the Unionist party into making a last-ditch stand? They were neither impoverished aristocrats nor political backwoodsmen. The vast majority of the ditchers were large landed proprietors, and in their ranks they counted not a few privy councilors, former cabinet ministers, imperial proconsuls, officers of the Unionist party, and leaders of the new social imperialist leagues. Their aggressive defense of the old and imperial regime was led by such towering notables as the dukes of Bedford, Norfolk, Somerset, and Westminster; the fourth marquess of Salisbury; the earls of Halsbury, Selborne, and Plymouth; Viscount Llandaff; and Lords Milner and Roberts.

It took two years to prevail on the peers to abandon their own intransigents and vote the bill to reduce the Lords' veto to a limited delaying power. This outcome was achieved only after the government had called an extraordinary general election, the king had intimated that the Lords might be packed with compliant peers, and Sir Arthur Balfour, the august Conservative leader in Commons, had thrown his full weight behind an accommodation.

Having lost what they considered only the first skirmish in their campaign to reclaim the political power essential to their economic, social, and cultural survival, the ultras moved to exploit the Ulster resistance for their own purposes. To brace themselves for this counteroffensive, they engineered the removal of the conciliatory Balfour in favor of the tough-minded Bonar Law, who became the first commoner without the aristocratizing passion to lead the Conservative party.

While the Conservatives in the Lords flexed their remaining constitutional powers by defiantly voting to delay the new Irish home rule bill in 1912 and 1913 (along with three other measures), Bonar Law all but supported Sir Edward Carson's extraparliamentary opposition. After endorsing the Ulster covenant Carson and his lieutenants proceeded to drill paramilitary volunteers and to organize gunrunning. Encouraged by high Tories and unrestrained by the crown, England's opposition leader and shadow prime minister justified direct action in contravention of law and parliament. In 1912 Bonar Law denounced the Liberal government for being "a revolutionary committee which seized by fraud upon despotic power," and declared that there were "things stronger than parliamentary majorities." He also asserted that should home rule be imposed on Ulstermen "they would be justified in resisting by all means in their power," eventually adding that he could "imagine no length of resistance to which Ulster [could] go in which [he] would not be prepared to support them." By late 1913, in a speech in Dublin, Bonar Law even incited British troops in Ulster to refuse to enforce home rule, if ordered to do so. These and similar pronouncements by other prominent Conservatives in Britain encouraged the mutiny of officers on the Curragh in March 1914 in which General Sir Henry Wilson, the Ulster-born chief of the general staff, was unabashedly complicit.

Meanwhile George V bent his neutrality in favor of the insurgent Ulsterites, who loudly professed obeisance to him while violating the laws he was sworn to uphold. Uncertain of the support of the king and the loyalty of the army, Asquith and his closest advisers hesitated to ask for Sir Henry's resignation. Instead they sought to appease the extremists in Ulster and their coadjutors in England. Indeed, the Liberal cabinet was at an impasse, and so was England's parliamentary system: to prosecute or arrest diehard Orangemen might necessitate the arrest of Carson, and a move against Carson could escalate into a move against Bonar Law, the leader of the Opposition. The coming of the war in July–August 1914 helped the Liberal administration and the parliamentary system out of an explosive stalemate. This political impasse was a direct consequence of the refusal of the tempestuous landed peers in the upper house and their aggressive associates in the Unionist party to accept a stringent curtailment of their privileged and unrepresentative power.

If England's upper chamber was so intractable well into the new century, its German equivalent could hardly be expected to be less refractory. Since Prussia practically controlled the German Confederation, its own parliamentary institutions were quite as important as those of the Imperial Diet. The Prussian Herrenhaus, or house of peers, was entirely a creation of the king, who was free to make as many appointments as he wished provided he made them hereditary or for life. In 1913 this chamber had 402 seats, divided into three classes. The first category consisted of 117 hereditary princes of royal blood *(erbliche Berechtigungen):* 1 head of the House of Hohenzollern; 22 heads of the princely houses of the erstwhile Holy Roman Empire; 51 peers *(Fürsten, Grafen, und Herren);* and 43 members of noble families who had been awarded hereditary entailments by royal command. The second category included 105 life members, 4 of whom occupied Prussia's highest state offices, and other ranking personalities of exceptional fidelity to the crown. The remaining 190 lifetime seats went by royal appointment to individuals nominated by corporate bodies: 3 by religious bodies, 126 by associations of noble landowners, 10 by universities, and 51 by cities.

In social-professional terms three-fourths of the membership of Prussia's upper chamber was noble. Without counting any of the 117 hereditary members, there were alone 71 agrarians and 106 military officers (59 retired, 47 on active service). Such an assembly of grand peers, great landowners, and prominent state notables was certain to be intensely loyal to the Prussian king and authoritarian tradition.

This Prussian house of peers shared its power with a Landtag, or representative chamber, which, given its mode of election and composition, was really a second upper chamber. Although the principle of popular suffrage was recognized, the Prussian franchise, fixed in 1849–1853, was glaringly unequal, indirect, and nonsecret. In other words, whereas the eviscerated federal Reichstag that so disquieted the feudal element was elected by universal male franchise, Prussia's lower house, which wielded considerably greater power, was chosen by an electoral law that even Bismarck once characterized as uniquely "senseless and wretched." But neither the Iron Chancellor nor his four successors, who except for an interval under Caprivi simultaneously served as minister-presidents of Prussia, ever proposed a thorough reform of this extravagant franchise precisely because it assured them a second upper house in the guise of a popular assembly.

Above all, this franchise was unequal, in that in each electoral district all eligible voters—the primary electors—were divided into three classes according to the amount of taxes they paid: the first class consisted of the electors paying the first third of the combined tax roll, the second of those paying the second third of the total, and the third of those paying the remaining third, including those who paid no taxes at all. The voters in each of these three groups voted separately, by absolute majority, and by open inscription (ballot) one-third of the electors to which their district was entitled (one elector for every 250,000 inhabitants). In their turn, these electors chose the representatives.

Regardless of the actual number of primary voters in each of the three electoral classes, each class voted the same number of electors. The result was a tremendous disproportion in favor of the wealthy ruling class and against the lower orders. Taking Prussia as a whole in 1908, of every 10,000 eligible voters 382 voted in the first class, 1,386 in the second, and 8,232 in the third (in 1914: 3 to 5 percent, 10 to 12 percent, 85 percent). Out of a total of 29,000 electoral districts there were 2,200 districts in which a single voter constituted the entire first class, as in the case of Krupp in Essen. Since 1848 Prussia had, of course, experienced major population shifts and changes in favor of cities and industrial districts. Even so, there had been only minimal reapportionment and redistricting, with the result that Prussia's lower house remained preeminently rural and agrarian. In 1913, 140 out of 440, or slightly over 31 percent of all the representatives, were landowners, as over 28 industrialists and 9 merchants. The representation of the parties reflected this same disproportion between country and city: while the 16.6 percent of the primary electors who voted Conservative secured 48.2 percent of the total representation, the 23.8 percent who voted Socialist secured a bare 1.4 percent. Ultimately the noble Junkers in eastern Prussia were the principal beneficiaries of this three-tiered suffrage, for in the elections of 1913 the Conservative and Free Conservative parties, which were their primary political vehicles, still captured 148 and 54 seats, or 202 out of a total of 443 seats. In addition, they had common interests with the Catholic Centrists, who were substantially agrarian and won 103 seats, and with the "industrialist" National Liberals, with whom they logrolled and who secured 73 seats. As for the Social Democrats, they had to settle for barely 10 seats although they polled nearly the same popular vote as the Catholics.

By virtue of the three-class franchise and the congealed apportionment and districting, the feudal element controlled the Prussian house of representatives in addition to dominating the Prussian Herrenhaus, ministerial council, bureaucracy, and army, as well as the Hohenzollern throne and court. In turn, this essentially coherent political society spawned the Prussian delegation to the Bundesrat, or upper chamber of the Second Empire's bicameral parliament, whose lower house was the Reichstag. Instead of representing the people of the confederation's member states, the delegations in the Bundesrat represented the state governments. The imperial constitution assigned each state a fixed number of votes in rough proportion to its size, population, and general importance. For example, the three free cities had a quota of one vote each, Brunswick had two, Baden three, Saxony four, and Bavaria six. Although less than proportionate to its overall demographic and economic weight, Prussia's seventeen votes gave it by far the single largest and most decisive voice in the Bundesrat. Under the constitution, the premier state had an absolute veto in military and tax matters and sufficient votes to block constitutional amendments. Moreover, since Prussia virtually controlled the three votes of Waldeck and Brunswick, it needed to corral only ten additional votes to dispose of an absolute majority.

The Bundesrat, in which Prussia was supreme, was not a deliberative assembly but a council of ambassadors from member states. Each member state was prepresented by a delegation of appointed state officials—usually including a minister or even the minister-president—who cast the votes of their state as a single bloc on explicit instructions from their home government. In addition to fielding the most formidable delegation, Prussia held further sway because the emperor-king appointed the imperial chancellor, who both presided over the Bundesrat and was a member of the Prussian delegation. Moreover, Prussia dominated the twelve committees in which this upper chamber dispatched all important work behind closed doors.

To the extent that Germany had a bicameral parliament, effective power was vested in this federal council rather than in the Reichstag. For the emperor-king appointed the chancellor, who used his commanding position in the Bundesrat to move that upper chamber to adopt the bills which he then placed before the lower house. Although it was highly desirable to win the approval of the popularly elected Reichstag, it was not essential. After all, the chancellor and his ministers were exclusively responsible to the crown, which, along with them and the Bundesrat, governed in the name of Prussia's feudalistic civil and political society.

In the Dual Monarchy the upper houses were equally archaic. The Herrenhaus of the Reichsrat, or parliament of Austria, was composed of princes of the imperial family, of archbishops and other high prelates, of the heads of big and noble landowning families who were granted hereditary seats by the emperor, and of between 150 and 170 notables with lifetime appointments. Similarly, the Table of Magnates (Förendihaz), or upper house of the Hungarian parliament, was an assembly of some 300 eminent noble magnates who held hereditary seats along with the highest dignitaries of the Catholic, Protestant, and Greek Orthodox churches, as well as 50 lesser magnates and 50 other personalities with lifetime appointments. Although the emperor-king elevated ennobled businessmen, professionals, and academicians into the high chambers of Vienna and Budapest, they went unnoticed in what were preserves of the landed aristocracy.

Russia also had a State Council, or upper chamber. The tsar appointed fully one-half of the councilors from among high civil and military state servants. Large estate owners, the nobility, the clergy, and provincial zemstvos dominated by an unprogressive gentry elected the other half. In all, only 18 seats were assigned to notables drawn from industry, commerce, and the professoriate.

The Italian Senate shared many family resemblances with all these upper chambers. Inevitably there were the princes of the House of Savoy, who, being prerogative members, gave this assembly its royal imprint. All the other members were lifetime appointments by the king, guided by the nominations of the prime minister. Of 360 to 400 senators, 100 were high civil, military, and judicial officials; 100, ex-deputies (having served at least six years); and 100, wealthy notables paying over 3,000 lire in taxes. The remaining 60 to 100 senators were chosen from among prominent members of learned societies, including universities, and other individuals who had served the nation with exceptional distinction. Since there was no membership limit, at least 40 new senators were appointed all together on three separate occasions—1886, 1890, 1892—in order to break the Senate's veto or delay of legislation voted by the Camera (chamber of deputies). Clearly, between the two houses, the upper chamber was by far the more conservative, not least because it was weighted with a substantial feudal element.

Even the upper chamber of the third French republic contained vestiges of this legacy. Following the fall of Louis Napoleon and the crushing of the Commune, above all the divided monarchists pressed for the establishment of a senate. They looked to an upper chamber to check the radical impulses of the lower house and to serve as Trojan horse to subvert the nascent regime in the interest of a royal restoration. Admittedly, the ultramonarchists became altogether irreconcilable. But impressed by the stabilizing influence of both the notables and the peasants of rural France, especially the center right, led by the duc de Broglie, decided to support Thiers's republic on condition that it be tempered by a safe senate. Needless to say, any such chamber and compromise were anathema to ultrarepublicans. But in spite of this radical opposition—or because of it—the center left of pragmatic republicans decided to accept the senate in exchange for the center right's acquiescence to a republic that the two centers were equally determined to keep conservative.

The law of February 1875 fixing the composition of the Senate was one of the fledgling republic's major constitutional transactions, and also one of its supporting arches. Of 300 senators, 75 were chosen for life by the two chambers sitting jointly (as the National Assembly). Special electoral colleges in each department selected the other 225 for a term of nine years, one-third of the senators to be replaced every three years. The electoral college of each department was made up of officials previously elected to other public offices: the members of the Chamber of Deputies, the members of the General Council, the councilors of the arrondissements, and one delegate from each of the communal councils. All in all, this electoral arrangement was designed to guarantee the wanton overrepresentation of the villages and towns over Paris and the major cities. The Senate became a chamber of political and administrative officials who were rooted in small towns of between 600 and 5,000 inhabitants, which down to 1914 changed ever so slowly and whose economic, social, and cultural moderation was sustained by the large farmers and small peasants of the surrounding countryside.

Nor was the Senate purely decorative and impotent. One of its powers was to sit jointly with the lower chamber to elect the president of the republic, and certainly the conservative impulsions in the Senate significantly helped Poincaré's election to that office in January 1913. In addition, quite apart from its power of initiative in all but fiscal matters, the upper house had to approve the bills passed by the lower house. In this regard it demonstrated a remarkable capacity to delay, not to say obstruct, the legislative process. Especially as of 1907 the Senate systematically blocked social, tax, and electoral reform and opposed the lowering of the military service from three to two years as part of a comprehensive drive for social defense orchestrated by Poincaré. Clearly, the Senate not only cemented but also acted to preserve stagnant against dynamic France—rural over urban France—and as such contributed to the political stalemate, the rock on which inchoate cabinets kept foundering.

Of all the institutions of political society the lower house of parliament was the only one to register and promote the pulsations of industry and commerce centered in rapidly growing cities, industrial zones, and mining basins. In a broad European perspective, however, these popular chambers were not only seriously flawed but also beleaguered. Whether the franchise was universal or limited, the electoral arrangements in all countries gave disproportionate weight to the rural areas in the lower legislatures. In England and France, which had general male suffrage, this rural bias may well have mitigated the intense clash between their lower and upper houses in 1910–1914. However, in the lower houses of Germany and Austria, which were also chosen by universal franchise, this same bias made it that much more difficult to mount an effective challenge to absolutism. The result was that in mid-1914 the German Reichstag was in gangrenous limbo while the Austrian Reichsrat, which was also weighed down by ethnic conflicts, was suspended indefinitely. In Hungary and Russia the franchise was deliberately framed to make the lower houses safe for the landed estate. Even so, in 1914 the Table of Deputies (Képriselöhaz) was prorogued in Budapest while the Duma was living on borrowed time in St. Petersburg. In Rome, meanwhile, the precipitate and politically inspired adoption of universal male suffrage in mid-1912, which overnight expanded the electorate fourfold, unsteadied a Camera that was congenitally frail.

Universal manhood suffrage for the popular house made its way gradually. While France reconfirmed it in 1875, England effected it in three stages between 1867 and 1918, Germany in 1871, Austria in 1907, and Italy in 1912. In Russia the revolt of 1905 unexpectedly gave the general franchise a fleeting but aborted life. In Hungary, meanwhile, the Magyar governing class resolutely stood against the democratic vote even at the price of prolonging Budapest's subordination to Vienna. Only England, France, and Germany dispensed with property, tax, and educational qualifications before the turn of the century. But even in these three countries, as in all others, apportionment, districting, and gerrymandering continued to weight the elections for the lower houses in favor of villages and towns over cities, of agriculture over industry. The force of deference and religion also furthered the rural vote disproportionately. Deferential attitudes forged in social relations almost naturally spilled over into political behavior. Since the predisposition of the lowborn to venerate and follow the highborn was more pronounced in old, small, and slow-moving rural and provincial communities than in rapidly growing, sprawling, and restless cities, local notables were the chief beneficiaries of the conversion of social into political deference.

As ranking members of the local notabilities, clergymen—priests, pastors, ministers, rabbis—were particularly well placed to mobilize and channel the political preferences of their flock, usually in support of spokesmen for feudal, agrarian, and preindustrial elements. In fact, with the extension of the franchise and the rise of political parties to muster the votes of the urban middle class, *petite bourgeoisie,* and proletariat, the men of God put their prestige and congregations in the service of conservatives generally and feudal elements in particular. Except in France, the political champions of the old regime were able to harness the deferential sway not only of the altar but also of the crown, the sword, and the flag. And even in France, notwithstanding political society's anticlericalism, the Catholic Church, along with the army, the tricolor, and the empire, became an increasingly important moderating force among republicans.

The franchise extensions and electoral reforms of the last third of the nineteenth century certainly hastened the political contraction of the landed elites in England. In 1868 landowners, notably the wealthier and most aristocratic among them, still claimed two-thirds of the seats in Commons, preeminently on the Conservative benches. By 1886 they had dropped to one-half, and after 1906, when the expanded franchise began to tell, they were reduced to little more than one-tenth of the house membership. Of course, this decline became particularly pronounced with the victories of the Liberal party, which the landed gentry had long since abandoned for the Conservatives. In fact, the Conservative-Unionist party became the choice meeting ground of the old nobility of land with the new nobility of finance, commerce, and industry. Although the landed interest lost its numerical primacy in this mighty amalgam, it maintained much of its influence and power, partly by virtue of its political leverage in the countryside. With their tenants beholden to them, the aristocratic landlords remained pre-eminent in the "rotten" counties, which continued to outvote the boroughs in parliament and which provided the Conservatives in particular with an overly large proportion of their seats. In 1902, 50 percent of all Conservative MPs were landowners, and in 1910, 26 percent, as over 7 percent of all Liberals.

But the landed classes did not yield political control commensurate with this decline in the number of their candidates for and members of Commons. Above all, they and their associates stayed in command of the Conservative cabinets. The landed aristocracy and gentry provided over half of the members of every cabinet until 1905, when the Liberals, led by Campbell-Bannerman, began to govern by leave of the Irish and Labour. The old aristocrats were now outnumbered in government. Finally, in 1908, they were also dislodged from the premiership, Asquith being the first "commoner" since Disraeli to climb to the top.

The Liberal party and cabinets were significantly less aristocratic, especially once many of the Whig notables had defected to the Tories. In 1910 only 7 percent of the Liberal MPs were landowners, while 66 percent came from commerce and industry and 23 percent from the liberal and learned professions. The party was broadly based in the middle class of the boroughs, and many of its leaders shared that social provenance.

Even so, the Liberals were far from being purely or dominantly middle class. While Campbell-Bannerman was the son of a wealthy businessman who, after acquiring an estate in Scotland, had secured the title of James Campbell of Strathcaro, Asquith was an attorney with aristocratic pretensions. Although commoners were in the majority in both their governments, from 1906 to 1916, 49 percent of the cabinet ministers (25 out of 51) came from families with hereditary titles, or, using a more rigorous definition, 34 percent were descendants of families with hereditary titles dating back at least two generations. Furthermore, of the 51 ministers of the three Liberal administrations, 20 had studied at Oxford and 16 at Cambridge, and 25 had gone to select public schools, 12 of them to Eton and 5 to Harrow. These educational institutions specialized in blending the sons of prominent and successful commoners into a ruling and governing class whose ethos continued to be markedly more aristocratic than its membership. Moreover, notwithstanding the prominence of a few middle-class politicians of modest means, especially under Asquith, most of the cabinet members had either inherited or married wealth, which made them upper middle class and meant that they had closer associations with the time-honored establishment than with their middle-class base.

In France the concern for social order and moderation that shaped the Senate in 1875 also left its imprint on the electoral arrangements for the Chamber of Deputies. Even the republicans, not to mention the center rightists and monarchists, faced the larger cities with caution, not to say apprehension. Admittedly, in the late Second Empire and after the fall of Sedan the republicans had made their political fortunes in the dynamic parts of France, notably in the major cities, and especially in Paris. But then the *communaux* rose not only in the capital but also in Lyons, Marseilles, and Bordeaux, with the result that the republicans began to both fear and abhor the urban masses. No doubt Thiers and his rightist supporters deliberately overreacted to the Paris Commune, denouncing as a savage and irreconcilable socialist insurrection what they knew to be a patriotically infused explosion of Jacobin republicanism. Even so, all but a few republicans rallied around the *versaillais* and condoned even their worst excesses during and after the infamous *semaine sanglante* of late May 1871.

In any case, trapped in the logic of preventive counterrevolution, unable to dispense with Thiers, and fearful of the urban plebs, the republicans themselves were eager to envelop the cities by overweighting the lower chamber in favor of rural society, including the *petite bourgeoisie* of provincial towns. Accordingly, the electoral system was designed to magnify the weight of immobile over dynamic France in *both* houses of parliament.

Admittedly the number of large and medium landowners in the lower chamber declined from 141 out of 576 in 1889 (25 percent) to 90 out of 597 in 1910 (15 percent). But though these delegates of the commercialized sector of French agriculture lost much ground, the same cannot be said of the representatives of the small peasant proprietors and tenants of the villages and the closely related lower middle class of provincial towns. For the electoral system divided the nation into arrondissements, each of which was entitled to one deputy. Should the inhabitants in these original election districts exceed 100,000, they could claim an additional representative for each additional 100,000 or fraction thereof, the districts being divided into a corresponding number of arrondissements. Obviously, this apportionment and its attendant districting made for rural overrepresentation, since the countryside had many arrondissements of considerably less than 100,000 and several of a mere few thousand voters. In 1875, northern France was assigned only 220 deputies even though it had a population of 19 million, while the 16 million of the less industrial and urban southern half were allotted 280. For having 3 million fewer people, the south received a bonus of 60 deputies.

Moreover, the *scrutin d'arrondissement,* which except for the election of 1885 survived down to 1919, favored the local notables. Needless to say, the old landed lords continued to reign by virtue of the fixed deference, loyalty, and mentality of rural populations, and often they had the collaboration of the clergy, which was in the enviable position of being able to influence and deliver votes. But with time the "new" notables of the decentralized Radical party surpassed them in importance. These Radical politicians extended their control over the open countryside and villages by virtue of their prestigious positions in provincial towns, where they were either professionals—lawyers, notaries, physicians, veterinarians—or grain, wine, and cattle dealers. These provincial "bourgeois," not unlike time-honored landlords and priests, claimed to be exceptionally well placed to understand the peasant mind and interest. In the assembly these landlords, most of them latent or avowed monarchists, and these inurbane bourgeois, most of them opportunist republicans, formed a farm block ranging from some 300 deputies around 1890 down to 200 around 1910.

In the face of what was perceived as a mounting urban and industrial challenge, especially after the Dreyfus case, the royalists reluctantly rallied to the republic while the Radicals modulated their anticlericalism. In times of normalcy these

rural elements provided pivotal support for centrist governments that improved the status quo with flexibly conservative
economic and social policies. But in times of unsettlement
when politics became polarized, the agrarian alliance became
a force for unpliant conservatism, not to say reaction. Of
course, the electoral geography of nonurban France was very
diverse, there being enormous variations in economic structure, patterns of settlement, religious practice, and political
tradition: while the west, *massif central,* and east were distinctly
right-wing and clerical, the south, the center, the north, and
the area around Paris were republican and religiously temper-
ate. Still, even the most "leftist" rural regions were relatively
moderate in economic, social, and cultural terms, and they
became ever more so after the turn of the century.

Even though the Reichstag in Germany was severely shack-
led, its franchise was carefully regulated so as to constrict the
voice of urban and industrial districts. From the outset in 1871
the 397 one-member constituencies were unequal. As a general rule each district was to have 100,000 inhabitants, or
roughly 20,000 voters. In practice many constituencies had
considerably smaller or larger populations, and these deviations from the norm increased with time. Even though Germany's population jumped from 40 million to 65 million
between 1870 and 1914, the constituencies remained unchanged for the entire life of the Second Empire. Solidly implanted in the countryside, the Conservatives and Catholic
Centrists strongly opposed either reapportionment or redistricting for fear of losing their privileged electoral leverage to
the cities that were not only the principal sites of this demographic explosion but also the magnets for internal migration.

Naturally enough, under the federal principle even midget
states like Schaumburg-Lippe and Waldeck, which had only
around 10,000 electors each, were entitled to their deputy. But
they contributed less to rural overrepresentation than eastern
Prussia, Pomerania, Silesia, and Posnan. The electoral districts
of these predominantly agricultural provinces retained their
seats in spite of their stationary or declining populations. Not
surprisingly, in 1907 the Conservatives secured 45 of their 60

seats in these territories, and in 1912 only 4 of their 43 seats came from outside Prussia. In turn, the feudalistic and agrarian elements of these and other rural districts resisted any increase in the representation of the fast-growing industrial provinces of western and central Prussia as well as of Saxony, and of cities like Hamburg, Bremen, and of course Berlin. Accordingly, while the number of eligible electors all along remained essentially unchanged and below the national average (15,500 in 1912) in the agrarian provinces, it rose to over 100,000 in Bochum in the Ruhr and to over 200,000 in one of the circumscriptions of the imperial Prussian capital. In fact, even with nearly 1 million qualified electors Greater Berlin continued to be limited to its original 8 deputies.

Ultimately this freeze of the electoral system enormously bolstered the representational base of the old order. In 1907 the Conservatives won each of their 60 Reichstag seats with an average of around 26,000 votes, though they needed only 10,500 votes to capture each of their 20 seats in Prussia. The Social Democrats were not nearly so well placed. Although they polled more than twice as many votes as the Conservatives in Prussia, they returned only 6 deputies, each with an average of 77,500 votes, or seven times the Conservative average. In national terms their disadvantage was considerably smaller, but not trivial. Each of the 43 Socialist deputies became the spokesman for an average of 69,000 electors, or 43,000 more than the Conservative average. Incidentally, thanks to their rural bastions the Catholic Centrists scored proportionately better results than the Social Democrats: with nearly the same popular vote they elected close to two and a half times as many deputies, each of them representing 29,600 electors, which was close to the Conservative average.

To be sure, the Socialists reduced their handicap by electing 110 deputies with 4.25 million votes in 1912. Even so, with 34.8 percent of all the votes they returned only a bare 28 percent of the deputies, and each deputy still spoke for as many as 40,000 electors. Understandably the leaders of Social Democracy were dispirited by what they realized was a hollow victory: not only was the Reichstag impotent, but even now that they had by far the largest parliamentary delegation the Socialists were unable to effect a change in the electoral arrangements of the empire and the three-class franchise of Prussia, both of which disproportionately served the *ancien régime.*

In the other European countries, which were overwhelmingly rural and where the suffrage either broadened gradually or remained altogether constricted, the feudalistic and agrarian bias was hardly less pronounced. Initially less than 2.5 percent of the population was eligible to vote in postunification Italy. The first reform of the all-male franchise came in January 1882. Reducing tax requirements from 40 to 19 lire and the voting age from twenty-five to twenty-one tripled the electorate to 2 million, or 6.9 percent of the population, of whom only around 60 percent, or 1.2 million, exercised their franchise. While the literacy test remained fully in force for a population that was 62 percent illiterate—the illiteracy rate being much higher in the south and the countryside—the tax qualification was waived not only for those making relatively substantial mortgage or rent payments but for members of academies, university professors, and high functionaries, most of whom were in any case well off. At any rate, the entire system favored local notables, who used the force of their deference and patronage, as well as the pork barrel, to win and hold small electorates in single-member districts, the majority of which were rural and safe. With the industrial bourgeoisie practically nonexistent until the turn of the century—even up north—the old urbane elites continued to dominate the cities. An amalgam of latifundists, merchant capitalists, and high public officials, these municipal ruling and governing classes rather easily lorded over the *petite bourgeoisie,* whose political participation was modest and unobtrusive.

When the number of eligible voters reached about 9.5 percent of the population in 1892, some 900,000 were stricken from the electoral rolls for inadequate literacy, with the result that in 1895 and 1897 the roll was again down to less than 7 percent. In the meantime, the Socialists and advanced Democrats in particular pressed for unrestricted male suffrage.

Eventually in June 1912, when illiteracy was down to 38 percent and receding rapidly, Giolitti had the universal franchise enacted as part of his pre-emptive strategy of integrating the lower urban and rural orders into the existing civil and political order. The danger of destabilization seemed to vanish as Pope Pius X allowed the Church to abandon the *non-expedit* to enter the lists for the forces of order. Of course socialist, syndicalist, and anarchist leaders made every effort to rally the urban and rural proletariat as well as sectors of the artisanate. But Catholic leaders, both clerical and lay, managed to counterbalance and countervail them by rallying the still heavily illiterate small and medium peasantry and the lower middle class of towns and cities, leaving a moderately reformist governing class to run political society.

In any case, under the new franchise the electorate rose from 2.9 million in 1909 to 8.4 million in 1913. With the Gentilone pact the Church enjoined Catholics to vote not only for Conservatives but even for Liberals in constituencies where a three-cornered contest risked leaving the seat to the defiant forces of change, which were also anticlerical. That there was neither reapportionment nor redistricting to take account of population changes in nonrural Italy was an additional guarantee that the Camera would not be lost to industry, the new urban centers, and the proletariat.

For forty years the lower house of the Austrian Reichsrat was elected by a singularly restrictive and complicated franchise. All eligible male voters were divided into four classes that tended to vote as a body for the representative of their district, except for the great landowners, who, save for those of Bohemia and Galicia, elected their representatives on a separate ticket. The house consisted of 253 seats with a fixed number of seats assigned to each class. In 1873, out of a population of 20.5 million, 1.2 million, or 17 percent, cast their unequal ballots as follows: the 4,930 great (noble) landowners elected 85 deputies, or one for every 59 voters; the 1.1 million voters in rural communes (indirectly) elected 129 deputies, or one for every 8,400 voters; the 500 members of the chambers of commerce, 21 deputies, or one for every 23 voters; and 186,300 city voters, 118 deputies, or one for every 1,580 voters. Clearly, this suffrage was tailored to suit in particular the great noble families and prosperous peasants—they kept hold of over 60 percent of the seats—but also wealthy businessmen, notably merchants.

It took until 1896 for the imperial regime, under Count Casimir Badeni, to give an unrestricted but minor voice to the lower orders. It created a fifth curia of general voters and increased the house membership to 425. Presently some 3.1 million elected the additional 72 deputies, or one for about every 69,500 voters. Although the franchise was not significantly democratized, the fifth class did offer greater representation to the national minorities.

Finally in 1907, again in the face of stiff opposition from the Austro-German landed nobility, Max Vladimir von Beck managed to put through the universal male suffrage. Indeed, in the elections of 1911 the grand nobles were all but eliminated from the popular house, which was left with only one duke, one prince, and four counts. But instead of expiring peacefully, the German Conservatives threw their weight to the Christian Socials, who mobilized the lower middle class of the major cities to destroy what remained of the Liberals. With 96 deputies the Christian Socials became the single largest parliamentary group, followed by 87 Social Democrats. But these figures were not all that meaningful, for the number of seats had been raised to 516, of which 45 percent were apportioned to the Austro-Germans, 21 percent to the Czechs, 16 percent to the Poles, and 18 percent to the other national minorities.

Whereas the old electoral system had encouraged representation by class and status with only limited regard for national impulses, the new national quotas reversed the process. Accordingly, the Reichsrat of 1911 was saturated with 36 essentially national factions. Even though these three dozen mini-groups tended to draw together into a dozen national "clubs" or delegations, no effective majority could form. There were simply too many irreconcilable cross-pressures not only among but also within the major national groups.

With few exceptions, they were heavily mortgaged to agrarian interests and rural constituencies; this was the case even for the Czechs. At any rate, the constitutionally cramped chamber became ever more divided, chaotic, and deadlocked until finally, in 1914, the emperor prorogued it, earning himself the plaudits of Austro-Germany's overweening ruling and governing class.

Compared to Austria's pre-Beck electoral system, Hungary's was both simpler and more preclusive. All nobles were entitled to vote, and so were all commoners making tax payments whose level varied regionally according to the property or income that was assessed. Moreover, to be eligible, voters had to be able to speak Magyar, since balloting was public and by voice. The 6 percent of the population that was eligible was certain to return a chamber that was predominantly agrarian and Magyar. In 1910, of the 413 members—the Croatian diet elected an additional 40 deputies—some 42 percent were gentry and 16 percent were landed aristocrats. Barely 5 percent were commoners by provenance and economic activity. Whatever the dissensions within the house—and they were acute—they reflected cleavages within the narrow Magyar ruling and governing class rather than between them and either the bourgeoisie or the national minorities.

With the Socialists much weaker in Transleithania than in Cisleithania, there was little pressure for radical suffrage reform, even after the turn of the century. Just the same, to soothe the bad conscience of small but respected circles of enlightened intellectuals and aristocrats, in 1913 Count Stephen Tisza introduced two changes to make the electoral system appear less undemocratic: balloting became secret in the cities, and the voting prerequisites became educational instead of fiscal. Although there was, of course, a high correlation between wealth and education, the electorate increased from about 6 percent to 10 percent of the population. Even so, the Magyar magnates and service nobles maintained their primacy in the chamber, not least because the time-worn districting unduly benefitted them.

Like that in Vienna, the lower house in Budapest was suspended in 1914: Count Tisza adjourned the Table of Deputies, not to silence the subject nationalities, but to throttle defiant Magyar magnates and their gentry associates. Almost simultaneously he closed down the diet of quasi-autonomous Croatia in Zagreb, partly to appease these same backwoodsmen who were bent on compensating for their own decline by rigidly enforcing, not to say intensifying, Magyar hegemony over all the minority peoples.

Defeat in the war with Japan in 1904–1905 momentarily destabilized Russia's *ancien régime* to such a degree that Nicholas II was forced to yield some of his absolute power. With extreme reluctance the tsar eventually decreed the establishment of a Duma, or lower chamber, with purely consultative powers, to be elected by a limited franchise and indirectly through four curiae. Moreover, he relied on the State Council, or upper chamber, that was a redoubt of the old order, to act as a check on the popular house. As in the two other semiabsolutist or semiparliamentary empires, not only the premier but all the ministers answered to the crown alone and not to the lower house. Moreover, although the Duma was elected for five years, the tsar reserved the right to dissolve or suspend it at will and to rule by executive decree under article 87 of the fundamental laws of 1906, which specified that all powers not specifically delegated to others remained the crown's prerogative.

In spite of a franchise favoring the reliable elements of civil society, because of simmering unrest after the revolt of 1905 was squashed, the first two Dumas of April 1906 and February 1907 proved too contentious for the tsar, the landed nobility, and the state bureaucracy. About one hundred peasant deputies of the Trudoviki faction teamed up with Constitutional Democrats, Socialists, and national minorities to demand not only genuine parliamentarianism but also land reform. Increasingly self-confident and pressed by the landed nobility, the zemstvo gentry, and the far right, Nicholas summarily dissolved the first two Dumas (July 9, 1906; June 3, 1907). He instructed Peter Stolypin to narrow the franchise before the election of the third Duma, fixed for September 1907.

The new first minister, who continued to be his own interior minister, was a perfect exemplar of the nobility of land and service. A member of the provincial gentry, Stolypin, who had a university degree, owned 5,000 acres in Kovno and Penza; he married into a noble family that had an estate of over 14,000 acres in Kazan and was close to the imperial household; and he served as a marshal of the nobility before moving up in the state bureaucracy. Even though sectors of his own "class" eventually balked his moderate land and local government reforms, Stolypin's suffrage restriction benefitted the large agrarians, especially those noble proprietors who still owned over 50 percent of all private lands in European Russia and who had privileged access to the court and the uppermost bureaucracy. The revised franchise, issued by imperial ukase, raised the number of electors allotted to landowners from 32 percent to 51 percent. The result was that in the third and fourth Dumas each gentry deputy represented 16,000 instead of the earlier 28,000 voters. Simultaneously, the number of electors assigned to the peasants was reduced from 42 percent to 23 percent, which meant that each peasant deputy represented 1,700,000 instead of 800,000 voters. Moreover, except for the five major cities, the cities that heretofore had voted separately were merged into gentry-dominated rural districts, and the small core of wealthy residents were given as many votes as the rest of the urban population.

In the two "black" Dumas of 1907 and 1912 around 220 or 50 percent of the deputies were landowners. One-half of these owned over 2,000 acres, 195 of them were nobles, and about 30 were marshals of the nobility. No less significant, among the 150 Octobrist deputies who constituted the single largest bloc in the Duma, there were around 110 gentry landowners, 70 of them with estates of over 2,700 acres. Meanwhile, the number of peasant deputies was reduced by nearly one-half, to around 20 percent of the membership.

In sum, even though the provincial gentry accounted for barely 1.5 percent of the population, thanks to its control of the zemstvos and the altered franchise it dominated the third and fourth Dumas. As of the fall of 1907 the large and titled landed nobles in particular, seconded by 46 to 48 thoroughly conservative priests, played as important a role in the emasculated lower chamber as they did at court, in the State Council, and in the bureaucracy. After Stolypin's assassination in 1911 the Duma increasingly balked the central bureaucracy, using its incipient budgetary powers to obstruct policies detrimental to the vital interests of the provincial gentry, notably the reform of local government. The resulting impasse prompted the ministries of Count Kokovtsev and Ivan Goremykin to consider reducing the lower chamber in 1913–1914. As elsewhere in Europe, cleavages in the ruling and governing class rather than mounting pressures from the peasantry, the proletariat, or even the middle class occasioned this impasse.

The feudal element also more than held its own in the civil and military bureaucracies that were the "steel frames" of Europe's political societies. Without a doubt, the influx of educated sons from middle-class and bourgeois families diluted the prebourgeois nucleus of these bureaucracies. But this influx was due less to the openness of the old governing class than to its inability to staff the rapidly expanding state apparatus. In addition to being relatively small in number, the nobility lacked the skills to man the higher echelons in the ministries of war, finance, agriculture, and justice. Accordingly, recruitment was streamlined to facilitate the access of qualified commoners, and promotion increasingly hinged on service performance and qualification instead of on birth or social connection. Certainly in recruitment and advancement social class was yielding important ground to education and in-service achievement.

But this is not to say that the civil service had become a career open to talent. Certain branches of state service—army, foreign office, diplomatic corps—remained a privileged preserve of the old nobilities with their ascriptive claim to authority. Moreover, throughout the entire state apparatus the nobilitarians continued to enjoy preferment in appointments and promotions. Above all, the highest positions still were reserved for them, which is not to deny a rising level of education and training among their sons. In addition, as the gentry became less landed it became more avid in the pursuit of public offices and their benefits.

At the same time, civil servants of humble origins dissembled their past and internalized the noble code in order to move ahead. This bent to conformity was spurred by the table of ranks, whether automatic or discretionary. Quite apart from proving, not to say exhibiting, their social and political fealty, the aspirants of humble background assimilated the old public service ethos and mentality. In imitation of their superiors and role models, they struck an aristocratic pose, which included contempt for the work ethic and profit motive. Torn between noble archetype and performance imperative, upstart officials strained to pressure and display their acquired posture even to the point of social and psychological hernia and incongruity.

There is no denying that the bureaucratic establishment of the governing class was being permeated by the bourgeoisie and middle class. But were these new men carriers of bourgeois values, mind-sets, and world-views? Did service in state ministries make them into agents of bureaucratic rationalism and professionalism, as defined by Max Weber? Or, like the ruling class, did the service nobility of the old governing class aristocratize commoners who were bent on scaling the ladder of officialdom? Although both processes went on simultaneously, the aristocratic pull was the stronger of the two. Rather than promote parity between the old and the new, the bureaucracy remained a public service aristocracy, both civil and military, whose dominant ethos and operational code were nobilitarian. To be sure, some branches of officialdom were more traditional than others. Whereas the diplomatic service endured as a patrician stronghold, the finance ministry became an outpost of technocracy. There were also vast national differences. In France the civil service was predominantly middle class in provenance, spirit, and conduct; in Hungary it was conspicuously gentry.

The bureaucracies were not politically neutral institutions but instruments of system maintenance, even when promoting modernization. This built-in tendency favored the feudal element in the state apparatus. In addition to being conservative by provenance and training, bureaucrats became conservative by function, and their professional mind and interest predisposed them to routine and caution. Moreover, all along and particularly in times of crisis, reflexive conservatism—not neutrality—was a prerequisite for promotion, especially to the higher administrative and executive echelons. In turn, the bureaucracy's political consistency cemented the social cohesion of the old ruling and governing class by giving it an aura of disinterested, efficient, and severe service to the commonweal.

The military was still at the center of the bureaucratic steel frame, also symbolically, all the more so because the extravagant growth of standing and reserve armies called for ever more officers. The armed services were needed for war; they were the strategic reserve of the internal security forces; they were a formidable socializing agency; they embodied the national idea; and they played a prominent role in state ceremonials. The uniformed generals were not only decorative and conspicuous but also powerful members of Europe's civil and political societies. With few exceptions, the topmost generals were of high birth, and those who were of common lineage had long since adopted the ethos, mentality, and carriage of the exalted world in which they had risen. This was as true of Conrad von Hötzendorff, who was knighted, as it was of Erich Ludendorff, who refused ennoblement. Within these long-standing military establishments all officers, regardless of social origin and class identification, embraced the traditional social, religious, and cultural outlook. As they moved up in the hierarchy, officers also acknowledged their conservative or reactionary political valuations, most explicitly in times of stress. There was little if any chance for officers of overtly liberal or democratic persuasion to reach a high rank, since deviants from the conservative norm were discreetly screened out.

In Great Britain the key positions in the foreign office, the diplomatic corps, the armed forces, the imperial service, and

the judiciary continued to be special strongholds of the nobility. With public schools and elite universities reinforcing their
ingrained disvaluation of business and science, young men of
noble background sought government careers that were honorific, that fulfilled their vocation of public service, and that
were compatible with the gentlemanly life. Quite often the
appropriate starting positions were obtained through influence, patronage, or even purchase.

On paper, the purchase of army commissions and promotions was abolished by 1871 and entry into the officer corps
was regulated by open competition. In actual fact, the officer
corps remained highly exclusive and selective. The military
continued to be a gentlemanly and leisurely calling, with little
concern for technical competence. While there was an overall
decline in the role of grand aristocrats in the army, their place
was taken by the sons of landed gentry and, above all, by public
school graduates of respectable stock. Many officers came
from southern rural counties and border countries, notably
Ireland. Woolwich and Sandhurst were the main sources of
new officers. Down to 1914, 50 percent of the cadets of these
two military academies were sons of officers, two-thirds of
them sons of lieutenant colonels and above. About 14 percent
were of gentlemanly background, and at least as many were
sons of gentlemen of leisure. As in most Continental countries, the landed aristocracy continued to monopolize the
higher ranks of the officer corps and most especially the uppermost leadership. To the extent that nobles lost ground in
absolute terms, they sought refuge in elite regiments, such as
the 1st Life Guards and Royal Horse Guards. On the whole,
the democratization and bourgeoisification of the upper
reaches of the army proceeded very slowly until 1914, though
the pace was somewhat more rapid in the artillery and the
engineers.

Similarly, the social base of recruitment and promotion in
the civil service continued to be narrow. With the gradual
introduction of official examinations, the chances for inbreed-
ing were lessened. Candidates for higher positions now
needed advanced schooling, which few Englishmen could

afford. Between 1905 and 1914, 75 percent of the 283 entrants into the administrative class of the home service came from public schools and nearly all of them were graduates of Oxford and Cambridge. Moreover, having passed the written test, candidates were summoned to a personal interview in which the poise, manner, accent, and appearance of a gentleman weighed very heavily, if not decisively. After the establishment of a professional selection board for the foreign service in 1907, candidates were prescreened for social pedigree before being granted an interview. Needless to say, because salaries in the army as well as in the home and foreign services were nominal, high state functionaries needed a private income to indulge their avocation of public service.

The governors general of the Dominions and the viceroys of India were peers, usually of proven and distinguished lineage. But colonial governors, notably in Africa, were of more modest provenance, most of them being sons of middle-level civil servants, military officers, and professional men. Service overseas facilitated social advancement in nobilitarian directions. Especially the proconsuls assumed courtly airs. From majestic government houses they presided over spectacular ceremonies calculated to integrate indigenous notabilities, intimidate "natives," and dramatize the imperial idea for back home. As part of this same political theater these satraps ostentatiously held court for white colonial society, including its nabobs. Both at their sham courts and when traveling, they wore splendidly decorated uniforms and followed a strict and conspicuous protocol punctuated by honor guards and gun salutes. As representatives of the crown the proconsuls awarded medals and orders in the territories over which they ruled. In turn, they counted on being ennobled, possibly even raised into the peerage, on completion of their mission.

The feudal element all but dominated the civil and military bureaucracy of the second German empire. No doubt the Junkers and old nobles lost ground throughout the state apparatus, there being a rising proportion of newly ennobled and untitled individuals in the civil, diplomatic, and military services. Even so, the force of the time-honored nobility's prestige and prototype remained undiminished, the more so because the nobilitarians continued to monopolize the highest posts in Prussia and to be only marginally less pre-eminent in the imperial administration.

From 1871 through 1914 close to 25 percent of the ministers of the Prussian state government in Berlin were Junkers, while close to 75 percent were nobles. These percentages were even higher at the top of Prussia's field administration. In 1907 only 1 of Prussia's 12 provincial governors was untitled. The picture was not all that different in Bavaria, Württemberg, and the other states. Taking the empire as a whole, 25 of the 36 *Regierungspräsidenten* were nobles; 6 of the 12 *Oberpräsidialräte;* 35 of the 131 *Oberregierungsräte;* 140 of the 690 *étatsmässige Regierungsmitglieder* (inclusive of the 131 *Oberregierungsräte* and 36 *Verwaltungsdirektoren*); 217 of the 540 *ausseretatsmässige Regierungsmitglieder;* 121 of the 278 *Regierungsassessoren;* and 271 of the 467 *Landräte.* This service nobility included 2 princes, 63 counts, and 148 barons.

Commoners were truly the exception at the highest levels of national government. All the chancellors were high nobles, and so were most of the cabinet ministers and state secretaries. In 1914, 8 of the 10 top officials of the foreign office and all but a few of Germany's ambassadors were titled nobles. Many of these senior imperial officials earned their original spurs in the Prussian bureaucracy, and all of them demonstrated their political conservatism as they rose to the top of a governing class that excluded progressives, socialists, and Jews.

In the army the Prussian officers remained pre-eminent in spite of their falling numbers, in part because the Hohenzollern emperors embodied and exalted their imperious conduct. Between 1860 and 1913 the percentage of noblemen in the officers corps declined from 65 percent to 30 percent. Actually, the dilution was most pronounced in the lower ranks. In 1913, 73 percent of all captains and subalterns were of non-noble birth. The decline of wellborn officers was much more limited in the higher ranks: over a period of fifty years the percentage of born noblemen among generals and colonels fell from 86 percent to 52 percent, or to only 56 percent counting in-service ennoblements. Moreover, into the twentieth century virtually all generals and field marshals were noblemen, one-third of them from old Junker families. The East Elbian nobility provided the top officers for the general staff, the war ministry, elite cavalry regiments, and to a lesser extent, infantry and artillery units.

Even so, there were those Prussian officers and their reactionary political associates who wanted to refeudalize the military by tightening their hold on select guard and cavalry regiments and on choice garrisons. More important, despite their fierce nationalism and bellicosity, they opposed any further expansion of the army immediately before 1914 for fear that the need for additional officers of non-noble origin would sap the Junker ascendancy. Actually, these ultras vastly exaggerated the *embourgeoisement* of Germany's military establishment, for even though the social provenance of officers was becoming more middle class, the Junker military ethos continued to pervade the army's command structure and war colleges.

Austria had a somewhat less exclusive public service nobility than Germany. In the army there was room for a relatively large number of Jewish and Czech reserve officers, though the elite regiments remained closed to them. Of course, neither Jews nor other minorities were represented in the uppermost reaches of the army and civil service, which were firmly in the hands of the Austro-German aristocracy. Admittedly, Conrad von Hötzendorff, the exceptionally talented but also belligerent chief of staff, was of non-noble origin. But quite apart from being an exception, he had recently been ennobled. On the whole he shared Francis Ferdinand's archnobilitarian and retrogressive world-view. In addition to the first echelons of the army, those of the foreign ministry and diplomatic corps were an exclusive preserve of the high Austro-German nobility.

Especially in Hungary, where the magnates became fewer but bigger and wealthier, the economically declining gentry looked to government positions for material security, social status, and political sway. Between 1867 and 1914 some 90,000 petty nobles found employment in a state bureaucracy that during that half-century increased from 30,000 to 233,000 civil servants, not counting the railroad and postal personnel. Without either court or foreign office, and with only a small autonomous military constabulary, this service nobility was singularly lackluster and short of legitimizing symbols and ceremonies. As if to bolster their meager accreditation, these gentry-bureaucrats relentlessly appropriated the ideological and social capital of the class and milieu in which they originated. Although driven out of the seignorial domain, even officials living in Budapest affected more than ever the ethos and life-style of the landed estate. Moreover, claiming to be the rightful heirs and agents of Hungary's national mission, this boisterous office nobility pressed for the extreme Magyarization of subject peoples and eventual independence from Vienna. Not that non-Magyars and nongentry were barred from the bureaucracy. But in order to be admitted they first had to deny their origins, master the Magyar language, and assume aristocratic manners. With Jews as their competitors for the civil service and the liberal professions, the service gentry became increasingly anti-Semitic. At the same time it joined the beleaguered small and middling landed gentry in opposing the large magnates in and out of government who collaborated with the barons of capital, most of whom were Jewish, charging these magnates with desecrating Hungary's national and cultural heritage.

In Russia also, the sons of noble proprietors sought posts in the civil and military bureaucracy to compensate for the deterioration of their landed fortunes. Especially after the abolition of serfdom in 1861 there was an influx of declining gentry into state service. By 1890 only about 30 percent of the 600 officials in the second and third highest ranks of the civil service had family estates, most of them inherited, and of these some 35 percent, or 180, had large holdings of over 1,000 dessiatines, or 2,700 acres. More than likely these percentages did not change significantly during the following quarter-century. All this time, however, officials with landed interests occupied a large place at the very top of Russia's political pyramid, which included the tsar's entourage.

Of course, the automatic table of ranks integrated all high bureaucrats, including or especially landless officials, into a public service nobility whose social ethos and political charge were to maintain the *ancien régime* that was inextricably interwoven with the landed estate. In turn, the sons of these service nobles were assured of preferential access and advancement in the civil administration. Although in the late nineteenth century officials of noble birth claimed only about one-third of all positions, they continued to be predominant in the four highest ranks. Even after October 1906, when the noble estate was stripped of all legal advantages in the state bureaucracy, noble descendants remained favored for promotion. An important reason for their persistence was the privileged access of the nobility's sons to elite schools for bureaucrats. Originally intended only for scions of the highest titled families, as of 1890 the Imperial Alexander Lycée and the Imperial Legal Institute admitted nobles regardless of provenance. The graduates of these *grandes écoles* chose to make their careers in the all-important interior and justice ministries. There they were spared service in the two lowest grades, the most capable among them even being selected to start in the ninth rank. Once these elite schools became oversubscribed, noblemen sent their sons to the gymnasia, where they made sure to live separate from students of middle-class background, who were in the majority.

Admittedly, after 1905 officials of noble and landed stock lost some ground among the senior personnel of the interior ministry to men of non-noble origins, who advanced mostly by virtue of their education, talent, and performance. Still, at this high level in 1914, traditional noble elements continued to claim 77 percent of all posts, having declined from 88 percent in 1905. Moreover, in the ministry of the interior, as in other ministries, landed nobles and particularly those with large holdings remained overrepresented in the highest and most prestigious posts. Evidently, despite changes in society at large and in the condition of the traditional ruling and governing class, the nobility retained a commanding position throughout the higher civil bureaucracy.

Much the same was true of the higher military echelons. Again, the intake of non-nobles into the officer corps quickened after 1905—by 3 percent in 1911–1912—at the same time that the table of ranks was relaxed to confer personal honors on newly commissioned officers and hereditary honors on anyone reaching the grade of colonel. Nevertheless, the bias toward sons of noble birth was not significantly attenuated. The highborn still advanced much more easily than non-nobles and claimed the lion's share of the top commands. The loftier an officer's pedigree, the speedier his rise through the ranks, any prince or count being almost certain of promotion to full general.

The officer corps of Russia's rapidly growing imperial army expanded from 19,500 in 1860 to 42,800 in 1900, and in 1914 to close to 46,000, of whom only about 50 percent claimed noble birth. But at the turn of the century, 10 of the 140 full generals were members of the imperial family and 78 were of noble ancestry, of whom 47 had little or no land. The percentage of hereditary nobles was at least equally high among lieutenant and major generals, though the great majority of them were landless.

Not surprisingly, the cavalry and artillery were considerably more select than the infantry. The officer corps of the cavalry came close to being noble to a man, and even in 1911 all its generals were of noble birth. The mounted guard regiments were still more socially exclusive, since only hereditary nobles were eligible. After attending the same prestigious military schools, notably the Page Corps and Nicholas Cavalry School, the guard officers advanced rapidly and as late as 1912 still provided the imperial army with well over 50 percent of its generals. It was a measure of the feudal nature of the tsarist regime that the cavalry, including the guards, engaged a full 12 percent of the officer corps though it accounted for only about 6 percent of Russia's military effectives. By comparison the artillery had 16 percent of the standing army and 13 percent of the officers, most of whom were of better than average preparation and general intelligence. As for the infantry officers, they trailed those of the other two branches in social position, education, and extramilitary influence. Appropriately, a large proportion of the lower officers of Russia's soldiery were of peasant origin, without secondary education. No more than 40 percent at best of the officers of line infantry units were of noble origin, though the 60 percent of humble birth were of course assured of personal ennoblement at a minimum. Ultimately, Russia's political class preserved the noble character of its military forces, which were also its praetorian guard, by maintaining the socially exclusive military schools as the required avenue to the higher echelons of the officer corps.

Down to 1914 the "steel frame" of Europe's political societies continued to be heavily feudal and nobilitarian. In spite of vast national and constitutional variations, there were significant family resemblances among all the regimes. Perhaps this affinity was rooted first and foremost in the enduring importance of landed interests and of rural society throughout Europe. While in England land was more a source of social status and political ascendancy than of economic and financial power, in France it provided the principal material understructure of the Third Republic, and most notably of its ruling and governing class. Although the Revolution of 1789–1794 had swept away the monarchy, it had reinvigorated the agricultural estate: quite apart from leaving many of the landed notables as well as the praedial Catholic Church in place, it expanded and strengthened small and medium peasant holdings. Throughout Europe upper houses, legislatures, bureaucracies, and armies drew their lifeblood from land-enveloped villages, towns, and provinces rather than from industrializing cities or regions. Moreover, except in France, king and court, like the nobilities, were inconceivable without the wealth, income, and nimbus generated by large landed proprietorship.

To the extent that this landed society was in relative economic decline, political society was there to brace it. King and court served an overall agglutinating function in the politics of economic, social, and cultural defense, France being the exception that proved the rule. By virtue of ancient custom or constitutional convention, or both, the strength of the old ruling class was magnified not only in local and provincial councils but above all in central government. The two houses of parliament and the public service nobilities worked to preserve or reinforce the preindustrial civil society. They passed protective tariffs for uncompetitive agriculture and manufacture everywhere except in England and provided prestigious government positions for embattled nobles and aspiring commoners. No less important, they blocked tax, suffrage, educational, and social reforms that threatened to hasten the erosion of the old order.

Chapter 4

OFFICIAL HIGH CULTURES AND THE AVANT-GARDES

EUROPE'S OFFICIAL CULTURES conspicuously mirrored the tenacious perseverance of preindustrial civil and political societies. In form, content, and style the artifacts of high culture continued to be anchored and swathed in conventions that relayed and celebrated traditions supportive of the old order. The eclectic revival and reproduction of time-honored and venerable styles dominated not only in architecture and statuary but also in painting, sculpture, and the performing arts. Museums, academies, churches, and universities actively promoted this congruent academic historicism, and so did the state, which enlisted historicism to articulate national and regional purposes. Overall, the hegemonic arts and institutions maintained

189

sufficient inner vitality and synoptic coherence to invigorate the *anciens régimes.*

Of course, between 1848 and 1914 Europe's official cultures experienced discordant modernist movements in the arts as well as in the churches and higher schools. But these defections were easily contained, above all because they were no match for the reigning cultural centers. Admittedly, most defectors were young, spirited, and aggressive experimentalists and innovators, and many of them eventually won recognition. Even so, successive waves of the avant-garde hit against the official cultures, which, like breakwaters, survived intact. In the long run the victory of the modernists may have been inevitable. In the short run, however, the modernists were effectively bridled and isolated, if need be with legal and administrative controls. Despite or because of relentless challenges and gibes from the avant-garde, the producers and guardians of official academic traditions remained at once imperious and adaptive. Like kings and nobles, they learned to defuse ascending rivals through calibrated assimilation and co-optation. And just as outworn economic interests made the most of their political leverage to secure protective tariffs and fiscal preferments, so eminent artists used their influence in key hegemonic institutions—academies, salons, museums, ministries of culture—to rally support for their timeworn idioms.

Compared to the vanguard, the cultural establishment and its rear guard were above all protective. But even though the historicist legacy for and with which they did battle was aesthetically impoverished, it was far from spent. Historicism was not an archaic, lifeless, and inert accretion that trailed far behind the economic and social developments of the nineteenth century. In fact, between 1848 and 1914 historic academicism declined no further than the rest of preindustrial civil society. To be sure, it lost in vitality as fixed form prevailed over idea, imitation over authenticity, ornateness over artlessness, and pomp over sobriety. But historicism was no less useful and effective for being turgid and specious.

The major historical styles—classical, medieval, Renaissance, Baroque, rococo—were part of the storehouse of symbols and images that served to thwart, dignify, and disguise the present. Historicism provided critics of modernity with an inexhaustible reservoir of representations with which not only to glorify and reinvigorate their own privileged though beleaguered world but also to censure and traduce the rival new society. Landed and service nobilities, political catonists, and Arcadian social critics each had their own reasons for harking back to time-honored metaphors and emblems.

But the makers and bards of modernity also had recourse to ancient tropes as they set out to justify their project and make it fathomable. While capitalist entrepreneurs excelled at creative destruction in the economic sphere, they took care not to tear the inherited cultural fabric. Indeed, in their quest for divine sanction and social recognition they enveloped their exploits and themselves with historical screens. This use of and solicitude for historical culture substantially mitigated and disguised the stress of fitting modernity into pre-existing civil and political society.

For the political classes high culture was an important ideological instrument. Not only public buildings, statues, and spaces but also the pictorial, plastic, and performing arts were expected to exalt the old regimes and revalidate their moral claims. The ruling classes took an equally functional view of the arts. Whereas new men enlisted them to display their wealth, taste, and aspiration, well-established families used them to reaffirm their fortune and status. For the two factions the consumption of high art and culture was both badge and sacrament of achieved or coveted positions of class, prestige, and influence in what remained distinctly traditional societies. Having assigned art such practical functions, the governing and ruling classes were disinclined to sponsor vanguards that balked at ratifying and extolling the *anciens régimes* and their elites in the accustomed ways.

In an age in which the declining old order easily held down the rising new society, traditional conventions, tastes, and styles only gradually yielded to breakaway visions and representations. Unlike those of the Renaissance, most new wealth-holders did not become patrons of modernism, no doubt because the avant-garde was oblivious to their thirst for flattering portrayals of their interest, mission, and standing. During the quattrocento, artists had adapted motifs and themes of classical antiquity to ratify and celebrate the rise of burghers to commanding positions in the pre-eminently noble ruling and governing classes of Italy's seignorial and republican cities. Straining to capture and express the expansive consciousness of their patrons, these artists had launched a movement of taste that eventually acquired a life and momentum of its own.

From the Middle Ages through the nineteenth century Europe's ruling and governing classes used art as much for practical purposes as for aesthetic enjoyment. The function of art was to celebrate God, patron, dynasty, regime, class, and nation. Until the eighteenth century artists were dependent on royal, aristocratic, patrician, and ecclesiastic patronage for both income and fame. Thereafter, as the *anciens régimes* began to live on their accumulated cultural capital, artists lost their traditional patrons. Forced to pursue art for art's and their own sake, they had to solicit clients and publics to support their irreverent quest. Hard pressed to find individual benefactors and public commissions, secessionists in particular looked to private and institutional customers to purchase modern along with traditional art. With rare though notable exceptions, however, the new barons of capital, driven by the rage for nobility, confined themselves to collecting "classical" paintings and art objects, to buying or building "historical" country manors or city mansions, and to patronizing the traditional performing arts. Instead of encouraging and appropriating the modern quest, they bought into the historicist legacy which remained too vast and alien for them to make their own. The economically radical bourgeoisie was as obsequious in cultural life as it was in social relations and political behavior. By espousing and consuming the conventional arts, the bourgeoisie reinforced ruling classes and official cultures that were disproportionately oriented to the preindustrial and prebourgeois world.

On the whole the reigning high cultures continued to incarnate and propagate officious realism, rigid conformity with the past, moral and religious rectitude, and national pride. The era was one of custom, not fashion, in which art and culture were "the magic and lively mirror of a past that was still alive . . . and fully confident of its own future." It was an age of "infatuation with one's country rather than with one's times," stimulated by patriotic cults. The injunction was to reproduce and diffuse that which was "not only known, but also liked, admired, or adored." This meant portraying religious legends and saints, historical epics and heroes, and everyday life and customs with studied references to the death of Prometheus, the affliction of Oedipus, the drama of creation, and the lore of popular fables. Rather than solicit the visual, plastic, and musical arts "for new impressions, [artists] were asked to intensively express and reproduce impressions and beliefs that were tried and tested."

But there was also a modernist movement, an avant-garde of artists radically critical and contemptuous of the historical outlook. The term "avant-garde" was actually drawn from military discourse. For friend and foe alike it conjured up visions of forward patrols of artists leading sympathizers in storming the fortress of official culture. In each country the vanguard consisted of numerous coteries that formed and reformed in relation to each other and in reaction to their losing battles with the cultural establishment.

Some groups mixed advanced art with radical politics, at least until it became clear that the modernist campaign would be difficult, slow, and wearing. Others confined themselves to mounting aesthetic challenges which usually also contested the social and political mission of art. But whatever the divisions both within and among the various formations of the avant-garde, all of them were driven by the same exasperation with the hardened historical posture of the major branches of high culture. Individually and collectively the avant-gardists rebelled, not against hegemonic institutions as such, but against their asphyxiating vise. With their relentless assaults they meant to force a relaxation of this strangle hold in order to create more public and private space for experimentation in technique, style, and subject matter.

The second half of the nineteenth century was, however, a difficult season for artists. While the ranks of artists expanded rapidly, the old ruling classes and the churches cut back on patronage. The spineless bourgeoisie, in the meantime, invested in certified "classical" art instead of sponsoring the modernist experiments of contemporary art and artists. The result was that government subsidies assumed ever greater importance at the very moment that artists prized their new-found autonomy and denounced high culture's continuing subservience to state and society.

With the growth of cities the production of officially funded art expanded significantly between midcentury and 1914, uninterrupted by the economic cramps of 1873 to 1896. Public authorities built government offices, town halls, museums, libraries, and universities; commissioned murals, monuments, and statues; organized world fairs and public festivals; and founded research institutes. Politicians and bureaucrats planned and administered these activities in close consultation with artists, intellectuals, and academics pledged to the reproduction and diffusion of traditional culture. Indeed, most of these collaborators were products of staid academies and conservatories which forced young artists seeking recognition and patronage to uphold the conventional canons. The directors and teachers of these academies fixed the curriculums, staffed the juries, and awarded the prizes that perpetuated traditional genres, controlled access to salaried careers, and regulated professional and social advancement into prestigious official circles.

The avant-garde was foiled on all sides. Buoyed by the old elites, the hegemonic institutions stood their ground, refusing both compromise and sponsorship. Similarly, offended by the charge of philistinism, the new plutocrats resolutely spurned or ignored the modernists. Nor did the vanguard find encouragement among the *petite bourgeoisie,* the working class, and the peasantry. The fourth estate was totally indifferent if not hostile to the modern quest.

Unable to make a dent in the historical culture, the coteries of the avant-garde became increasingly alienated first from the bourgeoisie and then from society as a whole. Rather than collaborate with the political vanguard, the artistic vanguard withdrew into what became a sprawling subculture. Insisting on the nobility of their calling and declaring themselves answerable to no one but themselves, the secessionists became champions of art for art's sake and extreme aestheticism. They attributed an absolute value to art and made it the object of a cult, not to say a religion, essentially disconnected from everyday life. Although they became resigned to having only each other as viewers, auditors, and critics, they nevertheless hoped, even if unconsciously, that their defiant innovations would with time discredit and overturn the prevalent styles and their curators, writ large. In sum, the vanguardists internalized their social protest and abandoned direct confrontations with the official order and culture in favor of permeating and subverting it. Except for the Futurists and the Left Expressionists, they became the Fabians of the modernist movement.

Meanwhile, shut out of official circuits, the vanguard spawned and resorted to alternate networks. Painters in particular organized their own exhibits without juries and prizes at the same time that sympathetic and enterprising art dealers and critics set about creating publics and markets for heterodox contemporary works. Occasionally grand orchestras and theaters presented avant-garde compositions and plays. But far more often amateur circles and offbeat cabarets performed modernist works. Paradoxically, instead of reclaiming their autonomy, avant-garde artists exchanged the fetters of official culture for those of the competitive and speculative market.

Prior to 1914 these new channels for the promotion and recognition of experimental art were incipient at best, largely because the bourgeoisie, which was most inclined to use the marketplace, remained antipathetic to modernism. As yet, the conspicuous consumption or patronage of untried contemporary art was not expected to further the social ambitions of the *nouveaux riches.* Admittedly, here and there a few *grands bourgeois* became clients of the moderns, as did scattered worldly aristocrats. But this incidental patronage no more loosened the iron grip of the old cultural hegemony than the modernization of agriculture, bureaucracy, and army softened that of the landed and service nobilities.

No doubt architecture was the most exemplary cultural mirror. Along with public statuary and urban space it both reflected and dignified the established cultural and social order. Judging by the style of official architecture in the nineteenth and early twentieth centuries, the period was one of unrelenting historicism. Although postmercantile capitalism kept forging ahead it never found or inspired an architectural language of its own. As in the other arts, except in literature, the steadfast industrial revolutions failed to incite new visions, symbols, and canons. Especially in larger cities, including those of rapid economic growth, public buildings kept assuming a variety of both pure and eclectically blended historical styles. Having abandoned the search for a distinct unitary style for the emergent society, architects prided themselves on mastering the art of imitating the major styles of Europe's past—Grecian, Roman, Byzantine, Romanesque, Gothic, Renaissance, Baroque. Depending on the country, some decades were given over to Neo-Hellenism, others to Neo-Gothicism, and still others to French Renaissance style. But there were also years when architects won fame with buildings combining two or more ancient styles. At all times religious and civic structures were conceived to summon up or reinforce sentiments and attitudes supportive of the *ancien régime.* Certainly the growing size of public buildings served this representational purpose.

In an atmosphere of straitened pluralism churches were more often than not built in Gothic style, and so were town halls that evoked the rebirth of municipal life at the end of the Dark Ages. Parliament buildings were given a classical or Gothic cast; military barracks took the form of medieval fortresses or castles; universities were designed to convey the spirit of Periclean Athens, the cloistered Middle Ages, or Italian Renaissance humanism; and museums frequently were made to pass for Greek temples. While banks were patterned after Florentine palaces, the city mansions of new men were given ostentatious Baroque façades. By using this tested historical vocabulary architects enabled growing and changing cities to maintain or acquire a premodern aura.

Although England was in the forefront of industrialization and urbanization, architecturally it remained firmly anchored in the past. In London after 1840, not only the Houses of Parliament and numerous churches but many office and civic buildings were built in Neo-Gothic style. In fact, by the turn of the century the nerve center of British and world capitalism had a more grandiose historical, notably Gothic, physiognomy than ever before. Much the same was true of Manchester, the capital of the first industrial revolution. The Gothic revival, in particular, endowed this city and others with a cultural legacy calculated to reconcile the accomplishments and ravages of capitalism with the old order.

While intended as a forum for democratic expression, the German Reichstag was given a stern mien, its heavy Baroque walls connecting its four corner towers. Moreover, located on Berlin's Königsplatz, it faced the headquarters of the general staff, one of the command centers of feudalistic Prusso-Germany. In this regard as also in their statuary program, the Hohenzollerns were more severe than the Habsburgs. Vienna's Reichsrat faced the less terrifying Hofburg, the emperor's Baroque residence, and its central hall was built like an exalting Greek temple prominently emplaced on a former military parade ground. This house of parliament was only one of an array of monumental, not to say mammoth, buildings erected along the new Ringstrasse, conceived during Austria's fleeting "liberal" era, where a Gothic town hall (Rathaus), a Baroque theater (Burgtheater), and a Renaissance university displayed Europe's major historical styles and allegorical motifs. In addition to setting the limits for visual expression the Ringstrasse was a microscopic reflection of the bourgeoisie's passion for historical borrowing that unceasingly helped relegitimate the old order in which it was subordinate.

As if to dissimulate its unreconstructed authoritarianism, Hungary's governing class erected a huge parliament building in Budapest that was perhaps the most colossal of Europe's Neo-Gothic structures. In Rome, meanwhile, the political class avoided having to contrive an imitation home for Italy's Camera and Senate by simply buying the muted Baroque Palazzo Montecitorio and the High Renaissance Palazzo Madama. There was an understandable reluctance to practice the art of imitation in civic construction, since architects from all over Europe came to Rome to study the ancient city's "original" masterpieces. As if to compensate for not using artists as they were being used elsewhere, Italy's governors commissioned large numbers of them to create the immense Victor Emmanuel II Monument. This white marble memorial to the ideals and struggles of Italian unification engaged at least five of Italy's leading architects and countless sculptors. Topped by a bronze equestrian statue of united Italy's first king, this towering structure dressed in classical Greek style recalled imperial Rome's penchant for ponderously splendid columns, bas-reliefs, monumental and statuary sculptures, trophies, and emblems. The governing class, notwithstanding its republican ancestry, herewith confirmed its allegiance to the House of Savoy that presumed to check parliament.

Throughout Europe the forging of direct, living links with the past went on apace. As part of this backward binding, a mixed classical and northern Gothic façade was finally affixed to the grand cathedral in Milan, and the Gothic cathedral in Cologne was completed at last. Simultaneously in the major cities, including Milan and Cologne, the forebuildings of grandiose railroad stations characteristically flaunted historical arches, columns, towers, and domes devised to conceal alien iron and glass train sheds conceived and built by engineers. Railroad terminals may well have become to post-1848 Europe what monasteries and cathedrals had been to the thirteenth century, but their arched and colonnaded head-houses were hardly expressive of the emerging industrial age. While these temples of transport glorified the new means of transport in an accepted way, they also marked a reaction against the quickening rhythm of life and speed of transport and alluded to slower-moving preindustrial times.

Of course, not all newly wrought constructions were masked by archaic fronts. Architects and engineers began to cooperate in the utilization of cast iron and glass, and then of steel and concrete. The Crystal Palace of 1851 in London was the first blatant use of a new architectural language that evoked nothing of the past. The next major probe was the Eiffel Tower erected in 1889 in Paris. But both of these daring and brash constructions were set in world exhibitions that were temporary expressions of emergent manufactural and industrial capitalism. These marginal and ephemeral "pantheons of art and industry" consisted of exhibition halls hailing the potentials of modern materials and design. In contrast to Gothic churches Joseph Paxton's Crystal Palace and Victor Contamin's Palais des Machines maximized width, unbroken space, the penetration of natural light—and bareness. Distrusted for profaning the ancient capitals which remained relatively untouched by the new industrialism, these "secular cathedrals of glass and steel" were eventually extruded: the Crystal Palace was moved from Hyde Park to Sydenham, while the Machine Palace was dismantled altogether. The Eiffel Tower may well have been left in place because, despite its steel girders, it was so conspicuously nonutilitarian and therefore a harmless landmark spatially disconnected from Paris's manufactural and urban bustle.

The Grand and Petit Palais of the world's fair of 1900 survived in a more central location, but by then such halls were decorated to blend into the historical cityscape. Besides, at all the universal exhibitions in Paris the glass and metal palaces were considerably more modern than the displays inside them, which featured more manufactural than industrial wares. This was also the case in Milan, where the glass and metal roof over the cruciform and cathedral-like Galleria Vittorio Emanuele II, with its triumphal-arch entrance, housed exclusive specialty shops and cafés.

Admittedly, between 1900 and 1914 a few architects struggled to free themselves from the shackles of tradition and the snares of ornamentation. By then architects not only faced pressing scientific, technical, and social challenges but also

encountered new aesthetic, visual, and spatial concepts, notably those of a Cubist tendency. In other words, the availability
of steel and reinforced concrete by itself was not enough to
inspire Otto Wagner, Joseph Olbrich, Josef Hoffman, and
Adolf Loos "to get out of historicism into a new style for a new
century." The new materials merely facilitated a defection that
was fired by a quasi-mystical ideal of austere purity and culminated in a crusade against ornamentation, including the
evanescent Art Nouveau. Convinced that "only what was practical could be beautiful," Wagner gave not only a flat and
unadorned façade but also a streamlined interior to his Postal
Savings Bank on Vienna's Ringstrasse (1904–1906), a building
intended to serve a living function. No doubt Wagner and his
Austrian colleagues were among the leading heralds of a "new
style untainted by historicism." But theirs were isolated statements with as little impact as the buildings of H. P. Berlage in
Holland and of Henry van de Velde in Germany, or the paper
projects of Tony Garnier. In fact, outside the embattled avant-
garde, the new style owed its notoriety primarily to hostile
reactions by defenders of historicist imitation. The inveterate
architectural idioms accorded too effectively with existing civil
and political society to be dismissed as mere *Kitsch*.

   Painters at the *fin du siècle* were as tradition-bound as architects. Both came out of academies that taught and enforced
a linear conception of European culture and drilled students
in the major styles and masterpieces of the past to the point
of stifling their originality. Painters were steeped in the Bible,
classical mythology, and folk ballads, and so were their well-to-
do clients. Neither of them questioned the "great chain of
being" in pictorial art in which historical, mythological, and
portrait paintings extolling the social order ranked way ahead
of genre, landscape, and still-life pictures. The grand salons
of painting held in prominent public buildings and under high
political patronage perpetuated this general ordering. Heads
of state or top ministers presided over the ceremonial distribu-

tion of prestigious prizes awarded by juries consisting of tried academicians who moved in high society. Gold medals and "academic" appointments were but first steps for up-and-coming painters, followed by official decorations and, except in France, ennoblement. Along the way successful artists exalted the ruling class with flattering portraits of its members and their social poses. While this amalgam of art, politics, and high society originated in a distant past, it was neither archaic nor sterile, judging by the effectiveness with which secessionists were excommunicated or reclaimed by the cultural establishment.

This continuing efficacy was due, in part, to the growth of certain hegemonic institutions. While private collections in particular were being closed, public museums proliferated and expanded, notably after midcentury. No doubt there were progressive aspects to this development. Public museums, not unlike public libraries, enlarged access to high art and became beacons of tolerance by virtue of the diversity of their holdings. But museums had elitist and obscurantist sides as well. From their beginnings during the Napoleonic era they were closely tied above all into the social and political projects of the regimes that created and operated them. Although they claimed to be agents of democratic enlightenment, in practice the great museological institutions became exclusive aesthetic churches devoted to glorifying a past that was parent to the present.

To begin with, the Greek, Renaissance, and Romanesque façades of these temples of art induced reverence and awe even among the initiates. Once past the portico, visitors were further daunted by the austerity of the central hall, where they collected themselves before entering the sanctuary to worship enshrined art objects that were authenticated by an ordained priesthood of curators, art historians, and connoisseurs. Museum-goers reverently contemplated the exhibited relics without reference to the societal and artistic context in which they had been conceived and crafted.

By the very nature of their holdings museums profiled and glorified the seductive and abashing splendor of leisure-class society. Until 1914 the high priests of museums felt little if any obligation to democratize or popularize their exhibits. Although their intellectual discipline and aesthetic refinement had a certain autonomy, museum directors were cultural elitists by social provenance, training, and osmosis. Accordingly, they presented visions of the past which upheld the ruling classes that also made up the bulk of Europe's museum patrons and publics. In fact, the museum's principal social function was to further the integration of the aspirant bourgeoisie into these ruling classes on terms favorable to the old elites. Nor were the grand museums politically innocent. As of the late nineteenth century they were named for Alexander III, Frederick William III, and Victoria and Albert. It rarely if ever occurred to the middle and lower classes to enter these forbidding pantheons of high art, which they took to be exclusive preserves of the ruling and governing class.

Of course, the capitals and major cities of the principal European countries, except for Italy, launched their museums during the era of the French Revolution. London got a slow start in that the Corinthian-style National Gallery was not completed until 1838 and the British Museum, cast as an Ionic temple, was only opened in 1847. But eventually Britain made up for time lost, increasing the number of its museums from 59 in 1850 to 295 in 1914. In particular the expansively Romanesque Natural History Museum (1871–1881), the eclectically Renaissance and Romanesque Victoria and Albert Museum (1891–1909), and the bombastic neoclassical Tate Gallery (1897) amplified the historicist monumentalization of England's capital.

In the Germanies, Munich, Dresden, and Darmstadt were in the vanguard, their museums originating in the splendid dynastic collections of their ruling houses. Not to be left behind, the Hohenzollerns of Prussia constructed the Old and New Museums (1823–1828; 1843–1855) on a special museum island in Berlin to rival not only the rich *pinakothekai* of the houses of Wittelsbach, Wettiner, and Hessen but also the Louvre in Paris. For reasons of prestige and power William I and William II strained to surpass their forebears by building

Berlin's National Gallery as a Corinthian temple (1876) and the Kaiser Friedrich Museum, designed by Ernst von Ihne, in seventeenth-century Baroque (1897–1903). Taking Germany as a whole, some 180 museums were built between 1900 and 1914 alone. To be sure, in Germany as elsewhere a good many museums were given over to ethnology, archaeology, and the applied arts, while in Prague and Budapest they were charged with firing nationalist sentiments. But everywhere the grand museums of the high visual and plastic arts remained the principal centers of cultural worship. Certainly such was the case in Vienna, where the Museum of Art History outclassed that of Natural History even though the two blazoned forth the same Baroque grandiloquence.

But St. Petersburg had perhaps the most archaic and revealing museological face. Both the old Hermitage and the new one, built in the 1840s, were integral parts of the imperial Winter Palace. The Romanovs were the last to "nationalize" their dynastic collections. Until the mid-sixties the Hermitage was used for grand receptions. Because visiting the museum meant visiting the imperial family, visitors had to follow a dress code and to be announced. Even after the Hermitage's sumptuous interiors and majestic collections of Western European masters were nationalized, the ministry of the imperial court continued to administer and finance them along with other museums, theaters, operas, and ballets.

It should come as no surprise that the avant-gardes found it difficult to penetrate these formidable museological bastions. Not that they remained completely shut out. Paradoxically, by 1914 German museums held some two hundred French paintings from Ingres to the Cubists, although such works were not necessarily prominently displayed. Notwithstanding the dismissal of Hugo von Tschudi for acquiring Impressionists for Berlin's National Gallery, the museums of the ironbound Second Empire were relatively open to the vanguard. In part this was so because Germany's decentralized museum system permitted Darmstadt, Dresden, and Munich—where Tschudi was welcomed—to pursue an independent course in defiance of Prussian bombast. By comparison the centralized museums of the presumably unrepressed, not to say licentious, Third Republic held less than one hundred French moderns. In 1890 Monet, Degas, and Rodin headed a national subscription for 20,000 francs to present Manet's pioneering *Olympia* to the Luxembourg, where it lingered in relative obscurity until Georges Clemenceau helped to secure greater visibility for it. Finally, in 1907, it was consecrated by being moved to the Louvre. In the meantime, the weight of traditions and biases complicated the acceptance of the bequest of Gustave Caillebotte, the realist painter who when he died in 1894 left some sixty-five paintings, mostly Impressionist, to the state on condition that they not be hidden in the Luxembourg or in provincial museums. Eventually the officials of the Beaux-Arts accepted thirty-eight of these pictures, not least because by so doing they integrated the still-controversial Impressionists into the Luxembourg without spending any of their meager acquisition funds and without risking budgetary battles. Besides, particularly following the Dreyfus affair, the cultural guardians viewed the Impressionists with somewhat greater favor, in part as a *ruse de guerre* against the socially more dangerous post-Impressionists, and by 1914 there were nine Monets, seven Renoirs, and six Pissarros in the Luxembourg, which also accepted a small *nature morte* by Gauguin. Moreover, in 1911 the bequest of Isaac de Camondo put works by Cézanne, Degas, Renoir, and Toulouse-Lautrec into the Louvre, and in 1914 the Pierre Goujon gift put one Van Gogh there. Still, until 1900 Jean-Léon Gérôme, Adolphe-William Bouguereau, and Carolus Duran, and after the turn of the century Joseph-Léon Bonnat and Paul-Albert Besnard, overshadowed their modernist challengers. All five were members of the Académie des Beaux-Arts of the Institut de France.

Compared to architecture and most of the performing arts, painting was an individual and personal art form, which partly accounts for its role as the locomotive of the modern movement. Vanguard painters were free to experiment, and as they rebelled against first classicism and then realism, they defied the academic and social mores of the art world. Impressionism was the start of an ever quicker succession of discontinuous but not unrelated modernisms. But as always, contemporaries overperceived the radicalism of the break with reigning canons and official cultures. And in retrospect the modernist quest appears to follow a linear trajectory from figurative to nonrepresentational art.

Actually, the Impressionists were radicals only to the extent that they rose against the fossilized academic conventions, abandoning the sterile imitation and reproduction of the past for vigorous representations of modern life. It was Manet, their *avant-courier,* who first proclaimed that he wanted to be "of his time" and to paint "what he saw." In other words, inspired by Courbet, the Impressionists were first and foremost realists who swore off Christian legends, social flattery, and academic aesthetics in order to reveal, not interpret, the world about them. Rejecting the time-honored view that painting was a cerebral activity, the Impressionists, in their optical assays, trusted the human eye to transmit reality without mental mediation. Accordingly they moved out of their murky studios into the broad daylight of society, city, and countryside. Although contemporaries of Zola and naturalism, except for Degas they tended to register a rather serene reality. Judging by the subject matter rather than the conception, technique, and color of their canvases, the Impressionists' eyes neglected much of the modern world. Though ethereal, Monet's exquisite *Gare Saint-Lazare* was unrepresentative, and before long he also moved down the banks and tributaries of the Seine to capture the sun-soaked landscapes that became a distinctive emblem of Impressionism.

On the whole, unlike realists such as Alfred-Philippe Roll and Jean-François Raffaëlli, the Impressionists fixed on the countryside and peasants rather than cities and proletarians. To the extent that cityscapes entered their line of vision they recorded artisanal ateliers, poultry markets, and the frolicsome pastimes of the Parisian middle class and *petite bourgeoisie.* Indeed, theirs was a fugitive rendering of urban life, devoid of the turbulence of factories and crowds, and with only occasional glances at the *haut monde.* Moreover, forever striving and hoping for official recognition, the Impressionists refrained from defaming their opponents. Manet's acceptance of a medal for a minor work in 1881 and his decoration with the Legion of Honor foreshadowed Cézanne's later claim that "he wanted to make Impressionism into something as stable and enduring as the art of museums."

The resolve to free themselves from "the dead hand of the past" continued to be the principal motor of the avant-gardes until 1914. Accordingly the Neo-Impressionists Seurat, Signac, and Luce were driven to register a less idyllic, elegiac, and quiescent social reality than the main body of painters, who were fellow travelers but not adherents of the Impressionist movement. While the Expressionists and Cubists tacitly disdained official culture, the Futurists thundered their animus against it from the rooftops.

In contrast, the creators of Art Nouveau—Jugendstil, Liberty Style, Sezession Stil—placated academicism by tempering rather than execrating its overornamentation. Uncertain whether the year 1900 would mark the dawn of a new age or the sunset of the old order, they hoped to use art to revitalize handicrafts in a time of growing mechanization. Although they looked for a reconciliation of art and industry, their estrangement from machines reinforced their artisanal bent. Particularly in France, but also elsewhere, Art Nouveau left its mark primarily through the applied and decorative arts. It grafted its ahistorical motifs into pre-existing craft traditions, notably in cities which, like Paris, were centers of luxury production in furniture, clothing, jewelry, and glassware.

With few exceptions, Art Nouveau was not architectonic. Instead of venturing into structural design and flouting monumentalism, it tamed decorative façades and lightened interiors by suffusing them with finely and individually crafted *objets d'art*. To be sure, its floral, vegetable, and animal themes were antitraditional statements. But unable to choose between the past and the future, Art Nouveau artists painted and forged sinuous, swirling, and fluid lines, thereby creating the illusion rather than the reality of movement. This effort to simulate motion and to miniaturize actuality in a time of crescive change was bound to misfire, and Art Nouveau vanished in record time, like a cultural meteor. Unable to reconcile their aesthetic calling with the dictates of factory production, these would-be artist-artisans became custom craftsmen and portraitists to wealthy clients. Most of their patrons were aristocrats or *grand bourgeois* aesthetes who, like themselves, reproved the official culture's excessive rigidity. In any case, Art Nouveau was overtaken in no time by a classical reaction on one side and by the irrepressible modernist currents on the other. Perhaps the haunting fantasy of the animated but circular movement of some of Debussy's and Ravel's scores should be seen as part of the Art Nouveau legacy that included Alfred Guibert's Shaftsbury Fountain, Hector Guimard's Métro entrances, Émile Gallé's Nancy vases, Gustav Klimt's society portraits, and Henry van de Velde's manifestos.

Meanwhile Art Nouveau artists agreed with the Post-Impressionists, excepting Cubists and Futurists, on two major scores. Distrustful of visual sensations, all alike abandoned realism and naturalism for the expression of inner emotions and sense stimulations. In addition, save for Left Expressionists, they were estranged from the city, the factory, the proletariat, and the masses. In particular the advancing urban city unsettled and alienated even the cosmopolitans among them. While Art Nouveau artists sought to screen out this invading ferment, most Post-Impressionists sought to either escape or excoriate it, even if indirectly. In this regard Cézanne, Van Gogh, Gauguin, and Munch were at one not only with Kirchner, Kokoschka, and Schiele but with Kandinsky. Indeed, the urban Babylon and moloch—as yet more spectral than real —nurtured the frustration, anxiety, dread, anguish, and horror of nearly this entire avant-garde of modernism. At once decadent and dynamic, repellent and magnetic, the city threatened to destroy the high culture and society which they themselves were attacking in another key. Not knowing where to turn, some vanguardists externalized their unresolved inner agony by distorting natural and human forms, while others cautiously stepped beyond recognizable objects, situations, and persons to experiment with abstract and nonrepresentational constructs. After 1905 German Expressionism, to be discussed below, most strikingly revealed this duality.

Neither Cubism nor Futurism shared this torment and pessimism. Despite enormous differences between them, both aimed at conceiving an art for the onrushing world of unbound cities and machines, which they faced with confidence.

Focusing on ordinary manmade and machine-made objects, Cubist painters experimented not only with new materials—paper, wood, metal, sawdust—but with new visual concepts. Rather than revealing the world as the Impressionists had done, they explored the interactions of structure, space, and representation with emphasis on form, not subject. Repudiating inert pictorial figures, the Cubists presented their interactive and synchronized geometric forms in a hermetic vacuum without reference to nature, economy, or society. Even the city, with which Braque and Picasso were reconciled, was eliminated from canvases designed to penetrate the dynamic processes of the modern world and psyche.

The Futurists, for their part, energized pictorial figures against the background of the urban city they glorified. Their verbal and written rhetoric was by far more militant than their visual vernacular, not least because of the public they were out to address. Whereas the Cubists fashioned an aesthetic language with which to speak to Europe's artistic subculture, the Futurists deliberately seceded from that subculture, including its bohemian branch, to brazenly court or harangue the masses. Accordingly Filippo Tommaso Marinetti's manifesto of February 1909 first appeared on the front page of *Le Figaro*. Paradoxically, though a "modern" medium, this newspaper was elitist, conservative, and Catholic, and as such stood for all the values the Futurists scorned.

In successive broadsides and "happenings" the Italian Futurists launched a uniquely comprehensive and virulent assault on Europe's official culture. For them Italy was "a land of the dead . . . a gigantic Pompeii," crowned by a "cancerous abscess of professors, archaeologists, tourist guides, and antiquaries." Children of the industrial north, notably Milan, the Futurists lashed out against Naples, Rome, Florence, and Venice as festering "wounds of passeism." While Venice just then captivated Europe's aesthetes, they satirized it for being a "market for fake antiques . . . a magnet for snobs and fools . . . a jeweled sitzbath for cosmopolitan courtesans . . . and the largest brothel of all time." In sum, Venice was infested with the "syphilis of sentimentality" and with gondolas that were "swings for idiots." But the Futurists' outcry was intended to reverberate beyond Venice and Italy. Railing against tradition and history, they presented themselves as a commando to lead Europe's vanguard in breaking out of the past once and for all, if need be by burning libraries, bombing academies, and flooding museums.

No doubt as poet and playwright Marinetti allowed his rhetoric to outrun the insurgent thrust of Futurist painters, sculptors, and architects. Nonetheless they all joined to defy the cult of official culture with a countercult of youth, irreverence, science, technology, movement, and speed. On one level, then, the Futurists were champions of industry, innovation, and progress, in that they extolled the dynamic rhythms of factories, automobiles, airplanes, and electric turbines with both words and brush strokes. On another, they allied themselves with conservative forces. To be sure, they attacked the monarchy, the Church, and the Vatican. But they also denigrated parliament, elections, and the philistine bourgeoisie, and distanced themselves from socialists and workers, the political vanguard of social progress. Instead, they trusted in extreme Italian nationalism, imperialism, and war to clear the ground for the machine age and culture, regardless of the human, social, and political cost. Inspired by Nietzsche, whose ode to delusional antiquity they transmuted into an ode to aerial modernity, the Futurists denied equality, opposed the leveling of society, and believed in an aristocracy of the spirit and the arts.

Few if any of the paintings of the Futurists corresponded to the inner mood of their printed manifestos and verbal declamations. Leaving behind the serene cityscapes of respectable society, Umberto Boccioni, Carlo Carrà, Ardengo Soffici, and Gino Severini portrayed urban streets, factories, and mechanized transport pulsating with the movements, tensions, and conflict of workers, unemployed, and deviants. While they convincingly rhapsodized northern Italy's urban dynamism—which, as we saw, was an enclave in an overwhelmingly pre-industrial society—they were unable to evacuate the social question from their pictures to make room for the patriotic frenzy and external conflict against either Austria or Libya. In fact, rather than abandon themselves to social protest or countenance Marinetti's modernist nightmare, Boccioni, Severini, and Carrà drew closer to Cubism's psychologically and socially less frenetic search for a modern style. But by 1914 both Futurism and Cubism had peaked and could hardly be said to be alarming to the *chiens de garde* of official culture.

While academic painting and museums furnished the contemplative gravity of artistic worship and reproduction, the theater, opera, and ballet provided its emotive leaven. In a conglomerate of styles the dramatic arts remained sufficiently authentic for the ruling classes to recognize themselves in the Baroque productions of courtly plays at the Comédie-Française in Paris and the Burgtheater in Vienna.

But between 1848 and 1914 the opera became the queen of Dionysian art forms and cults. Of Baroque origin, like the museum it moved out of its courtly environment into the public sphere, bringing along most of its architectural and repertorial endowment. In fact, the opera never ceased to be courtly, and after 1840, by moving into new houses and acquiring a new repertoire, it became increasingly stately. Behind grandiose historical façades, the grand staircases, tiered loges, and mannered foyers were ideally suited for the rites of imitation that promoted and reflected the aristocratization of the bourgeoisie. Steeped in historical lore and received musical constructs, the operatic librettos, scores, and productions were no less conducive to this lasting renobilization of Europe's ruling classes. Quite fittingly the crowned heads of Germany, Austria, and Russia took a special interest in the opera houses of their capitals, and all governments, including those of the Third Republic, allocated a disproportionately large share of their meager budgets for the arts to this exclusive and sacramental cultural activity.

Until after the turn of the century Richard Wagner was the only genuine innovator, giving a tremendous impetus to the apotheosis of grand opera. Himself a writer, composer, and conductor, and student of ancient Greek drama, Wagner set out to forge a *Gesamtkunstwerk* (complete work of art). In his hands opera became the vehicle for the integration of the major arts into a total and collective art form: architecture, painting, drama, poetry, music, song, and dance. All these media were synthesized to make a harmonious whole that was qualitatively greater than and distinct from its component elements. Instead of creating new musical and dramatic languages, Wagner ingeniously assembled prefabricated units to generate maximum theatrical effect. The principal ambiguity of his super-opera was whether music was the servant or the master of drama. But this very ambiguity was central to Wagner's purpose. Less and less interested in entertaining or achieving some ideal of stylistic purity, he turned to celebrating and reconsecrating the social order of the second German empire. Like his close friend Gottfried Semper, the preeminent architect of Baroque monumentalism in Central Europe, Wagner constructed music dramas of colossal pomp and self-possession calculated to mystify and spiritualize life inside and beyond the operatic temple.

That temple, in the form of the Festspielhaus, was constructed in Bayreuth from 1872 to 1876, when it was inaugurated with a performance of the complete *Ring Cycle* in the presence of Emperor William I, King Louis II of Bavaria, and a bevy of German princes. Soon it appeared that Wagner diverged from his model of Greek tragedy on two scores: he catered to an elite audience rather than a cross-section of the polity, and his aspirations were German-centered, not universal. In any case, the visitors who flocked to Bayreuth to participate in the incipient Wagnerian cult were wealthy and educated, which meant that they could afford luxurious travel and were able to read Wagnerian myths and legends. Moreover, despite the heavy Germanic flavor of the cult and ritual, aristocrats and *grands bourgeois* from all over Europe participated in the yearly pilgrimage even in times of rising national antagonisms. Eventually Thomas Mann claimed that Bayreuth became "a musical Lourdes . . . a miraculous grotto for the voracious credulity of a decadent world."

This was also the judgment of Max Nordau, author of the highly polemical *Degeneration,* first published in 1893 and within a few years translated into some twenty languages. According to Nordau, it became "a mark of aristocracy . . . among the snobs" of wealth and education to go to Bayreuth to witness operas that were a "bleating echo of a faraway past . . . and the last mushroom on the dunghill of romanticism [rather than] the art work of the future." Nordau considered that as a dramatist Wagner was "a historical painter of the highest rank" with a genius for imagining and re-creating "fêtes, pageants, triumphs, and allegorical plays . . . [whose] pictorial allurements were perceptible even to the eye of the crassest philistine." He also regarded Wagner as an "atavistic" composer who debased music "to conventional phonetic symbol," made use of the "vague recitative of savages," subordinated "highly differentiated instrumental music to music-drama," and avoided "more than one person singing on stage and vocal polyphony."

All in all, the cult and diffusion of Wagner, as of Nietzsche, grew apace after his death, more particularly from the turn of the century to 1914. His *oeuvre* may be seen as a reflection, prophecy, and tool of the persistence of the old order not only in Germany but in Europe as a whole. Certainly it was neither the funeral march nor the herald of the bourgeois age. Once he repudiated his qualified enthusiasm for the liberating springtime of 1848, Wagner more and more acclaimed heroic kinghood over law, abetted emotion over reason, and sanctioned romantic nationalism over poised cosmopolitanism.

Richard Strauss, not Claude Debussy, was the first to break with the traditional operatic mode as well as the Wagnerian ascendancy and vogue. Seeing himself as an Expressionist,

Strauss moved toward vocal dissonance and vehement psychologism, hesitantly in *Salome* (1905) and with full force in *Elektra* (1909). But the reception was so hostile, in Vienna and elsewhere, that he retreated to the pre-Wagnerian operatic genre. Thoroughly Mozartian and interlaced with Viennese waltz rhythms *Der Rosenkavalier* (1911) was a "capitulation and adaptation" to Europe's musically conservative opera-going public.

The musical avant-garde neither displaced nor beleaguered grand opera any more than it radicalized the rebirth of the ballet, which was sparked by Serge Diaghilev. A mere tastemaker and impresario, Diaghilev nevertheless became the Wagner of the ballet by remolding it into a *Gesamtkunstwerk* without effecting major stylistic departures. Not surprisingly, the ballet burst forth from the most intact of Europe's *anciens régimes*. An aristocratic art form which was perfected in the eighteenth century, it had continued to flourish in Russia under the patronage of the Romanovs. During the nineteenth century popular and patriotic motifs were assimilated into the ballet's classical choreographic and costumery tradition. Beginning with Glinka, the great Russian composers—Borodin, Tchaikovsky, Rimsky-Korsakov—wrote musical scores enabling the ballet to pioneer in the rediscovery and celebration of Russia's indigenous cultural heritage that animated the Russian avant-garde after the turn of the century.

Attuned to the artistic secessions of the West, Diaghilev became a moving force in opening Russia to Impressionism. Having done so, he next turned to reanimating his own country's past. Of noble ancestry and with intermittent imperial support he promoted a Russian renaissance through journals, exhibits, and artistic circles at home before becoming its plenipotentiary abroad.

In the wake of the Revolution of 1905 Diaghilev spent three years introducing Paris to Russian icons, orchestral music, and opera. Then, beginning in May 1909, he dazzled the French capital with the Ballets Russes. Audiences and critics were overwhelmed, not by the novelty of this musical dance, but by the regenerated life and splendor of what was an old art form.

Above all Nijinsky displayed the newfound vitality of linear, frontal, cyclical, but rigorously classical steps. Moreover, he and the corps of dancers conveyed an enormous range of unthreatening moods and sentiments through conventional corporeal movements and gestures.

Diaghilev's genius was to invest this fixed choreography with colorful and flamboyant stage settings and costumes. Designed by Bakst, Benois, and Larionov—and eventually also by Derain, Matisse, and Picasso—this *mise en scène* suffused the entire production with a wondrous luminescence. Meanwhile Diaghilev also invited Stravinsky to compose scores for his ballet, whose repertory was heavily "old" Russian. Just then Stravinsky, too, was caught up in the surging revival of folk culture—tales, music, dance, and song. Certainly *The Firebird* (1910) and *Petrushka* (1911) carried that imprint, as did *Le Sacre du printemps* (1913), which evoked "scenes from pagan Russia" in a musical language that marked a revolutionary break-through.

Whether at home or abroad, the Ballets Russes performed under august auspices and before highly exclusive audiences that were anything but champions of the cultural avant-garde. To be sure, in 1913 the dissonant but rhythmic *Sacre du printemps* shocked a first-night Parisian audience, and both *Petrushka* and Debussy's *Après-midi d'un faune* got a cool reception in Vienna. But in 1911 the Ballets Russes successfully presented a gala evening of dance and opera at Covent Garden as part of the festivities marking the coronation of George V. Moreover, that same year Emperor William II, Europe's supreme antimodernist, was in the glittering first-night audience in the Kroll Theater in Berlin. After the performance he sent for Diaghilev to compliment him, especially for *Cléopatra*.

"While in St. Petersburg folk music renewed the ballet tradition by way of great composers, in Vienna it was destroyed by the waltz, which was operetta-like, and therefore neither popular art nor ballet." In their commercialized operettas Franz Lehár *(The Merry Widow)* and Johann Strauss *(Die Fledermaus)* projected a world that was as aristocratic, sensual, and frivolous as that in Jacques Offenbach's *Vie Parisienne* under Napo-

leon III. But compared to the *tableaux vivants* of French imperial society, which were tinged with cynicism, those of Habsburg high life were crassly roseate and titillating.

Most of the great palaces for the performing arts were cast
in the same imposing architectural mold as the museums. But
compared with visiting a museum, going to the theater, opera,
or ballet was much more of a public and ostentatious act. The
price and location of seats, especially at gala performances,
were in the nature of an order and code of precedence. In fact,
the stately audiences of the performing arts mirrored the
changing ranks in the ruling class better and faster than court
or salon society. The overrepresentation of prosperous assimilated Jews among the patrons of the performing arts, especially in Central Europe, expressed not only their traditional
esteem for the life of the mind and nonrepresentational art but
also their turning to culture to compensate for their continuing social and political ostracism. In any case, most of these
Jews were middle class rather than bourgeois, and together
with the *Bildungsbürgertum* (educated and cultivated bourgeoisie) they eagerly participated in a cultural life that remained
embedded in the old society.

The clothes of the time, notably the vestments worn on
grand social occasions, echoed and fostered this adaptation.
No doubt, during the nineteenth century the aristocracy tempered its ostentation and distinctiveness, and men left it to
women to be the pacesetters of fashion. But on the whole
fashion remained subservient to custom, clothes being custom-
made and not imaginatively conceived. Above all, while the
nobleman dressed down so as to be less grandiose, the *grands
bourgeois* assumed the aristocracy's ingrained predilection for
discriminate distinction. Accordingly, dress continued to mark
status levels. But for the well-to-do, to be fashionable was not
to be original, flashy, or extravagant. Along with manners and
bearing, clothes were cut and worn to fit in with the
nobilitarian establishment.

Ultimately clothing conventions served not only to demar-
cate the ruling class but also to cement its internal cohesion.
As in so many other spheres of upper-class life custom was the

fashion, and it was custom that dictated a dress code whose spirit and make-up dated from before midcentury. If modes were conservative and slow-moving it was largely because the bourgeoisie was out to join rather than challenge the old elites. The latter periodically reasserted their primacy by parading their decorations or uniforms at official receptions and stately social and cultural occasions. Between Louis-Philippe, the citizen-king who put away his uniform and medals to dignify dark suits and cutaways, and Paul Poiret, the couturier who in 1910 scarcely started to liberate society women from their strait-fronted corsets, fashions marked time to the refined beat of the old society.

Until 1914 even Europe's most industrial, urbanized, and imperialist nation had a singularly traditional official culture. In public building, except in church architecture, the Gothic revival of England's Victorian era gradually receded, giving way to the Baroque revival of the Edwardian years and the classical revival of the decade before 1914. As of 1890 architects adopted the Baroque (or English Renaissance) style to express the high noon of Greater Britain's economic prowess and world hegemony. Predictably the swaggering Edwardian Baroque broke forth in government buildings in London, in the municipal halls of Belfast and Cardiff, and in the memorial to Queen Victoria in Calcutta. But it was also the style in which John Belcher designed the Institute for Chartered Accountants in London, Matear and Simon the Cotton Exchange in Liverpool, and the Skipper brothers and J. J. Burnett the headquarters of insurance companies in Norwich and Glasgow. Moreover, judging by Belcher's Ashton Memorial (1905–1909), commissioned by Lord Ashton to celebrate his family's linoleum firm in Lancaster, local tycoons seized upon High Edwardian Baroque to proclaim their assimilation into the old society.

Partly as a backlash against this heavy gaudiness, which the arts and crafts movement never really managed to temper,

English architects after the turn of the century opened themselves, cautiously, to the French Beaux-Arts influence. Seeking
the simplicity and refinement of classical proportions, they
adapted a neomannerist style for both public and business
constructions. But though free of florid decorations, behind
their stripped classical exteriors the Ritz Hotel (1903–1906)
and the Automobile Club (1908–1911) in London harbored
the same atmosphere of gentility that swathed the sentient
Proust in the Ritz in Paris.

The world of visual arts was dominated by the thoroughly
inbred Royal Academy, which monopolized art instruction and
the prestigious summer exhibitions at which the Arts Council
made regular purchases. Under the presidency of Frederick
Leighton, who after being ennobled (1886) was raised into
the peerage (1896), and John Everett Millais, who also was
knighted (1885), the Academy promoted painting that was
severely traditional in every respect. During these same years
George Frederic Watts painted frescos in the recently built
House of Lords and numerous stilted portraits of notables,
which eventually earned him the Order of Merit. There was a
nationalist, not to say nativist, side to this aesthetic conservatism. Impressionism was spurned not only for being novel and
impious but also for being the carrier of the lethal bacteria of
French degeneracy, *légèreté,* and radicalism. Only small segments of England's snobbish upper middle class were open to
influences from across the Channel. Chafing under the cramp-
ing cultural and aristocratic atmosphere of Edwardian and
post-Edwardian England, they patronized exhibits of modern
art in London's private galleries.

The National Gallery, which in 1904 refused a gift of a
Degas, was a treasure house of Italian, Flemish, and Dutch
masters, while the works of English painters were relegated to
the South Kensington Museum. Both national and social impulses moved Henry Tate, a wealthy sugar refiner, to press for
a London equivalent of the Luxembourg in Paris. He donated
not only his own collection of English paintings, which was
heavily academicist, but also the funds to build a major museum on a site provided by the government. In mid-1897 the

Prince of Wales conspicuously inaugurated this new Gallery of Modern British Art, constructed in a fustian neoclassical style. A year later Tate was rewarded with a baronetcy, which no doubt induced him to make additional gifts of paintings and of funds to enlarge the exhibition halls.

Needless to say, the word "modern" in the name was meant in a purely temporal sense, since the Tate Gallery was to acquire recent and current "academic" works. Hereafter the Treasury subsidized the growth of this collection of national art. It also compensated private donors who helped the National Gallery buy old Continental masters that were being sold by some of England's greatest peers (e.g., the duke of Marlborough, the earl of Radnor of Lanford Castle, the duke of Norfolk) and that were in danger of being lost to foreign museums or private collectors. The moderns, both British and foreign, remained completely shut out of Royal Academy and museums alike.

The resistance to modernity was no less apparent in drama and literature. Plays by Ibsen, Maeterlinck, and Sudermann as well as Strauss's *Salome* were banned, as were books by Zola. While this resistance to new art and thought was not without xenophobic overtones, the chief examiner also censored Oscar Wilde's *Salomé* (which was written in French) and two playlets by George Bernard Shaw.

Eventually, in 1907, although only 4 out of 536 licenses were refused, some seventy prominent writers petitioned the government to review the censor's powers as they applied to plays. Once a number of MPs took up the cause in 1909 Asquith finally appointed a joint parliamentary committee of inquiry. After four months of hearings this committee, more sensitive to producers and audiences than to writers, recommended that the lord chamberlain's prerogatives be kept essentially intact.

Although some of the ideas and attitudes of Continental avant-gardists started to resonate in England by 1914, this echo remained rather faint. Asquith and his Liberal associates kept their distance from the moderns for fear of alienating their middle-class base and of further inflaming the schism in

Britain's ruling class. Besides, the Liberal cabinet was not exactly composed of cultural radicals. It was as suspicious of "decadents" and "aesthetes" as it was of artists in search of an artisanal revival.

As the only republic among Europe's major powers France was in the forefront of de-royalization, de-aristocratization, and de-Christianization. The recessive antirepublican elements sought to use both the Boulanger and the Dreyfus affairs to narrow or close the historical break dating back to 1789. Although their bids for royal restoration misfired, French political society remained seriously fractured, in large part because so much of civil society remained unchanged. During both abortive sallies, and also during the nationalist eruption after 1905, the catonists demonstrated their capacity to rally a large popular following in Paris. Evidently the capital was no less torn than rural and provincial France. The result was that Paris remained a formidable bastion of national academicism at the same time that it towered as the mecca not only of France's but of Europe's avant-garde. The overweening official culture both fostered and exploited the chronic stalemate of the Third Republic, which inordinately benefitted the old order.

Although beginning with Jules Ferry's first government in 1881 the stalemated regime vigorously pushed the secularization, democratization, and nationalization of education, notably on the primary and secondary level, it hesitated to use state power to promote a cultural and artistic project of its own. In fact, rather than encourage experimentation, successive administrations adopted a policy of benign neglect, which resulted in the official assimilation and reproduction of classic academicism inherited from past regimes. The fragility of both government and regime and the cultural diffidence of the new political class, which was *petit* rather than *grand bourgeois,* dictated this circumspection.

The endemic cabinet instability of the Third Republic fortified the quasi-permanent undersecretaries of the principal ministries, including those dealing with the arts. Educated and socialized in the *grandes écoles* and academies, this state-created elite, regardless of social origin, was programmed to presume classical high culture as an indispensable substructure of the established order that it was trained and sworn to uphold. Henry Roujon directed the state administration of fine arts for twelve years from 1891 to 1903 while also a member and then permanent secretary of the Académie des Beaux-Arts. But H. Dujardin-Beaumetz, who between 1905 and 1912 served as undersecretary of state for fine arts under six different governments, personified this continuity. An academically trained painter and a staid opportunist republican who was first a deputy and then a senator, Dujardin-Beaumetz was a cultural conservative. It even took considerable pressure from premiers Clemenceau and Briand for him to appoint André Antoine director of the Odéon and Gabriel Fauré director of the Conservatoire. After selecting Bonnat, historical painter and knight of the Legion of Honor, to head the École nationale supérieure des beaux-arts, Dujardin-Beaumetz commissioned numerous orthodox sculptures for conspicuous public emplacement and refused to buy even a single painting by Cézanne. His successor, Léon Bérard, was hardly less unprogressive.

In addition to brittle cabinets and long-serving bureaucrats, there were the four sovereign academies with their lifetime or immortal members. Through their hold on the foremost teaching establishments, notably on the Beaux-Arts and the Conservatoire, these academicians were the guardians and apostles of the regnant cultural doctrine and style, not to say dogma. They controlled the committees which awarded the prizes that gave painters, composers, and architects prestigious visiting fellowships at the Villa Medici in Rome, the city that was Europe's leading pedagogic museum. To win and make good on these awards was to be favored not only in state exhibits or repertories but with regard to government commissions, decorations, and academic positions.

The republican regime's self-confinement in the cultural

matrix of its predecessors was prominently reflected in the
vacuous public and monumental architecture typified by the
new Hôtel de Ville and the Sacré-Coeur. Rather than venture
authentic but indeterminate statements, France's governors
limited themselves to works of restoration, decoration, and
preservation. For obvious reasons the first step was to scrupu-
lously reconstruct the historical buildings damaged during the
bloody week of the Commune. Thereafter the interiors of the
Théatre Français and the Opéra-Comique were renovated
rather than modernized, and laws were passed in 1887 and
1913 to protect the capital's architectural heritage, the number of *édifices classés* rising from 1,702 in 1902 to 3,560 in 1913.

Clearly, the Third Republic settled into a public environment that was built and "furnished" by previous regimes. It
behaved, not like a proud master commissioning his own
buildings and testimonials, but like the dutiful curator and
tenant of an old patrimony. Only in part for reasons of economy, the regime avoided new constructions, preferring to
move key civil and political institutions into the grandiose
palaces of France's royal and imperial past. Although French
engineers were ready with steel frames and reinforced concrete, their *génie* remained largely untapped. They were
pressed into service only for the world fairs which were meant
to signal the regime's resolve and ability to cope with the
future. Accordingly, the Palais des Machines and the Eiffel
Tower gave a patently modernist stamp to the centennial fair
of 1889. By comparison the Grand and Petit Palais of 1900
were more guarded statements, in that both had Baroque exteriors.

Similarly, academic painting and sculpture easily held their
own down to 1914, with stress on repetition and imitation of
past art forms, motifs, and masters. The neoclassicists dominated the École des Beaux-Arts and the salons. They also
secured all public commissions, both national and local, and
were supported by wealthy patrons. Moreover, with little difficulty they kept the Impressionists and their successors firmly
at bay. With few and unspectacular exceptions the *haut monde*
remained hostile to the Post-Impressionists, notably the

Fauves and the Cubists. In turn, most of the French secessionists voluntarily withdrew into self-enclosed artistic sects that
were indifferent to the social and political battles of their day.
They disdained rather than attacked the establishment and
continued to yearn for official recognition and for private patrons, especially since such art dealers as Kahnweiler, Durand-
Ruel, and Vollard had only begun to develop substitute
galleries and markets.

The Dreyfus affair unexpectedly turned into a campaign by
marginal intellectuals and artists to prevent France from being
put entirely back on European time. The confrontation that
nearly polarized the nation revealed the extent to which integral conservatism permeated the Third Republic's cultural
institutions. The anti-Dreyfusards found massive and prestigious support in the academies, the Conservatoire, the Beaux-
Arts, the theater, the university, and the church, as well as
among established and best-selling novelists, playwrights, and
journalists. The Dreyfusards, for their part, came primarily
from among the intellectual and artistic avant-gardes, but also
from among professional sociologists, historians, and philosophers who strained to provide the fragile republic with a sorely
needed legitimating ideology. If the Dreyfusards of the first
hour succeeded in stopping a would-be royalist restoration, it
was largely because they mobilized the independents and
secessionists of the intelligentsia and creative arts, who tended
to be unpolitical, thereby mounting a challenge that political
society could not ignore. Although many of the new believers
scorned Zola for his prosaic naturalism and popularity, it was
his voice, carried by the republican press, that gave theirs such
extraordinary force. Barrès and the anti-Dreyfus newspapers
were confounded, along with their aristocratic and academic
supporters.

The republic weathered the storm. With Premier Émile
Combes showing the way, successive cabinets reduced if not
entirely eliminated royalist and clerical influences in vital sectors of the public service. But this *épuration* of the state apparatus was neither accompanied nor followed by a liberalization
of the cultural establishment, let alone of *tout Paris*. Although

the avant-gardists eagerly returned to their cultural ghettos, they continued to be more suspect than ever. By having joined with socialists and advanced republicans they justified the old cultural and intellectual elites in their view that artistic modernism and social as well as political radicalism were linked inextricably. The labor unrest of 1906 to 1910 further stiffened the illiberalism and conservatism of important sectors not only of the ruling and governing class but also of the cultural establishment. The critique of the modern movement became increasingly moral and political. At the same time, a boisterous arrière-garde called for a neoclassical revival to bolster the inveterate artistic and cultural order against the avant-garde and its socialist and anarchist fellow travelers.

The conservative backlash manifested itself in the access of superpatriotism in the university and in the silencing of the "modernists" in the Catholic Church. In 1913 Stravinsky's *Sacre du printemps* was jeered by erstwhile sympathizers of the modern, and Debussy's *Jeux* did not fare much better, even though both composers were totally out of sympathy with the left and its internationalism. Perhaps understandably, despite intense anti-German feelings Wagner's pietistic *Parsifal* received a warmer reception when it was finally produced at the still imperial Opéra, which absorbed more than one-third of the state budget for the performing arts. Meanwhile the pressure to bar the Cubists from the next Salon d'Automne gave rise to an interpellation in the Chamber of Deputies on December 3, 1912. Significantly, even a Socialist deputy considered it "absolutely inadmissible that France's national palaces should be used for such obviously antiartistic and antinational purposes." But another Socialist, Marcel Sembat, promptly retorted that while viewers had every right to prefer some paintings to others they had no right "to call in the police." Although there was no follow-up to this debate, it was a sign of the times that it even took place. Certainly the France of Poincaré, who had engineered his own election to the Academy in 1909, was not about to unbend an official culture whose chief minstrel was Maurice Barrès. Both Poincaré and Barrès were natives of Lorraine and members of the Academy, but only the author of *Les Déracinés* played a spirited role in the royalist Action Française and the incipient cult of Jeanne d'Arc.

The culture of the second German empire was manifestly and relentlessly traditional. Even or especially after 1890 the emphasis continued to be on the imitation and reproduction of a conventional art that was oblivious to the country's rapid economic, demographic, and urban change. State and government, especially in Prussia, fostered this venerable *Kultur,* which also spawned the iconography glorifying the new German nation.

More than any other sovereign William II spoke out on the functions of art, even to the extreme of denouncing art that violated "the laws and limits" set by him as anti-art. Moreover, he considered the plastic and performing arts, along with the schools and universities, as so many "weapons" and "tools" in his political armory.

The kaiser made his fullest and most revealing cultural pronouncement on December 18, 1901, immediately after unveiling thirty-two statues of past rulers of Brandenburg-Prussia along both sides of a *Siegesallee* running from Berlin's Siegessaüle through the Tiergarten to the Rolandplatz. Addressing the artists who had executed this extravagant memorial to the Hohenzollern dynasty, William II vaunted himself on his close association with them. He stressed that with the counsel of Professor Reinhold Koser, his court historian, and Professor Reinhold Begas, his court sculptor, he had personally given the assembled artists their general directives without in any way restricting their "absolute freedom" of execution. Of course, the emperor presupposed broad agreement on the virtues of classical models and on the eternal laws of beauty and harmony. He gave his artists what was his highest praise by pronouncing their white marble statuary to be "nearly as accomplished as that of nineteen hundred years ago." Fortunately German sculpture remained immune to "so-called modern trends and currents," most of which were foreign and perverted the word "freedom" with their "laxity, boundlessness, and arrogance." In the kaiser's view high culture had no greater task than to educate the public, especially the lower classes, by forcefully portraying virtue, beauty, and honor. Whereas to project these lofty classical ideals was to uplift the German people morally and spiritually, to depict and exaggerate human misery was to "sin against it."

Even before bequeathing this Siegesallee to Berlin the emperor commissioned the construction of the neo-Romanesque Kaiser Wilhelm Memorial Church near the Kurfürstendam. Dedicated on the twenty-fifth anniversary of the victory at Sedan and named to honor the incumbent emperor's grandfather, this shrine was meant to join together and glorify throne, altar, and nation, also by insculpting the names of Roon, Bismarck, and Moltke between two portals. Since it was rather a new departure to christen religious buildings for political figures, this bold temple was seen as setting an imperial style which before long was reproduced in countless statues of William I and in official portraits of William II in military poses and flaunting bombastic uniforms.

Although William II was too brash and unpliant for sober conservatives and liberals, the ruling and governing class as a whole quite approved or at least tolerated his playing such an active role in official culture. He not only conspicuously acclaimed undistinguished authors like Ludwig Ganghofer and Ludwig Pietsch but also appointed Anton von Werner, his court painter, to preside over the Prussian Academy of Fine Arts, including its art school. Known for his evocations of Prussia's history, Werner could be trusted to oppose experimentation, naturalism, and Impressionism. Such gestures and appointments were intended to embolden officials throughout Germany's cultural institutions to block and harass recusants, critics, and secessionists. Though widely honored abroad, Gerhart Hauptmann was systematically rebuffed for his naturalist treatment of the wretchedness of Silesian weavers in *Die Weber* and for his derision of Prussia's authoritarian penchants in *Der Biberpelz*. As of 1890 the Berlin police and censor hindered and delayed the performance of Hauptmann's plays—along with those of Ibsen and Sudermann—and William II personally countermanded the jury that had awarded Hauptmann the Schiller prize.

Frank Wedekind did not fare much better. Because of his corrosive satire in *Simplicissimus* and his profanation of moral —notably sexual—codes, he repeatedly ran afoul of the censor and even was sentenced to seven months honorable confinement in the Königsstein fortress. Although Wedekind completed his *Frühlings Erwachen* in 1890, it was not until 1906 that Max Reinhardt finally staged it in a censored version in Berlin. The kaiser's dictum that drama should elevate the individual soul and nurture patriotism fueled this official chicanery. While he saw to it that the Royal Theater presented suitable morality plays, the empress used her influence to delay the production of Richard Strauss's *Salome* and *Rosenkavalier* at the Berlin Opera, in which William II took a special interest. The emperor also interposed himself in the graphic and visual arts. In 1898 he vetoed the awarding of a gold medal to Käthe Kollwitz for her drawings of *The Weavers,* which were inspired by Hauptmann's naturalist play, and eleven years later he dismissed Hugo von Tschudi, the director of Berlin's National Gallery, for purchasing Impressionist paintings which were too untraditional for his taste.

The different secessions were a remonstrance or revolt against this politically inspired and ungainly enforcement of an unenlightened academic art and imperial culture. Certainly the Berlin Secession of 1898, like the Vienna Secession of the year before, was meant to loosen rather than break academic constraints. Max Liebermann, a member of the Berlin Academy, and Julius Meier-Graefe, the respected art critic, merely asked that a *salon des refusés,* with a separate jury, be fitted into the yearly exhibition of the Prussian Academy in Berlin. When Anton von Werner, backed by the emperor, refused, Liebermann led the secessionists in organizing their own salon in which French moderns served to legitimate the showing of German Impressionists such as Lovis Corinth and Max Slevogt. Actually, the defectors were not all that radical artistically, since their objective was to catch up with Impressionism. With few exceptions they abjured social criticism and politics. Admittedly, for twenty years Liebermann had devoted himself to painting realistically natural portraits of the social problems of contemporary Germany for which he won official plaudits, including prizes and membership in the Academy. Even so, feeling hedged in, he turned to Impressionistic renderings of the leisure world of the *grande bourgeoisie,* to which he belonged. Eventually the emperor disparaged Liebermann and his associates as "gutter" artists, but less for being experimentalists than for no longer reproducing the imperial style. This very conservatism prompted Max Pechstein and the "new" secessionists to break away from Liebermann in 1910.

But while both the old and the young Berlin Secession remained a loyal opposition, Expressionism had the makings of a countercultural movement. At first the Expressionists also far more clearly impugned Germany's asphyxiating traditionalism than they articulated a new aesthetics. As Rudolf Kurtz proclaimed in the first issue of *Der Sturm* (March 3, 1910), the young rebels meant to expose imperial society's crushing solemnity, self-satisfaction, and sham. While rebelling against fathers, professors, officers, and governors, they identified with indigents, prostitutes, psychotics, youth, and women. But the Expressionists did not go so far as to denounce the bourgeoisie and its middle-class associates for exploiting workers and supporting superpatriotism. Instead, incensed that the pioneers of economic progress had embraced an archaic culture instead of promoting the modern movement, the Expressionists scorned them for being abject philistines.

The Expressionists admired the Impressionists more for having broken out of academicism than for their serene view of society, their optic recording of the external world, their promiscuous infatuation with color, and their obsession with perspective. Moved by the tortured strokes and anguished solitude of Van Gogh and Edvard Munch, and distrustful of sense perceptions, they looked to Rouault, Rousseau, and Delaunay for help in projecting their own internal feelings on the external world. The Expressionists undertook to give form to the interpenetration of their psychic dispositions with the real world outside. While they spurned the constricting and factitious imperial society, they remained at a loss to imagine an alternative to it.

Except for their common disenchantment with the world and their urge to escape all artistic conventions, the German Expressionists were as internally divided as any avant-garde. Some were radically irrational, others mystical, and still others humanitarian. Another line of division ran between active aesthetes and political activists, there being few recluses among them. In addition to lacking internal coherence, they were temporally out of phase. The more radical aesthetic and social elements among them did not really coalesce until 1910–1911, when Germany was in the grip of an ultraconservative resurgence.

Besides, *Die Brücke,* which was launched in Dresden in 1905, was only marginally Expressionist. Ernst Kirchner and his associates (Emil Nolde, Erich Heckel, Karl Schmidt-Rottluff, Max Pechstein) never really broke radically with figurative art. To be sure, their spasmic landscapes, distorted bodies, and melancholically violent colors articulated their spiritual malaise, their vibrant sensuality, and their repudiation of art as a cosmetic and sanctifying medium. Even so, while the *Brücke* group violated the kaiser's norms, it did not probe for a new aesthetic paradigm. When the journal and the group expired in 1913 Kirchner occupied a middle ground between the cautious Berlin Secession and the latest ultramoderns of the avant-garde.

From its very start in 1911, the *Blaue Reiter* in Munich disavowed the *Brücke* for being excessively impulsive, spontaneous, and egotistical, and insufficiently experimental and reflective. Instead of expressing elementary life-impulses and sacrificing medium to message, Wassily Kandinsky and Franz Marc called for an intellectualized expression of spiritual and mystical sensibilities. They wanted tomorrow's paintings, including their coloring, to become speculative symbolic reports on the psychic and spiritual state of artists liberated from yesterday's aesthetic shackles. Taking these criteria, Kandinsky held that the works of the *Brücke* did not qualify for inclusion in the *Almanach* in which he and Marc featured paintings making a "decisive contribution to the elaboration of contemporary art." The first *Blaue Reiter* exhibit of 1911 similarly excluded them.

In the meantime Herwarth Walden began publishing *Der Sturm,* which became the principal organ of the aesthetic avant-garde of all the arts. Eclectic in his modernist sensibility and taste, Walden opened his journal and also his gallery—inaugurated in 1913—to all genuinely experimental statements, both domestic and foreign, including the nascent Futurism and Abstractionism. But along with Kandinsky, whom he judged to be of pivotal importance, Walden was a crusader for the new, essentially apolitical aesthetics that looked to make a place for itself within the *ancien régime.* The "blue riders" were prophets of anxiety and despair rather than confident revolutionaries. Distancing themselves from society, let alone from socialism, and insulating art from politics, they had a premonition of world catastrophe. To the extent that Kandinsky and Marc expected a *vita nuova* to emerge from an impending cataclysm, they anticipated and craved a spiritual rather than an economic, social, and political rebirth. On close inspection the horse and rider on the cover of their *Almanach,* which were still drawn figuratively, conveyed a supernatural vision: the blue rider was a conflated representation of Saint George and Saint Michael, the Horseman of the Apocalypse slaying the dragon of materialism. Besides, the horseman was a symbol of European nobility, and blue evoked fealty and a romantic yearning for spiritual salvation.

Having turned their backs on materialism and empiricism, Kandinsky and Marc looked for guidance and consolation to whatever industrial and commercial civilization had not defiled. They sought inspiration in the art of an idealized, distant past and in the folk, children's, and "primitive" art of the contemporary world. To be sure, they meant to explode the "crust of convention" and cast away the "crutches of habit." But their rejection of the "used-up inheritance" went hand in hand with their repudiation of scientific progress.

Moreover, instead of adopting a constructive or critical social posture, Marc and Kandinsky aspired to be like "the disciples of early Christianity who found the strength for inner stillness amid the roaring noise of their time." In addition they vaingloriously and intentionally walked an elitist path that was "too steep" for the masses, whose "greed and dishonesty" were bound to destroy or debase any crusade "for pure ideas."

It was left to the *Aktion,* guided by Franz Pfemfert, to affirm that the battle for a new aesthetics was inseparable from the battle for a new society. Not that the *Aktion* group was either Marxist or tied to the Social Democrats, who were paragons of cultural conventionality. Paradoxically the painting and literature of revolt sought stimulation in anarchism, which was almost totally alien to Germany, except in a Dostoevskian and Nietzschean guise.

Indeed, few of the Expressionists squarely faced up to the novel tensions generated by the forced-draft implantation of modern industry into Germany's traditional society. Unlike the French Impressionists, they were not drawn to the countryside, nor were they fascinated by the measured gentility of city life. They were addicted to urbanizing cities that quickened their restlessness and anguish. Many avant-gardists may have started out in Dresden (population in 1880: 221,000; in 1914: 550,000) and Munich (population in 1880: 230,000; in 1914: 600,000), but few resisted the gravitational pull of Berlin. Compared to Paris, the German capital was a major industrial center whose population rose from about 800,000 in 1870 to over 2 million in 1914, or to 3.75 million with its suburbs. Berlin was a mammon that embodied and magnified the explosive contradictions of imperial society and polity. For nearly all Expressionists the modern city became a festering obsession and an unsettling enigma: a crucible of wealth and poverty, of hope and frustration, of novelty and atavistic tradition, of emancipation and alienation, of lust and numbness—but also and above all, a fount of high culture. Although it was one of their central preoccupations, the urban city remained peripheral or blurred in the Expressionists' artistic vision.

Eventually Ludwig Meidner—activist painter, playwright,

and poet—complained about the avant-garde's excessive preoccupation with primitive peoples and Christians of the early Middle Ages. He summoned Expressionists to admit "that they were living in Berlin, in the year 1913, that they went to cafés, that they constantly argued and did a great deal of reading." This being the case, the time had come to "paint the city, which was their country . . . and universe and which they loved deeply." Unlike their Impressionist mentors, the Expressionists "could not set up their easels in bustling streets," for these foiled the unmediated reading of the "monstrosity and drama of queues, railroad stations, factories, and chimneys . . . the elegance of iron bridges . . . the howling colors of buses and express locomotives, the undulating telephone wires . . . and the night . . . the night of the big city." To render the city's pulsations artists needed to "appropriate" totally new means of observation and expression. After walking the pavements to "gorge themselves with optical impressions" they would have to withdraw to their studios to "boldly and deliberately translate them into compositions . . . that penetrate to deeper levels of reality . . . than the ornamental, decorative, and surface fillings" of Kandinsky or Matisse. Because nature was presumed "not to have straight lines and not to be mathematical . . . ever since Ruysdael straight lines were banned from landscapes and artists avoided putting new buildings, new churches, and new castles into their paintings," preferring the picturesqueness of "irregular" houses, ruins, and trees. But as contemporaries of engineers, Expressionist artists needed to "sense the beauty of straight lines and geometric forms," which had a still "deeper meaning" for the Cubists. Above all, a straight line need be "neither cold nor stiff." If drawn in "excitement" and with close attention to its trajectory, it could be seen and shown to alternate between being "fine and thick . . . and animated by light and nervous vibrations." According to Meidner, the cityscapes were "mathematical battles," and this was the time to come to terms with "the triangles, squares, polygons, and circles that assault us in the streets."

In 1914 the Berlin Secessions of 1898 and 1910 as well as

the *Brücke* of 1905 were burned out, while the *Sturm* and the *Aktion* had yet to prove their staying power, notably in an increasingly illiberal political climate, also in Munich. Presumably a regime that knew how to curb the Social Democrats and to co-opt the bourgeoisie would also know how to constrain and defuse this cultural challenge. This task would be facilitated by the schisms within the avant-garde and also by its divorce from polity and society.

The Vienna Secession, which began formally in April 1897, was also an outcry against a stifling official culture. Until 1905 Gustav Klimt acted as "president" of a coterie of young architects, painters, and engravers bent on opening Vienna to the cultural modernisms of the rest of Europe in order to legitimate their own rage to experiment. In this metropolis of overwrought historicism they commissioned the architect Joseph Maria Olbrich, a secessionist of the first hour, to design an exhibition palace that opened in 1899 across from the stultifying Academy of Fine Arts, which had prompted their rebellion. In the coming years, in what Olbrich had designed as an ahistorical pagan temple, they showed their paintings and sculptures alongside those of European Impressionists, naturalists, and symbolists.

In the meantime, in 1897, they had launched *Ver sacrum* (Sacred Spring), a journal through which they diffused their dissenting vision while also forging links with the literary arts. Usually illustrated by Klimt and Koloman Moser, *Ver sacrum* featured, among others, Hugo von Hofmannsthal, Rainer Maria Rilke, and Peter Altenberg, until it expired in 1903. Convinced of the organic unity of all the arts, in particular Joseph Hoffmann and Moser, inspired by Klimt, also founded the *Wiener Werkstätte* in order to infuse the applied arts with the spirit and style of Art Nouveau.

From the very start the secession was internally torn between moderate and absolute aesthetes. The former, notably Klimt and Hoffman, were inclined to graft their innovations in concept, form, and technique onto the existing artistic and cultural matrix. But there were also the irreconcilable purists, above all Adolf Loos, the functional modernist, and Oskar Kokoschka, the instinctual and nihilist Expressionist. Eventually, by 1905, this composite secession suffered multiple fractures.

In the meantime Klimt's uneasy relationship with the cultural establishment left no doubt but that the secession lived on borrowed time. Klimt first made his reputation as a painter-decorator for Ringstrasse Vienna. His major commissions included historical murals for the Burgtheater and the Museum of Art History, which earned him the emperor's prize in 1890. Having proved his orthodoxy and loyalty, Klimt was commissioned by the minister of culture in 1894 to design three large ceiling panels for the *Aula* of Vienna University. While Klimt was charged with producing allegories of philosophy, medicine, and jurisprudence to represent three of the university's four faculties, Franz Matsch was asked to do the panel for theology. Actually, it took until 1898 for the contract to be signed, for the honorarium of 30,000 kronen to be paid, and for Klimt to settle down to work. Although Klimt had seceded by then, both he and the authorities proceeded as if artistic experimentation and service to official culture were not necessarily incompatible.

Once Klimt unveiled his preliminary drawings for the philosophy panel some two years later, however, this assumption turned out to be unfounded. Having repudiated the canons of classicism, Klimt did not provide a symbolic representation of "the triumph of light over darkness" that was in keeping with the Renaissance style and traditional ethos of the old-new university on the Ringstrasse. Instead, driven by his recent discovery of man's deeper instinctual stirrings, Klimt poured his own psychological and social disquietudes into a symbolically and aesthetically unshaped and arcane rendering of the philosophic quest.

Understandably, the academic world was incensed by this affront to the time-honored idiom and spirit of symbolic self-representation. The rector, Professor Wilhelm von Neumann, rallied eighty-seven faculty members to protest the panel and demand that the ministry of culture not accept it. This opposition intensified with the display of Klimt's equally unorthodox and defiant sketches for medicine and jurisprudence at the secession palace in 1901 and 1903 respectively. Only ten faculty members stood by Klimt, but they were no match for the conservative and liberal custodians as well as the arrière-garde of the classical tradition.

By then the government had also become involved in the controversy. The council of art advisers and the standing art committee of the ministry of culture were less inclined to traduce Klimt, in large part because his work was technically far superior to Matsch's classical creation. Even so, the government found it difficult to stand up to its critics, who included not only extreme rightists and clericals but mainline conservatives. In 1901 the medicine panel prompted Wilhelm von Hartel, the enlightened minister of culture, to be asked in the Reichsrat whether his patronage of Klimt meant that a style "which grossly violated the aesthetic feelings of the majority of people was about to become Austria's official art." Von Hartel not only forswore any such intention but also denied the existence of any "official art," declaring his ministry to be committed to "complete freedom of artistic creation." Just the same, von Hartel eventually resigned in September 1905, probably because he was unable or unwilling to shield Klimt, who was also denied a professorship at the Academy of Fine Arts.

Earlier that year, on May 25, 1905, Klimt asked the government to return his three panels to him. Convinced that he had become an acute "embarrassment" for von Hartel, Klimt decided to disengage: "Enough of censorship. I will have recourse to self-help. I want to free myself. I decline all state aid, and renounce everything." Three months later the government allowed Klimt to repossess his panels for the original 30,000 kronen, which Klimt secured from August Lederer, a wealthy Jewish businessman. In December Matsch was commissioned to redo the three frescos, confident that they would be suitable.

In the meantime Klimt had withdrawn from the public to the private sphere. He now gave himself to painting wealthy society women, mostly Jewish, portraying them as highly refined and placidly erotic members of Vienna's ruling class. By comparison Egon Schiele's nudes were altogether more violent, with pronounced satirical overtones. As a consequence the authorities raided Schiele's studio. In addition to serving a short jail sentence Schiele experienced the destruction of one of his drawings by an imperial magistrate.

But Kokoschka's searing portraits were the most extreme of all. He rejected tradition, pictorial representation, and the Jugendstil, and hence his master Klimt as well. In addition he conveyed his intense despair and angry denial through iconoclastic plays, poems, and programmatic pronouncements which anticipated the aesthetically radical Expressionism that he helped to shape in Berlin starting in 1910. Characteristically, the irascible Francis Ferdinand thought that Kokoschka "deserved to have every bone in his body broken," and for emphasis struck one of his pictures with his riding whip. Almost simultaneously Adolf Loos, Kokoschka's close friend, came under attack for his uncompromisingly modern building on the Michaelerplatz, opposite the Baroque gates of the Hofburg, which the aged Francis Joseph vowed to avoid now that they were defiled.

In fact, the Vienna Secession also foundered on the rocks of official resistance in the architectural arts, notably on the Ringstrasse. Between 1860 and 1890 the construction of twelve massive public buildings in the major historical styles had made Austria's *via triumphalis* into an unambiguous hegemonic statement. But from 1890 to 1905 the master planners relaxed their conventional blueprint to accept and assimilate elements of novelty. These were the years of stylistic unsteadiness and promiscuity that saw not only the impression of Art Nouveau ornamentation on traditional façades and monuments but also the emplacement of Olbrich's secession palace (1899) and Wagner's Postal Savings Bank (1904).

This is not to say that the secessionists ever made a significant breach in architectural tradition. Even during the Indian summer of Vienna's Belle Époque the Ringstrasse continued to be the site for classical construction. Moreover, the concessions to the architectural insurgents provoked the same traditionalist backlash that eventually defeated Klimt.

Indeed, the years 1905 to 1914 witnessed a revival of historicism on the Ringstrasse, promoted or even teleguided by the heir apparent and his ultraconservative supporters. Fixed in the Baroque tradition, they relied on neoclassical monumentalism to negate the modern style and reaffirm the undaunted power and will of the old order. This "retrospective art" guided Ludwig Baumann, Francis Ferdinand's favorite architect, in the completion of the Neue Hofburg and the construction of a new war ministry. In tune with this officially orchestrated counteroffensive, the historical spirit of the Ringstrasse was fortified by two private structures commissioned by patrons who might have been expected to speak in a less archaic idiom: both the association of merchants and the association of industry instructed their architects to give their new headquarters a palatial and monumental cast, with Baroque façades.

This systematic reaffirmation of historicism on the Ringstrasse was of infinitely greater symbolic and political force than the scattered modernist statements that Vienna endured but did not absorb. At any rate, the latest Baroque additions overshadowed the two pioneering houses that Loos built for private clients in 1910 and the unexecuted designs of Wagner, who no longer had any public other than avant-garde architects.

The performing arts, notably music and opera, remained similarly congruent with the *ancien régime.* Although Arnold Schönberg and his devoted disciple Alban Berg created the first glimmers of a new idiom, they were barely known outside rarefied music circles. Besides, Schönberg's early compositions, notably the *Verklärte Nacht* (1899) and the *Gurrelieder* (premiered in 1913) were still tonal works influenced by Hugo Wolf, Debussy, and Richard Strauss and, above all, by Wagner and Brahms. While he completed a first atonal work (Pieces for Piano opus 11) in 1908, Schönberg needed another fifteen years to complete his own emancipation from the "tyranny of tonality" and to perfect his dodecaphonic technique. To be sure, *Pierrot Lunaire* provoked controversy when it was first performed in 1912. It is worth noting, however, that it was premiered in Berlin, not in Vienna, and that it shocked less for its atonality than for its *Sprechgesang,* Schönberg's new vocal expression that fell halfway between song and declamation. Berg broke into atonality only in 1913–1914, when he composed Three Pieces for Orchestra opus 6, which were not performed until later.

In any case, although Schönberg and Berg (and Anton von Webern) were genial innovators, they were isolated. Vienna's musical tone was being set not by them but by Gustav Mahler, Hugo von Hofmannsthal, and Richard Strauss. Mahler made his mark less with his own compositions than as director-conductor of the Hofoper from 1897 to 1907. During those ten years he applied most of his enormous creative energy and talent to producing Richard Wagner's operatic works, thereby feeding the Wagner frenzy and cult that seized musical society, high and low. By the time Mahler retired, the Wagnerian corpus dominated the Imperial Opera's repertoire. Between 1907 and 1914 the majestic Hofoper put on some fifty-five performances of Wagner's major works every year. By then the Wagnerian musical drama was also a staple at the Volksoper.

Of course, both Hofmannsthal and Strauss were profoundly influenced, not to say captivated, by Wagner's "music of the past." Both had the same functional view of art that Wagner shared with Europe's ruling and governing classes. Hofmannsthal in particular intended his works to revitalize Austria's and Europe's time-honored values. Not surprisingly, therefore, he was closed or even hostile to whatever was radically new in literature, poetry, painting, and music. Along with so many Viennese of the *fin du siècle,* Hofmannsthal distrusted the modern movement for subverting and dissolving the *ancien régime,* which he worshipped. His association with Richard Strauss, the latter-day Wagner, began in 1907 and was to yield six operas. Evidently their *Elektra,* which had its premier in March 1909, was too severe, complex, and eerie even for

Vienna's sophisticated operatic public. But their *Rosenkavalier*, first performed in Vienna in April 1913, instantly struck a more receptive chord. To be sure, even after they had tempered the first act to appease the censor, the opening bedroom scene and Ochs's rendering of his amorous escapades were too lascivious for parts of the audience. Just the same, the *Rosenkavalier* accurately mirrored the lives, loves, and pretensions of Vienna's *haut monde.* Set in the time of Maria Theresa, it celebrated the enduring aristocratic world of barons, noblemen, princesses, and their retainers, leavened by exquisite melodies and graceful waltzes. In this comic opera there was no Figaro to satirize the recently ennobled and vain Herr von Faninal, who had made his vast fortune as an army contractor. Admittedly the lechery of the blue-blooded Baron Ochs auf Lerchenau was ridiculed. But ultimately the venerable virtues and conventions of the old society triumphed through the reluctantly but gracefully aging Feldmarschallin Fürstin Werdenberg, the young and fetching nobleman Octavian, and the still younger Sophie von Faninal, who consulted Austria's *Almanach de Gotha* as she pursued her family's social ascent.

Academicism and historicism were at least as overbearing in Russia as in the other major European countries, leaving only limited breathing space for avant-gardes. Following a modest flurry of Art Nouveau, which scandalized the cultural establishment, Russia's artistic vanguards swung into the obsessive search for national roots and authenticity that marked its artistic experimentation down through 1914. Instead of seeking renewal among "primitive" cultures across the oceans, Russian painters probed the depths of their own pluricultural national past. Following in the footsteps of the great Russian composers who since midcentury had sought inspiration in folksongs and legends, the restless painters explored the techniques, colors, and motifs of Russo-Byzantine icons, peasant woodcuts, and folk art generally. This compulsion drove even those artists who were intensely tuned into the secessions of

Vienna, Berlin, Munich, and Paris to affirm the distinctly Russian character of their quest. By drinking so deeply from the well of their own country's cultural heritage the vanguardists dulled the subversive edge of their antihistoricism and anti-academicism, so that even Tsar Nicholas II occasionally sponsored and encouraged them.

The Revolution of 1905–1906 momentarily radicalized many members of the avant-garde, prompting them to politicize both their rebellion against the official culture and their unorthodox artistic pursuits. But once the tsarist regime recovered its balance and reimposed its absolute grip, politically and culturally, a combination of disillusionment, despair, and impotence drove Russia's secessionists to depoliticize their revolt against historicism and to take refuge in pure subjectivism and art for art's sake. Unlike the "Itinerants" of the 1880s, whose criticism of the traditional Academy of Arts had a populist dimension, the post-1905 rebels intensified their repudiation of the social function of art which dated from the *fin du siècle.*

The private art market was undeveloped, compared to that in Central and Western Europe, and the public space for artistic defection was constricted. This accounts, in part, for the crucial importance to the avant-garde of six wealthy patrons, one from St. Petersburg and the rest from Moscow. Moreover, Savya Mamontov was the only modern "industrialist" among them, and this railroad mogul's sponsorship of the arts was cut short by an ultimately stillborn indictment for fraud. The other five belonged to the merchant estate of consumer manufacturers and traders in the tradition of merchant princes whose horizons stretched beyond Russia. Sergei Shchukin, the first and most daring of these patrons, was an importer of textiles. By 1914 his art collection included 221 French Impressionist and Post-Impressionist paintings, including 54 works by Picasso, 37 by Matisse, 19 by Monet, 13 by Renoir, and 26 by Cézanne. Shchukin hung these pictures in his large Moscow home, an ornate Trubetskoy palace which was open to the "public" on Saturday afternoons. While Shchukin concentrated on Post-Impressionists after 1905, Ivan Morosov,

Russia's largest textile manufacturer and a painter himself, never ventured quite that far. His was a more conventional collection. Except for one Picasso, he confined his purchases of contemporary paintings to the Impressionists, which he too displayed in a sumptuous mansion. Significantly, Shchukin and Morosov bought and hung not Russian but French moderns. They provided local painters, most of them in modest circumstances and hard put to it to travel abroad, with a convenient window onto Paris, the capital not only of artistic innovation but also of the tsarist empire's principal ally, which encouraged Franco-Russian cultural exchanges.

The other three patrons supported native artists. Although Shemshurin acquired few paintings himself, he hung the canvases of young Russian painters in his home, where he welcomed artists for dinner. As for Nikolai Ryabushinsky, he edited *The Golden Fleece,* and the artists of the vanguard group by the same name held one of their principal exhibits in his opulent Moscow villa.

As in the rest of Europe, the schismatics in Russia were internally torn and without coherence, except for their common resolve to expose the stultifying mendacity, formalism, and eclecticism of official art. Serge Diaghilev was the principal moving spirit of the *World of Art,* Russia's pioneering *frondeurs,* who held the first of a series of exhibits in Moscow in 1897. More attentive to the secessions of the German-speaking world than of Paris, they proclaimed the interrelatedness of all the creative and performing arts, exhibited in the fusion of music, drama, and the dance in Diaghilev's renewal of the Russian ballet. Typically the experimentalists disputed art's civic mission at the same time that they looked to Russia's national heritage for enrichment. Rather than reject historicism wholesale, they called for authentic and enlivening readings of ancient styles and traditions. In particular the drawings of Mikhail Vrubel reflected his exposure to the two-dimensional medieval Byzantine style while restoring the frescos of Kiev churches. Leon Bakst and Alexander Benois left their imprint first and foremost with mysterious, erotic, and brilliantly colorful stage designs for thoroughly classical Russian plays and ballets.

With a subsidy from Mamontov in 1899 Diaghilev founded and edited *The World of Art,* a journal which served as a focal point for Russian vanguard circles. Precisely because the tone of this journal was so impeccably national, Nicholas II became one of its patrons when Mamontov withdrew his support later that year. The tsar knew that he was not taking any risks, since in addition to reveling in Russian lore, the *World of Art* denounced as decadent whatever pointed in nonfigurative and abstract directions.

The *World of Art* circle also included architects who were no less fixed on Russia's past than the painters. Together they pressed for a "revival of imperial and aristocratic St. Petersburg," which they considered a treasure-trove of visual images and spatial arrangements that "met both their aesthetic and their social inclinations." The architects among these cultural revivalists also "pandered to the social ambitions of a considerable number of merchant princes, equipping them with mansions in the style of Russian classicism which proclaimed their equality with the old nobility." These architects were the forerunners of the post-1905 renewal of romantic classicism that characterized "the monuments and buildings erected for the tricentennial" of the Romanov dynasty in 1913.

Although the *World of Art* served as a conduit for Impressionism's breach of lifeless historicism, "at heart it remained aristocratic and conservative," and it never ceased to move in the orbit of the official culture. Eventually, at the time of the Tauride Palace Exhibition, Diaghilev himself conceded that because he and his associates had "plunged into the depths of the history of artistic images," they were immune to the "reproaches of extreme artistic radicalism." Anticipating a cataclysm in which the "new, unknown culture would sweep aside those who had been its midwife," he raised his glass "to both the ruined walls of the beautiful palaces and the new behests of the new aesthetics." Though he declared himself "an incorrigible sensualist," in Nietzschean fashion he wished that the "impending struggle would not abuse the aesthetics of life and that death would be as beautiful and radiant as the Renaissance."

But before striking this catastrophic pose, in late 1906 Diaghilev helped to form the *Blue Rose* circle, which was fully confident of the future within the imperial society. The paintings of Pavel Kusnetsov, whose Moscow residence became its exhibition hall, produced a soothing, joyful, and mystical effect with warm colors, curved strokes, and flowing lines. Natalia Goncharova and Mikhail Larionov were at the center of this *Blue Rose* circle by the time the *Golden Fleece* magazine and exhibitions, which Ryabushinsky subsidized, were launched. The first two *Golden Fleece* salons of 1908 and 1909 revealed the rising importance of the Franco-Russian connection. By prominently featuring French Post-Impressionists and Fauves, these exhibits helped the Shchukin and Morosov collections to redirect the artistic community's attention from Berlin and Munich toward Paris. To be sure, the unorthodox French paintings reinforced and legitimized the antihistoricism and antiacademicism of Russian artists. With the third *Golden Fleece* exhibit of December 1909–January 1910, however, the usual Russianizing reaction was in full swing. By this time Larionov and Goncharova nearly monopolized the show with works that revealed their engrossment in Russian folk and iconical art.

The first and second *Knave of Diamonds* exhibitions of late 1910 and 1912 in Moscow were heavily Russian affairs, though entries by members of the *Brücke* and *Blaue Reiter* re-established contact with the German vanguards. Given the importance of Kandinsky's contribution, the major foreign entry may be said to have been of good Russian stock as well. In any case, having established their pre-eminence in Moscow the intensely nationalist Larionov and Goncharova scorned the degenerates of Munich and Paris as well as their Russian fellow travelers, and openly broke with the eclectic *Knave of Diamonds* circle.

Presently they joined Kasimir Malevich and Vladimir Tatlin in what became the all-Russian *Donkey's Tail* exhibition of the following year. Even though the *Donkey's Tail* was intended to affirm the authentically Russian avant-garde's separateness from the Central and Western European centers of militant experimentation, they had a number of common traits. Above all, the *Donkey's Tail* paralleled Munich's *Blue Rider* with its interest in folk art and the peasantry. Moreover, Larionov chose *The Target* exhibition to issue his "Rayonnist Manifesto," thereby taking another step away from civic art. He now proclaimed: "We do not demand attention from the public, but [in turn] ask it not to demand attention from us." At the same time both Larionov and Goncharova developed momentary affinities with Italian Futurism. In his manifesto, not his painting, Larionov acclaimed "tramways, buses, airplanes, railroads, magnificent ships," while Goncharova, shelving her hatred of cities, painted cyclists, factories, railroad stations, and dynamo machines to convey a sense of speed and mechanized motion. Finally, in 1914, both went abroad as designers for Diaghilev's traveling ballet, no doubt to serve their country by helping to propagate what was one of old Russia's most authentic and traditional art forms.

Malevich and Tatlin alone, though profoundly rooted in native traditions, groped in directions that coincided with the most daring experimentation on the Continent, notably in France. Although he made rural and peasant life his subject matter, in 1910–1912 Malevich captured figures and movements in geometric, mechanical, and Cubist compositions that paralleled Fernand Léger's work of these same years. As of late 1913, however, under the influence of Braque and Picasso he abandoned Cubo-Futurism in favor of compositions that were both abstract and fanciful.

Tatlin had a similar evolution. After working closely with Larionov and Goncharova between 1910 and 1913, he broke free of the shackles of the Russian past. Captivated by Picasso's Cubist constructions, he made his way to Paris to learn at first hand, not to carry the torch of Russian culture. As of late 1913, when he returned to Moscow, he applied himself to conceiving and constructing three-dimensional space, using materials other than canvas and paint. But neither Tatlin's constructionist *Painting Reliefs* (1913–1914) nor Malevich's abstractionist *Head of a Peasant Girl* (1913) was likely to undermine the foundations of Romanov official culture. Nor would they overshadow the core of the avant-garde, which was swaddled in Russia's historical heritage.

Notwithstanding a long-drawn secularization and a decline in piety throughout much of Europe, the Church continued to be a centripetal support of the old order. Actually, de-Christianization had not gone very far among the peasants of the villages, the lower middle classes of provincial towns, and the ex-peasants in cities. Nor had the ruling classes deserted the Church. Though irregular congregants, even workers who enrolled in socialist parties and trade unions took the sacraments, primarily because they looked to be married, baptized, and buried in the faith of their parents.

But above all the altar remained closely tied with both state and nation. No doubt this tie was least direct and transparent in France, where Catholicism nevertheless permeated political society. In the other major countries crowned sovereigns boldly presided over religious establishments that were the ecclesiastic organs of their regimes. Constitutionally subordinate to the state, these sacred hegemonic institutions used their prestige, awe, and magic to legitimate the political and social status quo.

King, emperor, and tsar either appointed or prescreened the head of the national church. Wherever there was a general synod, the crown knew how to influence its proceedings. Moreover, there were intimate ties between the nobility and the hierarchy. Many of the top church officers, also in the Roman Curia, were highborn, were educated in elite schools, and, if non-Catholic, married into noble families, giving them the entry into high society. In fact, along with ranking bureaucrats and generals, leading churchmen were an integral part of upper classes that were heavily rooted in land and in state service. The lower clergy ministered to the peasantry and provincial lower middle class in which it originated. These rank-and-file clerics were influential confessors, confidants, advisers, and predicators for their flock, the more so because once assigned to a parish or congregation they tended to serve it for life.

The churches performed a wide range of functions, beginning with the strictly religious ones: holy services and sacraments; rites of passage (birth, communion, marriage, burial); high holidays; and pilgrimages. In all this ministering, iconography, symbolism, and ceremonial ritual carried greater weight than the spoken word and reproduced and reinforced time-honored beliefs and observances. Particularly in Catholic and Orthodox countries or regions religious processions were grandiose spectacles, and many of them graphically dramatized the interconnection of altar, throne, ruling class, and nation, as did royal coronations and funerals.

In addition to their religious and moral mission, the churches, even in France, were active in community work and education. Except in Russia they still operated many hospitals, orphanages, old-age homes, asylums, and charitable trusts. Especially in Catholic countries the delivery of health and social services, in which nuns played a decisive role, created a vast reservoir of goodwill for the ecclesiastic establishment.

The churches were even more important in the sphere of education. Of course, they had their own seminaries and convents. In civic terms, however, it was of greater importance that the churches remained deeply involved in schoolteaching, above all on the primary level. They either owned and operated most elementary and secondary schools or else were paid to delegate clerics to teach in public institutions. Quite apart from providing religious instruction the men of God were trained to teach a full curriculum, including basic natural science. Especially in villages and provincial towns, but also in cities, schoolteachers, whether parochial or public, were highly respected, not least because they could send gifted and ambitious pupils on to higher schools that practically guaranteed upward social mobility. If in 1914 even France still had almost half as many priestly as lay schoolteachers, no doubt there were many places in which clerics actually outnumbered civil schoolmasters in public education. They also enjoyed greater prestige.

Nor was the political suasion of churchmen negligible. Although prone to authoritarian and deferential politics, the churches eventually provided conservative parties with a corps of preaching friars to help fight their electoral battles. To support the conservative cause, clerics used their pastoral influence and their pulpits. They also became party activists, ran for elective office, and sat in upper chambers.

Not that the churches were monolithic. There were tensions between doctrinal dogmatists and revisionists, as well as between social conservatives and reformers. But by any standard, the churches remained unbending and hierarchical. Moreover, fearful of urban centers, industry, and labor, the ecclesiastic elites developed the same siege mentality as the landed and public service nobilities. Although they exaggerated the weakening of organized religion, there was no denying it altogether. Church attendance declined especially in fast-growing cities, where politically motivated and orchestrated anticlericalism was most prevalent. For the immediate future only Europe's villages and provincial towns seemed safe for formal piety, and even they were being pushed back by the growth of industry. Meanwhile, because the churches had much of their wealth in rural land, falling rent rolls and profits strained their finances at the same time that their expenses were rising. The new and projected urban parishes, which provided commissions for architects and artists of classical religious styles, were not self-sustaining in either endowments or donations. In addition, as in all other bureaucratized service institutions, training costs and salaries climbed sharply as the churches struggled to remain effective pedagogic and cultural organs in modernizing society.

Paradoxically, the internal difficulties of the churches increased their dependence on those segments of the ruling and governing class that proposed to bolster the hegemonic role of the clerical order. More than ever church leaders looked to government to maintain them in their old privileges and functions, not least by giving them additional credits and subsidies. The churches were particularly eager to protect and expand their educational mission in developing societies with a growing need for educated and skilled workers.

As of the turn of the century conservative forces, overfearful of socialism, favored increased public support for the churches. In exchange for continuing to consecrate the throne, the sword, the flag, and the established social order, the churches received government aid that helped them surmount a conjunctural fiscal crunch and modernize their social services. One of the consequences of this heightened mutuality, not to say complicity, of interests between the *ancien régime* and the altar was a growing intolerance for modernists and reformists *within* the churches. In fact, between 1900 and 1914 the zealous integrists of the churches were the counterpart of the ultraconservatives in Europe's polities and official cultures. Moreover, churchmen became careful not to criticize the domestic and foreign policies of governments or political forces that were their natural allies.

In the Catholic Church the severe pontificate of Pius X (1903–1914) followed the relatively open reign of Leo XIII (1878–1903). As a tolerant traditionalist, Pope Leo both condemned exegetic error and sought to come to terms with the new order, which he expected to bring "immense benefits" to all mankind, not only to the "civilized peoples." In 1891, in *Rerum Novarum,* Pope Leo outlined the Vatican's attitude to the social and economic processes that were creating the *rerum ordo in terris futurus.* Admittedly, this celebrated papal epistle censured the intemperance of economic and social liberalism —specifically the inordinate usury, profits, and fortunes of capitalists—at the same time that it lamented the misery and overexploitation of workers. But the Roman pontiff also, or above all, denounced socialism and trade unions for being irreligious and for feeding on the plight of the proletariat. Moreover, having declared private property inviolate and part of God's natural order, he looked to the state to "protect lawful owners from spoliation" and to save workers from the "seditious arts of disturbers," who had to be restrained. All in all, the multitude needed to be kept within "the line of duty." The lot of humanity was to "suffer and endure." Accordingly Leo XIII exhorted workers not to strike, to spurn socialism, and to rejuvenate guilds to check the worst abuses of capitalism. This statement of Christian social policy was anything but even-handed: whereas it ratified industrial capitalism, it urged the workers to trust in preindustrial forms of self-defense. That Pope Leo XIII had an unprogressive bent became even more evident in his denunciation of contemporary biblical criticism in the later years of his pontificate.

But it was left to Pius X to assail modernism, which he tended to treat as a heresy that needed to be quashed. Convinced that by making both exegetical and social concessions his predecessor had invited laxity and defiance, he proposed to retighten the reins of discipline. To be sure, upon his election Pius X conceded that a return to the past was as impossible as change was inevitable. Even so, he devoted his entire pontificate to reconsolidating the church that he considered in danger of disintegration. Accordingly he resacralized traditional values, customs, and practices, advanced the age of first communion, and upgraded Gregorian chants in the liturgy. But above all he reaffirmed the inerrancy of the Scriptures and declared an internal and spiritual regeneration to be the key to the future.

Pius X was, of course, reacting to revisionist stirrings that had begun around 1890 within a number of national churches. Touched by the *fin-de-siècle* winds and preoccupied by the mounting discordance between the Christian faith and current scientific thought, a few clerics and theologians enlisted the new biblical and historical criticism to harmonize Catholic doctrine and practice with their times. In the words of Alfred Loisy, the avant-garde wanted "to adapt Catholic theory to the facts of history and Catholic practice to the realities of contemporary life." There was a similar concern for the reconciliation of theology and science in the Protestant and Orthodox churches, where it also remained confined to a vanguard of exegetes. In any case, in their critical writings restive Catholic thinkers questioned the literal interpretation of revelation, argued for a more symbolic reading of the Scriptures, and stressed Christ's historical rather than divine origins. In fact, unlike the artistic avant-garde, which sought to break out of history, the religious vanguard meant to renew the Church by coming to terms with its historicity. Following the lead of Adolf von Harnack, the church historian and animator of liberal Protestantism in Germany, the Catholics Loisy in France and George Tyrrell in England harnessed the history of religion, including the critical reading of sacred texts, to argue that many miracles reported in the Scriptures and the Church's dogma itself were latter-day, corrupting accretions. By implication they called for a return to the purity and simplicity of a primitive church with ingenuous sacraments, hierarchies, and rituals. They also stressed the "this-worldly" aspects of God's kingdom, thereby pointing to the social message of the Gospels.

Like the academies, the churches had their guardians of orthodoxy. Not only the Vicar of Christ but above all the Roman Curia and the national hierarchies, dominated by noncompromisers, were determined not to tolerate this challenge to dogma and authority. Within a few months of his election Pius X put Loisy's works on the Index, and five years later, in 1908, he even excommunicated him. Tyrrell was denied a Catholic burial.

In the meantime, in 1907, the Holy Father had issued two condemnatory encyclicals: *Lamentabili* (July 17) and *Pascendi dominici gregis* (September 8). It was these papal circulars that affixed the label "modernist" to the ideas of those who were now treated as infidels. Pope Pius X denounced "the absurd tenets of the Modernists" in exceptionally impetuous language. These tenets were "profane novelties . . . foolish babblings [and] ravings . . . and poisonous doctrines taught by the enemies of the Church [who were] lost to all sense of modesty." Actually, by the pope's own admission, the ideas of the misbelievers were unsystematic. Moreover, this avant-garde, like most others, was too theoretical to have any instant following among the rank-and-file faithful and clergy. Even so, as if to justify his overreaction, the pontiff portrayed the modernist heresy as a dangerous and widespread movement. In inquisitorial fashion the Vatican even ordered the establishment of councils of vigilance in each diocese and, as of 1910, required an antimodernist oath of all clerics.

This fierce and unrelenting reaction by the Vicar and Curia of Rome encouraged the hard-liners and integrists in all the national churches. They felt licensed to oppose change, to denounce errors, and to collaborate with political forces sworn to battle modernism in society at large. By 1914 nothing remained of the intellectual challenge of the *fin du siècle*.

But the call for reform had another dimension as well. There were the beginnings of a Catholic social movement, dedicated to extending Leo XIII's *Rerum Novarum*. Not surprisingly, the Apostolic See and the hierarchies were as determined to contain social as intellectual modernism. Interestingly, though, while the encyclicals of 1907 attacked doctrinal deviations, they discreetly ignored social and political errancy. Some of the revisionists called on the Church to lead workers in reviving ancient guilds to protect their welfare while summoning capitalists to act in a spirit of responsible paternalism. Others envisioned a reorganization of industry to allow for codetermination of workers, the social accountability of employers, and the humanization of the labor process. But apart from remaining vague, these and similar reformist prescriptions elicited little response among either workers or employers. Even so, the French episcopate severely censured both Albert de Mun and Marc Sangnier. Especially Sangnier caused alarm, because he, through his journal *Le Sillon,* advocated democratic self-rule and the lessening of class differences, thereby inviting defamation as a cryptosocialist. In a climate of ecclesiastic intolerance, the bishops of France intensified their campaign against social modernism, and in August 1910 Pius X issued his own reproof of Sangnier and his associates. The pope assailed them for doctrinal transgressions and indiscipline, and also charged them with "working not for the Church but for humanity." Sangnier promptly and obediently recanted and stilled both the written and the spoken voice of the *Sillon.* That this arraignment and foreclosure spurred practically no popular protest was a measure of the evanescence of social Catholicism.

Unlike Germany and Austria, the France of the Third Republic had no Catholic political and syndical movement. In Germany the Center party, together with the Catholic trade unions, fought to improve the lot of Catholic workers without incurring the wrath of the Vatican. But Germany's Catholic social movement had no luminaries to preach a democratic and humanitarian gospel. In certain regions employers cooperated with moderate Catholic unions to counteract free trade unions and their Social Democratic sponsors. Besides, the Deutsche Protestantenverein, which championed social and political modernism within Protestantism, notably in southwestern Germany, was also in reflux by 1910.

But even in Germany, which had a relatively large industrial sector and labor force, the Catholic Church continued to stand on intrinsically preindustrial foundations: the faithful were heavily peasant and lower middle class, the clergy originated in these same social strata, the material base of the Church was in land and agriculture, and the vast majority of parishes were in villages and provincial towns. Estranged from this preindustrial environment the modernists, both intellectual and social, were attuned to the scholarship of urban universities and to the social problems of city workers. They believed that the world of religion should and could adapt to what they saw as a rapidly changing civil society. Steeped in sacred texts, the modernists wanted the Church to sanctify and guide rather than defame, ignore, or obstruct the new order.

But while the microscopic minority of dissenters sought to hedge against the new order of the future, the leaders of Catholicism became altogether unbending. Even at the risk of alienating the Church's intellectual and social avant-garde, including its lay elements, they resolved to maintain and reproduce ancient beliefs and practices that were as congenial to their tradition-bound parishes as to themselves. No doubt the Holy See and the national priesthoods sought to protect the religious creeds and customs of their preindustrial flock, which was the rock of the Church. But their own archaic mentality also inclined them to bolster and regenerate time-tested structures and practices, fearful that to adapt to the contemporary world was to capitulate to it. Moreover, the interests of the Church disposed its leaders to keep in step with their principal associates and benefactors in the ruling and governing class, who looked to the Church to consecrate and support their own remitment.

While in Russia the religious reform movement was as embryonic as in the rest of Europe, the revolt of 1905 gave it a considerable impetus. But once this rebellion was crushed and the Duma bridled, reforming bishops and school principals were either removed or put under strict surveillance. The Eastern Church resumed its pivotal place in tsarist Russia's official triad of Orthodoxy, Autocracy, and Nationality. As an extension and branch of state power it both mirrored and fostered the reaction that gripped the Romanov Empire down to 1914. The Holy Synod and upper clergy became increasingly inflexible and ideologically aggressive. Prominent Orthodox churchmen blessed pogrom banners, condoned the trial of Mendel Beilis for ritual murder, and headed the right-populist Union of Russian People. That neither the Holy Synod nor the tsar ever disavowed, disciplined, or demoted any of these zealots meant that they encouraged or at any rate condoned them.

Especially after Stolypin's *coup d'état* of June 1907 the clergy took an active part in party, electoral, and parliamentary politics. Needless to say, they militated exclusively in reactionary and conservative formations. There were some 46 Orthodox priests in the third and fourth Dumas, or 10 percent of the total membership. While only 16 of them were with the ultra-conservatives, all of them stood emphatically to the right of the Octobrists. Certainly these priest-deputies, along with the Holy Synod, backed the tsar and those of his advisers who worked to eviscerate the Duma even though it nearly doubled church subsidies between 1908 and 1914.

Still, this patently political support of the autocratic regime was of lesser moment than the controlling influence that the

Orthodox establishment exercised through pomp and ritual in a society of poor, illiterate, and superstitious peasants and laborers. Chastened and hardened by the convulsion of 1905, the Church made certain that it would not harbor another Father Gapon.

Higher education was aligned with the other hegemonic institutions and like them was a solid pillar of the *anciens régimes*. In addition to being bastions of traditional high culture, the higher schools were charged with mediating society's adaptation to the present and its advance into the future. On balance, however, secondary schools and universities were less locomotives of progress than regenerators and conveyors of the preindustrial and prebourgeois cultural heritage that upheld the established order. But this is not to say that they were oversized obstacles to change, responsible for a disproportionate lag between archaic and residual ideas, meanings, and values on the one hand and new economic and social realities on the other. As we have seen, the old elites that embodied the former were still more potent than the bourgeoisie and upper middle class. In addition, the newer social strata's obsessive craving for assimilation into the old culture and society predisposed them to look to prestigious elite schools to facilitate the social ascent of their sons.

At any rate, the "public schools" in England, the *lycées* in France, the *ginnasi-licei* in Italy, and the *Gymnasien* in Germany, Austria-Hungary, and Russia were vehicles for the reproduction of the world-view and learning of the old notables, and the universities played the same role. Between 1848 and 1914 classical studies were central to this enterprise in all European countries regardless of their level and rate of capitalist modernization. This curriculum prevailed in higher education whether the schools were public, private, or parochial. The administrators and teachers of the educational establishments were themselves fiery champions of classical learning. However, their pedagogic conservatism was anchored not only in the inner life of their institutions and disciplines but in their own personal, social, and political valuations.

By themselves, these internal factors were not enough to account for higher education remaining so firmly locked into its classical course. Embedded in heavily preindustrial civil societies and, except in France, in nobilitarian authority systems, it served first and foremost to form upper cadres of the civil service, clergy, and learned professions. By stressing the general education appropriate to all these callings except medicine, the higher schools reinforced the negative stigma attached to commercial, industrial, and technical vocations. In fact, one of their principal missions was to fuse the sons of bourgeois and middle-class families into the old ruling class on terms acceptable to the latter. The guilded professoriate accomplished this task by forming men of gentility and broad cultivation rather than of specialized and practical knowledge.

Bourgeois and middle-class fathers who instinctively adopted the ethos and life-style of landed and public service nobilities wanted their sons to formalize and internalize this conversion. To this end they enrolled them in higher schools that initiated them into a status-elevating humanistic culture and peer group. In the course of the nineteenth century the classics actually assumed an ever larger place in the curriculum of these schools. The mastery of Latin in particular became the prerequisite for membership in an upper class that devoted itself to running the state and official culture, including churches and higher schools, rather than to making money. The dominant view was that only the study of classical texts could provide this elite with the norms and models for heroic action, civil service, and gentlemanly bearing.

Whatever their social mix, successive age cohorts shared a common intellectual, cultural, and moral patrimony by the time they completed their higher education. In England as on the Continent the novices of the upper classes, including those who were lowborn, were or pretended to be gentlemen of classical *Bildung* or *culture générale*. Moreover, the higher schools, and in particular the highest among them, cleansed their students' spoken language of all distinctive social traits and regional dialects. Once they graduated, their homogenized speech became not only a code of intramural recognition but also a badge of public distinction and influence even beyond national borders. Where the geographic dispersion of higher schools defied this purification of language, this conspicuous code and badge took the form of the *Tonsur* (dueling scar) or of dress conventions.

Tracking was the chief mode of selection and segregation. Especially for commoners, a university or university-level degree became an absolute precondition for advancement into or within the upper class. In turn, access to a university was contingent upon completing secondary schooling in which classical languages and literature claimed at least half of the curricular time. Accordingly there were two tracks that formally started at age eleven or twelve but in fact reached back to family wealth and environment, and therefore to elementary schooling as well. The fixedly narrow classical pathway channeled preselected students into prestigious universities and reputable university-level institutions, while the ever broadening avenues of nonclassical instruction prepared sons of more modest families and life-chances for vocational institutes or in-business training.

Interestingly enough, the subordinate grafting of modernity into pre-existing structures that worked so well in the economy, polity, and army was considerably more difficult and less successful in higher education. Rather than incorporate new disciplines into their classical curricula and new social elements into their select student bodies, upper schools remained closed to both, thereby forcing the establishment of a separate and unequal educational network. On the secondary level, English grammar schools, French *collèges municipaux,* and German *Realschulen* were created to de-emphasize classical in favor of modern studies. While these essentially de-Latinized and declassicized secondary schools usually foreclosed access to the ancient and prestigious universities, they gradually opened alternative roads to new university-level institutions. For like the elite secondary schools the great universities all but froze their traditional curricula, with the result that new universities and institutes had to be founded to provide space for the theoretical and applied sciences, including engineering. Except in Scotland and following the foundation of London University in the early nineteenth century, the United Kingdom saw the development of "red-brick" universities. Germany expanded her *technische Hochschulen* and established the Kaiser Wilhelm Institutes for physics and chemistry, which were all but independent of the universities. In France, meanwhile, the École supérieure des mines, the École des ponts et chaussées, and the École polytechnique not only trained experts for a highly centralized state bureaucracy but also raised the status of certain practical studies and professions, though nowhere near the level of time-honored gentlemanly callings.

It may well be that by the turn of the century the classical revival had peaked in the secondary schools. Even so, the classics remained the central control valve of a finely tuned screening mechanism down to 1914, and beyond. The purpose of this screening was not to block the upward mobility of the sons of peasants, workers, and *petit bourgeois*. Since higher education remained an affair of the elites rather than the masses, it fixed the conditions and allurements for the co-optative integration of the sons of magnates of business and the professions into the ruling class. It thereby impeded the formation of a counterelite and counterhegemony. In sum, the classical higher schools promoted the subordinate merger of recently risen social strata into upper classes dominated by the old established notables. By providing the offspring of the bourgeoisie with the general education that was the precondition for higher positions in the civil service and liberal professions, these schools certified and enhanced the status of newcomers in the old society rather than their moneymaking capacity in the new economy.

Europe's pioneering industrial and capitalist nation was singularly retrograde in matters of education. Particularly on the level of primary schooling, England's elites were slow to live up to their civic pretensions. It was not until the 1890s that elementary education finally became compulsory. But even in 1914 it was not yet free, and the school-leaving age was still less than fourteen years. Moreover, the level of instruction in English primary schools was too low for their pupils to qualify for higher education.

Similarly, until the turn of the century the public sector of secondary education was practically nonexistent. Although the Education Act of 1902 was intended to correct this situation, private institutions continued to dominate this critical avenue of learning and social promotion well into the twentieth century.

The bourgeoisie of manufacture and trade that emerged with the industrialization and urbanization of the nineteenth century never developed an educational project of its own. To be sure, the entrepreneurs and professionals of the manufacturing cities at first shunned the elite public schools for being outposts of the establishment that snubbed them. But before long they conceded in spite of themselves that there was no other channel of social advancement. The new men decided to entrust their sons to the public schools despite the fact that the old elites and schoolmasters, most of them Anglican clergymen, used their educational monopoly for co-optative purposes.

Although the nineteenth century saw the rapid growth of "grammar" as well as "proprietary" schools, these remained very much in the shadow of the prestigious and expensive public schools after which they were modeled. Most of them of Anglican denomination, England's public schools were perfectly geared to foster the continuing primacy of the aristocratic element in civil and political society. But even within this rarefied universe there were only nine schools that really mattered: Eton and Harrow, followed by Charterhouse, Merchant Taylors, Rugby, Shrewsbury, St. Paul's, Westminster, and Winchester.

Unlike secondary schools on the Continent, where the most distinguished were centered in capitals and old cities, those across the Channel were secluded in the countryside. In fact, the public schools, including the newer ones, boarded boys between the ages of thirteen and nineteen in simulated country houses. Geographically isolated, these educational estates were designed to affirm the supremacy of the aristocrat's manorial life-style. Touched by pastoral nostalgia, prosperous city dwellers in particular gave up their sons to be initiated and entrapped into England's land-bound tradition.

No less important, classical studies claimed about three-fourths of the curriculum and nearly two-thirds of the faculty until well past midcentury. Admittedly, by the last third of the century most public schools had set up "modern" as well as "military" majors with more attention to science, modern languages, English literature, and history. Down to 1914, however, these new programs not only developed very slowly but were disvalued for catering to students with second-rate minds and pedigrees.

Sports were the fourth distinguishing characteristic of the public schools, after rural isolation, boarding, and the classics. Such sports as Rugby, invented at Oxbridge, trained members of peer groups to combine individual exertion with teamwork. Besides, just as the rural setting exalted the idea of country living, so outdoor sports accorded with the hunts and horse races of aristocratic society. Even though many of the grammar schools, including those that were publicly financed after 1902, came to locate in cities and to soft-pedal sports, they nevertheless maintained the classical curriculum and its gentlemanly stress on general rather than practical education.

Not surprisingly, in the foremost public schools the sons of aristocrats and gentry made up by far the largest single block of students. Although the offspring of entrepreneurial and commercial families gradually claimed a larger share of enrollments, they continued to trail the sons of clergymen, professionals, and military officers.

The situation was much the same at Oxford and Cambridge, the university extensions of the nine public schools. At the colleges of both, the emphasis continued to be on classical and humanistic studies. Except for theology, professional training was all but excluded. To be sure, University College in London was established as early as 1826, largely to break the Anglican, classical, and upper-class vise of Oxbridge. Moreover, around 1860 the University of London inaugurated its external-degree program, for which completion of public school was no longer a prerequisite. The growth of "red-brick" universities at Birmingham, Bristol, Leeds, Liverpool, Manchester, and Sheffield also was concentrated in the years 1880 to 1914. Although the curriculum of all these institutions of higher learning incorporated the generalist tradition, the new universities, unlike Oxbridge, opened and enlarged professional tracks, notably in science, medicine, and technology. But London University, including its Imperial College of Science and Technology, did not graduate an appreciable number of students until after the turn of the century. Furthermore, although by 1900 London and the "red-brick" universities had more students than the two dominant elite institutions, their academic and social standing did not rise commensurably. A pure scientist or mathematician on occasion gained grudging respect in England's *haut monde*, but on the whole, science and technology continued to be considered not fit for true gentlemen. At Cambridge and Oxford, Greek was required past 1914. Although Cambridge was somewhat more flexible, both universities as of 1880 continued to neglect chemistry, physics, and engineering, not least because of their tenuous financial and social links with industry and commerce.

At midcentury around 60 percent of the students at Cambridge were sons of landowners and clergy. Easily over 50 percent of the graduates still went into the Anglican ministry, 15 percent into landowning, 10 percent into the liberal professions and public service, and another 10 percent into teaching. Even though a modest 5 to 10 percent of Cambridge students came from banking and industrial families, nearly all of them abandoned their fathers' disesteemed occupations for nobler callings. Between 1850 and 1914, and particularly beginning in 1900, both the social provenance and the career choices of Cambridge students changed considerably without, however, making this university a fief of industrialists, merchants, and engineers. To be sure, during the second half of the nineteenth century the sons of the landed class were reduced from 31 percent to 19 percent in the student body, and they turned their backs on manorial pursuits. But the sons of clergymen remained as numerous as before, and over 35 percent of Cambridge graduates continued to enter the Church. The sons of businessmen, for their part, rose to only about 15 percent. But instead of choosing business careers, they, like many sons of landowners, entered the professions and civil service. Specifically, the percentage of Cambridge students going into law, medicine, teaching, and public administration reached close to 14 percent by the turn of the century. Oxford had much the same evolution. By the decades around 1900 the sons of landed families, the clergy, and the professions each claimed at least as high a proportion of student enrollments as the sons of businessmen. Roughly 20 percent of the Oxford student body came from industry and commerce, but only between 15 and 20 percent of all graduates entered the business world.

All in all, the top public schools and Oxbridge continued to serve the old elites as an effective filter and amalgamator. The ancient nine graduated the critical sector of those less than 2 percent of English students who completed secondary education immediately before and after 1900. From this small core came the majority of the students admitted to Oxbridge, who constituted 0.3 percent of their age group.

In particular once the ruling and governing class had overtly and aggressively assumed England's imperial mission, the public schools and Oxbridge commended themselves as uniquely qualified to prepare future generations for this heavy burden. They had, after all, solid experience in training character and body. The classics, notably the history of ancient Rome, were ideally suited to drill would-be colonial and imperial administrators in the precepts and opportunities of governing the sullen peoples of distant India and Africa that, according to Rudyard Kipling—and the missionaries—"were half-naked and half-child." In sum, in the late nineteenth century the exaltation of empire and country enabled the elite schools to re-energize themselves. Their trustees and alumni ardently supported the ultraimperialism that furthered the cause of social defense and that bolstered the pretense, ethos, and practice of government by a prescriptive elite rather than a meritocracy. Moreover, the headmasters and tutors of higher education were programmed to extol the romance and challenge not of business but of empire, public service, the army and navy.

Unlike that in England, the dominant religion in France contested rather than sanctified the political regime. The governors of the Third Republic were determined, therefore, to break the educational hold of the Catholic Church in order to reduce its secular influence. In 1881–1882, during his first ministry, Jules Ferry presided over the passage of laws making primary education compulsory and free. His aim was to have the schoolhouses rival the parish churches as missionary centers in which a secular clergy of government-paid teachers would spread not only basic education but also the republican gospel. Judging by the sharp decline in the number of parochial schools and pupils, by 1914 the republic had undoubtedly won the battle of primary education. Even so, its victory was far from complete. Some 12 percent of all boys and 25 percent of all girls continued to attend Catholic primary schools, and probably close to 40 percent of all the students in public and private secondary schools were enrolled in religious establishments. No wonder that around 1910 there were still half as many priests (60,000) as *instituteurs* (120,000), and that their influence extended even to students of the state schools. Moreover, though republican and presumably anticlerical, most schoolteachers stopped short of breaking with Catholicism. Of essentially provincial and *petit bourgeois* origin and status, the Third Republic's secular clerics not only were raised in the Church but also stayed in it for their family marriages, baptisms, and funerals. And last, although as of 1905 low salaries and resurgent ultraconservatism radicalized the republicanism of quite a few *instituteurs,* most of them never ceased to inculcate into their pupils a patriotism that was inherently conservative.

The passage from public elementary to secondary school was as difficult and rare in France as elsewhere in Europe. In the final analysis family wealth and environment remained decisive. Since primary schools were not intended as feeders for higher education, would-be *lycée* students had to enroll in special and costly preparatory schools or programs. Paradoxically, at the same time that Ferry's democratizing primary-education program was launched, Latin and Greek were upgraded in the curriculum of the *lycées,* and so were the methods of classical instruction in the humanities and rhetoric. Though governed by opportunist republicans of modest birth and status, the highest cadres of civil and political society received a general rather than a professional and practical education. In fact, the classics were an integral component of the *culture générale* that served a twofold purpose: it welded the old notables and new *grande bourgeoisie* of wealth and professions into a cohesive ruling class while at the same time creating bonds of ideological affinity with the less exalted political class.

The curriculum of the *lycée* was neither an expression nor a tool of *grand bourgeois* or entrepreneurial domination. Rather, in conformity with the official culture of the Third Republic, it venerated the enduring values of another epoch in which intellectual refinement was evidence of membership in a leisured upper class that preserved rather than transformed the world about it. Around 1900 well over one-half the learning time at the *lycée* was spent on classical languages, grammar, and rhetoric, compared with one-eighth on science. Curiously enough, the classically rather than vocationally oriented *lycées* did not prepare their students to take examinations for university-level schools that trained "practical" civil servants. As a consequence, and in response to a variety of pressures, modern and scientific programs were started in 1902 *within* the existing secondary schools. But these updated courses never acquired much prestige and numerical weight despite the fact that they had a classical component, were integrated into the lofty *lycée* system, and led to the fearsomely selective *baccalauréat.*

Just the same, these new departures incensed the champions of the classical and humanist *culture générale.* The professors of higher education rose to protect the hallowed pedagogic, intellectual, and institutional order. They were joined by those large sectors of the ruling and governing class that defended classical education as a cherished heritage, a conspicuous mark of nobility, and a valuable intellectual capital to be transmitted intact to their heirs. In any case, though the law declared modern and classical certificates to have equal standing, teachers continued to guide the least gifted students into the modern track, to classicize the instruction of the modern humanities, and to shrink from conceiving a way out of the encumbering culture of the past. Admittedly, the classical burden was much lighter in the *collèges municipaux* of small towns than in the *lycées* of large cities, not least because the *collèges* tended to offer a truncated course of study, to have less qualified teachers, and to be less costly.

Taken together, in 1910 there were some 77,500 students in France's public *lycées* and *collèges*, which amounted to about 2.75 percent of youngsters between twelve and nineteen years of age. Needless to say, the number that went the full seven years was considerably smaller: while about 5 percent of all students of secondary school age began higher studies, only 2 percent stayed to try for the *baccalauréat* examinations, which only 1 percent actually passed.

Clearly, down to 1914 secondary education remained confined to the children of the upper classes, a small contingent from the intermediate classes, and a few prodigies from the lower rungs of the social ladder. Moreover, "children" meant essentially boys. Girls accounted for less than one-seventh of enrollments, in part because Latin was thought not suitable for them. At any rate, unlike the primary school, the *lycée* was neither required nor free. Though the tuition was inexpensive, middle- and low-income families could not afford to support their sons for a seven-year program, the more so since the failure rate at the *bac* was so high. As for fellowships, probably no more than 1,500 were awarded during any one year before 1914, preference being given to the sons of loyal public servants, including teachers. Not surprisingly, therefore, enrollments in the classical *lycées* barely rose between midcentury and 1914. The expansion after 1880 was confined to the advanced elementary and vocational schools, which reproduced and enlarged rather than upgraded the world of the lower middle class.

Of course, the rarefied *bac* was required for admission to the universities, whose student body advanced from 10,000 in 1875 to 19,300 in 1891 and to 39,900 in 1908. About two-thirds of these students were in law and medicine, the remaining third being almost evenly divided between letters and sciences. University attendance compared unfavorably with the other European countries, largely because the theological faculty trained neither clergy nor classical schoolmasters. In turn, France had a complex network of university-level institutions of higher learning whose enrollments were far from negligible. But until 1914 few if any of the high intellectual, technical, and administrative cadres graduated by these specialized *grandes écoles* penetrated into the upper circles of the grand notables.

After an exceptionally difficult and competitive *concours* or super-*bac*, the École normale supérieure, the pacesetting *grande école,* accepted thirty to forty students. Probably half of them originated in academic families, and *all* of them, after excelling in the *agrégation,* were destined for choice teaching posts in *lycées* and faculties, where they held high the flame of undiluted general culture. In sum, the *normaliens*—there were as yet few *normaliennes*—were merely the elite guard of the corps of *agrégés* who became the proponents and drillmasters of classical studies and textual analysis of literary and philosophic texts—notably of the seventeenth century—throughout higher education. Regardless of field and faculty, the university professors, whose numbers rose from 500 in 1880 to 1,050 in 1910, and 30 percent of whom were of high social origin, prided themselves on their classical training. The same was true of the elite of 2,000 *agrégés* among the 9,000 to 10,000 professors in the *lycées* and *collèges.* More than likely these elite secondary school professors came from slightly higher-status families than the 7,000 to 8,000 ordinary secondary school teachers of *petit bourgeois* provenance, who both admired and resented their titled colleagues for surpassing them in cultivation, salary, and social standing. In provincial cities—but not in Paris, where the social barriers were steeper—a *lycée* professor could become a figure of some prestige provided he had the classical *agrégation.* A knowledge of Latin tended to make him acceptable even to local notables who might suspect his laic republicanism.

As for the presumably prestigious École polytechnique, it had, of course, a different profile from the École normale. Especially after 1880, it recruited its students increasingly from lower-middle-class families until by 1914 these students almost equaled the sons of well-placed businessmen, free professionals, and state officials in numbers. It is no less significant that during these same years the proportion of scholarship students rose from 31 percent to 57 percent and the percentage of graduates entering the armed services reached 74.

In the early twentieth century neither the Polytechnique nor the École des ponts et chaussées and the École des mines were elite schools in terms of the social origins of their students, the nature of their curricula, and the government posts their graduates came to occupy. Actually, these so-called *grandes écoles,* which admitted nonclassical *bacheliers,* provided their graduates with advanced but practical schooling and degrees which in protobourgeois France, as in the late-nobilitarian regimes, commanded only limited status. At any rate, they never rose into the highest reaches of France's administrative and political class, let alone of its social hierarchy.

Like France but unlike England, the German Empire had a public system of higher education. Notwithstanding their autonomy, the *Kultusministerien* of the member states financed and administered their secondary schools and universities along essentially uniform lines. Their teachers and professors were esteemed and intensely conservative civil servants. But unlike France, where the commanding heights of higher education were concentrated in Paris, and England, where they were set apart in the countryside, Germany had no towering locus of educational excellence and prestige.

Instead, the *Gymnasien,* which were of fairly equal quality, were dispersed throughout the cities and even towns of the empire. Likewise, Germany's distinguished universities were scattered in historic cities such as Bonn, Freiburg, Göttingen, Halle, Heidelberg, Munich, and Leipzig, and only latterly in urban centers like Berlin and Düsseldorf. But while secondary students attended the *Gymnasien* of their home towns, they left home after the *Abitur,* or final examination, to go to universities that did not, however, board them. In part because the *Gymnasien* were less socially exclusive than the great *lycées* and public schools, upward socialization was delayed until the university years.

It was at the university that the sons of the nobility of land and public service obtruded their social primacy. Of course, many students began their upward socialization between the *Abitur* and the first year of university study, while serving as officers in select army units, preferably cavalry regiments, a military experience that heightened the national, not to say nationalist, consciousness of provincial elites. Once at the university, students joined *Landsmannschaften,* or fraternities that sustained the quasi-feudal ethos. Obviously, the blue-bloods tended to keep to themselves in Bonn's "Borussen," Heidelberg's "Westphalen," and Leipzig's "Canitzer." But after proper hazing students of less exalted origins were admitted into these and other exclusive corporations. The student duel, that "bizarre survival of bellicose chivalry," was the most notorious of the ordeals used to determine the worthiness of fraternity postulants. Presumably this duel was fought as a test of courage and honor in which each contestant contracted a dangerous facial cut which left a permanent and conspicuous *Tonsur.* In actual fact, the eyes, the throat, the right arm, and the torso were so thoroughly shielded that what was billed as a risky combat was really a benign and ritualized facial operation. By the turn of the century, even heretofore liberal student fraternities assumed the brazenness of the unreconstructed *Landsmannschaften* as part of the conservative resurgence. To join any fraternity, therefore, was to subscribe to the aristocratic pretensions of the old regime.

Needless to say, the higher schools saw to it that the intellectual and moral cement of this elite coalescence was premodern. While the study of Greek was dominant between 1789 and the mid-nineteenth century, as of the 1860s Latin became the pivot of a *Gymnasium* curriculum that now centered on the philological approach to the study of both classical and modern languages—the German counterpart of textual analysis in the French *lycée*. All told, well into the twentieth century the classics took up over 40 percent of the curriculum, compared with 20 percent for modern languages and literature, 10 percent for history, 8 percent for religion and philosophy, 14 percent for mathematics, and 7 percent for natural sciences.

As in the other European countries, family background, not performance in primary school, decided whether or not a child would prepare and qualify for higher education. Certainly the children—the sons—of peasants, workers, and the *petite bourgeoisie* were in no position to compete for places in the *Gymnasium,* which remained a citadel of the classes against the masses. Steeped in tradition and dispensing *Bildung,* this self-selective classical secondary school helped preserve the privileged position of the old ruling and governing classes as well as certify and promote the status of families that had improved their fortunes. The *Gymnasium* was the only avenue to the university, which in turn controlled access to ennobling careers in the civil service, the Church, the liberal professions, and higher education.

Germany, like the rest of Europe, showed no increase in the ratios of either enrollments or graduates of classical secondary schools between 1870 and 1914. In the *Gymnasien* the sons of the nobility of land and public service, the clergy, and the liberal professionals continued to outnumber the sons of prosperous businessmen. Predictably the classical schools reproduced or at best slightly altered Germany's professional and status structure. At the turn of the century close to 75 percent of the *Abituranten* looked to careers in the high civil service and the liberal professions, notably the law, the clergy, and the professoriate of higher classical education. Apparently less than 12 percent headed for engineering, commerce, and industry, occupations which continued to be disdained.

Of course, secondary education also had a modern section.

In fact, between 1870 and 1914 the 50 percent increase in the ratios of students and graduates in secondary education was entirely limited to this rapidly growing sector. Around 1910 the nonclassical high schools had nearly as many students as the grand *Gymnasien* and awarded 35 percent of all secondary school degrees. This less prestigious branch had three major trunks: the middle schools that provided postprimary instruction; the six-year *Realschulen,* or nonclassical high schools, that awarded a terminal degree; and the nine-year *Realgymnasien* that cut back classical studies, particularly Greek, in favor of modern languages and, to a lesser extent, of natural sciences. But even this half-classical and half-modern *Realgymnasium* recruited students from modest families, notably of the *Mittelstand.* Furthermore, it channeled them at best into middle-status industrial, commercial, technical, and civil service occupations. Only about 8 percent of them continued into the liberal professions and higher bureaucracy that required university degrees. Although after the turn of the century graduates of nonclassical secondary schools qualified for admission to all universities and university-level institutes, they continued to be excluded from the faculty of theology and from those civil service positions and liberal professions for which Latin and even Greek remained a prerequisite.

In sum, in Germany as in England and France the classical and modern tracks were sharply separated. Moreover, the student body of the *Gymnasium* remained as small and unchanging as that of the public school and the *lycée,* the number of graduates from all three ranging between 1 and 2 percent. All three, furthermore, had a select student body, offered traditional cultivation, and sent many of their graduates to the universities. In Germany as in England, the Protestant clergy remained of considerable importance in upper society, in teaching, and as an honorable profession.

On the whole, Germany's twenty-two universities were the continuation of the classical secondary schools, the more so since such a high proportion of *Gymnasium* graduates were university-bound. To a considerable extent Germany's university enrollments, notably in the faculties of law and philosophy, were so high because both the *Abitur* and a university degree were required for a broad range of bureaucratic posts and for accreditation in key liberal professions. Between 1890 and 1914 the enrollments in the philosophical faculties rose by close to 50 percent, though those in the Protestant theological faculties fell from 16 percent to 5 percent. In passing it should be noted that while the German professoriate served as the "intellectual bodyguard of the Hohenzollerns," its social and political conservatism was only marginally more extreme than that of the other European professoriates.

That the German university spurned modern exigencies as decisively as the German *Gymnasium* proved and reinforced the essential oneness of classical higher education. While the challenge of rapid industrialization failed to attenuate the antimodernism of the universities, it did hasten the development of the elaborate system of postsecondary institutes of technical and vocational training, some of them highly specialized. The *technische Hochschulen* were the most versatile and noteworthy of these establishments in that they pioneered in the professional instruction of the applied sciences and engineering. By 1914, 20 percent of all university-level students matriculated in Germany's eleven *technische Hochschulen.* Needless to say, despite their functional and numerical importance, these specialized institutes trailed the universities in academic and social status, not least because both their teachers and their students, as well as the latter's career objectives, were without classical leavening.

The educational scene was much the same in Austria-Hungary, except that advanced technical schooling was not as developed as in Germany. Higher education was confined to the sons of small elites, and the classics dominated the course of studies that prepared them for the world of yesterday rather than tomorrow. In addition to facilitating the reproduction of the old nobilitarians and their cultural values, the *Gymnasien* and universities assimilated not only the ever rising bourgeoisie and upper middle class of the Austro-German and Magyar master nations but also the elites of the subject nationalities. Moreover, university professors were state officials. It was not enough for a candidate for *Ordinarius* to be elected by an academic council; the minister of education had to confirm his election. Before assuming his post in Prague, Albert Einstein had to avow his belief in God and don a military-type uniform, complete with sword, in order to take the required loyalty oath to the Habsburgs. Although he might have welcomed them, Sigmund Freud was spared these officious rigors in Vienna, but only because he aspired to a mere *Extraordinarius,* which carried none of the perquisites and privileges of the full professorship. Prominent faculty members could look forward to being appointed to the Herrenhaus and even to ennoblement. Meanwhile students who aimed for government careers were likely to join *Burschenschaften,* which more than ever observed the rites of dueling.

Between the mid-nineteenth century and 1914, tsarist Russia's higher education was increasingly patterned after that of Western Europe, notably Prusso-Germany. As the most influential minister of education of the century, Dmitri Tolstoi, who served from 1866 to 1882, firmly implanted the eight-year classical *Gymnasium* in Russia's principal cities. Latin and Greek came to dominate the curriculum in schools whose principal function was to prepare students for universities that provided access to the public service nobility. Under the influence of Konstantin Pobedonostsev, the fundamentalist procurator of the Holy Synod, Ivan Delianov, who succeeded Tolstoi until 1898, introduced quotas for Jews, thereby accentuating privileged access for Orthodox and noble Great Russians to both gymnasia and universities. But except for such illiberal changes and a minor deflation of the classics after the upheaval of 1905, the gymnasium continued unchanged until 1914 and completely eclipsed the nonclassical *Realschule,* which Tolstoi had also modeled after the German original. Similarly, the universities kept their German cast, charged as they were with facilitating economic, bureaucratic, and military modernization with full regard for the integrity and discipline of the old order. No doubt this deep-seated conservative concern accounted for the tsarist regime all but neglecting the development of primary schooling for the lower classes as it expanded secondary and higher education for the elites.

As elsewhere in Europe, the corps of full professors was very small and firmly integrated into the establishment. Between 1860 and 1914 some 90 professors were elected in Russia. In 1914, 145 of a total of 475 chairs were unfilled, in part because the government wanted to brake the growth of universities that were seen as centers of subversive ferment. As high state officials the faculty were, of course, entitled to full bureaucratic privilege, including promotion by the table of ranks. Accordingly, while a rector rated the fourth highest *chin,* which conferred hereditary nobility, a full professor and even an *Extraordinarius* were in the fifth and sixth grades respectively. Moreover, a fairly high proportion of the professoriate was of noble provenance. Although after the turn of the century only about 18 percent of the full professors came from old and wealthy landed families, all told nearly a full 40 percent originated in the noble estate. Of the 90 professors at Moscow University 37 came from the nobility, 12 from high military families, and 12 from the clergy. The profile of the St. Petersburg and Kiev faculties was essentially the same. About 40 percent of the student body continued to be noble as well.

This is not to suggest that the universities were reliable and evangelizing outposts of the *ancien régime.* In 1899–1902 and again in 1905–1906 large sectors of the student body were in the vanguard of the liberal opposition, and they won the support or indulgence of a considerable number of faculty. But both times, and particularly in and after 1905, students and professors recoiled from collaborating with workers, peasants, and even liberal politicians, the struggle for university autonomy being their first concern. Many professors saw themselves, not unlike their German counterparts and models, as unpolitical scholars in the service of an objective and ultimately civilizing *Wissenschaft.*

In the heat of 1905 the faculty and students compelled the education ministry to enlarge their self-governance in matters of curriculum, examination, admissions, and appointments. But starting in 1907 and until 1914 the government pressed a counterreform in higher education as part of its general rehardening of the tsarist regime. Between 1908 and 1913 two ministers of education vetoed 58 appointments voted by academic councils at the same time that they held these councils responsible for maintaining the tranquillity of their institutions, if need be by expelling troublemakers. In 1910–1911 dissident students used the death of Lev Tolstoi to protest capital punishment and prison conditions rather than the constriction of political liberty and university autonomy. Even so, the government overreacted. L. A. Kasso, the ultraconservative minister of education, ordered the brief arrest of some 5,000 students and the expulsion of another 3,000 from the largest university centers. At the same time, he pressured the professoriate to expel agitators or transfer them to the provinces. Especially at Moscow University quite a few professors actively protested this government interference with university autonomy. Throughout Russia and also in Moscow, however, the faculty became increasingly circumspect, not to say wary. They feared that continuing student unrest would exacerbate the ultraconservative fury and encourage the curtailment of classical higher education in favor of *Realschulen* and specialized institutes.

Italy's higher education was also frozen into the classical mold. Although Count Gabrio Casati, the minister of education, was considerably more liberal than Count Tolstoi in Russia, between 1859 and 1877 he endowed Italy with an equally classical, elitist, and changeless system of higher education. Moreover, as in Russia, elementary schooling was neglected and significantly left to the Church. Around 1910, although about 80 percent of the children between six and ten were registered in primary schools, less than 10 percent of youngsters between eleven and fourteen stayed on. By the same token no more than 1 percent of youngsters between eleven and nineteen, or 63,000, attended the classical *ginnasi-licei*, three-fourths of them going to the state-run schools. Nearly all the graduates from these elite schools took the examination for university admission. The two-thirds of them who passed rushed the gates of universities because a university degree alone, not the gymnasium certificate, qualified them for respectable careers, including high public service. The funnel to the top remained quite narrow, the more so because the relative worthlessness of the gymnasium certificate without a university degree prompted middle-income families to send their sons to nonclassical high schools on the German model rather than to the classical *ginnasi-licei.* As for university professors, their appointments required government approval, they had to swear an oath to both crown and state, and they, too, took the ostensibly unpolitical German *Ordinarius* as their model.

Chapter 5

WORLD-VIEW: SOCIAL DARWINISM, NIETZSCHE, WAR

IN 1914 EUROPE WAS still too much of an old order for its reigning ideas and values to be other than conservative, undemocratic, and hierarchical. Postmercantile capitalism and its class formations were too weak for enlightened progress, liberalism, and equality to become hegemonic. To the extent that the axioms of nineteenth-century enlightenment made their way, they were forced to adapt to the pre-existing world-view of the imperious old regime, which excelled at distorting and defusing them. To be sure, throughout the century state and society had become ever more solicitous of the dignity, reason, and welfare of the common man. But this does not mean that a new bourgeois synthesis had supplanted the nobilitarian outlook and presumption. Indeed, European society continued to be firmly planted in traditions and values of preindustrial times. Rather than acting as midwives for the enlightened and democratic society of the future, the ruling and governing classes remained the bearers and guardians of the proud classical and humanistic heritage of the past. They succeeded in this holding operation partly because the snares of nationalism, the perils of socialism, and, in Central and Eastern Europe, the restraints of semiabsolutism kept asphyxiating and denaturing the liberal challenge.

After midcentury, scientific, technological, and material progress was increasingly hailed as the key to an ever greater and faster advance toward a plentiful, rational, and ethical life. There was the further presupposition that the inexorable and infinite ascent of man would go hand in hand with the growth of political liberty, religious toleration, and world peace. The faithful of this gospel of terrestrial progress came principally from the rationalist business and professional bourgeoisie, and the educated middle class. But too much of the old order remained intact for the new creed to tempt the dominant elites of land, public service, and culture or to make many converts among the peasantry, the *petite bourgeoisie,* and the laboring masses.

Because of their shallow social and political rooting the teachings of linear progress were vulnerable to attack. Admittedly, the early critics did not question progress as such. But they did warn that progress would be irregular and discontinuous. They also cautioned that rapid scientific and technological advances would cause severe social and psychological dislocations. By the *fin du siècle* this limited criticism gave way to outright hostility. Ever more intellectuals and artists disputed the positivism of social theory, the rationality of man, and the reality of progress.

Progress and liberalism were firmly yoked to each other. Both depended on capitalist and urban elites in heavily traditional societies. In addition to being intrinsically feeble, the carriers of liberalism were internally divided. Admittedly, the bourgeoisie expanded steadily between 1848 and 1914. But it squandered much of its growing strength on internecine battles between the supporters of free trade, democratic liberties, and informal empire on the one hand and economic protection, political illiberalism, and muscular imperialism on the other. The great price deflation of 1873 to 1896 eventually decided this conflict in favor of the national-conservative bourgeoisie by forcing the pace of protectionism, imperialism, and rearmament.

Although liberalism had grown to be more than embryonic between 1848 and 1873, it had never reached full maturity. Admittedly, during that quarter-century laissez faire and free trade became sovereign in the political economy of European and world capitalism. However, this golden age of unrestrained competition was but a brief parenthesis in the persistent reality of government regulation of economic life. In political society the attainments of liberalism were even more limited and transient. In other words, because of its narrow economic, social, and political base the liberal moment would have been stunted even without the "great depression," which merely hastened its demise.

Liberalism not only was inherently weak and divided but also faced uncommonly strong and active opposition. The old ruling and governing classes and their major cultural institutions were forever ready to stifle it. The landed classes, in which the nobilities figured so prominently, launched the ever impending counterthrust in the 1870s, when international competition threatened to undermine their material base along with their swollen social, political, and cultural status. Their demand for tariff protection and economic preferments for agriculture occasioned the rearticulation of the old society which lacked "a tradition or ideology of public liberties and parliamentary rule." In collaboration with the civil service nobilities the Continent's landed classes set out to choke "the market economy and its corollary, constitutional government." Standing firm against the liberal moment, they "produced the cross-currents of Prussian politics under Bismarck, fed clerical and militarist revanche in France, ensured court influence for the feudal aristocracy in the Habsburg [and the

Romanov] Empire, and made church and army the guardians of crumbling thrones." Before long big landowners also took the lead in remobilizing the old society in England. Throughout Europe the nobilitarians, seconded by churchmen and generals, bolstered their prestige "by becoming advocates of the virtues of the land and its cultivators" and by presenting themselves as "the guardians of man's natural habitat, the soil." With this stratagem the traditional elites won the backing of large sectors of the peasantry as well as of other groups that felt endangered by rapid industrial and urban growth.

The old elites reasserted themselves without too much difficulty because they had yielded relatively little ground during the heyday of liberalism. They made headway not only in the three semiabsolutist empires but also in England, France, and Italy, where their hold on political society had been drastically reduced. Liberalism was powerless to thwart this remobilization of the old civil and political society, not least because the unsteady bourgeoisie broke in two, leaving only its weaker preindustrial elements to resist.

The stronger national sector of the bourgeoisie increasingly looked to the *ancien régime* not only for tariffs, contracts, and public offices (for their sons) but also for armed protection against restive workers and nationalities at home and rival powers and colonial peoples abroad. Large business interests sought out their agrarian counterparts with a view to reactivating the state for their common benefit. While both needed government aid, only the agrarians had the political power and mythological sway with which to secure it. In exchange for help in acquiring state assistance business leaders jettisoned their liberal beliefs, embraced the conservative world-view of the traditional elites, and supported the politics of illiberalism. This realignment reduced elite conflicts and ideological debates in favor of a consensus heavily weighted toward the old moral, cultural, and political order.

In one respect England was an exception. Because the free-trading manufacturing, financial, and commercial interests outweighed the protectionist agrarian interests politically, the protectionist impulse misfired in London. But even though

England's tariff reformers failed to achieve their economic objectives, they succeeded in inducing a massive social and political reaction within the Conservative party, and they did so with an ideology in which appeals for a return to rural traditions figured prominently.

In any case, throughout Europe the unbound Prometheus of material progress helped to refurbish and harden the old order instead of liberalizing and weakening it. This, then, was the fatal contradiction that bewildered and unsettled so many men of ideas. Renouncing their faith in the Heavenly City of the nineteenth century, they became angry prophets of violent decay and self-destruction. Critical intellectuals were particularly incensed that the bourgeoisie should so readily extend its social and cultural infeudation into the ideological and political realm. Even so, they were careful not to attack the bourgeoisie directly or by name. Critics chose to lash out at unspecified philistines, hoping thereby to avoid a break with the bourgeoisie at a time when both were terrified by the rise of the masses. Not that they were afraid of socialism. What the bourgeoisie feared above all was the extension of the franchise and full democratic government, and this fear, which was economically motivated, hastened its capitulation to elite politics. As for the intelligentsia, it was deeply concerned about the future of high thought and culture under conditions of popular rule.

An ever larger number of concerned intellectuals seized on the city as the chief embodiment of the malignant impasse of European civilization. They saw capitalist modernization forcing not only the overnight growth of soulless urban centers but also the decomposition of Europe's grand historical cities. Their greatest torment was that the ancient cities were turning into caldrons of social and cultural leveling, in which the patrician minorities of education, reason, and taste would be at the mercy of the unwashed multitudes.

But for all their despair about the city, few of the Cassandras ever advocated a return to nature and the soil, even in their Arcadian reveries. As sworn metropolitans, they could imagine no alternative to it. They were at once appalled and fascinated by the neurasthenia, corruption, and boredom that undermined the city as a fount of creativity and learning.

Europe's advancing decadence was a fall from the classical city of elite politics, society, and culture, not from a state of pastoral innocence and purity. The decadence-mongers disdained, not to say feared, the coarse and sinister plebs for their reckless intrusion. Simultaneously they scorned the terrified upper classes for appropriating the humanistic tradition for their own self-defense. The disenchanted intelligentsia appeared to be pronouncing a plague on both houses. In actual fact it sided with the established social order, the guarantor of elite culture. This built-in conservative bias was confirmed after the turn of the century when, instead of escaping into genteel aestheticism and dandyism, many prophets of decadence rallied around either the established churches or the new cults of superpatriotism.

The idea of decadence was inseparable from that of *fin-de-siècle,* which conveyed a sense of psychic malaise and ideological uncertainty, an uneven blend of hope and fear. The year 1900 could usher in either the radiant dawn of a new society or the ominous sunset of the old order. With few exceptions, Europe's disquieted intelligentsia expected the heightened contradictions between humanistic cultivation and democratic entitlement to explode into a dark age.

The *idées-forces* of decadence and *fin-de-siècle* were absorbed into the mental stock and psychological disposition of the feudalistic and aristocratizing members of Europe's upper classes. They percolated into assumptions and beliefs that were "tacitly presupposed rather than formally expressed or argued for . . . that seemed so natural and inevitable that they were not scrutinized with the eye of logical self-consciousness." If these vague ideas gained widespread acceptance it was "because one of their meanings, or the thoughts which they suggested, were congenial" to the beliefs of the time. A pervasive sense of disintegration and beleaguerment became part of the elite's *Weltanschauung,* or world-view, in which "atheoretical and alogical but not irrational" spiritual attitudes and cultural statements were no less significant than "systematic philosophic theses . . . and theoretical ideas." The intellectuals and politicians who embraced the notions of decadence and *fin-de-siècle* did not see themselves as degenerates. Nor were they resigned to suffer what they considered a far-reaching crisis of authority, community, and values. Instead, they proposed to surmount and manage that crisis by restoring and transvaluing the old hierarchic society, not by reforming and democratizing it.

This sense of impending crisis provided the invasive setting, not the remote backdrop, for the revolt against scientism, positivism, and materialism. If socialism and the labor movement became the main target and victim of this revolt, it was because they had become the principal surrogate and executor for progressive liberalism, which was all but devitalized by the late nineteenth century. In other words, socialism and labor were attacked less for militantly pursuing their own revolutionary or revisionist project than for carrying on and democratizing the second enlightenment. To redeem that enlightenment the "intellectual innovators of the 1890s" would have had to engage socialism in a spirit of constructive criticism. But this was asking too much of them, for they saw socialism as promoting the mass democracy which threatened their world of classical culture and learning. Like the ruling and governing classes, the intelligentsia sought to insulate itself in order to preserve its critical values from the urban plebs. The precocious social Darwinist Ernest Renan dared say out loud what so many men of ideas avowed only to themselves: that large segments of humanity would have to be kept "in a subordinate role" for high culture and learning to thrive. Renan urged that instead of educating the ignorant masses, society should concentrate on creating "geniuses and [select] audiences capable of understanding them."

In any case, the intellectual innovators of after 1890 counted for little in their own day. Like most avant-garde artists they wrote primarily for each other, and only rarely if ever reached wider audiences in or near the seats of power. Not they but Darwin and Nietzsche were the towering figures of the time. Although both died before the start of that crucial quarter-century of 1890 to 1914, they still provided the driving ideas that were turned against enlightened progress. Such simplistic notions as "the survival of the fittest" and "the will to power" penetrated into the storehouse of antiprogressive and antiliberal ideas and attitudes. Diffused through respected opinion journals, newspapers, and salons, they permeated the common presuppositions of ruling and governing classes in search of ideational underpinnings for their counterattack against the demonic demos.

With the remobilization of the old order, social Darwinism became the dominant world-view of Europe's ruling and governing classes. Of course, the social Darwinist creed varied enormously in time and place. Even so, there is no denying that it evolved into a synoptic *Weltanschauung* whose "sacred words and phrases" won wide acceptance. Both the retreating liberals and the advancing socialists recognized that the cardinal tenets of social Darwinism were congruent with the hierarchical and antidemocratic purposes and mind-sets of the political classes.

Social Darwinism owed much of its immense importance to its syncretic quality: it was both science and faith in an age increasingly torn between the two. The antipositivists and antirationalist social thinkers of the late nineteenth century never called in question the natural sciences, which were the lifeblood of material and medical progress and military power. Social Darwinism enhanced its credibility through seeming to explain the laws of social development by applying the rational and empirical methods used to study natural evolution. It provided both a fiercely conservative and a mildly progressive reading of the struggle for existence: on the one hand, the Hobbesian war of all against all; on the other, the survival of the fittest as the validation of forward evolution. Social Darwinism's ambiguity about the nature of the struggle for existence and the criteria for selection assured it of a wide audience.

While the advocates of laissez faire could construe the principles of evolution and selection as warranting unlimited competition, agrarian and industrial protectionists could interpret them as sanctioning the new mercantilism. In other words, although social Darwinism never fixed specific norms of action and purpose, it did supply a general scheme into which individual preferences and collective projects could be inserted.

The Origin of Species by Means of Natural Selection, which inspired and braced the social Darwinist creed, was published in 1859. Marx and Engels almost immediately commended Darwin for evacuating religion, metaphysics, and ethics from the domain of the natural sciences. They also applauded him for formulating a unified causal theory capable of accounting for the automatic, irreversible, and structured process of evolution, with stress on conflict and forward change. More generally, they credited Darwin with establishing a common ground for all knowledge by showing nature, hitherto thought of as unchanging and harmonious, to have a historicity comparable to that of human society. This breakthrough so exhilarated Marx that in the introduction to the second volume of his *Capital* he professed to view "the evolution of the economic formation of society as a process of natural history." In 1883, in his eulogy at Marx's grave, Engels maintained that "just as Darwin had discovered the law of evolution in organic nature, so Marx had discovered the law of evolution in human history."

Simultaneously, however, Marxists began to censure the epigones of Darwin who projected the great naturalist's hypothesis into the social realm. Without denying the heuristic value of comparing natural and human development, the critics claimed that there were too many intrinsic differences between nature and man for the one to serve as model for the other. With Engels in the lead, Marxists insisted that man was, above all, a social and thinking creature, and that instead of obeying the blind forces of nature, he made his own history in accordance with the dictates of economic growth and the class struggle. In addition, Marxists postulated history as moving toward a conflictless and liberated society, if need be by revolutionary leaps, while Darwinians presumed society to be condemned to eternal struggle.

With the rebirth of statism, the accent shifted in the syncretic social Darwinist formulary from sanctifying the unruly competition of laissez-faire economics and politics to justifying the disciplined struggles of social imperialism, both domestic and foreign. By the late nineteenth century the organized struggle for survival between nations overshadowed the orderless conflicts within society. This transposition of permanent strife from the national to the international sphere coincided with a sea-change in the world-view of the ruling and governing classes: from confident and flexible traditionalism to pessimistic and rigid conservatism, not to say reaction.

The old elites were ready to use the resurgent primacy of foreign and imperial politics to buttress their domestic positions. Braced by the warrior caste, they could even claim to be particularly well qualified to direct the war of all against all in the world arena, where military victory would be the supreme test of fitness.

The second half of the nineteenth century was rich in lessons for the few big powers that were destined to vie for supremacy rather than bare survival. Prussia's conquest of the Germanies, the Piedmont's ascendancy in Italy, and the triumph of the North in the American Civil War had recently validated the law of the strong. In turn, the defeat of France in 1870, the surrender of Spain in 1898, and the discomfitures of England in the Boer War exposed the consequences of national weakness and decline.

The societal conflicts that were once glorified as a source and sign of vigor were now decried for impairing the external strength of the nation. But social Darwinists divided over how best to tame this dysfunctional domestic strife. The catonists among them opposed domestic reforms as devitalizing and divisive and trusted to the challenge of war to toughen individuals and forge national solidarity. The more modern and self-confident Darwinians reversed this prescription. They urged governments to effect basic social reforms in order to ensure the popular support so essential for war-making in an age of mass armies. These two major precepts coexisted within social Darwinism, along with as yet relatively inconsequential racist injunctions.

Social Darwinism justified rather than caused Europe's realignment in outlook and policy. It provided pseudoscientific support for the old ruling and governing classes which were reasserting themselves. Social Darwinism suited their elitist mentality, in which the idea of inequality was deeply ingrained. In their view men were unequal by nature, and so was the structure of society, which was forever destined to be ruled by a minority of those most fit to govern.

Social Darwinism and elitism grew out of one and the same subsoil. Both defied and criticized the enlightenment of the nineteenth century, and more particularly the pressures for social and political democratization. The value-laden term "elite" only came into its own in the late nineteenth century, and it received the widest currency in societies that were still dominated by the feudal element. But throughout Europe elite theories mirrored and rationalized current ruling practices while also serving as a weapon in the battle against political, social, and cultural leveling.

Nietzsche was the chief minstrel of this battle. Notwithstanding the purposely provocative contradictions and ellipses in his writing, his thought was coherently and consistently antiliberal, antidemocratic, and antisocialist, and it became more intensely so with the passage of time. Although he came to be particularly scornful of progress in the tragic delirium of his final years, he was no less critical of it in his years of extraordinary sanity. Nietzsche certainly recoiled from Darwin, in the sense that he rejected the progressive presumptions of evolutionary theory. But he was a confirmed social Darwinist, and a pessimistic and brutal one at that. For him the world was one of permanent struggle, not for mere existence or survival, but for creative domination, exploitation, and subjugation. To be sure, Nietzsche never conceived of the "will to power," the cornerstone of his thought, as mere brawn. In fact, he extolled the aspirations and achievements of artists and philosophers as the quintessence of that power drive. But Nietzsche was prepared to enslave the rest of mankind in the pursuit of high culture, to which he assigned absolute priority.

Nietzsche reviled his own age for permitting the masses to shackle the will to power of the "highest specimens." For him, classical Greece and the Renaissance were shining examples of elite societies in which small nobilities of aristocratic morals and taste promoted high culture with lordly disregard for the plebs, whose humanity Nietzsche all but denied.

Nietzsche was not above aristocratic pretensions himself, starting with his dubious claim to noble Polish ancestry. He admired his father for having tutored the four princesses of the House of Sachsen-Altenburg and for having received his pastorate from King Frederick William IV, on whose birthday Nietzsche was born and whose "Hohenzollern name" he bore with pride.

His exaltation of the will to power, high culture, and aristocracy was an integral part of his "critique of modernity." This excoriation was expansively political, though not partisan. Nietzsche considered all of Europe, except Russia, to be degenerating in will and authority under the corrosive influence of the bourgeoisie, which he obsessively despised. He was particularly appalled at imperial Germany becoming half-*gentilhomme* and half-*bourgeois* and undergoing a general impoverishment of high culture. Admittedly, Nietzsche criticized the old elites, and above all Bismarck, for their plebiscitary sops, their nationalist frenzy, and their sham monarchism and religiosity. On balance, however, he esteemed the Iron Chancellor for his peasant and noble origins and even respected him for deftly manipulating the Reichstag, thereby sparing Germany the "non-sense of numbers" and "the superstition of majorities." At the same time, Nietzsche urged the extrusion of English *Kleingeisterei,* or small-mindedness, and parliamentary principles from Germany, to be achieved in collaboration with Russia, which he admired for keeping its old order intact. At the minimum he hoped that the tsarist empire, which was primed to dominate both Asia and Europe, would incite Western Europe to abandon its *Kleinstaaterei,* or particularisms, and band together to become a "cultural center comparable to Greece under Roman rule." United Europe would have to produce a truly great statesman and a transnational ruling caste in order to reach this goal. For should Europe fall into the hands of mobs and parliaments its culture-center would be ground up in "the struggle between the poor and the rich."

But since a united Europe was not for the near future, Nietzsche sought to come to terms with the contemporary world. He was full of admiration for the cultural vitality of Paris. "The issues of pessimism and . . . Wagner as well as nearly all psychological and artistic questions were being discussed with much greater sophistication and thoroughness" in defeated France than in Germany, where the hubris of military success and great-power status was blunting the arts. Even so, to avoid the Third Republic's depraved decadence Nietzsche wanted Berlin to become more potent and obdurate and to move closer to St. Petersburg.

But while he reconciled himself to the cultural costs of Germany's rise to world power, Nietzsche never accepted the costs growing out of the ascent of the bourgeoisie. The latter were the "philistines," whom he scorned mercilessly for failing to provide the Dionysian impulse and dialectic tension indispensable for genuine creativity. He also thundered against them for devitalizing Germany with their affected imitation of traditional culture and their idolatry of the new state. Eventually Nietzsche even accused Wagner, his greatest idol, of catering to these philistines with his narcotic *Parsifal* in Bayreuth, which he considered an obscene shrine to Germany's counterfeit *Kultur-Staat*. Wherever upstart philistines mingled with authentic aristocrats, as they did at Bayreuth, they polluted the atmosphere with their spurious deportment.

The philistines, including the Jews among them, were the core of a new elite that was desperate to cloak its common origins and appearance. Unable to find a suitable costume in Europe's rich historical wardrobe, these parvenus started a perpetual "masquerade of styles" in which they kept "trying on, changing, taking off, packing, and above all studying" the major historical models. No other epoch ever schooled itself so thoroughly in the "morals, beliefs, aesthetics, and religions" of the past for what became "a permanent carnival." Nietzsche insisted that if the "democratic jumbling of classes and races" had not thrown Europe into a "bewitching and mad semibarbarism," the old order would not have had to develop this historical or "sixth" sense peculiar to the nineteenth century.

Indeed, the pretensions of democracy were the principal bane of modern times. Distrustful of "great human beings and elite society," democracy meant to enthrone popular majorities and parliaments through which "herd animals made themselves masters." Nietzsche denounced Rousseau as the "idealist and *canaille*" who had infused the revolution with a "morality and doctrine of equality" that were the "most poisonous of all poisons." Only courageous "new philosophers" —such as Nietzsche himself—could provide the necessary antidote by formulating counterideals and "transvaluing as well as reversing eternal values." As the "immoralists" and "enraged pessimistic idealists of their day," these *nouveaux philosophes* would also lend support to the battle against socialism. Compared to democracy, this latest scourge had no virtue other than that of goading Europeans to remain sober, cunning, manly, and warlike.

Ultimately, though, Nietzsche looked for a caste of superior masters to arrest and reverse the onrush of philistines and slaves by articulating and implementing the transfigured visions and values of an imagined aristocratic past. Nietzsche proudly acknowledged that his proclamation of the crisis of modernity and his call for a clean moral sweep were anchored in "aristocratic radicalism." After all, he was concerned first and foremost with the excellence and aesthetic refinement of aristocratic minorities at the expense of the vile majority. But his concern was not exclusively with spiritual aristocracies as procreators and cognoscenti of philosophy, literature, and the arts, notably music. Not the least of Nietzsche's paradoxes was that in pursuit of positive decadence he simultaneously extolled the aesthetics of aristocratic high culture and the brutality of aristocratic power politics.

Whether by blood or nurture, genuine aristocrats were ever ready to be cruel and "to sacrifice, with a clear conscience, vast numbers of human beings who, for the benefit of noble men, had to be pressed down and reduced to be lesser humans, slaves, or mere instruments." This attribute of elite ruthlessness was the moving force of "life itself," whose essence was violence, oppression, and exploitation. In brief, "life was nothing less than the will to power" untempered by sympathy, compassion, or benevolence toward inferiors.

This noble man striving for both spiritual self-perfection and brutal power was also an accomplished warrior. According to Nietzsche the crisis of modernity had a dual face: the furious irruption of herd man and negative decadence within the state, and "tremendous wars, upheavals, and explosions" abroad. War was as essential to the nation-state as slavery was to society. Above all, external struggles could be used to quicken the will to power. Since "paradise was in the shadow of swords," the coming era of unparalleled wars would enable the aristocracy to display its virility and swagger and bolster its honor and heroic leadership. All in all, in his apocalyptic vision Nietzsche hailed the fires of war for fueling the transmutation of Europe's crisis from a negative and putrefying decadence into one that would be positive and creative.

Nietzsche's ideas were an early expression and timely stimulant of the self-doubt, pessimism, and despondency that gnawed at Europe's ruling and governing classes at the *fin du siècle.* They accorded with the burning melancholy and fears of haughty and self-conscious elites preparing to do battle for a future in which Dionysian life-forces would be released to maintain and expand the life of high culture. Like Nietzsche, who finally repudiated Schopenhauer's "paralyzing and debilitating pessimism" and espoused a "dynamic decadence of strength," these elites assumed that their essentially reasonless quest for eternal recurrence would fit into rather than explode the established order. Nietzsche himself had prophesied as much: "If men will read my works, a certain percentage of them will come to share my desires as regards *the organization of society;* these men, inspired by the energy and determination which my philosophy will give them, *can preserve and restore aristocracy, with themselves as aristocrats or (like me) sycophants of aristocracy,*" and thereby "achieve a fuller life than they can have as servants of the people."

Between 1890 and 1914 social Darwinist and Nietzschean formulas permeated the upper reaches of polity and society. Because of their antidemocratic, elitist, and combative inflection they were ideally suited to help the refractory elements of the ruling and governing classes raise up and intellectualize their deep-seated and ever watchful illiberalism. They provided the ideational ingredients for the transformation of unreflective traditionalism into a conscious and deliberate aristocratic reaction. Clearly, social Darwinist and Nietzschean ideas did not express and generate a revolt against the liberal state and bourgeois society. Rather, they embodied and fostered the recomposition of those conservative forces in the *ancien régime* that were determined to block all further liberal and democratic advances or to dismantle some that had been realized in the recent past.

Darwinist and Nietzschean precepts were a principal ideational source and tributary of the broadening stream of pessimistic irrationalism that threatened to sweep away the fragile conquests of nineteenth-century enlightenment. These precepts undermined the higher strata's tolerance for the self-extension of reason, progress, and democracy. They also summoned willful elites to use power and myth to harness the instinctual temper of the masses for conservative purposes. The social Darwinist and Nietzschean credos stressed the permanent division of society between ruling and governing minorities with their superior qualities and multitudes with their demeaning passions. Although the attributes of the dominant minorities were never spelled out with precision, they

were presumed to have the capacity to make deliberate, rational, and moral decisions that would be forever beyond the
reach of the masses. In addition, the elites commended themselves for their honor, courage, and honesty. The bourgeois
was unfit to join the political class because he not only lacked
these time-honored qualities but was suspected of aiding and
abetting the dissolution and decomposition of the old order.
But rather than attack the bourgeois outright, Darwinists and
Nietzscheans railed against the philistine and the Jew. In the
new demonology the Jew in particular became a convenient
surrogate for the bourgeois. In contrast to the noble, who had
all the ancient virtues, including racial purity, the Jew embodied everything that was democratic, liberal, anticlerical, cosmopolitan, and pacifist. Moreover, being merchants and
traffickers, Jews were seen as deceitful and greedy. All in all,
the Jews were the antipodes of the agrarians, friars, and soldiers who were the tried bearers of Europe's feudal-aristo-
cratic traditions and values. *A fortiori* the bourgeois, whether
philistine or Jewish, was unqualified for political and military
leadership in an era of heightened international and imperial
conflict.

As previously noted, there was no need to read the Darwinian and Nietzschean texts closely in order to extract argu-
ments in support of the mounting aristocratic reaction. Their
teachings were, of course, uncommonly complex, and not
without progressive and humanitarian passages. But at the
time they were drawn upon recklessly and selectively, with
exclusive attention to their elitist, vitalist, and cruel declamations. Precisely because the Darwinian and Nietzschean discourse was unsystematic and contradictory, in addition to
being full of plausible aphorisms, it invited abuse by nimble
ideological and political warriors. In this sense the new *Weltanschauung* was anything but innocent. Nietzsche's nihilistic max-
ims, which he himself presumed to transcend and transvalue,
were quoted out of context—a technique that became the hall-
mark of the *terribles simplificateurs* of the postprogressive era. It
was easy enough for well-meaning aesthetes to seize on Nietzsche's iconoclastic sallies against the hypocrisy and decadence

of contemporary life and his clarion calls for the regeneration of high culture along patrician lines without taking note of his fervor for political despotism. Similarly, the literati and politicos of the aristocratic reaction ignored Nietzsche's ironic vilification of the establishment as they appropriated his merciless scorn for human equality and compassion to reinforce their social Darwinist writ. Whatever there was of optimism and humanity in Darwinian and Nietzschean thought, the prophets of decadence boldly ignored it, and they did so with complete impunity. Although many of them wanted the armies modernized for the great wars of tomorrow, they spurned any call for genuine progress and reform.

Both the scribes and the zealots of the new *Weltanschauung* were consumed by acute anxieties and fears. Nietzsche's paradoxical pronouncements appealed to literati who were perplexed by the formless uncertainties of their time, which they inflated in their feverish imagination. The Darwinists, for their part, felt threatened by concrete and finite political, economic, and social dangers at home and abroad. Of course, there were overlaps: many neurasthenics also perceived real dangers, while many of the rational fear-mongers were overstrung. In any case, once converted to social Darwinism, the governing elites were disposed to canalize the fears they themselves stirred up into external aggression and war. They thus became Europe's most formidable *classe dangereuse.* Their bellicosity was conditioned and sustained by a *Lebensphilosophie* of will, power, and myth whose dynamic *idées-forces* they pretended to serve.

The diffusion of Darwinian and Nietzschean ideas, though difficult to measure, must have been considerable. The intentions behind these ideas were less important than the needs of the individuals who accepted and used them to express their feelings and justify their actions. Accordingly, the spread of Darwinian and Nietzschean thought was more an effect than a cause of historical change. While they remained remote for most of the population, they became immensely meaningful and valuable to the elites engaged in reaffirming their dominance. Moreover, because of the relative smallness and concentration of these elites in the major cities, the social Darwinist and Nietzschean tenets could easily touch many if not most of their members. Indeed, they became a central component not only of the *Weltanschauung* but also of the persuasive belief system of the ruling and governing classes.

Darwin and Nietzsche were the common spiritual and intellectual source for the mean-spirited and bellicose ideological assault on progress, liberalism, and democracy that fired the late-nineteenth-century campaign to preserve or rejuvenate the traditional order. Presensitized for this retreat from modernity, prominent *fin-de-siècle* aesthetes, *engagés* literati, polemical publicists, academic sociologists, and last but not least, conservative and reactionary politicians became both consumers and disseminators of the untried action-ideas.

Oscar Wilde and Stefan George were perhaps most representative of the aristocratizing aesthetes whose rush into dandyism or retreat into cultural monasticism was part of the outburst against bourgeois philistinism and social leveling. Their yearning for a return to an aristocratic past and their aversion to the invasive democracy of their day were shared by Thomas Mann and Hugo von Hofmannsthal, whose nostalgia for the presumably superior sensibilities of a bygone cultivated society was part of their claim to privileged social space and position in the present. Although they were all of burgher or bourgeois descent, they extolled ultrapatrician values and poses, thereby reflecting and advancing the rediscovery and reaffirmation of the merits and necessities of elitism. Theirs was not simply an aesthetic and unpolitical posture precisely because they knowingly contributed to the exaltation of societal hierarchy at a time when this exaltation was being used to do battle against both liberty and equality. At any rate, they may be said to have condoned this partisan attack by not explicitly distancing themselves from it.

Maurice Barrès, Paul Bourget, and Gabriele D'Annunzio were not nearly so self-effacing. They were not only conspicuous and active militants of antidemocratic elitism, but they meant their literary works to convert the reader to their strident persuasion. Their polemical statements and their novels promoted the cult of the superior self and nation, in which the Church performed the holy sacraments. Barrès, Bourget, and D'Annunzio were purposeful practitioners of the irruptive politics of nostalgia that called for the restoration of enlightened absolutism, hierarchic civil society, and elite culture in the energizing fires of war.

But the most brutal and reckless Darwinists and Nietzscheans were the writers of lesser rank, such as Gustave Le Bon in France and Julius Langbehn in Germany. Judging by the circulation of their principal writings, Le Bon and Langbehn were the most widely read and perhaps the most famous propagators of the somber and fiery faith. Both were driven by contempt for democracy and the masses, reverence for soil and ancestry, and belief in perpetual struggle. An ex-socialist, Le Bon became more haunted by the populist and democratic implications of Marxism than by its socioeconomic defiance. Convinced as he was of the fixed instinctual unreason of the masses, his *Psychology of Crowds* (1895) and subsequent writings became pleas or apologias for elitist and authoritarian rule.

Langbehn's musings went in that same direction. While they had none of Le Bon's Bonapartist overtones, they had a distinct, if not central, anti-Semitic vein. In late 1889 Langbehn persuaded Nietzsche's mother to allow him to minister to her son, who by then was in acute agony in a psychiatric clinic in Jena. His idea was to place Nietzsche at the head of a company of spiritual nobles to lead the fight against the democratization and leveling of German society. Although within a month he abandoned this project and his efforts to save Nietzsche from self-destruction, he did write a book of social and cultural criticism reflecting the Nietzschean temper. Rambling and incongruous, Langbehn's *Rembrandt als Erzieher* (1890) was nevertheless an authentic expression of elitist aestheticism and power. Following Nietzsche, he approved of the Junker-run Second Empire except for its gratuitous universal franchise. Langbehn was anything but an unpolitical German. He considered politics the essential "lever" for the revival of the moribund arts which he—contrary to Nietzsche—wanted to be nationally rather than individually ennobling. He called on the hereditary aristocracy to reclaim full political control and forge the herdlike "fourth estate" into an obedient *Volk,* to be enlisted against the philistines. Because they were the "enemy of both the warrior and the artist" the philistines should be "crushed" between the upper millstone of the "noble minority" and the lower millstone of the common people.

Admittedly, Langbehn excoriated Jews, insisting that "a Jew could no more become a German than a plum could become an apple." But he vilified only assimilating Jews, not the "genuine and old-believing Jews who had something noble about them, in that they belonged to that ancient moral and spiritual aristocracy which was being forsaken by modern Jews." As was so common at the time, Langbehn cried out against Jews and philistines as an indirect way of assailing liberals, democrats, and revolutionaries. Following their initial betrayal in 1848, the Jews had masterminded the liberal-progressive opposition to Bismarck and organized social democracy. By now they occupied strategic positions in public and cultural life, which enabled them to spur on "materialism, skepticism, and democracy."

Langbehn portrayed the Jew as the obverse of the aristocrat. There is no denying that he spoke of "Aryan blood," but for Langbehn this rarefied blood was, above all, "aristocratic blood." In other words, he never called for new and pure overmen to take command. Instead, Langbehn trusted the old nobility to retain and stiffen its control and preside over the regeneration of Aryan Germandom as part of a regress into the past.

There were also academic intellectuals to expound somewhat more orderly versions of the baleful creed of permanent struggle, elitism, and unreason: Karl Pearson in England; Ernest Renan, Alfred Fouillée, and Georges Vacher de Lapouge in France; and Ernst Haeckel, Ludwig Gumplowicz, and Gustav Ratzenhofer in Germany and Austria. But these formularists of the ideological onslaught on progressive liberalism were not the only academics to face up to the quandaries of the *fin du siècle.* The upcoming social scientists had to recognize that the old regime was still fully capable of dictating the terms for the absorption and taming of the forces of modernity. Max Weber's inaugural lecture at Freiburg in 1895 was symptomatic of this resignation. He chose a solemn academic and scholarly occasion to give a political valedictory in which he conceded that although the industrial magnates successfully logrolled with the Junker agrarians in pursuit of their common economic interests, the former were in no position to challenge the latter's superior status and power. Indeed, throughout Europe, and not only in Germany, preindustrial elites managed to maintain themselves by containing and manipulating the thrust for popular participation and by co-opting members of rising counterelites.

Gaetano Mosca, Vilfredo Pareto, and Robert Michels led the way in probing the dynamics of this elite staying power. Scornful and fearful of popular participation and control, they focused on the recruitment and renewal of governing classes responsible to no one but themselves, even within socialist parties. While Mosca looked to rising social classes to supply fresh talent, Pareto saw recruitment dictated by the organic necessity for governing elites to maintain a proper balance between "lions" and "foxes."

Inspired by Machiavelli, Pareto modeled the lions of the elite after the feudal element. He portrayed them as extolling traditional institutions and sentiments, suspecting and resisting novelty, exercising economic caution, and sacrificing the present to the future. Moreover, they were ever ready to use force against foreign and domestic enemies. As for Pareto's foxes, they were almost the exact mirror-image of the lions, or the incarnation of bourgeois ambition. Their economic innovation, risk-taking, and spending were said to go hand in hand with their shrewd, crafty, and flexible pursuit of gradual change. Unlike their ever cautious senior associates, the foxes tended to discount the future for the present and to trust their wits rather than muscles.

Pareto's great regret was that the equilibrium in the governing elites was being disturbed in favor of foxes and lions of foxlike dispositions. He censured even Napoleon III and Bismarck, let alone the governing class of the Third Republic, for making unwarranted concessions to universal suffrage. Moreover, he held the cunning foxes in the governing elites of England, France, and Italy responsible for coddling domestic troublemakers and for appeasing hostile nations, notably by allowing social spending to cut into military budgets. Ultimately, though, he was confident that the dictates of international politics would enable the lions to keep the upper hand.

Whatever their differences in substance and emphasis Mosca, Pareto, and Michels were agreed on the separation though not the independence of the governing class from the ruling class at large, the relative autonomy of politics within this governing elite, and the unfitness of the masses to overturn this closed and insulated system. Ever less fearful of the proletarian underclass and less admiring of the bourgeoisie, these elite theorists were increasingly in awe of the upper class in which the bourgeoisie willingly acceded to its subaltern position.

Max Weber was similarly awed. As a class-conscious member of the bourgeoisie and a chastened liberal, he too was daunted by the tenacity with which the Junkers preserved their positions and the zeal with which the German bourgeoisie continued to do political and social obeisance. Despondent about the prospects for true parliamentarism, Weber placed his hopes in higher education. He looked to the university to train experts of middle-class and bourgeois extraction to staff the state apparatus, confident that the exigencies of disciplined study and bureaucratic service would subvert and lessen the seduction of the nobiliar society, to which he himself was far from immune. Like so many liberal elitists of the turn of the century, Weber disregarded the extent to which educational institutions were instruments for the reproduction of rather than change in the status quo.

With time Max Weber became skeptical of the possibility of permeating the Second Empire's feudalized bureaucracy with liberalizing officials and ideas. By the turn of the century nearly the entire political class, including the high civil servants, accepted the urgent necessity for *Weltpolitik*, which further reinforced the feudal element throughout the polity. Even so, Weber fell in line, enthusiastically. Through both his political and his scholarly writings he contributed to the theoretical, perhaps even ideological, vindication of the new departure in foreign policy, of which industrial capitalism was by no means the only or the prime mover. To be sure, Weber all along had considered conflict an enduring and vital motive force of the social system, notably of class relations. But once Germany launched its drive for world power he upgraded its importance and value, insisting that the international system of sovereign states was replacing the social system as the main arena of social strife. For the time being the Darwinian struggle among nations would have to take precedence over the Marxian class struggle, with which Weber never ceased to wrestle theoretically and politically. He realized only too well that by sanctioning the primacy of foreign policy he was helping to fortify the primacy of the Prussian agrarians, the hidebound industrialists, and the feudal element throughout the state apparatus. With the simultaneous growth of industrial capitalism and contraction of political liberalism the *ancien régime* faced mounting tensions at home and abroad. To break the impasse without fatally tearing the fabric of legitimacy, Weber considered recourse to a great leader: it would take a charismatic, plebiscitary figure to curb the feudal-industrial combine while at the same time rallying popular support for *Weltpolitik.* Not surprisingly, Weber attributed essentially aristocratic qualities to the charismatic leader. While he claimed grace and will to be characteristic of all superior beings, Weber saw heroism and cunning as particularly salient traits of parvenu princes or demagogues. Significantly, by the time Weber elaborated his typology of domination in which the indeterminate charismatic element figured so prominently, he had not only gleaned the "disenchantment of the world" but also developed considerable affinity for Nietzsche's thought as well as for the arcane aristocratism of Stefan George and Friedrich Gundolf.

Eventually Weber's *Weltanschauung* crystallized into an uneven blend of Marx, Darwin, and Nietzsche. He confronted and appropriated their thought selectively and sequentially. In the first instance, he came to terms with Marxist theory, inserting status as a significant variable between class and power. His encounter with social Darwinism resulted in his stressing the permanency of struggle, not for the survival of qualitatively superior societies, but for the relative and temporary supremacy of nations. Acutely confounded by the explosive incongruities of imperial Germany's civil and political society, Weber became susceptible to such Nietzschean motifs as the exaltation of creative elites or overmen and the celebration of high culture. He did not, however, accept either Nietzsche's strictures against nationalism or his apocalyptic pessimism. Indeed, Weber was prepared to risk the very cataclysm he dreaded because, for reasons of social control, he attributed the highest value to state, nation, and empire. Unlike Nietzsche, who presaged an essentially existentialist and spiritual catastrophe, Weber knew that the deepening crisis would be political and material as well.

The principal themes of the intellectual and cultural critique of modernity merged into and rejuvenated conservative political thought and action. Needless to say, conservatism was as divided internally as the other large political families. By the turn of the century the stolid leaders of traditional conservatism were flanked by the diehards of reaction and the fanatics of counterrevolution. These major factions differed over whether to freeze the status quo, return to a *status quo ante,* or force a spiritual regeneration. In the realm of strategy and tactics they disagreed over whether conservatives would have to play the plebiscitarian card in order to be effective in an age of heightened mass politics. But whatever their intramural wrangles, the main branches of conservatism had significant ideological affinities and organizational links which were forged in their common hostility to economic liberalism, political democracy, and social reform, not to mention socialism.

These closely related sectors of conservatism rummaged through the past in search of motifs to update and enliven their *Weltanschauung.* Even though each camp invoked a different usable past, they all claimed to incarnate the immemorial virtues of preindustrial times. Furthermore, they were equally inclined to designate culture and art as revealing indicators of the health of civil and political society. In altogether vague terms they denounced modern civilization for disfiguring and destroying high culture's vital and eternal styles, forms, and tastes. In tune with the disenchanted aesthetes and decadents of the *fin-de-siècle*, ultraconservatives in particular decried urban life as the main seedbed of the modernity they loathed and stood against. In turn, they advanced the wholesome towns and villages of peasants, burghers, clerics, and notables as a counterideal to the profligate city. Although this sprawling countryside still thoroughly enveloped European civilization, overanxious conservatives exaggerated the extent and speed of its decline. Not too surprisingly the glorification and defense of soil and peasant became prominently inscribed on the banner of truculent nationalism that eventually rallied all conservatives.

As an *idée-force* the nation was anything but nonpartisan, let alone reformist or revolutionary. Partly to counter the cosmopolitanism of the liberals and the internationalism of the socialists, it came to embody the established order and the political forces sworn to uphold it. Accordingly, the cult of the nation was used to bolster civil and political societies in which the feudal elements occupied pivotal positions, including or especially the principal command posts of swelling but heavily peasant armies. At the time the most zealous nationalists came to be the most radical conservatives. With the maintenance of the status quo as their minimum objective, these absolute national-conservatives pressed for the material and spiritual renewal of the *ancien régime,* to be fostered and tested in the ordeal of war in a Darwinian universe. With the full blessings of the churches, this campaign was intended to harden and spiritualize civil and political societies in which the landed and public service nobilities reigned supreme. Before long the fit became perfect: at the same time that they became the chief protagonists of the conservative resurgence, the feudal elements personified nation, soil, family, and religion, as well as the cardinal virtues of honor, service, and courage. Notwith-standing past conflicts between feudal lords and the centraliz-ing royal power, or the current tensions between titled bureaucrats and the crown, the noble strata vouched loyalty to king and country. In fact, they became more royalist and na-tionalist than the monarchs themselves.

If a crisis arose in Europe after the turn of the century, it was fueled not by *in*surgent popular forces against the established order but by *re*surgent ultraconservatives bent on bracing it. Within a decade and a half the labor movements and the subject nationalities suffered ever greater setbacks that ex-posed their own intrinsic weaknesses and made plain the strength and resolve of governments to contain them. Even the great popular upheaval in Russia in 1905–1906 followed this pattern.

In addition to breaking radical labor, peasant, and national-ist movements, conservatives who became increasingly inflexi-ble under the pressure of their own ultras turned back moderate reformism as well. Between 1907 and 1914 this con-servative intransigence either brought down or checkmated Stolypin, Beck, Bethmann Hollweg, Caillaux, Asquith, and Giolitti. Not the errors or tragic failings of these first ministers but an interest-motivated "aristocratic reaction" aborted what apparently were promising historical possibilities: the growth of an independent peasantry in Russia; the conciliation of national minorities in Austria-Hungary; the reform of the three-class franchise in Prussia; the adoption of a progressive income tax in France; the passage of home rule for Ireland in England; and the deepening of parliamentary government in Italy.

The landed elites were in the vanguard of this aristocratic reaction against prudent forward change or flexible conserva-tism. As we saw above, even in England their enormous social and cultural influence and disproportionate political power continued to be crucial despite their declining economic im-portance. But precisely because the agrarians feared that an accelerated deterioration of their economic fortunes would be certain to undermine their status, they became obsessed with preserving or even bolstering their hold on political society, the only dike capable of saving them from being swept away. In other words, they considered *continuing political control* essential for the survival of their extravagant but endangered economic, social, and cultural positions, which were embedded in preindustrial and prebourgeois structures. Moreover, given their authoritarian presumption and ethos the landed magnates, most of them noble or ennobled, pressed for an aggressive and timely use of power in defense of their class and status.

In this undertaking they were joined by industrial magnates. These, too, required government aid in the form of favorable tariffs, subsidies, contracts, and taxes. But they did so less to safeguard than to advance their interests. Paradoxically, by cooperating with the captains of industry the agrarians contributed, in spite of themselves, to the very modernization that was hastening their eclipse.

Agrarians and industrialists gradually recognized the insufficiencies of their politics of logrolling and deference in an era of rising democratic politics. In search of popular support for their hybrid project of radical reversion and controlled industrial development they conspired in the mobilization of those sectors of the urban and rural lower middle class which felt threatened by both economic modernization and social leveling. But rather than engage in popular politics themselves, they condoned and financed satellite politicians and leagues that rallied these crisis strata with slogans stimulating their fears and anxieties, flattering their vulnerable sense of status, and inflaming their jingoist nationalism.

While agrarians, industrialists, and their acolytes pressed their common offensive, they also sparred among themselves, especially once the lightning of militant socialism, syndicalism, and national self-determination had been deflected. With the public exchequer seriously strained they found it increasingly difficult to agree on pressing fiscal questions. In particular the soaring military and naval outlays had to be covered by new revenues if the state budgets were not to be gravely unbalanced. With higher indirect and regressive taxes politically dangerous or impracticable, there was no option other than levies on capital, income, or property. No issue could have been more divisive for the ruling and governing class than this fiscal crunch. Characteristically each major faction was determined to fight off taxes detrimental to its own interests. The result was that government became unsteadied or deadlocked in favor of intransigent elements in the state apparatus.

This crisis-generating fiscal crunch was an integral part of the aristocratic reaction whose drive to freeze or roll back the status quo was wrapped in superpatriotism. To be sure, ultranationalism served as a cementing ideology for conservatives with clashing interests at the same time that it gave them a selfless and populist aura. But this nationalist drum-beating also quickened the burdensome arms race and international tensions.

As champion anxiety-mongers the catonists, with their bunker mentality, foiled all possibilities for national and international appeasement. Rather than acknowledge the reformism of Europe's socialist and self-determination movements, they portrayed them as endorsing the inflammatory rhetoric and sporadic terrorism of their marginal militants. Similarly, they distorted the intentions and capabilities of rival powers abroad.

Europe's latter-day aristocratic reaction owed much of its effectiveness to the fact that, except in France, the ranking personnel of the state shared so much of its social provenance, ethos, and world-view. To paraphrase Schumpeter, the religiously anointed king was still the "centerpiece" of political societies in which the descendants of the aristocratic element "filled the offices of state, officered the army, and devised policies." Although this political class "took account of bourgeois interests" and harnessed industrial capitalism for its own purposes, it governed "according to precapitalist patterns."

After the turn of the century, and most particularly following the failed Russian Revolution of 1905–1906 and its fallout abroad, much of Europe experienced a conservative resurgence. In the major powers it made headway regardless of the nature of their authority system or the extent of their industri-

alization. Even though it was most evident in the three absolutist empires of Central and Eastern Europe, the radicalization
and recomposition of the right was no less real in the parliamentary regimes of Western Europe.

In each country this conservative incursion, sparked by the
diehards, produced a crisis, or "an [acute] state of affairs in
which a decisive change for better *or worse* was imminent." In
other words, the crisis of the early twentieth century was indeterminate. Since political society remained steady, it was
strongly bent not toward revolution but toward reaction or
Bonapartism, or a mixture of the two. Moreover, notwithstanding significant national variations, this tendency toward
historical regression was in evidence throughout Europe.
Hence, like any other of Europe's epochal tremors, this crisis
ran in international veins. No doubt contagion and imitation
were at work, but there had to be a certain "receptivity" for
them to take hold. Much as in the seventeenth century and the
era of the French Revolution, this "epidemic" in distempers
was due to the extreme susceptivity of Europe's social, economic, and political structures. Indeed, the major European
countries were like "separate theaters upon which the same
great tragedy was being played out simultaneously in different
languages and with local variations." Obviously, the furious
nationalism and arms race of these years aggravated and interlaced the domestic distempers of the big powers, thereby preparing the ground for total war among them.

The inner spring of Europe's general crisis was the overreaction of old elites to overperceived dangers to their over-
privileged positions. In their siege mentality they exaggerated
the pace of capitalist modernization, the revolt of the plebs,
the frailty of the state apparatus, and the breakaway of the
industrial and professional bourgeoisie. If the ultras managed
to impose this aggressive crusade for social defense, it was
partly because the "new philosophy" of irrationalism, elitism,
and cultural decay predisposed much of the ruling and governing class to share their fears. In turn, this *grande peur* among
the notables fostered the presumption of war as a general
prophylaxis and enhanced the importance of generals and

military calculations in the highest echelons of political society. Indeed, this encroaching militarization of society, politics, and politicians benefitted the old ruling and governing classes, who meant to resolve Europe's crisis in their own interest, if need be by induced war.

Throughout most of the nineteenth century Europe's civil and political societies had gone to war for limited, well-defined, and negotiable objectives. Their governments had used external conflict to achieve concrete territorial, economic, and military aims, which they defined and redefined without constant fear for their political survival or the overall stability of society and regime. After 1900, however, this realistic and limited warfare gradually receded. With the growth of crisis the motives and preconditions for international conflict became increasingly political. War ceased to be the continuation of diplomacy to become the extension of politics, Europe's governors becoming ever more prone to resort to foreign conflict to further domestic objectives. As the realignment of home politics became the principal end-purpose of foreign policy, war was called upon to serve ever more arbitrary, ill-defined, and unlimited diplomatic aims. In sum, internal conflicts of class, status, and power charged external war with absolute and ideological impulses. Not the logic of modern warfare and alliances but Europe's general crisis fomented this radicalization and universalization of war.

This mutation of war into an instrument of domestic politics involved a heightened predilection of governments to launch or accept external conflict despite enormous hazards. Besides, pressures by ultraconservatives for belligerence magnified the margin for miscalculation and imprudence among ranking civil and military leaders with highly politicized views of the functions of war. Their common mind-set predisposed them to fan smoldering fires of confrontation instead of exerting themselves to dampen or extinguish them. Precisely because this predilection for war was so pervasive in all the cabinets of the major powers, Europe's general crisis was freighted with catastrophe.

The upper reaches of society and polity ceased to deplore war as an extreme and sad necessity. In an intellectual and psychological atmosphere heavy with social Darwinist and Nietzschean influences, war was celebrated as a new cure-all. The violence and blood of battle promised to reinvigorate the individual, re-energize the nation, resanitize the race, revitalize society, and regenerate moral life. In addition to being a panacea, war was a fiery ordeal that tested physical prowess, spiritual soundness, social solidarity, and national efficiency. The idea of defeat became well-nigh unthinkable as victory was expected to provide irrefutable proof of personal, social, and political fitness.

This cult of war was an elite, not a plebeian, affair. To be sure, sectors of the ordinary people—peasants, lower middle classes, and workers—eventually joined the cult. However, there was no spontaneous clamor for war among the presumably aggressive and bloodthirsty masses. In fact, the established elites and institutions, including the Christian churches, had to inculcate the furor for war in their people—their young menfolk—and they did so with their habitual dexterity and success.

As European societies continued their politically motivated militarization, the armed forces increasingly became schools of the nation charged with diffusing martial virtues into society at large. The armies of professional and long-service regulars had, since 1871, been transformed into mass armies of short-service recruits without the old military caste losing its primacy. Moreover, except in France, the kings flaunted their military uniforms and conspicuously reviewed their elite guard regiments. Needless to say, the emperors of Germany, Austria-Hungary, and Russia exercised immeasurably greater military authority than the kings of England and Italy. Even so, all five were the supreme chiefs of armed forces that embodied the nation, and their closest blood relatives and courtiers occupied key commands. Moreover, officers of aristocratic and noble background rose to top positions by seniority and connections rather than talent and training.

Although the military elite became less gentlemanly and more professional, these noble and ennobled officers, and those who assimilated their ethos, continued to shine forth with their predilection for hierarchy, courage, and heroic sacrifice. To be sure, they commanded armies heavily dependent on rail transport and equipped with advanced weaponry. But this did not preclude their continuing to romanticize hand-to-hand combat—hence the bayonet—and cavalry charges. Moreover, the mystique of unflinching attack was congruent with the swords, stirrups, and horses that officers still sported despite or because of their uselessness beyond crowd control. Across Europe cavalry and guard officers and regiments remained peerless. Not unlike the ruling and governing classes in which the nobility outranked the bourgeoisie, the standing armies were military amalgams in which archaic elements more than held their own. Modern warfare was grafted onto huge standing armies in which an aristocratic officer corps trained cavalry regiments for mounted charges and infantry divisions for pitched field battles. Army recruits were drawn, first and foremost, from the illiterate and semiliterate peasantry. They also came from the laboring and lower middle classes of villages and provincial towns rather than from industrial cities and zones. In 1911 even in Germany 65 percent of all conscripts hailed from rural areas and 22 percent from small towns. The draftees of the other Continental armies were still more heavily from nonindustrial regions. Soldiers of rural origin were, of course, conditioned to be submissive and blindly obedient to traditional leaders who were not likely to be particularly sparing of their lives.

Admittedly, in the early twentieth century the British home army shared few of the dominant characteristics of its Continental counterparts. Above all, it remained volunteer, small, and professional. The navy together with the colonial service and army were England's and the empire's principal shield. Yet as we saw in an earlier chapter, the officer corps of England's fighting services, notably in the top ranks, continued to be a highly exclusive body. By birth and training it was steeped in a gentlemanly code of service, austerity, duty, valor, and

team play. Although with time ever more volunteers originated among unskilled laborers in the industrial center of
England, the military elite still had its strongest roots in southern rural counties as well as in border districts. Not surprisingly, the Ulster rebels, many of them of noble standing,
claimed this ethos as their own when they armed a force of
paramilitary volunteers to protect their heavily landed interests in a region of the United Kingdom in which manufacture,
trade, and industry had not swamped the feudal-agrarian sector. Moreover, the insurgent Orange aristocrats won not only
the sympathy but the support of large numbers of officers,
high and low, who like themselves were more royalist than the
king in their defense of the old order.

Notwithstanding the post-Dreyfus *épuration,* the French
army remained a strongpoint of reaction. It may have been a
citizen army with an unaristocratic officer corps, yet in the
main the citizen-soldiers and noncoms did not originate in the
proletariat, middle class, or bourgeoisie but in the peasantry,
petite bourgeoisie, and artisanal working class. Their homes were
in the villages and towns of rural France, in which the governments of the Third Republic had only slowly and partially
implemented their declared project of secularized, liberal, and
socially conservative education, welfare, and magistracy. Similarly, although few of the officers were of wellborn lineage, an
ever larger number being of middle class and provincial background, they were solidly conservative with strong right-wing,
not to say antirepublican and monarchist, sympathies that
Saint-Cyr did little to counteract. While soldiers were closer to
their Catholic priests than to republican schoolmasters, generals felt more at ease in the company of bishops and old notables than of republican politicians, especially if the latter were
of center-left persuasion. The rising tide of nationalism, approved by the episcopacy, fostered the army's conservative
coherence still further. There was not only the cementing
force of the German threat. Once republican administrations
called on the army to repress industrial strikes, officers and
men discovered and acted out their common fear and suspi-
cion of the proletariat, which symbolized the threat to their

preindustrial world. With rare exceptions French generals, champions of *élan vital,* coached the militant conservatives who, having robbed the left of its patriotic heritage, called for a *levée en masse* less to face down the Central Powers than to stem the forces of change at home. Specifically, the three-year law was to integrate and subdue the workers, the prime carriers of progressive modernization, by forcing them into the army, the school of the conservative nation where they too would wear red trousers, obey bugle calls, and internalize the duty to rush the enemy in a paroxysm of patriotism and heroic self-immolation. While some republican politicians had scruples about their republic's ever closer alliance with the tsarist autocracy—even as a necessary counterweight to the German autocracy—the officers of the French general staff had an easy meeting of minds with their Russian counterparts: both were in command of massive peasant armies whose principal mark of modernity was their capacity to rush to the battlefields by rail instead of on foot. Needless to say, the Quai d'Orsay, an aristocratic stronghold even after the Dreyfus affair, also commended and spurred the Russian connection.

In the Central and Eastern European empires the army, headed by the soldier-king, was the main bulwark of the old order as well as the most visible and striking expression of political society's noble caste. The political and administrative summit of the Hohenzollern Empire was heavily aristocratic: all the chancellors and the overwhelming majority of cabinet members, state secretaries, foreign ministry officials, and ambassadors. The wellborn were even more in evidence in the government of Germany's largest and hegemonic state, judging by their absolute primacy in the Prussian cabinet, Herren-haus, and civil administration. However, the officer corps of the imperial army, that perfect and awesome embodiment of Prusso-Germany, represented the feudal element in its most concentrated form, especially in the higher ranks. While William II was its supreme and swaggering war lord, the crown prince of Germany, Prince Rupprecht of Bavaria, and the duke of Württemberg held important command posts. The successive heads of the general staff came from old landed families:

Helmuth von Moltke, Erich von Falkenhayn, and Paul von Hindenburg. Moreover, 77 percent of the generals in the three top ranks had an old pedigree. Of all the generals, regardless of rank, 40 percent were sons of East Elbian nobility. The extended von Goltz family alone provided one field marshal and six generals. In 1914 the leading clans were well represented among the active officers: 49 Puttkamers, 44 Kleists, 34 Litzewitzes, 30 Bonins, 20 Kamekes, and 16 Hertzbergs, Heydebrecks, and Zastrows. Such distinguished names as Bülow, Arnim, Wedel, Oertzen, Wangenheim, Schwerin, Prittwitz, and Knobelsdorff also figured prominently on the roster of active and reserve officers. Recent in-service ennoblements, controlled by the militarist kaiser, were an additional guarantee that the aristocratic ethos of unquestioning duty to the *ancien régime* should permeate the entire command structure. Admittedly, the officer corps was sharply divided over the continuing expansion of the army, which necessitated more officers and hence an accelerated dilution of the imperious Junker element and its martial spirit. But this internal wrangle was minor compared with the iron-tight consensus to keep liberals, progressives, and socialists from rising into the leadership. As a school of the nation, the German army was fiercely conservative. Its officers purged irreverent worker recruits of what they considered disloyal ideas and, if need be, garrisoned them in safe rural districts, far from socialist-infected industrial areas. But partly thanks to the primary schools and churches, loyalty never became a problem even in the cities, where officers ordered troops to break strikes or restrain dissident crowds without fear of defections. No one in authority ever seriously worried about the rank and file resisting the call to war, whatever the causes and objectives for taking the ultimate step.

The situation was much the same in the Habsburg Empire. In both halves of the Dual Monarchy the entire governing class, and particularly the army, was heavily nobilitarian. In public high officers may have been less obtrusive on Vienna's Ringstrasse than in Berlin's Tiergarten. Moreover, they certainly kept a low profile in Budapest so as not to rile unduly those refractory Hungarian noblemen who, dissatisfied with the Magyar-speaking but accessory Honvéd regiments, clamored for an army of their own. In fact the resurgence of ultra-Magyarism, which intensified this military claim, fueled ultraconservatism in Cisleithania, notably after 1907. Yet pushed by Francis Ferdinand, the heir apparent, Francis Joseph I and his advisers were more than ever determined to maintain the absolute predominance of the Austro-German officer corps, which was solidly aristocratic by birth and in-service ennoblement. Seeing themselves beleaguered at home and abroad, the governors of Austria looked upon the army as the indispensable agglutinant of their *ancien régime.* Overperceiving the strength and radicalism not only of the minority self-determination and socialist movements but above all of the Magyar defiance, which was rooted in fiscal and tariff conflicts, they expected to have to substitute force and violence for this failing consensus. To counteract the further advance of civil and cultural autonomy in both Cisleithania and Transleithania it was essential to maintain a cohesive army whose officers issued commands in German and who along with their multinational troops swore allegiance to the emperor, the principal unifying and legitimating symbol of the polyglot empire. More than any of the other regimes, the Habsburgs needed their army to serve as a unifying school for what was still only a would-be nation. Precisely because they despaired of having the time and finding the fiscal resources to transform empire into an integrated nation, the military, under General Conrad von Hötzendorff, proposed to induce war to reinvigorate and strengthen the primacy of the Austro-German ruling and governing class for an indeterminate but tolerable future. At any rate, if the high command pressed for war as part of an aristocratic reaction, it did so to bolster the regime at home and not to secure foreign-policy goals other than to reassure Berlin that Vienna was still a worthy diplomatic and military partner.

Once the Revolution of 1905–1906 was repressed, the Romanov Empire also experienced an aristocratic reaction. Successively Witte, Stolypin, and even Kokovtsev were

removed from the premiership for being excessively conciliatory. Led or encouraged by Nicholas II himself, resurgent
ultratsarists in the landed and public service nobility meant to
restore absolutism by castrating the recent constitutional settlement, notably the Duma. They, too, overestimated the insurgent power of socialism and the border nationalities as well
as the influence of moderate progressives in the political class
and intelligentsia.

Admittedly, some of the ultras, remembering the disastrous
political consequences of the war with Japan, which they had
pressed for essentially political reasons, ceased to urge war to
further their retrogressive project. Rather than take a chance
on another defeat, they advocated abandoning the distasteful
alliance with republican France in favor of a rapprochement
with the more congenial regime in Berlin. They opted for
external appeasement, confident that in case of need the army
could be trusted to stage a coup against the gravediggers of
tsarism at home.

But the clamorers for such a new course were in the minority
even among radical conservatives. Notwithstanding factional
rivalries at court and in the bureaucracy, Russia's conservatives in and out of government, encouraged by the tsar, pursued a policy of overreaction that was financially and militarily
dependent on the French alliance, which was fraught with the
possibility of politically motivated foreign war. Again the
army, closely held by the tsar, was pivotal. Grand dukes and
pedigreed generals claimed the highest command positions
and the officer corps was distinctly noble, in part owing to the
automatic table of honors. Even the archaic cadres, confident
of their peasant-soldiers, had no fears about modernizing
Russia's military machine. They eagerly increased the mobility
of their infantry steamroller by building the strategic railroads
to the western borders which Paris pressed on them. There
were no signs of disaffection among either officers or troops
when the army was asked to move against striking workers or
to enforce martial law in border provinces. Even when defeated in 1904–1905, the army had held together and returned
from Siberia to crush the rebellion in European Russia that

had exploited its departure to the front. After the Russo-Japanese War the army improved and expanded considerably, not least because nearly the entire Duma cheerfully approved military appropriations. Because there was even less peasant, labor, and student unrest than at the turn of the century, the risks of seeking or accepting war seemed minimal compared with a successful clash of arms which would refurbish the *ancien régime,* notably its absolutist and nobiliary components. Rather than give poor peasants the opportunity to become independent proprietors, the exploitative overlords impressed them into a mass army of foot soldiers geared for assault warfare in the interest of feudalistic elites.

By any historical standard the militarization of Europe assumed enormous proportions. In 1914 the standing and reserve armies of the major powers reached staggering levels, the rate of expansion having accelerated after 1905. Not counting "colonial" troops (160,000), France had a standing army of over 800,000 and Russia a standing force of 1.5 million, to be increased to 2 million by 1917. In the Central camp, Germany and Austria-Hungary fielded 761,000 and 500,000 men respectively. Counting the reserves the two opposing alliances, without England, could muster a total of 8 million men. In size the Italian army was also of its time. In addition, throughout Europe quite a few men and women were busy producing the military matériel and supplies that inflated the war budgets. Between 1850 and 1913 the major powers increased their expenditures for land armaments fivefold. From 1908 to 1913 alone they rose by close to 50 percent—approximately 30 percent in England, 53 percent in Russia, 69 percent in Germany, and 86 percent in France. In those same five years the rise in naval expenditures was even greater, ranging from close to 45 percent in Germany and 60 percent in England to 160 percent in Russia.

To be sure, the division of Europe into two opposing, not to say hostile, alliances quickened this competitive military and naval buildup, which in turn heightened the mutual distrust and belligerence of governments. Furthermore, by placing such heavy and divisive fiscal burdens on Europe's civil and political societies, the arms race increased the disposition of the governing classes not only to lance this abscess of internal discord by going to war, but to do so with an offensive strike for a quick victory that would spare them the self-destructive strains of a protracted campaign.

But this rupture of the international system into two rigid blocs, each with strategic plans contingent on ultrasensitive trip-wires—such as Germany's Schlieffen plan and Russia's mobilization timetable—was more effect than cause. Europe's military behemoth, at once enormous and grotesque, was an expression of the general crisis in which ultraconservatives were gaining the upper hand over less radical national-conservatives. They were the prime advocates and beneficiaries of a militarization that rehabilitated the nobilitarian officer corps in armies of peasant and *petit bourgeois* soldiers. While newfangled social Darwinist and Nietzschean ideas inclined their rivals-*cum*-partners in the hegemonic bloc, including the suppliant bourgeoisie, to support this preparation for war—or at least not to oppose it—ingrained deferential attitudes conditioned rural and provincial recruits to follow the orders of officers born, trained, and arrogated to command.

A salient and integral aspect of the aristocratic reaction, this military excrescence, which included the heightened sway of generals in the highest political councils, foreshadowed a general and conflict-oriented conflagration and not a small war for limited foreign-policy purposes. Significantly, among the informed publics the coming war was continually referred to as a European war, a world war, another Thirty Years' War, or a catastrophe. Moreover, the political end-purposes of war were discussed constantly. No one of stature stepped forward to question or deny the legitimacy of considering foreign and domestic policy as closely linked and of envisaging war and peace as instruments of domestic policy. Indeed, although Europe's ruling and governing classes did not have a closely reasoned understanding of the character of the war they were breeding, they had a general sense of its potential magnitude of scale, purpose, and consequence. To be sure, the politicians and soldiers of the major powers prepared for a quick and limited strike rather than a hyperbolic conflict. Even the advocates of "conflict-oriented" war hoped and promised that the bulging military machines were so finely tuned that a brief and successful encounter would achieve the desired results, both international and domestic. On another level of consciousness, though, they realized that the risks and costs of war had become excessive and that the cataclysm they were inviting defied advance preparation. Just the same, in this time of troubles the top civilian crisis managers, not only the generals, overestimated the probability of a swift victory for their own state and alliance, largely because their ostensibly rational capability analyses were permeated by the new *Weltanschauung.* Besides, the social psychology and politics of overreaction to overperceived domestic and foreign dangers predisposed politician-statesmen to gamble on a war that might be suicidal.

The socialists were in the vanguard of those who exposed the political purposes behind the drive to war, which they saw as primarily aimed at strangulating progressive liberalism and the rising labor movement. But concurrently with Bertha von Suttner, Ivan Bloch, Tolstoi, and eventually Norman Angel, who were not of their ideological persuasion, the socialists also warned of dire consequences for the ruling classes themselves. Like Friedrich Nietzsche, Friedrich Engels had a premonition of the coming crisis at exactly the same time, though he expected that despite its horrors it would benefit mankind, notably the underclasses. An exceptionally astute military analyst, Engels was among the first to grasp that the unbound military behemoth would not only steel the ruling and governing classes against revolution but would also entrap them in a fatal war spiral. In 1887, before the alliance system took form, he predicted that any future conflict among great powers could only be a "world war of hitherto unimagined extent and intensity." In this holocaust "eight to ten million soldiers would slaughter each other; the continent-wide ravages would be concentrated in three to four years; famine, disease, and generalized hardships would feed the savagery of soldiers and civilians; and trade, industry, and credit would be totally unsettled and sink into general bankruptcy." There was no way to prognosticate either the course or the outcome of such a cyclopean struggle. Although Engels prophesied that the general unsettlement would "*eventually* bring about the victory of the working class," in the first instance "old and traditional regimes would collapse and royal crowns would roll in the streets by the dozens, with *no one* to pick them up" (italics mine).

Some twenty years later, during the Morocco affair of 1905, August Bebel, the leader of German Social Democracy, reiterated the prediction of an early calamity from the floor of the Reichstag. He foresaw Europe being "consumed by a vast military campaign involving 16 to 18 million men . . . equipped with the latest murder weapons for this mutual slaughter." But Bebel also warned that this great general war would be followed by a "*grosse Kladderadatsch,*" or general breakdown, for which the socialists declined all responsibility. If Europe was moving toward a "catastrophe," it was because the upper classes themselves were driving it there, and they would have to reap the fruits of their own extremism in "the *Götterdämmerung* (twilight) of the bourgeois world." Six years later, in their election manifesto, Germany's Social Democrats denounced Europe's governing and ruling classes for preparing to inflict "a great European war" on their peoples, stressing that it would be a "*Vabanquespiel,* or high-risk gamble, such as the world had never seen," which might even turn out to be Europe's "terminal war." Despite these and similar anticipations of general doom, however, German socialists professed continuing confidence that tomorrow's socialist society could be forged even in the fires of cataclysm.

Similarly, by 1905 Jean Jaurès, speaking for French socialists, became increasingly preoccupied with the perils of general war. Admittedly, he too envisaged the possibility, even the probability, of such a conflict paving the way for a social-democratic Europe. Even so, Jaurès was loath "to take this barbarous gamble" and to stake the emancipation of workers and peasants on such a "murderous toss of the dice." For he feared that a general war could just as likely "result, for a long period, in crises of counterrevolution, of furious reaction, of exasperated nationalism, of stifling dictatorship, of monstrous militarism, of a long chain of retrograde violence and base hatreds, reprisals, and servitudes." Seven years later, at the time of the Balkan imbroglios and the battle of the three-year-service law, Jaurès forewarned that because the distempers of the time were Europe-wide, any local conflict would mushroom into "the most terrible holocaust since the Thirty Years' War."

Prophecies and premonitions of monstrous war and destruction were also rife in the cultural avant-garde. This agony broke through in paintings by Delaunay, Kandinsky, Klee, Kokoschka, Marc, and Seewald. Writers ranging from Alfred Kubin and Georg Heym to George Bernard Shaw and H. G. Wells similarly expressed their presentiments of impending disaster. Hardened Nietzscheans no doubt sneered at these anguished forebodings by the artistic and literary vanguard, but they could not dismiss them altogether. After all, Nietzsche himself had considered European culture, tortured by ever growing tensions, to be "moving toward a catastrophe," though he also half-thought that Europe was getting its just deserts for yielding to the lures of modernity. Anyway, Nietzsche anticipated that the deep-running spiritual battle between truth and falsehood would generate wars of unspeakable destructiveness which, like earth tremors, would "transplant mountains and valleys." Inspired by Nietzsche, the Futurists welcomed this impending Armageddon as "the only hygiene of the world."

But what deserves special emphasis is that the apprehension that Western civilization was moving into the eye of a historical hurricane also preyed on the minds of many of Europe's political masters who, though tormented, nevertheless continued to advance to the precipice. Theobald von Bethmann Hollweg was one such master. Born in 1856 on the family estate of Hohenfinow, he was raised as a Junker and groomed for public service. After having attended elite schools, served with the dragoons, and studied law, he entered the Prussian bureaucracy. Quickly recognized for his exceptional talent and loyalty, he became interior minister of Prussia in 1905, vice-chancellor and imperial secretary of the interior in 1907, and imperial chancellor in mid-1909.

In April 1913, during a debate of the military budget, Bethmann Hollweg declared that "no human being could possibly imagine the dimensions as well as the misery and destruction of a [future] world conflagration." In his judgment, "by comparison all past wars probably would appear as mere child's play." This being the case, "no responsible statesman would think of lighting the fuse that ignites the powder keg without careful consideration." In other words, the German chancellor did not rule out taking the fateful step, though he claimed that the "pressure" to take that step came not from the majority of public opinion but increasingly from "noisy . . . and passionate minorities" that knew how to take advantage of new democratic freedoms. In June 1914, in a letter to General of the Cavalry Baron Konstantin von Gebsattel, an ultra not of the streets but of high government circles, Bethmann averred that to compound the empire's domestic conflicts with external war would be to "create a situation similar to that which had existed in Germany during the Thirty Years' War and in Russia at the end of the Russo-Japanese War." That same month he told Count Hugo von Lerchenfeld, the Bavarian envoy, that while conservative circles "expected a war to restore the internal health of Germany," he was afraid that "a world war of uncertain consequences would strengthen Social Democracy immensely . . . and cause the overthrow of many a throne." Bethmann Hollweg remained in his post although he knew that William II, the ultimate authority, stood with the ultras, even if in early 1914 he spurned the proposal of the crown prince and Gebsattel to initiate a coup against the helpless Reichstag. In the meantime not only the chancellor and emperor but the entire top leadership must long since have been apprised of what General Helmuth von Moltke, the chief of staff, conceded on July 29, 1914, as he helped set the switches for war: that the war that had been planned "would destroy the culture of nearly all of Europe for decades to come." Despite the evident domination of hard-liners in the government, Jordan von Kröcher auf Vinzelberg, the president of the Prussian Landtag, had resigned in 1912 to protest any further temporizing for reasons of political caution: "the governing circles being incredibly blind, we are approaching the *grosse Kladderadatsch* with giant steps, and we can no longer have any other wish than to die like decent people."

The same general sense that any future war would likely be catastrophic prevailed in the ruling and governing circles of Vienna and Budapest. Notwithstanding tactical differences between the Austro-German and Magyar political elites, they were in broad agreement that a war would almost certainly strain the Dual Monarchy and Europe beyond the breaking point. Intermittently an explicit and forceful champion of induced war, whether against Italy or Serbia, Hötzendorff in mid-1914 spoke for all those who were convinced of the urgency to escape forward: "whereas in 1908–1909 war would have been a card game in which we could see everyone's hand . . . and in 1912–1913 one in which we would have had a good chance of winning, [by] now it was a *Vabanquespiel.*"

When Sergei Dimitrievich Sazonov, the Russian foreign minister, first heard of the text of Vienna's ultimatum to Serbia of July 23, 1914, which had been cleared and approved by Berlin, he immediately exclaimed that it would unleash a "European war." He told Count Friedrich Szápary, the Austro-Hungarian ambassador in St. Petersburg, that by "making war on Serbia" his country would "set fire to Europe" and that notwithstanding the justified grief and indignation of the Habsburgs over the assassination of their heir apparent, "the monarchic idea had nothing to do with it." In what was a monstrous test of nerve Szápary countered that he quite realized that any "conflict among the major powers . . . could not help but have the most horrid consequences, which meant gambling with the established religious, moral, and social order." For special emphasis he presented Sir Edward Grey's admonition against a "European war . . . in lurid colors . . . which Sazonov fully endorsed."

Perhaps it was only natural that the British foreign secretary should have stressed the economic side of the overhanging "breakdown of civilization." Born into the provincial nobility and to an equerry of the royal family, Grey was a leading member of Europe's most authentic liberal government, which staked its future on continuing free trade for the world's largest empire. When Count Albert von Mensdorff, the Austrian ambassador in London, informed him on July 23 of the ultimatum about to be served on Belgrade, he instantly cautioned that a war by the four major powers would spell the "economic bankruptcy of Europe" and that in "most countries quite a few institutions would be swept away, irrespective of victory or defeat." Immediately following this conversation, Grey reiterated his concern to Sir Maurice de Bunsen, England's ambassador in Vienna. A Continental war would involve such vast expenditures and interruptions of trade that it "would be accompanied or followed by a complete collapse of European credit and industry," which for "great industrial states would mean a state of things worse than that of 1848." The following day he told Prince Karl Max von Linchowsky, the German ambassador to the Court of St. James's, that the consequences of war "would be absolutely incalculable" but that whatever the outcome there "would be total exhaustion and impoverishment, industry and trade would be ruined, and the power of capital destroyed," which would generate "revolutionary movements like those of the year 1848." Grey returned to this theme with Mensdorff on July 29, insisting that with economic collapse and unemployment "the industrial workers would rebel" and in the process "the monarchic principle would simply be swept away." Except for his preoccupation with the economic dimension of an impending conflict which would imperil England's government and regime even if London remained neutral, Sir Edward—and his governing associates—shared the sense of the politician-statesmen of the Continent that a war would mean a European cataclysm.

The upper classes of Europe were prepared to take their peoples into a catastrophe from which they hoped against hope to draw benefits for themselves. In other words, though unprecedented, the catastrophe was not expected to be total. To be sure, there might be millions of victims, massive devastation, and severe unsettlement. Even so, a general war would not turn out to be "the end of history," though it would overload the circuits of military planning and control. Certainly the politicians and generals of the aristocratic reaction were accomplices rather than adversaries or rivals in the march to the brink. This is not to deny that there were strains between civil and military leaders and that the military plans, including their operational provisions, limited the freedom of action of politicians and diplomats. But these civil-military tensions were embedded in factional battles over means, not ends, within conservatism and the governing classes. Once the ultraconservative resurgence lifted the soldiers into the highest levels of government, the generals militarized the civilians no more than the civilians politicized the warriors. The latter left their mark not because of their expertise but because the civilians were in search of military solutions to political problems. What tied them together, quite apart from shared social and political attitudes, interests, and objectives, was a common commitment to struggle against political democracy, social leveling, industrial development, and cultural modernism. These *idées-forces,* wrapped in pugnacious patriotism, significantly influenced the making of strategic and tactical plans. To be sure, these required the expertise of generals. But military know-how alone did not dictate the stress on mass assault *à outrance* in pursuit of a swift battlefield victory, regardless of human cost. Besides, that know-how was obsolete. The generals meant to re-enact the lightning campaign of 1870, in which the first Moltke had overwhelmed France with his pioneering speed and concentration of infantry divisions, having overlooked the fact that since then Moltke's formula had been assimilated by all the general staffs. Furthermore, they deceived themselves into thinking that by using the railroads they were appropriating the latest technology for their own purposes, when as a military technique the rails for troop trains, immovably fixed in space, were nearly as much a legacy of the first industrial revolution as the officers were of feudalism.

At any rate, the civilian governors were not disposed to scrutinize the military's strategic and operational schemes. Not that they lacked the intelligence and knowledge to do so. But the statesmen were locked into the same impetuous worldview and political project as the generals. Accordingly, they screened out other options, such as defensive strategies which would have reduced the pressures of timetables and mutual fear. Clearly, the rigidity of diplomatic and military master plans was "as much in the mind as it was in the railway timetables." In addition, Europe's politician-statesmen refrained from questioning the wisdom of the quick and massive strike because of their gnawing realization that the *anciens régimes* were too fragile to support the burdens of a protracted war of attrition. In sum, their position was highly paradoxical, and more than likely they knew it.

Eventually, in July–August 1914 the governors of the major powers, all but a few of them thoroughly nobilitarian, marched over the precipice of war with their eyes wide open, with calculating heads, and exempt from mass pressures. Along the way not a single major actor panicked or was motivated by narrow personal, bureaucratic, and partisan concerns. Among the switchmen of war there were no petty improvisers, no romantic dilettantes, no reckless adventurers. Whatever the profile of their populist helpers or harassers, they were men of high social standing, education, and wealth, determined to maintain or recapture an idealized world of yesterday. But these politician-statesmen and generals also knew that to achieve their project they would have to resort to force and violence. Under the aegis of the scepter and the miter, the old elites, unrestrained by the bourgeoisie, systematically prepared their drive for retrogression, to be executed with what they considered irresistible armies. They, the horsemen of the apocalypse, were ready to crash into the past not only with swords and cavalry charges but also with the artillery and railroads of the modern world that besieged them.

For its own reasons and interests the capitalist bourgeoisie, symbiotically linked to the old elites, was ready and willing, if not eager, to serve as quartermaster for this perilous enterprise. The magnates of movable wealth calculated that the requisites of warfare would intensify the *ancien régime*'s need for the "economic services of capitalism." Like their senior partners, the bourgeois did not shy away from what they too knew would be absolute war, confident that it would be a forcing house for the expansion of industry, finance, and commerce and an improvement of their status and power. As for the industrial workers, they were too weak and too well integrated into nation and society to resist impressment, though theirs was the only class in which there was any marked disposition to do so.

Not that the labor movement was quiescent throughout Europe. Beginning in 1912 Russia was hit by a new wave of industrial unrest: there were some 200 strikes involving 725,000 workers in 1912, some 2,400 strikes involving 887,000 workers in 1913, and some 3,500 strikes involving 1,337,000 workers during the first seven months of 1914. This mounting labor unrest was concentrated in such key industrial centers as St. Petersburg, Moscow, and Baku. Especially in the capital, but also elsewhere, young semiskilled and unskilled workers were the prime carriers of militancy. Most of them ex-peasants who had recently arrived from the countryside, these laborers were poorly paid, badly housed, and psychologically unsettled. These were the workers who were most predisposed to spontaneous and instant action. Bolshevik and Social Revolutionary organizers merely reinforced this bent to action and helped to politicize the strike movement. The industrial turmoil reached its most intense point with the great but not general strike in St. Petersburg in July 1914 in which certain socialist and labor leaders ultimately restrained the new militants.

Although this labor turbulence of the immediate prewar years and weeks was without precedent, it fell considerably short of a general revolt and a prerevolution. The work stoppages were not only restricted to a few cities, but they also remained totally uncoordinated. Above all, except for minor stirrings in Moscow and a few cities of the western and Baltic provinces, the great strike of July 1914 was confined to the capital. Moreover, throughout urban Russia, including St. Petersburg, the striking workers were forced to go it alone. Neither students and intellectuals, nor the intermediate classes and their political representatives, made any move to help them. No less debilitating was the absence of agitation or unrest among the peasants of the countryside and of the nationalities in the border provinces.

Since the labor unrest was sequential rather than synchronized, and without support in other classes, it was relatively easy for the government to curb it. The state was steadier than in 1905–1906 and its forces of repression ready and loyal. In mid-1912 the authorities did not hesitate to order soldiers to move against the striking miners in the Lena goldfields in Siberia, with the result that 170 workers were killed and 372 injured. Following this massacre, which stimulated the labor upheaval in European Russia, the gendarmes, Cossacks, and soldiers reinforced the social and political isolation of the workers with a military quarantine. In July 1914, literally days and hours before Austria's ultimatum to Serbia, the constabulary contained the rebellious strikers within the factory and working-class districts of St. Petersburg. Quite apart from the presence of large coercive forces, the workers were handicapped in all these confrontations by the infiltration of police spies, who robbed them of the element of surprise, and by the lack of arms.

Even so, there was considerable concern, notably in Paris, that this labor insurgence might be sufficiently strong to deter the tsarist government, fearful of popular uprisings, from going to war should the need arise. By this time Raymond

Poincaré, the only bourgeois head of state of all the major powers, had sent a new ambassador to St. Petersburg. Like Poincaré himself, Maurice Paléologue was an intransigent national-conservative, impatient with the instability and would-be social reformism of republican cabinets. The new president of France, with his autocratic pretensions, wanted a trusted envoy to see that the tsarist government pressed ahead with preparedness and made no overtures to Berlin. He also expected full reports on the internal conditions in France's major ally. Accordingly, on May 21, 1914, almost immediately after taking up his post, Paléologue filed a dispatch on "the revolutionary forces in Russia and their likely behavior in case of general mobilization."

Paléologue saw the revolutionary forces as divided between intellectuals and workers. The intellectuals, most of them members of the liberal professions, "were nihilists . . . without discipline or cohesion and [with] a vague program full of sickly dreams, unsophisticated utopias, and pessimistic speculations." Estimated at 5,000 to 6,000 "leaders and soldiers," these nihilist intellectuals were ineffective, in large part because they were exhausted and disillusioned by the events of 1905–1906. Among students this lassitude even took the form of an "insolent recrudescence of suicide and of neurasthenia." Although the intellectual proletariat was capable of individual sacrifice, martyrdom, and assassination, it was unable to generate a "great social upheaval."

The industrial proletariat was growing rapidly because of Russia's recent economic development. In the industrial centers—St. Petersburg, Reval, Moscow, Lodz, Warsaw, Odessa, Baku—there was now a disciplined army of 500,000 workers sworn to "the integral destruction of autocratic despotism." The general staff of this army, whose membership was secret, was singularly effective. Whereas the intellectual proletariat had "no weapons other than theoretical propaganda and personal assassination," the proletariat of workingmen possessed the "terrible weapon of the general strike." The Jewish Bund of Poland—with its clandestine press, strike fund, and 35,000 members—was the "avant-garde of the workers' army." Although there was little sympathy and even mutual contempt between Jewish artisans and Russian workers, "they nevertheless constituted a formidable force for revolt and subversion."

But whatever the strength of these revolutionary forces, they faced formidable "forces of resistance and repression." Although Nicholas II was criticized in high society for being excessively secluded and susceptible to occult influences, the prestige of the tsar remained intact with the population at large, except with the Jews. To that day the revolution had not destroyed the "imperial illusion and the autocratic fetishism," so that the tsar's supremacy remained a "highly respected palladium for the regime."

After the crown, the police was the great bulwark of the state. "An enormous and shrewdly centralized bureaucracy," it counted 38,000 gendarmes, a secret chancellery (the Okhrana) with an extensive network of agents, and a budget of 162 million francs, plus a special fund of 25 million francs disbursed at the emperor's discretion. In times of trouble the government ruled by emergency decree under which the police was "omnipotent" and a cavalry of 25,000 Cossacks was primed for riot duty. But there was, in addition, a private police, which was perhaps "the most redoubted weapon of social conservatism." A vast "secret society, the Union of Russian People was in the nature of a counterrevolutionary league that had clandestine ties to the government." This society had its own press, which was "subsidized and controlled by the Okhrana." It also distributed political tracts and pamphlets "inciting popular fanaticism against the enemies of religion, emperor, and state." Paléologue even added that "our own Committee of Public Safety would have been envious of such a beautiful instrument of retaliation and domination."

As a last resort, there was a standing "army of 1.3 million men in peacetime, of which 30,000 formed the imperial guard." Paléologue's own information and the reports of his military attachés confirmed the "perfect loyalty of officers and men," which meant that "the army seemed not to have been contaminated by anarchist propaganda."

In conclusion, the balance was decidedly in favor of the

tsarist government. To be sure, in the event of general mobilization the main industrial centers would experience some unrest and sabotage. "But any serious outbreak would immediately be drowned in blood [*étouffée dans le sang*]." Judging by past experience, "in case of a national emergency the revolutionaries would certainly be treated with implacable rigor." If there was anything to the view that regimes were "overthrown not by revolutions but because governments abdicate power," the Russian government was not about to cede. Should its enemies strike, it would "retaliate ruthlessly." Westerners might consider "the repression of the Russian state inhuman," but that was irrelevant: "The Russian people was used to putting up with enormous doses of absolutism, and the present dose was not exceeding popular endurance." For good measure, Paléologue conjectured that if there was to be any real danger, "it would come not from the Revolution, but from the Reaction, and not as a by-product of war, but in peacetime."

Thereafter the French ambassador, himself a superhawk against Germany, kept reassuring General Joffre and others that notwithstanding the new strike wave, the revolutionary movement neither would nor could interfere with mobilization. Right down to July 1914 he remained firm in his conclusion that "the forces of autocratic tsarism far exceeded the revolutionary forces" and that in case of war, the Russian people could be trusted to fight, even with enthusiasm. As an afterthought, however, he added that "should the Russian armies not be victorious or should their victory be a mutilated victory," there would again be "an explosion of popular wrath, as there had been in 1879 and 1905." Paléologue's final conclusion, not unlike Trotsky's, was that "military defeat alone could overthrow tsarism."

Just as the Russian labor movement was too weak to deter the tsarist government from mobilizing, so East Central Europe's nationalist movements were too feeble and fragmented to give a second thought to Vienna. In the early twentieth century the subject nationalities, including the Serbs, were marking time. Their political programs, organizations, and strategies were as moderate as those of the social democratic parties of Central and Western Europe. With rare exceptions their leaders were confirmed gradualists, both because they were awed by the repressive powers of the state and because, like the leaders of the recent Italian Risorgimento, they were disinclined to mobilize the masses, notably the peasants, with radical social programs.

Significantly, the clandestine Black Hand and the youthful assassins of Francis Ferdinand were based, not among the allegedly seething Slavs within the Austro-Hungarian Empire, but across the border in Serbia. Moreover, theirs was an act not of confidence but of despair. The politics of symbolic assassination was, as always, the strategy of nationalist movements that were stalled, feeble, and divided.

Actually, the assassination of the archduke and his morganatic wife in the Bosnian capital was a microscopic reflection of Europe's general crisis. There were, on the one hand, the sporadic excesses of militants at the margin rather than the center of fundamentally moderate labor, socialist, and nationalist movements. In addition to being weak, the zealots of these forces of change were disavowed by their parent movements. Even so, the politics of overreaction tarred these movements with the same brush of extremism, with the result that they in turn were distrusted and spurned by the crumbling vital center.

On the other hand there were the steady excesses of ultraconservatives with close ties to the core of the ruling and governing classes and institutions. Far from being repudiated by their conservative associates in and out of government, the zealots of the forces of order exercised ever more influence over them.

Francis Ferdinand was the absolute incarnation of the resurgent ultraconservatism and the politics of overreaction that permeated the nerve-centers of power. He was not only a haughty aristocrat, arrogant absolutist, proud Austro-German, fervent Catholic, and imperious militarist; as an integral reactionary he was also an aggressive antidemocrat, anticapitalist, antilibertarian, antisocialist, anti-Magyar, anti-Slav, anti-Semite, and antimodernist. The heir apparent may have wavered between the politics of the pronunciamento at home and of induced war abroad. But few doubted that once on the Habsburg throne—Emperor Francis Joseph I was eighty-four in 1914—he would orchestrate a vigorous policy of historical retrogression. Meanwhile the army was Francis Ferdinand's primary preoccupation. Characteristically he became a lieutenant at the age of fourteen and quickly rose through the ranks. As of 1895 he was presumed to act as commander in chief in case of war, and in 1898 he took charge of a military chancery that soon became a diehard shadow government. The archduke expected the army to instill loyalty and discipline throughout the realm. Though charged with overseeing all aspects of the military establishment, Francis Ferdinand was totally uninterested in the new weaponry and tactics of infantry warfare. His confidence in the cavalry remained unwavering, in part perhaps because he considered the army at least as much an instrument of internal order as of external war.

Francis Ferdinand was merely the victim of the solitary terrorist commando that fired those fatal shots in Sarajevo. Behind the hapless victim was the larger target of venerable elites and institutions bent on prolonging their privileged life, if need be by force and violence. But this target was too vast, resilient, and resistant to be felled by a few terrorist bullets. It would take the two World Wars and the Holocaust, or the Thirty Years' War of the twentieth century, to finally dislodge and exorcise the feudal and aristocratic presumption from Europe's civil and political societies.

Bibliography
Index

Bibliography

INTRODUCTION

Anderson, Perry. *Lineages of the Absolutist State.* London: New Left Books, 1974.
Arendt, Hannah. *The Origins of Totalitarianism.* 3rd ed. New York: Harcourt, Brace & World, 1966.
Aston, Trevor, ed. *Crisis in Europe, 1560–1660.* New York: Basic Books, 1965.
Barraclough, Geoffrey. *An Introduction to Contemporary History.* New York: Basic Books, 1965.
Behrens, C. B. A. *The Ancien Régime.* New York: Harcourt Brace Jovanich, 1967.
Bloch, Marc. *La Société féodale.* Paris: Albin Michel, 1939.
Dahrendorf, Ralf. *Society and Democracy in Germany.* Garden City, N. Y.: Doubleday & Co., 1967.
Engels, Friedrich. *The Role of Force in History: A Study of Bismarck's Policy of Blood and Iron.* New York: International Publishers, 1972.
Furet, François. *Penser la Révolution française.* Paris: Gallimard, 1978.
Goubert, Pierre. *L'Ancien Régime.* 2 vols. Paris: Armand Colin, 1969–1973.
Gramsci, Antonio. *Selections from the Prison Notebooks.* New York: International Publishers, 1971.
Halévy, Élie. *The World Crisis of 1914–1918.* Oxford: Clarendon Press, 1930.
Hayes, Carlton J. H. *A Generation of Materialism, 1871–1900.* New York: Harper & Row, 1941.
Hobsbawm, E. J. *The Age of Revolution: Europe, 1789–1848.* Cleveland, Ohio: World Publishing Co., 1962.
———. *The Age of Capital, 1848–1875.* New York: Charles Scribner's Sons, 1975.
Kehr, Eckart. *Economic Interest, Militarism, and Foreign Policy.* Berkeley: University of California Press, 1977.
Lenin, V. I. *Imperialism: The Highest Stage of Capitalism.* New York: International Publishers, 1939.
Marcuse, Herbert. *Negations: Essays in Critical Theory.* Boston: Beacon Press, 1968.

Marx, Karl. *The Eighteenth Brumaire of Louis Bonaparte.* New York: International Publishers, 1963.

————, and Engels, Friedrich. *The German Ideology.* Pts. 1 and 2. New York: International Publishers, 1947.

Moore, Barrington, Jr. *Social Origins of Dictatorship and Democracy: Lord and Peasant in the Making of the Modern World.* Boston: Beacon Press, 1966.

Norman, E. Herbert. *Japan's Emergence as a Modern State.* In John W. Dower, ed., *Origins of the Modern Japanese State: Selected Writings of E. H. Norman.* New York: Pantheon Books, 1975.

Ortega y Gasset, José. *The Revolt of the Masses.* New York: W. W. Norton & Co., 1932.

Polanyi, Karl. *The Great Transformation: Political and Economic Origins of Our Time.* New York: Rinehart, 1944.

Schumpeter, Joseph A. *Capitalism, Socialism, and Democracy.* 3rd ed. New York: Harper Torchbooks, 1962.

Steiner, George. *In Bluebeard's Castle: Some Notes Toward the Redefinition of Culture.* New Haven: Yale University Press, 1971.

Tocqueville, Alexis de. *The Old Régime and the French Revolution.* Garden City, N. Y.: Doubleday & Co., 1955.

Tuchman, Barbara W. *The Proud Tower: A Portrait of the World Before the War, 1890–1914.* New York: Macmillan Co., 1966.

Veblen, Thorstein. *Imperial Germany and the Industrial Revolution.* New York: Macmillan Co., 1915.

Vovelle, Michel. *La Chute de la monarchie, 1787–1792.* Paris: Éditions du Seuil, 1972.

Williams, Raymond. *The Country and the City.* New York: Oxford University Press, 1973.

CHAPTER 1
The Economies: The Endurance of Land, Agriculture, Manufacture

Barral, Pierre. *Les Agrariens français de Méline à Pisani.* Paris: Presses de la Fondation Nationale des Sciences Politiques, 1968.

————. *Les Sociétés rurales du XXe siècle.* Paris: Armand Colin, 1978.

Bater, James H. *St. Petersburg: Industrialization and Change.* Montreal: McGill-Queens University Press, 1976.

Bechtel, Heinrich. *Wirtschaftsgeschichte Deutschlands im 19. und 20. Jahrhundert.* Munich: Georg D. W. Gallwey, 1956.

Blum, Jerome. *The End of the Old Order in Rural Europe.* Princeton: Princeton University Press, 1978.

Bouvier, Jean. *Histoire économique et histoire sociale: Recherches sur le capitalisme contemporain.* Geneva: Librairie Droz, 1968.

————. *Naissance d'une banque: Le Crédit Lyonnais.* Paris: Flammarion, 1968.

Brodrick, George C. *English Land and English Landlords.* London: Cassel, Petter, Galpin & Co., 1881.

Cairncross, A. K. *Home and Foreign Investment, 1870–1913.* Cambridge: Cambridge University Press, 1953.

Cameron, Rondo. *Banking and Economic Development.* New York: Oxford University Press, 1972.

Castronovo, Valerio. *Storia d'Italia.* Vol. 4, pt. 1, *La storia economica.* Turin: Giulio Einaudi, 1975.

Chandler, Alfred D., Jr. *The Visible Hand: The Managerial Revolution in American Business.* Cambridge, Mass.: Harvard University Press, 1977.

Clapham, J. H. *The Economic Development of France and Germany, 1815–1914.* 4th ed. Cambridge: Cambridge University Press, 1945.

Collinet, Michel. *Essai sur la condition ouvrière, 1900–1950.* Paris: Éditions Ouvrières, 1951.

Courthéoux, J. P. "Les Pouvoirs économiques et sociaux dans un même secteur industriel: La Sidérurgie." *Revue d'Histoire économique et sociale* 38 (1960): 339–76.

Crisp, Olga. *Studies in the Russian Economy Before 1914.* New York: Barnes & Noble, 1976.

Daumard, Adeline. "L'Évolution des structures sociales en France à l'époque de l'industrialisation." *Revue Historique* 502 (1972): 325–46.

Deane, Phyllis, and Cole, W. A. *British Economic Growth, 1688–1959: Trends and Structure.* Cambridge: Cambridge University Press, 1962.

Dobb, Maurice. *Studies in the Development of Capitalism.* New York: International Publishers, 1947.

Dovring, Folke. *Land and Labor in Europe, 1900–1950.* The Hague: Martinus Nijhoff, 1956.

Duby, Georges, and Wallon, Armand, eds. *Histoire de la France rurale.* Vol. 3, *Apogée et crise de la civilisation paysanne, 1789–1914.* Paris: Éditions du Seuil, 1976.

Eddie, Scott M. "The Changing Pattern of Landownership in Hungary, 1867–1914." *Economic History Review* 20 (1967): 293–310.

Erickson, Charlotte. *British Industrialists: Steel and Hosiery, 1850–1950.* Cambridge: Cambridge University Press, 1959.

Fridenson, Patrick. *Histoire des Usines Renault: Naissance de la grande entreprise, 1898–1939.* Paris: Éditions du Seuil, 1972.

Gerschenkron, Alexander. *Economic Backwardness in Historical Perspective.* Cambridge, Mass.: Harvard University Press, 1962.

Giedion, Siegfried. *Mechanization Takes Command.* New York: Oxford University Press, 1948.

Gross, Nachum. "Austrian Industrial Statistics 1880/85 and 1911/13." *Zeitschrift für die gesamte Staatswissenschaft* 124 (1968): 35–69.

Guiral, Pierre, and Thuillier, Guy. *La Vie quotidienne des domestiques en France au XIX siècle.* Paris: Librairie Hachette, 1978.

Häbich, Theodor. *Deutsche Latifundien.* Stuttgart: W. Kohlhammer 1947.

Halsey, A. E., ed. *Trends in British Society since 1900: A Guide to the Changing Social Structure of Britain.* New York: St. Martin's Press, 1972.

Hannah, Leslie. *The Rise of the Corporate Economy.* Baltimore: Johns Hopkins University Press, 1976.

Hobsbawm, E. J. *Industry and Empire: The Making of Modern English Society.* Vol. 2, *1750 to the Present Day.* New York: Pantheon Books, 1968.

Hoffman, Walther G. *The Growth of Industrial Economies.* Manchester: Manchester University Press, 1958.

Jones, Gareth Stedman. "Working-Class Culture and Working-Class Politics in London, 1870–1900: Notes on the Remaking of a Working Class." *Journal of Social History* 7 (1974): 460–508.

BIBLIOGRAPHY

Kahn, Alfred E. *Great Britain in the World Economy*. New York: Columbia University Press, 1946.

Kemp, Tom. *Industrialization in Nineteenth Century Europe*. New York: Humanities Press, 1969.

Kindleberger, Charles P. *Economic Growth in France and Britain, 1851–1950*. Cambridge, Mass.: Harvard University Press, 1964.

Landes, David S. *The Unbound Prometheus*. Cambridge: Cambridge University Press, 1969.

Laux, James M. *In First Gear: The French Automobile Industry to 1914*. Montreal: McGill-Queens University Press, 1976.

Lebovics, Herman. " 'Agrarians' Versus 'Industrializers.' " *International Review of Social History* 12 (1967): 31–65.

Lévy-Leboyer, Maurice. "Le Patronat français a-t-il été malthusien?" *Le Mouvement Social* 88 (1974): 3–50.

Lyashchenko, Peter I. *History of the National Economy of Russia to the 1917 Revolution*. New York: Octagon Books, 1970.

McBride, Theresa M. *The Domestic Revolution: The Modernization of Household Service in England and France, 1820–1920*. New York: Holmes & Meier Publishers, 1976.

Matis, Herbert. *Österreichs Wirtschaft, 1848–1913*. Berlin: Duncker & Humblot, 1972.

Mayer, Hans, ed. *Hundert Jahre österreichischer Wirtschaftsentwicklung, 1848–1948*. Vienna: Springer, 1949.

Mitchell, B. R. *Abstract of British Historical Statistics*. Cambridge: Cambridge University Press, 1971.

———. *European Historical Statistics, 1750–1970*. New York: Columbia University Press, 1975.

Moore, Barrington, Jr. *Injustice: The Social Bases of Obedience and Revolt*. White Plains, N.Y.: M. E. Sharpe, 1978.

Moss, Bernard H. *The Origins of the French Labor Movement, 1830–1914: The Socialism of Skilled Workers*. Berkeley: University of California Press, 1976.

Neuburger, Hugh, and Stokes, Houston H. "German Banks and German Growth, 1883–1914: An Empirical View." *Journal of Economic History* 34 (1974): 710–30.

Palmade, Guy P. *Capitalisme et capitalistes français au XIXe siècle*. Paris: Armand Colin, 1961.

Payne, P. L. "The Emergence of the Large-Scale Company in Great Britain, 1870–1940." *Economic History Review* 20 (1967): 519–41.

Pohl, Manfred. *Einführung in die deutsche Bankengeschichte*. Frankfurt am Main: Fritz Knapp, 1966.

Puhle, Hans Jürgen. *Politische Agrarbewegungen in kapitalistischen Industriegesellschaften*. Göttingen: Vandenhoeck & Ruprecht, 1975.

Samuel, Raphael. "The Workshop of the World: Steam Power and Hand Technology in mid-Victorian Britain." *History Workshop* 3 (1977): 6–72.

Sartorius von Waltershausen, A. *Deutsche Wirtschaftsgeschichte, 1815–1914*. 2nd ed. Jena: Gustav Fischer, 1923.

Saul, S. B. *The Myth of the Great Depression, 1873–1896*. New York: Humanities Press, 1969.

Sombart, Werner. *The Jews and Modern Capitalism*. Glencoe, Ill.: Free Press, 1951.

Statistisches Jahrbuch für das deutsche Reich, 1913. Berlin: Puttkamer & Mühlbrecht, 1913.

Statistiques internationales rétrospectives. Vol. 1, *La Population active et sa structure.* Brussels: Université Libre de Bruxelles, 1968.

Stearns, Peter N. *Lives of Labor: Work in a Maturing Industrial Society.* New York: Holmes & Meier Publishers, 1975.

Tremel, Ferdinand. *Wirtschafts- und Sozialgeschichte Österreichs.* Vienna: Franz Deuticke, 1969.

Tross, Arnold. *Der Aufbau der Eisen- und eisenverarbeitenden Industriekonzerne Deutschlands.* Berlin: Julius Springer, 1923.

Zorn, Wolfgang, ed. *Handbuch der deutschen Wirtschafts- und Sozialgeschichte.* Vol. 2, *Das 19. und 20. Jahrhundert.* Stuttgart: Ernst Klett, 1976.

CHAPTER 2

The Ruling Classes: The Bourgeoisie Defers

Baldick, Robert. *The Duel.* New York: Clarkson N. Potter, 1966.

Bergeron, Louis. *Les Capitalistes en France, 1780–1914.* Paris: Gallimard/Julliard, 1978.

Bourdieu, Pierre, and Passeron, Jean-Claude. *Les Héritiers.* Paris: Éditions de Minuit, 1964.

————. *La Reproduction.* Paris: Éditions de Minuit, 1970.

Bramsted, Ernest K. *Aristocracy and the Middle-Classes in Germany: Social Types in German Literature, 1830–1900.* Chicago: University of Chicago Press, 1964.

Bruce-Jones, Mark, and Montgomery-Massingberd, Hugh. *The British Aristocracy.* London: Constable, 1979.

Cecil, Lamar. "The Creation of Nobles in Prussia, 1871–1918." *American Historical Review* 75 (1970): 757–95.

Chaussinand-Nogaret, Guy, ed. *Une Histoire des élites, 1700–1848.* Paris: Mouton Éditeur, 1975.

Daumard, Adeline. *Les Bourgeois de Paris au XIXe siècle.* Paris: Flammarion, 1970.

Demeter, Karl. *The German Officer Corps in Society and State, 1650–1945.* New York: Frederick A. Praeger, 1965.

Du Puy de Clinchamps, Philippe. *La Noblesse.* Paris: Presses Universitaires de France, 1959.

Elenco ufficiale nobiliare italiano. Bologna: Forni, 1922.

Elias, Norbert. *Die höfische Gesellschaft: Untersuchungen zur Soziologie des Königtums und der höfischen Aristokratie.* Neuwied: Luchterhand, 1969.

————. *Über den Progress der Zivilisation.* 2 vols. Frankfurt am Main: Suhrkamp, 1978.

Ellul, Jacques. *Métamorphose du bourgeois.* Paris: Calmann-Lévy, 1967.

Emmons, Terence. "The Russian Landed Gentry and Politics." *Russian Review* 33 (1974): 269–83.

Engelmann, Bernt. *Krupp.* Munich: Wilhelm Goldmann, 1978.

Feguiz, P. L. *Il volto sconosciuto dell'Italia.* 2 vols. Milan: Antonino Giuffrè, 1966.

Fontane, Theodor. *Der Stechlin.* Berlin, 1899.

————. *Frau Jenny Treibel.* Berlin, 1893.

Fugger, Nora. *The Glory of the Habsburgs.* New York: Dial Press, 1932.

Giddens, Anthony. *The Class Structure of the Advanced Societies.* New York: Barnes & Noble, 1973.

Girouard, Mark. *Life in the English Country House: A Social and Architectural History.* New Haven, Conn.: Yale University Press, 1978.

Goblot, Edmond. *La Barrière et le niveau: Étude sociologique sur la bourgeoisie française moderne.* Paris: Presses Universitaires de France, 1967.

Görlitz, Walter. *Die Junker: Adel und Bauer im deutschen Osten.* Glücksburg/Ostsee: C. V. Starke, 1957.

Graña, César. *Bohemia Versus Bourgeois.* New York: Basic Books, 1964.

Groethhuysen, Bernard. *Origines de l'Esprit bourgeois en France.* Paris: Gallimard, 1927.

Guttsman, W. L., ed. *The English Ruling Class.* London: Weidenfeld & Nicolson, 1969.

Hamburg, Gary Michael. "Land, Economy and Society in Tsarist Russia: Interest Politics of the Landed Gentry during the Agrarian Crisis of the Late Nineteenth Century." Unpublished Ph.D. dissertation, Stanford University, 1978.

Huizinga, Johan. *The Waning of the Middle Ages.* Garden City, N.Y.: Doubleday & Co., 1954.

Jäger-Sunstenau, Hanns. "Statistik der Nobilitierungen in Österreich, 1701–1918." *Österreichisches Familienarchiv* 1 (1963): 3ff.

Jaray, Gabriel Louis. *La Question sociale et le socialisme en Hongrie.* Paris: Félix Alcan, 1909.

Karady, Victor, and Kemény, Istvān. "Les Juifs dans la structure des classes en Hongrie: Essai sur les antécédents historiques des crises d'antisémitisme du XXe siècle." *Actes de la Recherche en Sciences Sociales* 22 (1978): 25–59.

Kruedener, Jürgen von. *Die Rolle des Hofes im Absolutismus.* Stuttgart: Gustav Fischer, 1973.

Lewis, Roy, and Maude, Angus. *The English Middle Classes.* London: Phoenix House, 1949.

Machtan, Lothar, and Milles, Dietrich. *Die Klassensymbiose von Junkertum und Bourgeoisie in Preussen-Deutschland, 1850–1878/79.* Frankfurt am Main: Ullstein, 1980.

Mann, Thomas. *Buddenbrooks.* Berlin: S. Fischer, 1901.

Mayer, Arno J. "The Lower Middle Class as Historical Problem." *Journal of Modern History* 47 (1975): 409–36.

McCagg, William O., Jr. "Ennoblement in Dualistic Hungary." *East European Quarterly* 5 (1971): 13–26.

———. *Jewish Nobles and Geniuses in Modern Hungary.* Boulder, Colo.: East European Quarterly, 1972.

McMillan, James. *The Honours Game.* London: Leslie Frewin, 1969.

Manchester, William. *The Arms of Krupp, 1587–1968.* New York: Bantam Books, 1968.

March, Harold. *The Two Worlds of Marcel Proust.* Philadelphia: University of Pennsylvania Press, 1948.

Michels, Robert. *Probleme der Sozialphilosophie.* Leipzig and Berlin: B. G. Teubner, 1914.

Muncy, Lysbeth Walker. *The Junker in Prussian Administration under William II, 1888–1914.* Providence, R.I.: Brown University Press, 1944.

Musil, Robert. *Der Mann ohne Eigenschaften.* Hamburg: Rowohlt, 1956.

Oertzen, Friedrich Wilhelm von. *Junker: Preussischer Adel im Jahrhundert des Liberalismus.* Oldenburg: Stalling, 1939.

Painter, George D. *Marcel Proust.* 2 vols. New York: Vintage Books, 1978.

Perrott, Roy. *The Aristocrats: A Portrait of Britain's Nobility and Their Way of Life Today.* London: Weidenfeld & Nicolson, 1968.

Phillips, Gregory P. *The Diehards: Aristocratic Society and Politics in Edwardian England.* Cambridge, Mass.: Harvard University Press, 1979.

Ponteil, Félix. *Les Classes bourgeoises et l'avènement de la démocratie, 1815–1914.* Paris: Albin Michel, 1968.

Preradovich, Nikolaus von. *Die Führungsschichten in Oesterreich und Preussen, 1804–1918.* Wiesbaden: Franz Steiner, 1955.

Pritzkoleit, Kurt. *Wem gehört Deutschland?* Vienna, Munich, and Basel: Kurt Desch, 1957.

Proust, Marcel. *A la recherche du temps perdu.* 15 vols. Paris: Gallimard, 1919–1927.

Pumphrey, Ralph. "The Creation of Peerages in England, 1837–1911." Unpublished Ph.D. dissertation, Yale University, 1934.

Riehl, Wilhelm Heinrich. *Die bürgerliche Gesellschaft.* Frankfurt am Main: Ullstein, 1976.

Riese, Laure. *Les Salons littéraires parisiens.* Toulouse: Privat, 1962.

Romano, Salvatore. *Le classi sociali in Italia.* Turin: Giulio Einaudi, 1965.

Rothenberg, Gunther E. *The Army of Francis Joseph.* West Lafayette, Ind.: Purdue University Press, 1976.

Rubenstein, W. D. "Wealth, Elites and the Class Structure of Modern Britain." *Past and Present* 76 (1977): 101–26.

Schnapper, Dominique. *L'Italie rouge et noire.* Paris: Gallimard, 1971.

Schwering, Axel von. *The Berlin Court under William II.* London: Cassel & Co., 1915.

Siegert, Heinz, ed. *Adel in Österreich.* Vienna: Kremayr & Scheriau, 1971.

Sinclair, Andrew. *The Last of the Best: The Aristocracy of Europe in the Twentieth Century.* New York: Macmillan Co., 1969.

Sombart, Werner. *Der Bourgeois.* Munich and Leipzig: Duncker & Humblot, 1913.

Spring, David, ed. *European Landed Elites in the Nineteenth Century.* Baltimore: Johns Hopkins University Press, 1977.

Tarde, Gabriel. *Les Lois de l'imitation.* Paris: Alcan, 1895.

Thompson, F. M. L. *British Landed Society in the Nineteenth Century.* Toronto: University of Toronto Press, 1963.

Veblen, Thorstein. *The Theory of the Leisure Class.* New York: Huebsch, 1918.

Whittam, John. *The Politics of the Italian Army, 1861–1918.* Hamden, Conn.: Shoe String Press, 1976.

Wortman, Richard. "Court Ceremonial and Bureaucracy in Nineteenth Century Russia." Unpublished draft paper, 1979.

Zeldin, Theodore. *France, 1848–1945.* 2 vols. New York: Oxford University Press, 1973–1977.

Zunkel, Friedrich. "Industriebürgertum in Westdeutschland." In Hans-Ulrich Wehler, ed., *Moderne deutsche Sozialgeschichte.* Cologne and Berlin: Kiepenheuer & Witsch, 1966.

BIBLIOGRAPHY

C H A P T E R 3
Political Society and the Governing Classes: Linchpin of the Old Regime

Anderson, R. D. *France, 1870–1914: Politics and Society.* London: Routledge & Kegan Paul, 1977.

Armstrong, John A. *The European Administrative Elite.* Princeton, N.J.: Princeton University Press, 1973.

Beau de Loménie, E. *Les Responsabilités des dynasties bourgeoises.* Vol. 2, *Sous la Troisième république: De Mac-Mahon à Poincaré.* Paris: Éditions Denoël, 1947.

Beer, Samuel H. *British Politics in the Collectivist Age.* New York: Alfred A. Knopf, 1965.

Bernstein, Serge, and Milza, Pierre. *L'Italie contemporaine.* Paris: Armand Colin, 1973.

Bois, Paul. *Paysans de l'Ouest.* Paris: Flammarion, 1971.

Bolton, Glorney. *Roman Century, 1870–1970.* London: Hamish Hamilton, 1970.

Bromhead, P.A. *The House of Lords and Contemporary Politics, 1911–1957.* New York: Hillary House Publishers, 1958.

Cannadine, David. "The Context, Performance, and Meaning of Ritual: The British Monarchy and the Invention of Tradition, c. 1800–1977." Forthcoming in *Past and Present.*

Charle, Christophe. *Les Hauts Fonctionnaires en France au XIXe siècle.* Paris: Gallimard/Julliard, 1980.

Charnay, Jean-Paul. *Le Suffrage politique en France.* Paris: Mouton, 1965.

Charques, Richard. *The Twilight of Imperial Russia.* London: Oxford University Press, 1958.

Chastenet, Jacques. *Histoire de la Troisième république: Triomphes et malaises.* Paris: Librairie Hachette, 1964.

Chmielewski, Edward. "Stolypin's Last Crisis." *California Slavic Studies* 3 (1964): 95–126.

Coppa, Frank J. *Planning, Protection and Politics in Liberal Italy.* Washington, D.C.: Catholic University of America Press, 1971.

Desmarest, Jacques. *L'Évolution de la France contemporaine: Des Oppositions à l'unité, 1897–1914.* Paris: Librairie Hachette, 1977.

Feuchtwanger, E. J. *Prussia: Myth and Reality.* London: Oswald Wolff, 1970.

Florinsky, Michael T. *The End of the Russian Empire.* New York: Collier-Macmillan, 1961.

Gash, Norman; Southgate, Donald; Dilks, David; and Ramsden, John. *The Conservatives: A History from their Origins to 1965.* London: George Allen & Unwin, 1977.

Girardet, Raoul. *La Société militaire dans la France contemporaine, 1815–1939.* Paris: Plon, 1953.

Grusky, Oscar. "Career Patterns and Characteristics of British Naval Officers." *British Journal of Sociology* 26 (1975): 35–51.

Guttsman, W. L. *The British Political Elite.* New York: Basic Books, 1963.

Hosking, Geoffrey A. *The Russian Constitutional Experiment: Government and Duma, 1907–1914.* Cambridge: Cambridge University Press, 1973.

Jászi, Oscar. *The Dissolution of the Habsburg Monarchy.* Chicago: University of Chicago Press, 1929.

Katz, Robert. *The Fall of the House of Savoy.* New York: Macmillan Co., 1971.

Kelsall, R. K. *Higher Civil Servants in Britain: From 1870 to the Present.* New York: Humanities Press, 1955.

Kingsley, J. Donald. *Representative Bureaucracy: An Interpretation of the British Civil Service.* Yellow Springs, Ohio: Antioch College, 1944.

Kochan, Lionel. *Russia in Revolution, 1890–1918.* New York: New American Library, 1966.

Lowell, A. Lawrence. *Governments and Parties in Continental Europe.* 2 vols. Boston: Houghton Mifflin, 1896.

Lukes, Stephen. *Essays in Social Theory.* New York: Columbia University Press, 1977.

Manning, Roberta T. *The Crisis of the Old Order in Russia: Gentry and Government, 1861–1914.* Princeton, N.J.: Princeton University Press, 1981.

———. "The Zemstvo and Politics, 1864–1914." In Terence Emmons, ed., *The Zemstvo: An Experiment in Local Self-Government.* Cambridge: Cambridge University Press, forthcoming.

Massie, Robert K. *Nicholas and Alexandra.* New York: Dell Publishing Co., 1967.

Michels, Robert. *Political Parties.* Glencoe, Ill.: Free Press, 1949.

Miliband, Ralph. *Marxism and Politics.* New York: Oxford University Press, 1977.

Neufeld, Maurice F. *Italy: School for Awakening Countries.* Ithaca, N.Y.: New York State School of Industrial and Labor Relations, Cornell University, 1961.

Ostrogorski, Moisei. *Democracy and the Organization of Political Parties.* 2 vols. 1902. Reprint ed. Brooklyn, N.Y.: Haskell House Publishers, 1970.

Otley, C. B. "The Educational Background of British Army Officers." *Sociology* 7 (1973): 192–209.

———. "The Social Origins of British Army Officers." *Sociological Review* 18 (1970): 213–39.

Pares, Bernard. *The Fall of the Russian Monarchy.* New York: Alfred A. Knopf, 1939.

Pintner, Walter M., and Rowney, Don K., eds. *Russian Officialdom: The Bureaucratization of Russian Society from the Seventeenth to the Twentieth Century.* Chapel Hill: University of North Carolina Press, 1980.

Pritzkoleit, Kurt. *Das kommandierte Wunder: Deutschlands Weg im zwanzigsten Jahrhundert.* Vienna, Munich, and Basel: Kurt Desch, 1959.

Razzell, P. E. "Social Origins of Officers in the Indian and British Home Army, 1758–1962." *British Journal of Sociology* 14 (1963): 248–60.

Rebérioux, Madeleine. *La République radicale? 1898–1914.* Paris: Éditions du Seuil, 1975.

Robinson, Geroid T. *Rural Russia Under the Old Regime.* New York: Macmillan Co., 1932.

Seton-Watson, Hugh. *The Decline of Imperial Russia, 1855–1914.* New York: Frederick A. Praeger, 1956.

Shapiro, David, ed. *The Right in France 1890–1919.* Carbondale: Southern Illinois University Press, 1962.

Siegfried, André. *Tableau politique de la France de l'ouest sous la IIIe république.* Paris: Armand Colin, 1913.

Sorlin, Pierre. *La Société française, 1840–1968.* Vol. 1, *1840–1914.* Paris: Arthaud, 1969.

Stanworth, Philip, and Giddens, Anthony, eds. *Elites and Power in British Society.* Cambridge: Cambridge University Press, 1974.

Sternberger, Dolf, and Vogel, Bernhard. *Die Wahl der Parlamente und anderer Staatsorgane.* Vol. 1, *Europa.* Berlin: Walter de Gruyter, 1969.

Tannenbaum, Edward R., and Noether, Emiliana P. *Modern Italy.* New York: New York University Press, 1974.

Underwood, F. M. *United Italy.* London: Methuen & Co., 1912.

Walsh, W. B. "Political Parties in the Russian Dumas." *Journal of Modern History* 22 (1950): 144–50.

Weber, Eugen. *Peasants into Frenchmen: The Modernization of Rural France, 1870–1914.* Stanford, Calif.: Stanford University Press, 1976.

Wehler, Hans-Ulrich. *Das deutsche Kaiserreich, 1871–1918.* Göttingen: Vandenhoeck & Ruprecht, 1973.

Wildman, Allan K. *The End of the Russian Imperial Army.* Princeton, N.J.: Princeton University Press, 1980.

Zaionchkovsky, Peter A. *The Russian Autocracy Under Alexander III.* Gulf Breeze, Fla.: Academic International Press, 1976.

CHAPTER 4
Official High Cultures and the Avant-Gardes

Adorno, Theodor. *Dissonanzen: Musik in der verwalteten Welt.* Göttingen: Vandenhoeck & Ruprecht, 1972.

———. *Einleitung in die Musiksoziologie.* Munich: Rowohlt, 1971.

———. *Prismen: Kulturkritik und Gesellschaft.* Frankfurt am Main: Suhrkamp, 1955.

Asor Rosa, Alberto. *Storia d'Italia.* Vol. 4, pt. 2, *La cultura.* Turin: Giulio Einaudi, 1975.

Auerbach, Erich. *Mimesis.* Princeton, N.J.: Princeton University Press, 1953.

Balandier, Georges. *Anthropologie politique.* Paris: Presses Universitaires de France, 1967.

Baltzarék, Franz; Hoffmann, Alfred; and Stekl, Hannes. *Wirtschaft und Gesellschaft der wiener Stadterweiterung.* Wiesbaden: Franz Steiner, 1975.

Barea, Ilsa. *Vienna.* New York: Alfred A. Knopf, 1966.

Barzini, Luigi. *The Italians.* New York: Bantam Books, 1964.

Bastide, Roger. *Art et société.* Paris: Payot, 1977.

Baumgarth, Christa. *Geschichte des Futurismus.* Munich: Rowohlt, 1966.

Bazin, Germain. *The Museum Age.* New York: Universe Books, 1967.

Behrmann, N. S. *Duveen: La Chasse aux chefs-d'oeuvre.* Paris: Librairie Hachette, 1953.

Bence-Jones, Mark. *Palaces of the Raj.* London: George Allen & Unwin, 1973.

Benjamin, Walter. *Illuminationen.* Frankfurt am Main: Suhrkamp, 1977.

Bentmann, Richard, and Müller, Michael. *La Villa: Architecture de domination.* Brussels: Pierre Mardaga, 1975.

Berger, John. *The Success and Failure of Picasso.* New York: Pantheon Books, 1980.

———. *Ways of Seeing.* New York: Viking Press, 1973.

Billy, André. *L'Époque contemporaine, 1905–1930.* Paris: Jules Tallandier, 1956.

———. *L'Époque 1900.* Paris: Jules Tallandier, 1951.

Bobek, Hans, and Lichtenberger, Elisabeth. *Wien.* Graz and Cologne: Hermann Böhlaus, 1966.

Broch, Hermann. *Hofmannsthal und seine Zeit*. Frankfurt am Main: Suhrkamp, 1974.

Buckle, Richard. *Diaghilev*. New York: Atheneum Publishers, 1979.

Bürger, Peter. *Theorie der Avantgarde*. Frankfurt am Main: Suhrkamp, 1974.

Carassus, Emilien. *Le Snobisme et les lettres françaises de Paul Bourget à Marcel Proust, 1884–1914*. Paris: Armand Colin, 1966.

Charle, Christophe. "Champ littéraire et champ du pouvoir: Les Écrivains et l'Affaire Dreyfus." *Annales* 32 (1977): 240–64.

Crubellier, Maurice. *Histoire culturelle de la France: XIXe–XXe siècle*. Paris: Armand Colin, 1974.

Decker, Hannah S. *Freud in Germany: Revolution and Reaction in Science, 1893–1907*. New York: International Universities Press, 1977.

Dellheim, Charles J. "Medievalism in Modernity: Studies in the Victorians' Encounter with Their Historic Inheritance." Unpublished Ph.D. dissertation, Yale University, 1980.

Dufrenne, Mikel. *Art et Politique*. Paris: Aubier-Montaigne (10/18), 1974.

Egbert, Donald Drew. *Social Radicalism and the Arts*. New York: Alfred A. Knopf, 1970.

Eisler, Hanns. *Materialen zu einer Dialektik der Musik*. Leipzig: Philipp Reclam, 1973.

Elgar, F. "L'Académisme de l'art officiel sous la IIIe république." *Carrefour*, February 8, 1956.

Engelmann, Bernt. *Trotz alledem: Deutsche Radikale, 1777–1977*. Munich: Rowohlt, 1979.

Fremantle, Anne. *The Papal Encyclicals in Their Historical Context*. New York: Mentor Books, 1972.

Friedell, Egon. *A Cultural History of the Modern Age*. Vol. 3. New York: Alfred A. Knopf, 1954.

Gathorne-Hardy, Jonathan. *The Old School Tie*. New York: Viking Press, 1977.

Gaudibert, Pierre. *Action culturelle: Intégration et/ou subversion*. Paris: Casterman, 1972.

Gay, Peter. *Freud, Jews and Other Germans*. New York: Oxford University Press, 1978.

Gilbert, Alan D. *Religion and Society in Industrial England, 1740–1914*. New York: Longman, 1976.

Gilman, Richard. *Decadence: The Strange Life of an Epithet*. New York: Farrar, Straus & Giroux, 1975.

Giraudoux, Jean. *Pleins Pouvoirs*. Paris: Gallimard, 1939.

Golding, John. *Cubism*. 2nd ed. New York: Harper & Row, 1968.

Graña, César: *Fact and Symbol: Essays in the Sociology of Art and Literature*. New York: Oxford University Press, 1971.

Gray, Camilla. *The Great Experiment: Russian Art, 1863–1922*. New York: Harry N. Abrams, 1962.

Gregor, Joseph. *Kulturgeschichte des Balletts*. Vienna: Gallus, 1944.

Griffiths, Richard. *The Reactionary Revolution: The Catholic Revival in French Literature, 1870–1914*. New York: Frederick Ungar Publishing Co., 1965.

Grigoriev, S. L. *The Diaghilev Ballet, 1909–1929*. London: Constable, 1953.

Grover, Stuart R. "The World of Art Movement in Russia." *Russian Review* 32 (1973): 28–42.

Hall, Ron. "Family Backgrounds of Etonians." In Richard Rose, ed., *Studies in British Politics.* New York: St. Martin's Press, 1966.

Hauser, Arnold. *The Social History of Art.* Vol. 4, *Naturalism, Impressionism, the Film Age.* New York: Vintage Books, 1951.

Hess, Thomas B., and Ashbery, John, eds. *Art of the Academy.* New York: Collier-Macmillan, 1971.

Hinz, Berthold. *Art in the Third Reich.* New York: Pantheon Books, 1980.

Hynes, Samuel. *The Edwardian Turn of Mind.* Princeton, N.J.: Princeton University Press, 1968.

Janz, Rolf-Peter, and Laerman, Klaus. *Arthur Schnitzler: Zur Diagnose des wiener Bürgertums im Fin de Siècle.* Stuttgart: Metzler, 1977.

Johnston, William M. *The Austrian Mind: An Intellectual and Social History, 1848–1938.* Berkeley: University of California Press, 1972.

Kandinsky, Wassily, and Marc, Franz, eds. *The Blaue Reiter Almanac.* New York: Viking Press, 1974.

Kassow, Samuel D. "The Russian University in Crisis, 1899–1911." Unpublished Ph.D. dissertation, Princeton University, 1976.

Kohn, Caroline, *Karl Kraus.* Stuttgart: J. B. Metzlersche, 1966.

König, René. *Macht und Reiz der Mode.* Düsseldorf and Vienna: Econ, 1971.

———. *The Restless Image: A Sociology of Fashion.* London: George Allen & Unwin, 1973.

Lalo, Charles. *L'Art et la vie sociale.* Paris: Librairie Octave Doin, 1921.

Laurent, Jeanne. *La République et les beaux-arts.* Paris: Julliard, 1955.

Laver, James. *Taste and Fashion from the French Revolution Until Today.* New York: Dodd, Mead & Co., 1938.

Le Bot, Marc. *Peinture et machinisme.* Paris: Klincksieck, 1973.

Lecanouet, Édouard. *L'Église française sous la IIIe république.* Paris: Alcan, 1930.

Lenman, Robin. "Politics and Culture: The State and the Avant-Garde in Munich, 1886–1914." In Richard J. Evans, ed., *Society and Politics in Wilhelmine Germany.* New York, Harper & Row, 1978.

Lichtenberger, Elizabeth. *Wirtschaftsfunktion und Sozialstruktur.* Vienna: Böhlaus, 1970.

Lilge, Frederic. *The Abuse of Learning: The Failure of the German University.* New York: Macmillan Co., 1948.

McClelland, James C. *Autocrats and Academics: Education, Culture, and Society in Tsarist Russia.* Chicago: University of Chicago Press, 1979.

McManners, John. *Church and State in France, 1870–1914.* New York: Harper & Row, 1972.

Marraro, Howard R. *The New Education in Italy.* New York: S. F. Vanni, 1936.

Marx, Roland. *Réligion et société en Angleterre.* Paris: Presses Universitaires de France, 1978.

Masur, Gerhard. *Imperial Berlin.* New York: Basic Books, 1970.

Meeks, Carroll L. V. *The Railroad Station.* New Haven, Conn.: Yale University Press, 1956.

Minihan, Janet. *The Nationalization of Culture: The Development of State Subsidies to the Arts in Great Britain.* New York: New York University Press, 1977.

Minio-Paluello, Lorenzo. *Education in Fascist Italy.* 1946. Reprint ed. New York: AMS Press, 1979.

Moers, Ellen. *The Dandy: Brummel to Beerbohm.* New York: Viking Press, 1960.

Morgan, D. H. J. "The Social and Educational Background of Anglican Bishops." *British Journal of Sociology* 20 (1969): 295–310.

Moulin, Raymonde. *Le Marché de la peinture en France.* Paris: Éditions de Minuit, 1967.

Naumann, Michael. *Der Abbau einer verkehrten Welt: Satire und politische Wirklichkeit im Werk von Karl Kraus.* Munich: Paul List, 1969.

Nordau, Max. *Degeneration.* Reprint ed. New York: Howard Fertig, 1968.

Ogilvie, R. M. *Latin and Greek: A History of the Influence of the Classics on English Life from 1600 to 1918.* Hamden, Conn.: Shoe String Press, 1964.

Paret, Peter. "Art and the National Image: The Conflict over Germany's Participation in the St. Louis Exposition." *Central European History* 11 (1978): 173–83.

Pevsner, Nikolaus. *A History of Building Types.* Princeton, N.J.: Princeton University Press, 1976.

Pierrard, Pierre. *Le Prêtre français.* Paris: Blond & Gay, 1969.

Poggioli, Renato. *The Theory of the Avant-Garde.* New York: Harper & Row, 1971.

Poulat, Émile. *Église contre bourgeoisie.* Paris: Casterman, 1977.

Proffer, Carl and Ellendea, eds. *The Silver Age of Russian Culture.* Ann Arbor, Mich.: Ardis Publishers, 1975.

Prost, Antoine. *L'Enseignement en France, 1800–1967.* Paris: Armand Colin, 1968.

Richard, Lionel. *D'une Apocalypse à l'autre.* Paris: Aubier-Montaigne (10/18), 1976.

———. *Le Nazisme et la culture.* Paris: François Maspero, 1978.

Ringer, Fritz. *The Decline of the German Mandarins: The German Academic Community, 1890–1933.* Cambridge, Mass.: Harvard University Press, 1969.

———. *Education and Society in Modern Europe.* Bloomington: Indiana University Press, 1979.

Roazen, Paul. *Freud and His Followers.* New York: New American Library, 1976.

Samuel, R. H., and Thomas, R. Hinton. *Education and Society in Modern Germany.* New York: Humanities Press, 1949.

Sanderson, Michael. *The Universities and British Industry, 1850–1970.* London: Routledge & Kegan Paul, 1972.

Schoch, Rainer. *Das Herrschaftsbild in der Malerei.* Munich: Prestel, 1975.

Schorske, Carl E. *Fin-de-Siècle Vienna: Politics and Culture.* New York: Alfred A. Knopf, 1980.

Schüler, Winfried. *Der bayreuther Kreis von seiner Entstehung bis zum Ausgang der wilhelminischen Ära.* Münster: Aschendorff, 1971.

Sedlmayr, Hans. *Art in Crisis.* Chicago: Henry Regnery Co., 1958.

Service, Alastair. *Edwardian Architecture.* New York: Oxford University Press, 1978.

Shapiro, Theda. *Painters and Politics: The European Avant-Garde and Society, 1900–1925.* New York: Elsevier, 1976.

Starr, Frederick. *Melnikov.* Princeton, N.J.: Princeton University Press, 1978.

———. "The Revival and Schism of Urban Planning in Twentieth-Century Russia." In Michael F. Hamm, ed. *The City in Russian History.* Lexington: University of Kentucky Press, 1976.

Strobl, Alice. "Zu den Fakultätsbildern von Gustav Klimt." *Albertina Studien* 2 (1964): 138–69.

Stuckenschmidt, H. H. *Neue Musik.* Frankfurt am Main: Suhrkamp, 1951.
Swart, Koenraad W. *The Sense of Decadence in Nineteenth-Century France.* The Hague: Martinus Nijhoff, 1964.
Tisdall, Caroline, and Bozzolla, Angelo. *Futurism.* New York: Oxford University Press, 1978.
Vaisse, Pierre. *La Troisième République et les peintres: Recherches sur les rapports des pouvoirs publics et de la peinture en France de 1870 à 1914.* Thèse d'État, Université de Paris IV, 1980..
Williams, Raymond. *Marxism and Literature.* New York: Oxford University Press, 1977.
Wittlin, Alma S. *The Museum: Its History and Its Tasks in Education.* London: Routledge & Kegan Paul, 1949.
Wolff, Pierre. *La Musique contemporaine.* Paris: Fernand Nathan, 1954.
Yarwood, Doreen. *The Architecture of Italy.* New York: Harper & Row, 1971.

CHAPTER 5
World-View: Social Darwinism, Nietzsche, War

Althusser, Louis. "Idéologie et appareils idéologiques de l'état." *Pensée* 151 (1970): 9–21.
Ansart, Pierre. *Idéologies: Conflits et pouvoir.* Paris: Presses Universitaires de France, 1977.
Assoun, Paul-Laurent. *Freud et Nietzsche.* Paris: Presses Universitaires de France, 1980.
Bachrach, Peter. *The Theory of Democratic Elitism: A Critique.* Boston: Little, Brown & Co., 1967.
Bannister, James Mark. "The Survival of the Fittest Is Our Doctrine." *Journal of the History of Ideas* 31 (1970): 377–98.
Barzun, Jacques. *Darwin, Marx, Wagner.* Garden City, N.Y.: Doubleday & Co., 1958.
Beetham, David. *Max Weber and the Theory of Modern Politics.* London: George Allen & Unwin, 1974.
Bendix, Reinhard. *Max Weber: An Intellectual Portrait.* Garden City, N.Y.: Doubleday & Co., 1962.
Bergmann, Klaus. *Agrarromantik und Grossstadtfeindschaft.* Meisenheim am Glan: Anton Hain, 1970.
Bestuzhev, I. V. "Russian Foreign Policy, February–June 1914." *Journal of Contemporary History* 1 (1966): 93–111.
Bottomore, T. B. *Elites and Society.* London: Penguin Books, 1970.
Boudot, Pierre. *Nietzsche et les écrivains français, 1930–1960.* Paris: Aubier-Montaigne (10/18), 1970.
Brandes, George. *Menschen und Werke.* Frankfurt am Main: Literarische Anstalt, 1970.
Buci-Glucksmann, Christine. *Gramsci et l'état.* Paris: Fayard, 1975.
Burnham, James. *The Machiavellians.* London: Putnam & Co., 1943.
Clark, Linda Loeb. "Social Darwinism and French Intellectuals, 1860–1915." Unpublished Ph.D. dissertation, University of North Carolina, Chapel Hill, 1968.
Conrad-Martius, Hedwig. *Utopien der Menschenzüchtung: Der Sozialdarwinismus und seine Folgen.* Munich: Kösel, 1955.

Conry, Yvette. *L'Introduction du darwinisme en France au XIXe siècle.* Paris: Vrin, 1974.

Danto, Arthur C. *Nietzsche as Philosopher.* New York: Macmillan Co., 1965.

Drake, Richard. *Byzantium for Rome: The Politics of Nostalgia in Umbertian Italy, 1878–1900.* Chapel Hill: University of North Carolina Press, 1980.

Edelman, Robert. *Gentry Politics on the Eve of the Russian Revolution: The Nationalist Party, 1907–1917.* New Brunswick, N.J.: Rutgers University Press, 1980.

Fouillée, Alfred. *L'Évolutionisme des idées-forces.* Paris: Félix Alcan, 1890.

———. *Nietzsche et l'immoralisme.* Paris: Félix Alcan, 1920.

———. *La Psychologie des idées-forces.* Paris: Félix Alcan, 1893.

Gasman, Daniel. *The Scientific Origins of National Socialism: Social Darwinism in Ernst Haeckel and the German Monist League.* New York: Elsevier, 1971.

Geyer, Dietrich. *Der russische Imperialismus.* Göttingen: Vandenhoeck & Ruprecht, 1977.

Glick, Thomas F., ed. *The Comparative Reception of Darwinism.* Austin: University of Texas Press, 1974.

Goodheart, Eugene. *The Failure of Criticism.* Cambridge, Mass.: Harvard University Press, 1978.

Greiffenhagen, Martin. *Das Dilemma des Konservatismus in Deutschland.* Munich: R. Piper, 1977.

Guillaumin, Colette. *L'Idéologie raciste: Genèse et langage actuel.* Paris: Mouton, 1972.

Himmelfarb, Gertrude. *Darwin and the Darwinian Revolution.* Gloucester, Mass.: Peter Smith, 1967.

Hofstadter, Richard. *Social Darwinism in American Thought.* New York: George Braziller, 1959.

Hughes, H. Stuart. *Consciousness and Society: The Reorientation of European Social Thought, 1890–1930.* New York: Alfred A. Knopf, 1958.

Jackson, Holbrook. *The Eighteen-Nineties.* 1913. Reprint ed. New York: Humanities Press, 1976.

Janowitz, Morris. *The Professional Soldier: A Social and Political Portrait.* Chicago: Free Press, 1960.

Joll, James. *1914: The Unspoken Assumptions.* London: Weidenfeld & Nicolson, 1968.

Kaufmann, Walter. *Nietzsche.* New York: Meridian Books, 1956.

Kennedy, Paul M., ed. *The War Plans of the Great Powers, 1880–1914.* London: George Allen & Unwin, 1979.

Koch, H. W. "Social Darwinism as a Factor in the 'New Imperialism.' " In H. W. Koch, ed., *The Origins of the First World War.* New York: Taplinger Publishing Co., 1972.

———. *Der Sozialdarwinismus: Seine Genese und sein Einfluss auf das imperialistische Denken.* Munich: C. Beck, 1973.

Lammers, Donald. "Arno Mayer and the British Decision for War: 1914." *Journal of British Studies* 12 (1973): 137–65.

Langbehn, Julius. *Rembrandt als Erzieher.* Leipzig: G. L. Hirschfield, 1903.

Lichtheim, George. *Marxism.* New York: Frederick A. Praeger, 1961.

Lowi, Theodore J. *The End of Liberalism.* New York: W. W. Norton & Co., 1969.

Lukács, Georg. *Die Zerstörung der Vernuft.* Vol. 2, *Irrationalismus und Imperialismus;* Vol. 3, *Irrationalismus und Soziologie.* Neuwied: Luchterhand, 1974.

Mann, Thomas. *Nietzsches Philosophie im Lichte unserer Erfahrung.* Berlin: Suhrkamp, 1948.

Mannheim, Karl. *Essays on the Sociology of Knowledge.* New York: Oxford University Press, 1952.

Masur, Gerhard. *Prophets of Yesterday: Studies in European Culture, 1890–1914.* New York: Macmillan Co., 1961.

Mayer, Arno J. "Internal Crisis and War Since 1870." In Charles L. Bertrand, ed., *Revolutionary Situations in Europe, 1917–1922: Germany, Italy, Austria-Hungary.* Montreal: Interuniversity Center for European Studies, 1977.

Mitzman, Arthur. *The Iron Cage: An Historical Interpretation of Max Weber.* New York: Grosset & Dunlap, 1969.

———. *Sociology and Estrangement: Three Sociologists of Imperial Germany.* New York: Alfred A. Knopf, 1973.

Mommsen, Wolfgang J. "Domestic Factors in German Foreign Policy Before 1914." *Central European History* 4 (1973): 3–43.

Moore, James R. *The Post-Darwinian Controversies: A Study of the Protestant Struggle to Come to Terms with Darwin in Great Britain and America, 1870–1900.* Cambridge: Cambridge University Press, 1979.

Mosca, Gaetano. *The Ruling Class.* New York: McGraw-Hill Book Co., 1939.

Nasmyth, George. *Social Progress and Darwinian Theory.* New York: G. P. Putnam's Sons, 1916.

Nietzsche, Friedrich Wilhelm. *Gesammelte Werke.* 23 vols. Munich: Musarion, 1920–1929.

———. *Werke.* 3 vols. Ed. Karl Schlechte. Munich: Hanser, 1960–1962.

Pareto, Vilfredo. *The Mind and Society.* 4 vols. New York: Dover Publications, 1935.

Plamenatz, John. *Ideology.* New York: Praeger Publishers, 1970.

Podach, Erich. *Nietzsches Zusammenbruch.* Heidelberg: N. Kampmann, 1930.

Poulantzas, Nicos. *Pouvoir politique et classes sociales.* 2 vols. Paris: François Maspero, 1972.

Robinson, Ronald, and Gallagher, John. *Africa and the Victorians: The Official Mind of Imperialism.* New York: St. Martin's Press, 1961.

Rogers, James A. "Marxist and Russian Darwinism." *Jahrbücher für Geschichte Osteuropas* 13 (1965): 199–211.

Rogger, Hans. "Russia in 1914." *Journal of Contemporary History* 1 (1966): 95–120.

Russell, Bertrand. *A History of Western Philosophy and Its Connection with Political and Social Circumstances from the Earliest Times to the Present Day.* New York: Simon & Schuster, 1945.

Scally, Robert J. *The Origins of the Lloyd George Coalition: The Politics of Social Imperialism, 1900–1918.* Princeton, N.J.: Princeton University Press, 1975.

Schroeder, Paul W. "World War I as Galloping Gertie." *Journal of Modern History* 44 (1972): 320–45.

Schumpeter, Joseph A. *Imperialism and Social Classes.* New York: Meridian Books, 1955.

Semmel, Bernard. *Imperialism and Social Reform: English Social-Imperial Thought, 1895–1914.* Cambridge, Mass.: Harvard University Press, 1960.

Sheehan, James J. *German Liberalism in the Nineteenth Century.* Chicago: University of Chicago Press, 1978.

Steiner, Zara S. *Britain and the Origins of the First World War.* New York: St. Martin's Press, 1977.

Stern, Fritz. *The Politics of Cultural Despair.* Berkeley: University of California Press, 1961.

Sternhell, Zeev. *La Droite révolutionnaire, 1885–1914: Les Origines français du fascisme.* Paris: Éditions du Seuil, 1978.

Struve, Walter. *Elites Against Democracy: Leadership Ideals in Bourgeois Political Thought in Germany, 1890–1933.* Princeton, N.J.: Princeton University Press, 1973.

Sykes, Alan. *Tariff Reform in British Politics, 1903–1913.* Oxford: Clarendon Press, 1979.

Thatcher, David S. *Nietzsche in England, 1890–1914.* Toronto: University of Toronto Press, 1954.

Thayer, John A. *Italy and the Great War: Politics and Culture, 1870–1915.* Madison: University of Wisconsin Press, 1964.

Therborn, Göran. *Science, Class, and Society: On the Formation of Sociology and Historical Materialism.* London: New Left Books, 1976.

Vagts, Alfred. *A History of Militarism.* New York: W. W. Norton & Co., 1937.

Vucinich, Alexander. *Social Thought in Tsarist Russia: The Quest for a General Science of Society, 1861–1914.* Chicago: University of Chicago Press, 1976.

Weber, Max. *Gesammelte politische Schriften.* Munich: Drei Masken, 1921.

Weiss, John. *Conservatism in Europe, 1770–1945: Traditionalism, Reaction and Counter-Revolution.* New York: Harcourt Brace Jovanovich, 1977.

Wilkinson, Rupert. *Gentlemanly Power: British Leadership and the Public School Tradition.* New York: Oxford University Press, 1964.

Wolfe, Alan. *The Limits of Legitimacy: Political Contradictions of Contemporary Capitalism.* New York: Free Press, 1977.

Zmarzlik, Hans-Günter. "Der Sozialdarwinismus in Deutschland als geschichtliches Problem." *Vierteljahrshefte für Zeitgeschichte* 11 (1963): 246–73.

Zweig, Stefan. *Nietzsche: Le Combat avec le démon.* Paris: Éditions Stock, 1978.

Index

351

About the Author

Arno J. Mayer received his B.B.A. from the City College of New York and his Ph.D. from Yale University. He has taught at Brandeis, Harvard, and Columbia, and since 1961 has served as a professor of history at Princeton. Professor Mayer is a fellow of the American Academy of Arts and Sciences. His previous books include *Political Origins of the New Diplomacy, 1917–1918*; *Politics and Diplomacy of Peacemaking: Containment and Counterrevolution at Versailles, 1918–1919*, which was awarded the American Historical Association's Herbert Baxter Adams Prize; and *Dynamics of Counterrevolution in Europe, 1870–1956*.